WAR AT A DISTANCE

WAR AT A DISTANCE

Romanticism and the Making of Modern Wartime

Mary A. Favret

PRINCETON UNIVERSITY PRESS
Princeton and Oxford

Copyright © 2010 by Princeton University Press

Published by Princeton University Press, 41 William Street, Princeton, New Jersey 08540

In the United Kingdom: Princeton University Press, 6 Oxford Street, Woodstock,

Oxfordshire OX20 1TW

Library of Congress Cataloging-in-Publication Data

Favret, Mary A.

   War at a distance: romanticism and the making of modern wartime / Mary A. Favret.

      p.   cm.

   Includes bibliographical references and index.

   ISBN 978-0-691-14276-0 (hardcover)—ISBN 978-0-691-14407-8 (pbk.)   1. War and literature.

2. War and society.   3. Romanticism.   I. Title.

   PN56.W3F38   2009

   809'. 933581—dc22   2009010310

British Library Cataloging-in-Publication Data is available

This book has been composed in Adobe Garamond.

Printed on acid-free paper. ∞

press.princeton.edu

Printed in the United States of America

10 9 8 7 6 5 4 3 2 1

To Andrew, with love

and

In loving memory of

Patrick J. Favret 1956–1988

Sophia Patrick Miller April 9, 1996

CONTENTS

ILLUSTRATIONS

A Winter's Evening

On a winter's evening, a man looks into the fireplace and contemplates a world at war.

It is February of 2003; the poet has just turned off the evening news. The buildup to the U.S.-led invasion of Iraq goes without saying. Sleet is "slashing" outside on this "bitter evening," while C. K. Williams's attention wanders to the hearth.[1] There he sees a plastic coffee cup teetering "on a log for a strangely long time, / as though uncertain what to do" (7–8). The hesitation and subsequent collapse of this strange "creaturely" thing calls forth a series of meditations on distant violence: memories of a friend injured during the Vietnam War, thoughts of the upcoming invasion of Iraq, and the prospect of a world devastated by such violence. Suffering is made remote by time and geography but also, despite the marvels of modern telecommunications, by the limits of human perception and feeling. The experience of distant warfare is, for this man at home in the evening, clouded by uncertainties, hesitations, lapses, and collapses. Williams's "The Hearth" is a poem, in other words, of wartime, of the complex working of time-consciousness and feeling that accompanies and shapes the awareness—but also the unknown-ness—of modern, distant war.

Time teeters: past, present, and future all threaten to surrender to an obliterating violence. Seeing the melting cup, Williams remembers a friend "I once knew" who had been ravaged by flames in the Vietnam War after loading a faulty napalm shell. His skin now "lavaed with scar," his soul fails to learn "to not want to die" (24). The poet turns from this absent friend who cannot but wishes to die, to describe a present, impassive violence: an owl "here tonight, after / dusk" "helicoptered" in the dark to kill its prey. In this instance there is "nothing to mourn": "[I]f the creature being torn from its life / made a sound, I didn't hear it" (29–30, 33, 38, 39–40). The suffering outside happens at a remove, imaginable yet inaudible. Meanwhile, the flying predator, equipped

---

[1] C. K. Williams, *The Singing* (New York: Farrar, Straus and Giroux, 2003), 65–66.

with sophisticated night vision, has turned the poet's thoughts even further away—to a battlefield, and beyond, to prophecy:

> But in fact I wasn't listening, I was thinking,
> as I often do these days, of war;
> I was thinking of my children, and their children,
> of the more than fear I feel for them,
>
> and then of radar, rockets, shrapnel,
> cities razed, soil poisoned
> for a thousand generations; of suffering so vast
> it nullifies everything else. (41–48)

The fire blazes up when the "uncertain" plastic cup finally falls, fueling the flames. Against this burning light, the night outdoors becomes "even darker" (54) while the interior room is "barely . . . warm" (55). The poet stokes the fire again and "crouch[es] closer" (56).

On a winter's night a man looks into the fireplace and guides his mind away from war. It is February of 1798; Samuel Taylor Coleridge has been closely following the news from abroad. In the next few months he will compose poems in response to France's bloody invasion of Switzerland and to the "alarm of invasion" of his native country; but not tonight.[2] Now he's couched at the hearth at midnight, staring into its dying embers. An "owlet's cry" comes loud, "and hark, again! loud as before" (2, 3); otherwise all the "numberless goings on of life" are kept at a distance, "[i]naudible as dreams" (12–13). One "sole unquiet thing" seems to hover over the coals (16): a "film, which fluttered on the grate, / Still flutters there" refusing to die and calling forth "dim sympathies" from the poet (15–16, 18). "In all parts of the kingdom," he explains, "these films are called *strangers* and supposed to portend the arrival of some absent friend" (515n). A stranger's intrusion foretells the coming of a friend: the distance between thing and person, foreign and familiar, falters.[3]

The flimsy soul or thing is even less substantial than a melting coffee cup, yet its hovering too opens up mortal time, casting the poet backward into memories of his childhood with its loneliness and anticipations, only to throw

---

[2] Samuel Taylor Coleridge, *The Complete Poems*, ed. William Keach (New York: Penguin, 1997), 515–16. "Frost at Midnight" was written in February 1798 and revised in the following months. Coleridge wrote "France: An Ode" and "Fears in Solitude: written in April 1798, during an alarm of invasion" that April. The three poems were published together in a quarto volume by Joseph Johnson in October of that same year. Richard Holmes, *Coleridge: Early Visions, 1772–1804* (New York: Viking, 1989), 182–85, 201–4.

[3] Rei Terada suggests that Coleridge's use of phenomenal apparitions such as this unquiet "film" "occup[ies] a fluid middle ground where [the poet] has the opportunity to reimagine relations." "Phenomenality and Dissatisfaction in Coleridge's Notebooks," *Studies in Romanticism* 43.2 (Summer 2004): 262.

him forward to the present and to prophecies of the future. The breathings of the poet's child, asleep in the room, "[f]ill up the interspersed vacancies / And momentary pauses" that had opened (46–47). "[T]hou," the poet tells his child, "shalt learn far other lore / And in far other scenes" (50–51).

The fire in the hearth does not blaze up at this view of the future. The prophecy is underwritten instead by "the secret ministry of frost" (72). If the poet is fearful for his child's future in a world torn by war, the silent, shining icicles of the winter night are there to transform his fear. They signal the hope that something beautiful—not yet fallen or lost or nullified—may survive the wintry blast.

> Therefore all seasons shall be sweet to thee,
> . . . ; whether the eave-drops fall
> Heard only in the trances of the blast,
> Or if the secret ministry of frost
> Shall hang them up in silent icicles,
> Quietly shining to the quiet Moon. (65, 70–74)

On another "Winter Evening," a man sits by the fireside and reads about a world at war. It is 1783, the British had recently surrendered after two bitter and unpopular wars, one in North America, one in southern India. The newspaper arrives, and William Cowper retires to the hearth to read and ponder the teetering fate of empire.[4] A "freezing blast" and "frost" are "raging abroad," yet the coming storm "endear[s] / The silence and the warmth enjoy'd within" (IV: 303, 308–10). In elaborating his evening rituals, the poet aims to shut out the "noisy world" in the silence of his nightly reading (IV: 5).

> . . . I behold
> The tumult, and am still. The sound of war
> Has lost its terrors ere it reaches me;
> Grieves, but alarms me not. I . . .
> Hear the faint echo of those brazen throats
> And sigh, but never tremble at the sound. (IV: 99–102, 104–6)

His reflection on the news leads to no individual memory, just to "the comforts that . . . the hours / Of long uninterrupted ev'ning, know" (IV: 141–43). There are nonetheless birds on the wing, and they do rupture the quiet of the night. "Time, as he passes us, has a dove's wing, / Unsoil'd, and swift, and of a silken sound" but, Cowper continues, the "world's time" is "tinctur'd black

---

[4] William Cowper, *The Task*, in *The Complete Poetical Works*, ed. H. S. Milford, 4th ed. (Oxford: Oxford UP, 1967), 129–241. "The Winter Evening" serves as Book IV of William Cowper's six-book *The Task*, begun in 1783 and first published in 1785. In 1798, Coleridge thought Cowper "the best modern poet" (qtd. in Holmes 195).

and red" and leads to "untimely graves" (IV: 211–12, 213, 216, 219). In this quiet zone sounds the faint echo of Passover and blood sacrifice. Not memory, but sacred history invades the poet's "season of peace" (IV: 243). Later celebrating the pleasures of the hearth, the poet suddenly imagines that he sees in his mirror Goliath, the great enemy warrior, "tow'ring crest and all" (IV: 271).

In response to these strange invasions, the poet's unthinking "soul" gazes into the dwindling fire on the hearth where he sees "houses, tow'rs, / Trees, churches, and strange visages" amidst "the red cinders" (IV: 288, 289). The vision fades, not quite suggesting the ravages of war. His focus rearranges itself: now he watches "films that play" on the grate,

> Pendulous, and foreboding, in the view
> Of superstition, prophesying still,
> Though still deceiv'd, some stranger's near approach. (IV: 293–95)

As in Coleridge's poem, something from the superstitious, premodern past survives to call forth an unsure future. Home and hearth are invaded by strange worlds and other times and the poet is pressed to prophecy: "To-morrow brings a change, a total change!" (IV: 322). But uncertainty lodges itself in this lapsed time, in the "vacancies" of the poet's contemplative mind. He looks out the window and sees snow falling "with never-ceasing lapse" (IV: 327). It will "[a]ssimilate all objects" in its blank unreadability (IV: 329). Will change bring a new creation or, as Williams imagines, vast nullification?

Winter, night, the hearth, the news. Invasions, interruptions and flickering, foreboding strangers. Flights of memory and winged predators. Tumult and quiet; listening and not listening; thinking and not thinking; blaze and frost. Lapse, vacuity, absence, nullity. Uncertainty and prophecy. The poems here collected gather some of the recurrent motifs of this book and in doing so, reveal in small its claims. If in these works warfare itself occurs *at a distance,* outside and beyond our reach, the experience of wartime begins *here,* in such domestic settings: in the intimacies of the home and hearth, the wanderings of the mind, the interruptions and lapses—of time, knowledge, and feeling— that compose the everyday. The geographies of such wartime experience cannot be easily compartmentalized *there* and *here;* it overflows these spaces, somehow fugitive and omnipresent at once. At the same time, the sequence of poems presents wartime as something neither firmly sequestered in the past nor thoroughly our own. To be sure, Cowper's and Coleridge's poems speak of wars of one period, crossing the late eighteenth and early nineteenth centuries; and I will be arguing that the generation of writers from Cowper to Coleridge— artists as celebrated as William Wordsworth and forgotten as the anonymous poets of the periodical press—helped to construct the first wartime of modernity. C. K. Williams's poem alerts us to this overlooked history, the continuity between the way war figures in romantic writing and the way war figures today. But the wartime so constructed does not obey the enclosing actions of periodization; instead it presents a more unsettled and unsettling temporality. Shot through with expressions, imagery, and figures of speech assembled over two hundred years ago, wartime is a present experience handed down from a past uncertain of its future. We have inherited what wartime looks and sounds and feels like from this other time, which remains both strange and familiar.

Thus the young Robert Frost would draw on Cowper and Coleridge in the recently discovered "War Thoughts at Home," where a woman looks out her window at a "bird war" in a winter landscape (1918). More powerfully, his earlier "Snow" (1916) takes place at night in a Vermont farmhouse, during an obliterating snowstorm, and centers on a debate about whether or not the character Meserve, a bit of a prophet, ought to venture outdoors. Not unlike Cowper, he finds "I like it from inside / More than I shall out in it" (227–28).[5] In the end Meserve does leave, after explaining how the snowfall recruits his leaving: "Hear the soft bombs of dust / It bursts against us at the chimney mouth" (225–27). True to his name, he will serve:

> "Well, there's—the storm. That says I must go on.
> That wants me as a war might if it came.
> Ask any man." (260–62)

Before this climax, Frost substitutes for the hovering film on the hearth a wavering "something," the leaf of a book, perhaps a book of romantic poetry:

> Meserve seemed to heed nothing but the lamp
> Or something not far from it on the table. . . .
> "That leaf there in your open book! It moved
> Just then, I thought. It stood erect like that, . . .
> Trying to turn itself backward or forward,
> I've had my eye on it to make out which;
> If forward, then it's with a friend's impatience—
> . . . if backward
> It's from regret for something you have passed
> And failed to see the good of. Never mind,
> Things must expect to come in front of us
> A many times—I don't say just how many—
> That varies with the things—before we see them. . . ." (128–42)

Epistemological uncertainty and wavering temporality provide the very texture of this wartime meditation, of wartime as meditation. Frost, attentive to

---

[5] Robert Frost, *Mountain Interval* (New York: H. Holt and Company, 1916), 76–98.

the poetic tradition, discovers in the winter evening forms—the storm without, the ambivalent leaf or medium—for what we both recognize and fail to recognize.

Why would these poets of the twentieth and twenty-first century—Frost, Williams—find their coordinates for wartime in motifs taken from poetry of the late eighteenth century? Something from that past survives to call forth the future.

PART I

Modern Wartime: Media and Affect

CHAPTER ONE

Introduction: A Sense of War

This book considers how war becomes part of the barely registered substance of our everyday, an experience inextricable from sitting at home on an evening, recalling absent friends, staring at a fire, gazing out a window. As it looks back over two centuries, *War at a Distance* tells how military conflict on a global scale looked and felt to a population whose armies and navies waged war for decades, but always at a distance. For those at home, the task was to find sentient ground for what often appeared a free-floating, impersonal military operation, removed from their immediate sensory perception. The literature and art produced in Britain during its twenty-year conflict with France cultivated this ground obsessively—and in doing so, it established forms for how we continue to think and feel about war at a distance. As a wartime phenomenon, British Romanticism gives its distinctive voice to the dislocated experience that is modern wartime: the experience of war mediated, of time and times unmoored, of feeling intensified but also adrift.

Modern wartime refers first to the experience of those living through but not in a war. As writers in England in the late eighteenth and early nineteenth century went about their everyday routines, their country was sending men to kill and be killed across the globe. In the course of the eighteenth century the newly United Kingdom had crushed two armed rebellions at home; participated in a half dozen wars on the continent; expanded its imperial holdings on the Indian subcontinent, in the Caribbean, and in Africa; increased and then lost a good portion of its North American colonies—through warfare. At the turn of the new century, Great Britain entered a worldwide campaign, fighting first against regicides and Terror and later against an evil despot (the French Revolution and Napoleon, respectively), emerging in 1815 as the world's dominant military power.[1] The intensity and length of fighting have led historians to refer to the eighteenth century as a "Second Hundred Years War," and Linda Colley has shown that British national identity was decisively forged through

[1] Great Britain joined the First Coalition against Revolutionary France after the execution of Louis XVI in January 1793. The rule of Terror in France commenced that fall. Napoleon seized political power on November 9, 1799—the 18th Brumaire.

this century of nearly constant military action.[2] But that military action, again, was undertaken at a remove: after the defeat of Stewart loyalists at Culloden in 1745, distance—either geophysical or temporal—was increasingly built into the British nation's understanding of war. War on home turf happened back then; it was history. If it occurred now, it occurred beyond the reach of eyes and ears, somewhere else, over there.

In trying to capture this modern wartime, the chapters of this book take up materials as varied as meditations on *The Iliad*, the history of meteorology, landscape painting in India, popular poetry in the newspapers and periodicals, theories of history and the everyday, the work of dictionaries, and various modes of prophecy and prognostication; they contemplate forms of war and wartime that range from the early years of the eighteenth century to the present. Yet their primary material (their "hearth" as it were) is the literature of romantic wartime. This material makes clear that wartime responses move in several directions. In some instances the experience of war at a distance prompts a move toward abstraction, an increasing distance from the human body. Here the consolations of system, idea, and purpose hold sway: as from a bird's-eye view, you see patterns emerge; you comprehend why and when, where and how war operates. War becomes an object of knowledge, a universalizing abstraction; indeed, in wartime it threatens to become all you know. In other instances, the reverse occurs: wartime promotes a sense of atomism and despair which folds into the body so completely that inertia and apathy—lack of feeling—are its only signs. Wartime here defeats human responsiveness. There is a third, perhaps more productive response, suspended between and resistant to the polar pulls of abstraction and numbness. The last chapter of this book locates this third response visually and spatially in a "middle distance." But it surfaces throughout the book as a poetic or aesthetic response, a response that strives to produce and give form to feeling. And it is this third term, the productive aspect of wartime writing, which opens wartime—and the romantic writing that conceived it—to the present.

War at a Distance works, then, at the intersection of two academic fields: the study of wartime literature and the study of affect. The scholarship on wartime literature and culture—for example, Paul Fussell's masterpieces, *The Great War and Modern Memory* and *Wartime: Understanding and Behavior in the Second World War;* Bernard Bergonzi's important *Wartime and Aftermath: English Literature and Its Background, 1939–60;* Susan Gubar and Sandra Gilbert's *No Man's Land: The Place of the Woman Writer in the Twentieth Century;* Jay Winter's *Sites of Memory, Sites of Mourning: The Great War in European Cultural History;* or more recently, *The Writing of Anxiety: Imagining Wartime*

---

[2] Linda Colley, *Britons: Forging the Nation, 1707–1837* (New Haven: Yale UP, 1992).

in Mid-century British Culture by Lindsey Stonebridge or *Grief in Wartime: Private Pain, Public Discourse* by Carol Acton—has been weighted heavily toward the two world wars of the past century. In recent years, the categories of "wartime" and "wartime literature" have been extended to the period of the American Civil War when, as Drew Gilpin Faust puts it, "the United States embarked on a new relationship with death."[3] Even as I learn from this work, I reach back to a yet earlier, but still self-consciously modern period of war, to acknowledge its continued currency.

Reaching back brings up a question all these studies tend to overlook: the question of "war time" itself. How do we know or measure, how do we *tell* the time of war? What sort of historiography does it require? My answers to these questions derive in part from recent work in the second of the fields I mention, the history of affect, which studies modes of response or apprehension that lie outside of cognition per se. Affect often eludes the usual models for organizing time such as linearity, punctuality, and periodicity; it eludes as well the usual models for organizing history. If we take wartime less as an object of cognition bounded by dates—a period—and more as an affecting experience which resonates beyond the here and now, then wartime literature becomes an attempt to trace and give shape to such affect, to register its wayward power.

This introduction will begin to spell out some of the human consequences of war at a distance. These consequences were of the most fundamental sort: most strikingly, we will see that distant war unsettled basic temporal experiences of the British population. How time and knowledge were registered in daily life became newly uncertain. And with that uncertainty came a set of disturbing affective responses, including numbness, dizziness, anxiety, or a sense of being overwhelmed. In taking romantic writers as architects of modern wartime, I want to bring forth these relations of distance, temporality, epistemology, and affect: the felt distance from crucial events, the limits of knowledge in a mediated culture, the temporal gaps in the transmission of information, and, finally, the difficulty of finding sounds or forms to which feeling can attach itself.

The chapters which then follow divide themselves into three parts. The first deals in particular with the conversion of war at a distance into a matter of time, into wartime. Wartime, as many romantic writers realized in their work, was the effect of war mediated, brought home through a variety of instruments. As the poems discussed in the prelude already suggest, a mediated war sets in motion various and conflicting senses of time, and unsettled times

---

[3] Drew Gilpin Faust, *This Republic of Suffering: Death and the American Civil War* (New York: Alfred A. Knopf, 2008), xi.

unleash unsettled feelings. This opening section, therefore, sets out the complex temporal structure of wartime, understanding it as a zone of affect which troubles what we can know and especially what we can know of history. The second section, while still underscoring how war conducted at a distance intensifies time-consciousness and charges it with affective resonance, concerns itself more with the ways distant war invades and becomes implicated in the most familiar forms of the everyday. The chapters of this section center on the thought that the everyday itself, its peculiar status in modern thought, derives from its intimate relationship with war. Indeed, writing in the romantic period illuminates how war invades thought itself, threatening to become the very ground of thinking, understood in ways that make it—like the everyday—familiar and routine, easy to overlook. The final section of the book then turns from written to visual texts, in part to demonstrate continuities and discrepancies between romantic mediations of war at a distance and more contemporary mediations which privilege the visual and televisual: our own "films upon the grate." But in directing attention to representations of the landscape of war-torn India in the 1790s, my goal is also to insist upon the global nature of a war often taken to concern only Europe. The very idea of a world war, as it emerged in this period, poses anew a question which lurks throughout the study: the question of our modern intimacy with and response to the suffering stranger who, though seen perhaps fleetingly and at a distance, nevertheless comes almost daily into our homes.

War Mediated

Taking up "modern wartime," let alone something called "wartime literature," means entering into the history of war and mediation. When war is conducted at a distance, how one can know or learn of war becomes massively important, as do the obstacles (psychological, ideological, practical) to such knowledge. The epistemology of modern wartime is an epistemology of mediation. Consider again C. K. Williams's "The Hearth," written in the wake of television reports; consider too his poem "Doves," a 2003 response to media reports on the war in Iraq:

So much crap in my head,
So many rubbishy facts,
So many half-baked
theories and opinions, . . .
So much political swill.
So much crap, Yet

so much I don't know
and would dearly like to. . . . (1–4, 8–11)⁴

Or consider the familiar stories of soldiers found in remote places, still primed to fight because they have not heard what those back home know already, that peace treaties have been signed months before. These stories, circulating widely in the media, not only advertise the more "accurate" knowledge of the viewer or reader compared to the benighted warrior ("too close" to the action); they also provide an ironic fable of the larger indeterminacies of wartime (when does wartime begin or end? where exactly does it take place?) and their tight links to the work of communication.

But the roots of these familiar stories about the mediation and uncertainties of war reach down to an earlier period. If modern wartime is the experience of noncombatants in a time of war, it is worth recalling that it was in fact during the Napoleonic period that the term "noncombatant" as well as the popular understanding of "civilian" as nonmilitary first emerged in English; and the notion of "wartime" as a distinct category emerged along with them.⁵ With the advent of mass media, in the print culture that rose in the eighteenth century, and in an increasingly popular visual culture of prints, panoramas, and theatrical performances, wartime stepped forth as a mediated relationship to distant violence.

Caught within these examples is the revelation that, by calling up questions of epistemology, of certainties and doubts, a mediated war evokes as well the unsettled terrain of wartime affect. Within such conditions of mediated knowledge, feeling responds not only to the war itself but to one's privileged experience of it—the privilege of knowing war at a distance. A 1798 pamphlet, written to raise the alarm of invasion by French forces, could invoke this privilege almost smugly, insisting on the war's distance and invisibility:

[I]t has been our peculiar privilege, through the whole of this unprecedented War, to triumph over our enemies without ever seeing them, without any exposure of our personal security, without any interruption of our domestic quiet, while a great part of Europe has experienced all the horrors of War, while its cities have been sacked, and its fields drenched with blood. . . . [W]e have it in our power to frustrate the

⁴ Williams read his poem "Doves" in his acceptance speech for the National Book Award in Poetry in 2003. http://www.nationalbook.org/nbaacceptspeech_ckwilliams.html.
⁵ The *OED* quotes Gen. Wellington, writing in 1811 and 1813, for the first two instances of the use of the word "non-combatant." A "civilian" originally studied or followed civil, as opposed to canon law. "civilian, *n.*" *The Oxford English Dictionary*, 2nd ed., 1989, *OED Online* (Oxford UP), 30 August 2007, http://dictionary.oed.com/cgi/entry/50280633.

designs of the enemy without seeing our Country become the seat of
War,—without, even any violation of our Coasts.[6]

This sense of privileged security sits uneasily, though, in a work dedicated to
rousing its countrymen to a constant vigilance. Elsewhere, the author paints
scenarios of "violence and rapine" on British soil and reports on incendiary
speeches in Paris, making visible and proximate the very violence it hopes to
defend against. The picture of domestic quiet remains meaningless without this
threat of "interruption." Pamphlets like this one—and there were dozens—
mediated between the known and the unknown, seen and unseen, prompting
wild fluctuations of feeling. They could, for instance, be at once contemptuous
of France's ability to fund an invasion, and certain that the threat was real and
imminent. They offered the feeling of security always bundled with the feeling
of vulnerability.

The arrival—or not—of news from abroad was one determining factor of
wartime experience, of what you might know and how you might feel. Already in 1798, Samuel Taylor Coleridge could lament that reading the morning news only dampened his ability to respond feelingly to distant warfare:
the papers offer "dainty terms for fratricide; . . . mere abstractions, empty
sounds to which / We join no feeling and attach no form!" (113, 116–17).[7]
Coleridge's "un-joined" feelings"—un-articulated affect—were encouraged
not only by the newspapers' euphemism and abstraction but also by the sheer
facts of physical and temporal distance. In the late eighteenth century, news
of war came with considerable lag time; reports of a particular event, the loss
of a battle or the death of your brother, could take months to be communi-
cated home and confirmed. Today we depend on the illusion of immediacy
granted by instantaneous and unceasing news reporting, as if we can always
know what is happening elsewhere in the world as it occurs; yet un-joined
feelings persist. Such feelings—empty, lacking solid attachment—contribute
to the experience of any war at a distance. The wartime writing of the Revolutionary and Napoleonic period gives expressive form to this experience of
mediated distance—distance spatial, temporal, epistemological, and, in the
end, mortal—and the responses it generates. For these reasons, reading this
literature has taught me that wartime is not just a period of time that can be
got over or settled, but rather a persistent mode of daily living and a habit
of mind.

---

[6] *An appeal to the head and heart of every man and woman in Great Britain, respecting the threatened French invasion, and the importance of immediately coming forward with voluntary contributions.*
London, 1798, 118–19. *Eighteenth Century Collections Online (ECCO).* Gale Group. http://galenet.
galegroup.com/servlet/ECCO. My thanks to Lily Gurton-Wachter for pointing out this passage.

[7] Samuel Taylor Coleridge, *The Complete Poems*, ed. William Keach (New York: Penguin,
1997), 95.

In such circumstances, mediation itself becomes an object of emotion: of comfort, complacency, relief, anxiety, impotence, complicity. In response to the mediated versions of war we receive, we may admit, as William Cowper did while reading his newspaper in 1783, that "The sound of war / Has lost its terrors ere it reaches me; / Grieves, but alarms me not" (IV: 100–2).[8] Yet, at the next moment we may discover in the safe space of our living rooms, as he did, the fleeting presence—however imagined—of towering warriors and cities in flames, or towers in flames and cities full of warriors. Distant violence becomes at once strange and familiar, intimate and remote, present and yet not really here. "Being a spectator of calamities taking place in another country," Susan Sontag noted, "is a quintessential modern experience."[9] In saying this, she echoes a well-known radical preacher of the romantic period, Joseph Fawcett, who published his famous anti war poem, *The Art of War*, in 1795. In his later *War Elegies* (1801), Fawcett put succinctly the operation of wartime affect as it fluctuates somewhere between minds, hearts, and bodies, here and elsewhere. The misery of war, he remarks, consists in part "in the pain it inflicts upon the mind of every contemplator of its ravages, *at whatever distance* he stand from its theatre . . . whose heart can bleed at home along with the thousands whose bodies are bleeding in the field."[10] Appealing without apology to the bleeding heart in wartime, Fawcett asks us to reexamine this overworn figure as it presses closely on the problem of mediation: of what is far brought close, what outer made inner. Fawcett expects hearts and minds to respond to war conducted anywhere at all, at whatever distance from "home"—and yet it is difficult to pinpoint where and when such misery takes place. For Fawcett, what is at a great distance seems also somehow (through some unspoken mediation) to penetrate us.

As this thought suggests, war itself does not necessarily *make sense*. Indeed, wartime is often the experience of an undoing or damaging of rational sense— which is to say that war, even at a distance, works to dismantle the forms that prop up our sense of the world and our place in it. In *The Body in Pain: The Making and Unmaking of the World*, Elaine Scarry anticipates this thought, arguing that war has as its target "a people and its civilization (or . . . the realms of sentience and self-extension)."[11] In the face of such absolute destructiveness, she tries to give voice and shape to the "interior and inarticulate . . . sentience" that accompanies and registers the prosecution of war (60). Deprived

---

[8] William Cowper, *The Task*, in *The Complete Poetical Works*, ed. H. S. Milford, 4th ed. (Oxford: Oxford UP, 1967), 129–241.

[9] Susan Sontag, *Regarding the Pain of Others* (New York: Farrar, Straus, and Giroux, 2003), 18.

[10] Joseph Fawcett, *War Elegies* (London: J. Johnson, 1801), vii; emphasis added.

[11] Elaine Scarry, *The Body in Pain: The Making and Unmaking of the World* (New York: Oxford UP, 1985), 61.

of the fortifications of intellect and understanding, deprived even of the immediacy of empirical evidence, the inhabitants of modern wartime often rely
on another and less categorizable "sense" of what war is and does; affect is this
alternate sense or sentience. Usually associated with the body and autonomous sensation, it names an awareness, not distinctly psychological or physiological but sharing aspects of each, that remains at some remove, at a distance,
from rational comprehension.[12]

Fawcett and his contemporaries respond to the wars they live through according to this more extensive view of distance, knowledge, and affect. In this
they run athwart twentieth-century theorist Carl Schmitt, who, arguing from
the aftermath of the Treaty of Westphalia (1711), famously called up the Lines
of Amity to "bracket" eighteenth- and nineteenth-century European warfare
from violence conducted elsewhere on the planet. Warfare in Europe was so-
called limited war: limited to familiar and respectable enemies (*justis hostes*),
limited in scale, and, ultimately, limited in its ethical consequences.[13] Fawcett's
view partakes instead of the cosmopolitan perspective provisionally outlined
by Immanuel Kant in "Perpetual Peace: A Philosophical Sketch" (1795).[14] This
perspective admits the claims of that stranger we saw in the prelude, coming
from no matter how remote a place, who might intrude upon the winter eve-
nings of contemplators such as Fawcett, Cowper, or Coleridge. For Kant, the
stranger may claim

> a *right of resort*, for all men are entitled to present themselves in the soci-
> ety of others by virtue of their right to the communal possession of the

[12] See Kevis Goodman's discussion of the "*history* of the *sense of history*" in *Georgic Modernity and British Romanticism: Poetry and the Mediation of History* (Cambridge: Cambridge UP, 2004), 5, 145–46n12; Adela Pinch, *Strange Fits of Passion: Epistemologies of Emotion, Hume to Austen* (Stanford: Stanford UP, 1996); and Julie Ellison, *Cato's Tears and the Making of Anglo-American Emotion* (Chicago: U of Chicago P, 1999). For more general discussions of affect and feeling, see Eve Kosofsky Sedgwick, *Touching Feeling: Affect, Pedagogy, Performativity* (Durham: Duke UP, 2003); Rei Terada, *Feeling in Theory: Emotion after the "Death of the Subject"* (Cambridge, MA: Harvard UP, 2001); Brian Massumi, *Parables for the Virtual: Movement, Affect, Sensation* (Durham: Duke UP, 2002); and Denise Riley, *Impersonal Passion: Language as Affect* (Durham: Duke UP, 2005).

[13] In *The* Nomos *of the Earth* (New York: Telos, 2003), Carl Schmitt called the "bracketing of war" the great accomplishment of the European powers in the eighteenth and nineteenth centuries. This "bracketing" depends upon the concept of *justis hostes*, the just or respectable enemy, which structures war as a duel between personified sovereigns and as "war in form." His influential account argues that after the Treaty of Westphalia an international law prevailing within the Lines of Amity marked Europe as the supposed zone of limited war (among *justus hostes*). Outside these lines—notoriously in the colonial holdings of European states—war was exempted from this law. Schmitt can see the Napoleonic period only as an anomaly (140–47). See Garrett Mattingly, "No Peace beyond What Line?" *Transactions of the Royal Historical Society, 5th Ser.* 13 (1963): 145–62; Eliga H. Gould, "Zones of Law, Zones of Violence: The Legal Geography of the British Atlantic, circa 1772," *William and Mary Quarterly* 60.3 (July 2003): 471–511.

[14] Immanuel Kant, "Perpetual Peace: A Philosophical Sketch," in *Kant: Political Writings*, ed. Hans Reiss (Cambridge: Cambridge UP, 1991).

earth's surface, . . . since the earth is a globe, they cannot disperse over an infinite area, but must necessarily tolerate one another's company. (106)

Taking the globe as a finite space, Kant sees the line between near and far dissolving. The principle of hospitality consequently extends beyond the realm of the "civilized states . . . especially the commercial states" of Europe to all "foreign countries and peoples" (106).[15] To give that principle force, to make it felt, Kant turns from the abstraction of states (his main concern) to the figure of an individual stranger knocking, as it were, on the door to your home. Kant understands such visitations in a quite literal and geographically grounded sense: "when he arrives on someone else's territory" a stranger should not be "treated with hostility" (105–6). For Fawcett and other romantic writers, the visitations from other lands are stranger, both more intimate and more metaphysical. Fawcett draws his lines not geopolitically, but as the difference between an inner and an outer "bleeding": in the heart or on the field, invisible or visible to the outward eye. Or perhaps it would be more accurate to say that the bleeding that is not visible because it takes place at a geographical distance elicits this other invisible bleeding, located in the inner terrain designated by the conjunction of "heart," "mind," and "body." Such mediation between inner and outer worlds provides no improved access to sensory perception. Indeed, it puts the problem of distance on a new footing: how remote or accessible is this inner world? And yet the mediation produces a "sense" that movements across the globe can be felt and registered, can even inflict with pain the wartime "contemplator."

The wartime affect described by Fawcett, produced in response to wars which cannot be seen or heard, smelled or touched, might thus recall the "sense of History" Alan Liu describes as "the absence that is the very possibility of the 'here and now.'"[16] But precisely as a "sense" of History, the affect of wartime also resists such abstraction (resists the sheer negativity of "absence" or Kant's "infinite distances") to attach itself to a feeling body. Throughout *War at a Distance*, writing and art are attuned to this new sense of a war that has potentially no limits or end, whose scope expands both internally and externally. They ask: how can the human form, with its mortal limits, register and check what remains beyond its ken?

[15] Here Kant states his difference from the Grotius-Pufendorf school of international law and its Westphalian view of European exclusivity. In his critique of colonial violence (105–6), Kant echoes William Godwin's concurrent thoughts in *An Enquiry Concerning Political Justice, and Its Influence on Morals and Happiness*, vol. 2 (London: G. G. and J. Robinson, 1796), 156–57. See also Richard Tuck, *The Rights of War and Peace: Political Thought and the International Order from Grotius to Kant* (Oxford: Oxford UP, 1999), 219–25.

[16] Alan Liu, *Wordsworth: The Sense of History* (Stanford: Stanford UP, 1989), 39. Liu takes the concept of history structured as "absent cause" from Louis Althusser and Étienne Balibar, *Reading "Capital,"* trans. Ben Brewster (London: Verso, 1970), 188.

As I've been suggesting, and as the next chapter will develop at length, wartime is an affective zone, a *sense* of time that, caught in the most unsettled sort of present, without knowledge of its outcome, cannot know its own borders. It indicates a dislocation of the bounded terrain usually associated with war, and the extension of war into a realm without clear limits. To consider wartime then shifts attention from war on the battlefield to the experience of those at home, but also moves from objective events to this other, subjective arena, much harder to locate. When Paul Fussell introduces his book *Wartime* as a study of the "psychological and emotional culture of Americans and Britons" during World War II, he is following a course laid down two hundred years earlier, in a previous wartime.[17] His explanation of "wartime" confirms my sense of its pervasive as well as its elusive nature. Even as it is not easily amenable to reason, wartime makes war a matter of mind:

> The damage the war visited upon bodies and buildings, planes and tanks and ships, is obvious. Less obvious is the damage it did to intellect, discrimination, honesty, individuality, complexity, ambiguity, and irony, not to mention privacy and wit.

Such damage happens every day, imperceptibly, in the most trivial instances or utterances. And yet *War at a Distance* discovers not only the damaging but also the creative or productive nature of wartime: that wartime may establish something that war would otherwise destroy, namely a culture; and that wartime writing and art might be able to make the imperceptible felt. However fragile or compromised, the psychological and emotional culture called wartime provides its own responses and sometimes its own resistance to the destructiveness of war. The wartime culture called Romanticism has been tremendously influential precisely because it was a culture that could be felt and questioned and imitated in response to a war threatening to destroy the realm of sentience and the realm of its extension.

The task of capturing this history, torn as it is with knowing and not-knowing, feeling and not-feeling, was felt acutely by William Hazlitt, a writer supported but also troubled by the wartime growth of the periodical press.[18] Studying his writing will give a more concrete sense of the mediation of distant war in its seemingly endless complexity. Indeed Hazlitt's essay "The Letter-Bell" is an act of creative re-mediation, a self-reflexive meditation on

[17] Paul Fussell, *Wartime: Understanding and Behavior in the Second World War* (New York: Oxford UP, 1989), 1.

[18] David Minden Higgins, *Romantic Genius and the Literary Magazine* (London and New York: Routledge, 2005), 102–26, gives a lively account of Hazlitt's struggles with writing for the periodical press.

the very material conditions of mediation in wartime.[19] In this, the last essay
he wrote, Hazlitt broods over an unresolved age. As if in response to Coleridge's
worries about the "empty sounds" of journalism and Cowper's musing on the
sounds of violence muted by the newspaper, Hazlitt makes the memory of
sounds and various media of communication the objects of his attention. And,
in doing so, he draws together various strands which regularly follow from this
preoccupation with media: the structure and feeling of time; a sense of historical eventfulness that falls away into eventlessness; and wordless sounds or
"voices" which, if we could only discern them properly, would describe a world
of affecting interest.

"The Letter-Bell" surveys Hazlitt's career as a writer, beginning with the present moment in 1830 as he learns of the July Revolution that has driven the
Bourbons (again) from France, and extending back almost forty years to the
time of the execution of Louis XVI and the opening days of Britain's wars with
France.[20] Then was "my first entrance into life, the period of my first coming
up to town, when all around was strange, uncertain, adverse—a hubbub of
confused noises, a chaos of shifting objects" (203). Amid these reflections, the
ringing of a letter bell announcing coming news and departing missives organizes the chaos, awakening the young Hazlitt from "the dream of time" into a
sense of the momentous present (203). Enunciating that moment, the bell calls
Hazlitt into life and into writing. But its ringing simultaneously calls him into
what Scarry would call sentience and its extension: "[T]his sound alone . . .
brought me as it were to myself, made me feel that I had links still connecting
me with the universe, and gave me hope and patience to persevere" (203). The
musical sound thus grants Hazlitt a sense—heard and felt—of history; it situates him in the world and in his work. Thus he describes the end of a wintry
day, as he sits by the fireplace "while the Letter-Bell was the only sound that
drew my thoughts to the world without, and reminded me that I had a task to
perform in it" (205). Yet even as the sounding bell calls him to his historic role,
it recalls the distance between the world without and the world within: he has,
in fact, withdrawn from the world and lapsed in his attention to his task. In
signaling the moment, the letter bell also exposes the surrounding drift of

[19] On remediation, see Jay David Bolter and Richard Grusin, *Remediation: Understanding New Media* (Cambridge: MIT Press, 1999), esp. pp. 2–15 and 20–50. Celeste Langan and Maureen McLane argue for the specifically romantic preoccupation with remediation. "The Medium of Ro-mantic Poetry," in James K. Chandler and Maureen McLane, eds., *Cambridge Companion to British Romantic Poetry* (Cambridge: Cambridge UP, 2008), 239–62.

[20] "The Letter-Bell" was first published posthumously in *The Monthly Magazine*, March 1831. Hazlitt probably wrote in the aftermath of the "*trois glorieuses*"—the three days of revolution in Paris that ousted Charles X and resulted in Louis-Philippe's constitutional monarchy. *The Selected Writings of William Hazlitt*, ed. Duncan Wu, vol. 9 (London: Pickering & Chatto, 1998), 255n.

unsounded eventlessness; its punctuality carves out the alternative time of his "reveries" and the unsorted "dream of time" (203).

Hazlitt wants the play of these everyday sounds and rhythms to evoke their own historiography:

> The punctuating of time at that early period [during his early adulthood]—every thing that gives it an articulate voice—seems of the utmost consequence; for we do not know what scenes in the *ideal* world may run out of them: a world of interest may hang upon every instant, and we can hardly sustain the weight of future years which are contained in embryo in the most minute and inconsiderable passing events. (205)[21]

For a man of Hazlitt's generation, the letter bell might have announced the coming news of victories and defeats; and he drops in the word "alarm" (the bell "was a kind of alarm," he says) to hint at the years of invasion scares that troubled Britain during the wars; the bell was then a potent medium of wartime (204).[22] Yet Hazlitt asks us to understand the past four decades not by the content of the news which, presumably, we already know, but by these resonant forms or sounds which tell of what we may yet know and its companion feelings: anticipation, awakening, longing, regret, hope. For Hazlitt, the sound of the bell collapses content and form into a kind of history, an "articulate" if wordless voice that emerges from the chaotic "hubbub" to suggest the possibilities—still wordless, and perhaps never realized and only "ideal"—of any instant. The passing of the letter bell—its echoes passing through the streets of London, but also, now, passing away as a viable medium—itself becomes one of those "minute and inconsiderable passing events" that challenge the historian. The poignancy of the essay derives from the potential confusion of one instrument of communication (the writer's own words, printed up in the periodical press) with this other (the repeating, ringing bell of the moment); the identification of his evocative prose with this wordless sound; and the recognition that these passing "voices" carry a sense of the failures as well as the fullness of times.

And so Hazlitt ends by giving a history of wartime (that is to say, a history of war mediated) in the guise of an essay on aesthetics. In the final movement of the essay, he turns first to Cowper's *The Task* (the model for his own "task to perform") and quotes at length from the opening of Book IV, the noisy arrival of the post-boy. This poetic passage (and Hazlitt remains ambivalent

---

[21] Hazlitt's "On a Sun-Dial" also reflects on time-telling as a way into ideas of history. In *Selected Writings*, 153–60.

[22] Compare with Thomas De Quincey's triumphant "The English Mail Coach," in *Confessions of an English Opium Eater and Other Writings*, ed. Grevel Lindop (Oxford: Oxford UP, 1996), 183–233.

whether poetry may be another passing instrument) underwrites his closing meditation:

> In Cowper's time, Mail-Coaches were hardly set up; but he has beauti-
> fully described the coming in of the Post-Boy. . . . [He quotes IV: 1–22,
> where, in fact, Cowper describes both the coming and the passing of the
> post-boy.] And yet, notwithstanding this, and so many other passages
> that seem like the very marrow of our being, Lord Byron denies that
> Cowper was a poet!—the Mail-Coach is an improvement on the Post-
> Boy; but I fear it will hardly bear so poetical a description. The pictur-
> esque and dramatic do not keep pace with the useful and mechanical.
> The telegraphs that lately communicated the intelligence of the new
> revolution to all France within a few hours, are a wonderful contrivance;
> but they are less striking and appalling than the beacon-fires (mentioned
> by Aeschylus), which, lighted from hill-top to hill-top, announced the
> taking of Troy and the return of Agamemnon. (207–8)[23]

It would be easy, and probably not incorrect, to ally Hazlitt to a reactionary and nostalgic view of warfare. But we should understand first that his critique applies to the mechanization and systemization of communication, not war-fare itself; and that he mourns there (even as he reproduces) the passing of something "poetical," which mixes matters of geopolitical information with timing or "pace" and aesthetic effects. In calling attention to the "poetic" (for him a synonym for the aesthetic), Hazlitt's purpose is not necessarily to pro-mote a spectacular and sublime view of history or warfare: "appalling" fires and the fate of Agamemnon surely short-circuit sublime uplift. Rather he ac-centuates the lived sense and structure of history that such mediating instru-ments—be they bell or telegraph, film or Web site—might convey. From them, Hazlitt constructs his version of wartime as an everyday experience.[24]

The aesthetic investigated in the chapters to come, as in Hazlitt's essay, will shy away from the spectacular and sublime effects usually associated with the representation of war, inclining more toward the unconsidered or the com-monplace, akin to what Anne-Lise François describes as "uncounted experi-ence."[25] In not calling attention to themselves, such aesthetic strategies are

---

[23] Walter Scott lights similar signal fires in the opening of *The Lay of the Last Minstrel* (1805), then subjects them to mild parody in his novel *The Antiquary* (1816). Charlotte Smith invokes signal fires in "Beachy Head" (1807). More recent signal fires appear in Peter Jackson's film adaptations of J. R. R. Tolkien's *The Lord of the Rings, The Return of the King* (2003).

[24] Celeste Langan and Maureen McLane understand romantic "controversies surrounding the disputed term 'poetry' as precisely an attempt to generate both media theory and media history" "The Medium of Romantic Poetry," n.p.

[25] Anne-Lise François, *Open Secrets: The Literature of Uncounted Experience* (Stanford: Stanford UP, 2007), xix. François explores representations of uncounted experience in order to remove the

nonetheless—and maybe all the more—affecting, as they glide into the rhythms of ordinary life. Found in moments of gazing at the fireplace or hearing a bell, they also disclose themselves, I will show later, in the scene of a snow-covered field, in unremarkable accidents, in a drifting cloud, a makeshift bridge. Such figures invite the condescension we give to the picturesque, even though they all carry with them, like Cowper's post-boy, a sense of distant calamity. Like "The Letter-Bell," the chapters that follow will look backward to what is known to have happened, but put the backward turn in the service of contemplating "the weight of future years" pressing on that past. In making the present and past answerable to a distant future, wartime writers sustain in history a form of prophecy. They write, that is to say, both of and out of their time.[26]

"The Letter-Bell" demonstrates how the "task" of the poetic or aesthetic inspires Hazlitt and infiltrates his prose, even though that task is always at risk of being forgotten or passing unnoticed. In this tradition, *War at a Distance* takes its bearings from what may seem a singularly unlikely source, William Cowper's *The Task*, with its post-boy and its "Winter Evening" set by the hearth. Though Cowper's masterpiece has long been taken as a hymn to domesticity and Christian piety, Hazlitt and many other romantic writers recognized that in *The Task* Cowper provided materials and techniques that helped them construct a complex aesthetic for modern wartime; these materials and techniques have since been overlooked. When Hazlitt suggests that Byron, a poet more associated with the spectacular and sensational, might relearn how to read Cowper and thus rediscover the "marrow of our being," he challenges us to reread as well. In doing so, we may learn anew how to read and write about war.

Worlds Without and Within

What Cowper gave to his contemporary readers has been variously described as a model of nineteenth-century domestic subjectivity tinged with evangelical piety; an uneasy rehabilitation of the bachelor figure as suburban man; and a sensibility critical of the inhumanity of slavery and imperial expansion.[27] Francis Jeffrey could claim in 1802 that "every one is internally familiar" with

---

subject from ethical "claims" or "demands" and provide instead a certain "grace" (11–13, 10). In my account of the eventlessness of wartime, however, claims and demands still permeate the experience of the ordinary.

[26] Fussell suggests that wartime presents a world in which deadly blunders "are more common than usual" and explanatory narratives are difficult to achieve (35).

[27] Leonore Davidoff and Catherine Hall, *Family Fortunes* (Chicago: U of Chicago P, 1987), 162–67; Andrew Elfenbein, "Stricken Deer: Secrecy, Homophobia, and the Rise of the Suburban Man," *Genders* 27 (1998); Tim Fulford, Debbie Lee, and Peter J. Kitson, *Literature, Science and Exploration in the Romantic Era: Bodies of Knowledge* (Cambridge: Cambridge UP, 2004), 18–20, 62–66.

the "private feelings" offered in *The Task*; by 1838 the poem had been given the status of "household words." [28] Yet there remains a neglected aspect of the remarkable bequest of Cowper's poem, sent out from his refuge in Olney to a larger world. For romantic writers of modern wartime, a world hangs in nearly every line of Cowper's "The Winter's Evening," a world of barely discerned consequences and violence. I will frequently reread these lines in the pages that follow. For the moment, I want to note the "worldliness" of Cowper's thinking: the "world" and its putative distance are both the objects of his thought and the enabling conditions of that thought. Here is Cowper's description of reading the newspaper "at a safe distance" from the "roar" of that world:

> . . . I seem advanc'd
> To some secure and more than mortal height,
> That lib'rates and exempts me from them all.
> It [the world] turns submitted to my view, turns round
> With all its generations; I behold
> The tumult, and am still. (IV: 95–100)

The description is remarkably vexing but also canny: the poet might as well be watching the evening television news (and its trademark spinning globe) with the sound muted. "The sound of war / Has lost its terrors ere it reaches me," he adds (IV: 100–1). The modern experience of wartime can certainly adopt this detached, rational, and obviously privileged stance. But detachment and rationality sometimes give way in his poem to a closer, more intimate sense of war. Even as he reads the paper and remarks upon his peaceful parlour, Cowper glances up to see a fleeting image of the enemy warrior Goliath in the mirrors of the room (IV: 269–70). And later, though apparently exempt from the effects of war, Cowper discovers in the "indolent vacuity of [his] thought," uncanny reminders of war even within his cozy retreat (IV: 297). As Kevis Goodman discovers in her reading of *The Task*, the poem opens onto "certain haunted strangers that wander through it, each of them dispossessed or vagrant subjects touched by the effects of imperial expansion" (92). Goodman's reading upends conventional interpretations of the poem by finding in it a sophisticated and anxious outlook on the news and a larger world of suffering. Cowper's masterpiece fits within her larger theorizing of the complex mediation of affect and consequent revisions of history at work in the poetry of the long eighteenth century. Her insights have profoundly influenced this study,

---

[28] Jeffrey writes of Cowper in his review of "Hayley's Life of Cowper," *Edinburgh Review* 2 (1803): 64–86; the last citation comes from George Godfrey Cunningham, ed. *Lives of Eminent and Illustrious Englishmen*, 8 vols. (Glasgow: A. Fullarton, 1838), 6: 327. Jeffrey and *Lives* are cited in Elfenbein 11.

as subsequent chapters will make clear. For now it is enough to say that in discovering these haunting reminders, affective rather than intellectual, Cowper
sketched a bridge from immediate feeling and perception to a sense of distant
suffering. It is true that this bridge is tentative and uncertain: those crossing it
are liable, at any moment, to fall back into detachment or affective paralysis,
to behold the tumult and be still. But romantic writers after Cowper found in
his poem the tools by which to express their affective, un-joined, inarticulate
response to battles fought afar.[29]

One reason Cowper's poem was so powerful for those writers lay in its engagement with that powerful tradition in eighteenth-century moral philosophy which insists that our feelings diminish as the objects of suffering are removed by distance, temporal or geographical. Cowper reacts, that is, against
what we might call a prior theory of mediation. Thus for David Hume the
news is mildly but not deeply affecting:

> Any recent Event or Piece of News, by which the Fortunes of States,
> Provinces, or many Individuals, are affected, is extremely interesting
> even to those whose Welfare is not immediately engag'd. Such Intelli-
> gence is propagated with Celerity, heard with Avidity, and enquir'd into
> with Attention and Concern. . . . The Imagination is sure to be affected;
> tho' the Passions excited may not always be so strong and steady as to
> have great Influence on the Conduct and Behaviour.[30]

Intelligence from abroad grabs your attention, but does not move or penetrate
you. Elsewhere, in fact, Hume warns against making distant suffering "present
and intimate":

> [I]f we confine ourselves to a general and distant reflection on the ills of
> human life, *that* can have no effect to prepare us for them. If by close
> and intense meditation we render them present and intimate to us, *that*
> is the true secret of poisoning all our pleasures, and rendering us perpet-
> ually miserable.[31]

---

[29] Cowper does this in response to, even in competition with, the reigning media form: the
newspaper (*Georgic Modernity* 78–91). See also Ian Baucom, *Specters of the Atlantic: Finance Capital,
Slavery, and the Philosophy of History* (Durham: Duke UP, 2005), 238–39.

[30] David Hume, *An Enquiry Concerning the Principles of Morals* (London: A. Millar, 1751), 90.

[31] David Hume, *Essays and Treatises on Several Subjects*, 2 vols. (Edinburgh and London: George
Caw, Cadell and Davies, 1800), 1:188; emphasis original. Adam Smith reiterates and extends this
thought in *The Theory of Moral Sentiments* (Amherst, NY: Prometheus, 2000): "All men, even those
at the greatest distance, are entitled to our good wishes. . . . But if, notwithstanding, they should be
unfortunate, to give ourselves any anxiety upon that account seems to be no part of our duty" (197).
On Smith and long-distance sympathy, see Ellison 10–11; Baucom 234–41; and Christopher Herbert, *Culture and Anomie: Ethnographic Imagination in the Nineteenth Century* (Chicago: U of Chicago P, 1991), 79–89.

This passage, from Hume's essay "The Sceptic," provides an extreme counter to the sentimental tradition, promoting instead the fantasy of a formidably insular individual. Nevertheless it shrewdly highlights the two faces or "two cosmopolitanisms" available in the sentimental tradition: on the one hand the "general and distant reflection" usually assigned to a figure like Adam Smith's "impartial spectator," kin to Cowper's "lib'rated and exempted" reader; and on the other the "close and intense meditation" of the melancholic, one who cannot help, as Smith also says, "changing places in fancy with the sufferer . . . and be[ing] affected by what he feels" (4).[32] As Cowper showed with special force, this oscillation between abstraction and intimacy, detachment and invasion, proves fundamental to the psychological and emotional culture of modern wartime.

When prosecuted on the scale of the planet, as it was at the turn of the nineteenth and again in the twentieth century, war took shape as forces spanning the globe. But as Cowper realized, recognition of the global sweep of the war lent only new urgency to the cultivation of an interiority which comprehended the interior spaces of England itself, its cottages and hearths, its "domestic quiet," but also, and increasingly, its inner psyche. As both Cowper and Hazlitt understood it, wartime was a matter of both the world "without" and a world within.[33] If, as Georg Lukács argued, the "inner life of a nation is linked with the modern mass army in a way it could not have been" prior to the French Revolution, the inner life of individuals cannot escape this militarized context. Indeed, as the three poems in my prelude, and as Hazlitt's bell—it was "like an alarm" and "brought me . . . to myself"—all suggest, wartime makes it hard to determine whether or not those psychic spaces had been conjured precisely to register war's intrusion.

Describing the "calamitous years" of foreign warfare in "The Ruined Cottage" (1797), William Wordsworth begins to develop some of the affective and rhetorical possibilities that lie within this conception of wartime.[34] In that temporally layered and highly mediated tale, written in 1797 but first published in 1814, the poet works out a "strange discipline" to coordinate the operations of worlds without and within.[35] The poem's narrator tells of repeated

---

[32] In his analysis of Smith's *Theory of Moral Sentiments*, Baucom identifies "the two cosmopolitanisms": that of the disinterested spectator, with its systematic view of the world; and that of a "dejected" system of a widely ranging sympathetic fancy independent of distance (Baucom 240).

[33] Georg Lukács, *The Historical Novel* (Lincoln: U of Nebraska P, 1983), 24.

[34] William Wordsworth, *The Excursion*, book I, line 549 in *Wordsworth: Poetical Works*, ed. Thomas Hutchinson, rev. Ernest de Selincourt (Oxford: Oxford UP, 1904; 1981), 597. All further citations from this text.

[35] William Wordsworth, "Reconciling Addendum" to "The Ruined Cottage," in *Poetical Works of William Wordsworth*, ed. Ernest de Selincourt and Helen Darbishire (Oxford: Clarendon, 1949), 5: 400.

visits to Margaret in her rural cottage and charts her decline into poverty and misery after "the plague of war" hits. First come disease and drought, the effects of which push her husband Robert to sell himself to join "a troop / Of soldiers, going to a distant land" (I: 676–77). The historical referent seems to be the American War of Independence, but the timing remains unclear; in any case the poem rehearses and then is itself rehearsed as a wartime narrative.[36]

Margaret is left no note, just a blank sheet of paper with the money Robert raised; she understands little but that he wanted to keep her from following and "'sink[ing] / Beneath the misery of that wandering life'"—that is, the not uncommon practice of accompanying her husband to war (I: 680–81). Yet as the effects of distant war accumulate, Margaret does take to a desperate wandering:

> "I have been travelling far; and many days
> About the fields I wander, knowing this
> Only, that what I seek I cannot find;
> And so I waste my time: for I am changed;
> And to myself," said she, "have done much wrong." (I: 764–68)

When her body grows too weary, her mind wanders in a sort of vacancy or waste of time reminiscent of Cowper's "lost hour":

> . . . in yon arbour oftentimes she sate [the narrator reports]
> Alone, through half the vacant sabbath day;
>   . . . On this old bench
> For hours she sate; and evermore her eye
> Was busy in the distance, shaping things
> That made her heart beat quick. (I: 876–77, 879–82)

This wandering of body and mind, answering to and mirroring the invisible movement of troops in distant lands, proves infectious not only to Margaret, but to the storyteller, later named "The Wanderer" in the version that appears in Book I of *The Excursion*. He too has "wasted" an hour staring at a "desolate" "spot" (I: 730, 740). Often in his walks, the Wanderer says, "A momentary

---

[36] In its first version, the narrator tells of his visits to Margaret's cottage and relays her version of what happened. In the later version, embedded in *The Excursion*, the narrator now known as the Pedlar repeats a tale told him by the Wanderer, who conveys Margaret's tale in a narrative full of interruptions and digressions. In a note dictated to Isabella Fenwick, Wordsworth does not exactly clarify the history, mixing the War of Independence and the more recent wars with France:

> I was born too late to have a distinct remembrance of the origin of the American war, but the state in which I represent Robert's [the husband's] mind to be I had frequent opportunities of observing at the commencement of our rupture with France in '93. . . . (Qtd. in William Wordsworth, *The Poems*, ed. John O. Hayden vol. 2 (New Haven: Yale UP, 1977), 955n)

trance comes over me; / And to myself I seem to muse" on someone who has either died or been "borne away" (I: 784–86).

This vagrancy of affection derives in part from the epistemological quandary these characters inhabit. Margaret, for instance, "had . . . [n]o tidings of her husband" gone to war (I: 818). "She knew not that he lived; if he were dead, / She knew not he was dead" (I: 819–20). But the wandering of affect has another source, one closely related to this unanswerable question of living or dead, and one which makes evident the relation between the trope of wandering and the oscillation of detachment and intimacy we first saw in Cowper. As Alan Liu argues, Wordsworth's poem portrays a world where feeling humanity wavers before a system or "pattern" of unfeeling things (I: 320–21): the "uncouth figures" carved by a disconsolate Robert "on the heads of sticks," the broken bowls, the omnipresent weeds, the ruin of the cottage. For all the Wanderer's belief that the "secret spirit of humanity" survives in the "plants, and weeds, and flowers" that cluster around the ruins of the cottage (I: 927–29), Liu points out that *there is also something shockingly dehumanizing about* [such] *imagery*" (320; emphasis original).[37] Not merely the individual objects but patterning itself, the translation of disparate things (and persons) into formal or conceptual organization, powerfully challenges a felt or feeling life. Even as Robert exchanges his vital presence for much-needed cash (which is soon dispersed); even as his happy domesticity with Margaret yields to larger economies that put him in a "troop" transported to a "distant land"; even as Margaret neglects her infant because her mind is pathologically "busy at a distance"; so the pattern of the poem leaves the reader, like Margaret, gazing after absent people while "shaping things" in a futile effort to "made [the] heart beat." " 'Tis a common tale," according to the Wanderer: part of a pattern, one might say, and common now to Margaret and reader alike (I: 636). And in becoming common, the poem pulls away from felt immediacy: "A tale of silent suffering, hardly clothed / In bodily form" (I: 638–39). (Wordsworth's tropes are characteristically complex: read backwards, the sentient body is a "form" converted through metaphor to insensate clothing, which is then nearly removed from the "tale.") Indeed, as Liu implies, in its complex formal patterning, in its layers of temporal and narrative mediation, "The Ruined Cottage" provides as much distanced comprehension of a "common" situation as moving testimony grounded in the suffering of human bodies.

The poem's affective and epistemological unease is located in the discrepancy between these two realms: between sensible feeling and comprehensive pattern. This discrepancy serves, in fact, as the motor for the poem's vagrancy,

---

[37] Liu takes his cue from Cleanth Brooks, "Wordsworth and Human Suffering: Notes on Two Early Poems," in *From Sensibility to Romanticism* (London: Oxford UP, 1965), 373–88. On the Stoic *apatheia* or un-feeling at work in *The Excursion*, see also Goodman 118–26.

its restlessness of mind and body. In his momentary trance, Wordsworth's Wanderer calls up a figure from the purgatory between the felt and the unfelt: "I seem to muse on One . . . / A human being destined to awake / To human life, or something very near" (I: 785–89). Margaret performs her own constant "tracing" and retracing of this purgatorial zone, a moving into the distance and returning to the cottage, toward absent people and back to present things. Each performs this perpetually frustrated sort of cognitive mapping, the movement of their feet in the outside world corresponding to the wandering of their minds. Against Cowper's more privileged newspaper reader, sitting at home while the world turns submitted to his view, these characters are externally and internally moved, unsettled, sent wandering from home. Even as they attempt to map this sentient ground, they realize nothing will be settled or ascertained here. "I wander," Margaret explains, "knowing this / Only, that what I seek I cannot find" (I: 765–66). Such purgatorial figures, "not dead but never fully alive, either animated things or deanimated persons," haunt Wordsworth's poetry more generally, as David Simpson notes. They are "ghosts who are not fully of the present yet seem bereft of accessible pasts—haunting the present from the present itself."[38]

When Wordsworth wants to disclose the coordination of the world within and the world without, he stages it as an incursion on what we might call the present frame of mind by distant violence. Like Cowper, Coleridge, Hazlitt, and Williams, Wordsworth literalizes this incursion in a winter scene by the hearth. For poor, abandoned Margaret, the security and exemption Cowper found in his retreat are far past. Her home and the very frame of her inner world are permeable to the ruinous forces of the world without, in ways that belie the supposed division of inner and outer:

> Meanwhile her poor Hut
> Sank to decay; for he was gone, whose hand,
> At the first nipping of October frost,
> Closed up each chink. . . .
> And so she lived
> Through the long winter, reckless and alone;
> Until her house by frost, and thaw, and rain,
> Was sapped; and while she slept, the nightly damps
> Did chill her breast; and in the stormy day
> Her tattered clothes were ruffled by the wind,
> Even at the side of her own fire. (I: 900–10)

[38] David Simpson, "Derrida's Ghosts: The State of Our Debt," *Studies in Romanticism* 46.2 (Summer–Fall 2007): 183–202.

I will have more to say later about the long winter of wartime and the chilling numbness that it spreads. For the present, I merely want to note that if "The Ruined Cottage" seems a raw or stripped down version of the wartime created in the other poems, it nonetheless comes to us through the mediation of the man of letters, Wordsworth's initial narrator and then the Wanderer. In each case, the narrator works diligently to put this history and its woes to rest. "My Friend! enough to sorrow you have given," the Wanderer chides his listener, as if sorrow had its own economy (I: 932).[39] Yet, as we have seen, the tale itself presses against all manner of laying to rest and moves in upon the present audience, eliciting that troubling sorrow. In its emphasis on the turnings and re-turnings that place the narrators on common ground with Margaret—"I turned aside in weakness," says the narrator for a second time, when the tale is done, "Then towards the cottage I returned" (I: 919, 925)—we see how the poem constructs wartime as a particular and recurrent (retraceable) geopolitical condition, the very ground of an experience that is nevertheless always in some sense removed, re-moved.

If the conduct of the Napoleonic wars prompted General Carl von Clausewitz to theorize "war without limits," an idea which led a century later to the theory and practice of what we now call total war, that military theory was accompanied and supported by another feature of those wars. As Wordsworth's "strange discipline" hints, writers found the capacity to represent war as an adaptive system with a global reach, moving impassively and extensively but also intensively and minutely—without limits. War in this era was shown to operate both globally and, simultaneously, within the everyday, cultivating what Samuel Taylor Coleridge calls, in "Frost at Midnight," "dim sympathies" between present and absent realities. Taken as a ubiquitous system, war was at once unremarkable and nearly imperceptible; something nonevident that could not always be made evident. Felt and unfelt, impersonal and intimate, war became for those experiencing it at a distance a not-fully-conscious awareness that could flare up and flicker out, even as they went about the routines of the day, read the paper, watched TV, or turned and stared, as many did, at something else—or nothing at all. In their histories of modern wartime, the texts of Romanticism do not disclose what had been hidden or repressed, but ask us to attune ourselves to the signs of what was always elsewhere.

[39] The Wanderer was strongly influenced by Wordsworth's encounters with Joseph Fawcett, the preacher and poet cited earlier. Wordsworth mentions that Fawcett's "Poem on War [*The Art of War*, 1795; later published as *Civilised War*, 1798], which had a good deal of merit . . . made me think more about him than I should otherwise have done" ("Notes" in *Poetical Works* 315).

Wartime Without Limits

Periodization flourishes within wartime. The desire is powerful to put period to and step outside of the time of war, to contain and manage it, to behold it and be *still*. This is one form by which war at a distance is mediated, a form which replaces geographical distance with the distance of chronological classification, even in the simple form of today's news occluding the news of yesterday. As we'll see Raymond Williams remark in the next chapter, such mediating structures of feeling (like any form of mediation) can allow both the transmission of experience and its obstruction. Channeling war into delineated periods of time with definite beginnings and ends—or, thinking spatially, with obvious insides and outsides—allows and heightens certain responses to war but also keeps it at a remove. Periodizing, in other words, resists or aims to close off the ongoing "presentness" or incomplete "present tense" of history, as Williams conceives it. The "periodization strategy," Russell Berman has argued polemically, is "designed to separate the readers of th[is] present from the claimants of the past"—that is, from the claimants of a present marked as different and over: yesterday's news.[40] It's not hard to understand, then, why wartime generates a rush to such forms of separation and ending, a warding off of those troubling ghosts that Simpson perceives "haunting the present from the present itself" (185).

And yet my survey of wartime writing indicates wartime also has trouble measuring its distance from other times of war: it produces a history of the present always permeable to other presents, other wartimes. Recall the structure of Wordsworth's "Ruined Cottage," its turns and returns fusing the wartime of the early 1800s with that of the 1770s, and those with an imagined future wartime of the reader. In another way, the "films" that Coleridge sees on the fire grate anticipate the strange films that invade our living (or media) rooms. And so my writing also, now and then, lets in such strangers from another time, hazarding a confusion of proper historical placement, introducing anachronism. It does so not—or not simply—to shake off the constraints of historicism, with its emphasis on periodizing, nor to generate topical relevance. (In fact, the anachronism of wartime is as likely to fling up wars from the ancient past as more historically recent conflicts.) Instead, this study participates in anachronism in order to be true to its topic.[41] Rather than provide

[40] Russell Berman, "Politics: Divide and Rule," *MLQ: Modern Language Quarterly* 62.4 (2001): 325.

[41] On anachronism see Srinivas Aravamudan, "The Return of Anachronism," *MLQ: Modern Language Quarterly* 62.4 (2001): 331–53; James Chandler, *England in 1819* (Chicago: U of Chicago P, 1998), 107–8, 500–2; and Jerome Christensen, *Romanticism at the End of History* (Baltimore: Johns Hopkins UP, 2000), 3–41.

the history of a past period, it records the vestiges of an unlimited present, sentient of a war without limits. These vestiges are ways of experiencing and telling war that have not been fully acknowledged, yet affect us still.

Over the ten years while I was writing it, *War at a Distance* became, as if by accident, a wartime history of modern wartime. When and where it actually begins thus is difficult to say: During the first Gulf War, when I initially turned my attention to this earlier wartime? Or during the Vietnam era, when Betty T. Bennett assembled her anthology of *British War Poetry in the Age of Romanticism*, the discovery of which stimulated my own research?[42] Or, indeed, during the years of the Revolutionary and Napoleonic wars, to which my reflections on twenty-first-century wartime return, again and again? Under the ever-present possibility of unlimited war, wartime itself seems increasingly difficult to restrict or seal off, always vulnerable to invasion from other wars. The problem is not solely mine. Throughout this contemporary wartime, the questions remain hotly debated: Is the United States again fighting in the quagmire of Vietnam? Or is it engaged in the noble mission of World War II? Or a reopening of the Crusades? Where and when did this time of war begin? And why do these past wars suddenly seem not to have been settled, once and for all? Elsewhere, perhaps more quietly, the present wartime gives increasing currency, if not explanatory value, to the Napoleonic adventure and its worldwide effects, as in Peter Weir's recent screen adaptation of Patrick O'Brien's novels *Master and Commander: The Far Side of the World* (2003), in the *Pirates of the Caribbean* movie franchise, or in the 2005 public vote on "The Greatest Painting in Britain," which went to *The Fighting Temeraire*, J.M.W. Turner's rendering of a battleship celebrated for its role in the 1805 battle of Trafalgar (an event whose bicentennial was celebrated with enormous fanfare throughout the British Commonwealth).[43] But I note also the brooding presence of this earlier wartime among intellectuals. In 1999, Booker Prize–winner Barry Unsworth published *Losing Nelson*, narrated by a man obsessed with, and compelled to reenact in contemporary London, the career of Admiral Horatio Nelson, hero of Trafalgar. Susan Sontag's eloquent essay on war photography, *Regarding the Pain of Others* (2003), has as its cover a (prephotographic) image from Francisco Goya's chilling series *The Disasters of War*, his record of the ravages of war in Spain circa 1810–14. Economist and *New York Times* columnist Paul Krugman tells readers that his eyes were opened to the chicanery of the George W. Bush administration when he began to study the political

---

[42] Bennett's anthology remained more or less neglected by scholars of Romanticism until this century, when an updated edition was made available online under the auspices of *Romantic Circles* at http://www.rc.umd.edu/editions/warpoetry/.

[43] The vote was sponsored by BBC Radio 4's *Today Programme* in association with the National Gallery.

maneuverings of Castlereagh and Metternich in Europe in 1812–15 (Krugman had been reading *A World Restored*, a study of the two statesmen written years earlier by Henry Kissinger, architect of foreign policy during the latter part of the Vietnam era).[44] I have already cited C. K. Williams's poem "The Hearth," with its echoes of Cowper and Coleridge; it is the most reprinted poem from his prize-winning collection *The Singing* (2003). In the acclaimed last novel by the German émigré W. G. Sebald, the lost history of his hero is filtered through a name, Austerlitz, which asks the reader to recall Napoleon's great victory, as well as the grand train station in Paris which commemorates that triumph and serves as the switchboard of Europe. But *Austerlitz* (2001) also insists that we hear in its title the garbled transmission of a more recent history, for which Auschwitz serves as the proper noun. Why does the Holocaust survivor Austerlitz, orphaned by the Nazi concentration camps, wandering adrift from his own past, carry with him a talismanic relic from the grave of Marshall Michel Ney, Napoleon's great accomplice in war? Sebald's work worries over the pained forgotten-ness of European history and in *Austerlitz*, as in his previous novel, *Vertigo*, the Napoleonic era marks the heart of what, forgotten or unnoticed, yet moves and motivates our world.

Several years ago, Jerome Christensen proposed that Romanticism, the intellectual and aesthetic movement that accompanied the rise of Napoleon and its aftermath in Europe, had rehearsed (or previewed?) the predicament of the turn of the twenty-first century: that is, it had wrestled with the "end of history" in ways that might illuminate our own condition.[45] That proposition was offered before the "end of history" was blown apart by the events and aftermath of September 11, 2001. It seems now that the condition of the romantic period which speaks most pressingly to the current day is its sense of a history of warfare that, however distant, keeps not ending: not in 1793 with the death of the French King; not in 1795 with the end of the Terror; not in the 1802 Peace of Amiens; not in Napoleon's first abdication in 1814; not in the seemingly decisive battle of Waterloo in 1815 (echoed in 1819 at the disaster of Peterloo); and certainly not in 1989 or 2001. If anything, it is a traumatized sense of history we have inherited from the romantic and Napoleonic era, one that disrupts any settled sense of period, context, or linearity.[46] When, for instance, Katie Trumpener characterizes the genre of the national tale circa 1814, she characterizes as well an aspect of other contemporary wartime writings: the exploration of "the coexistence of multiple layers of time in place and the

[44] Paul Krugman, *The Great Unraveling: Losing Our Way in the New Century* (New York: Norton, 2004).
[45] Christensen, see esp. 1–41.
[46] Philip Shaw probes the unclosed "wound" of the battle of Waterloo in *Waterloo and the Romantic Imagination* (Basingstoke, UK: Palgrave Macmillan, 2002), 1–34.

discontinuities of place in time."[47] In contrast to the progressivist histories of the Scottish Enlightenment, given imaginative form in many of Walter Scott's *Waverley* novels, this alternate view attends to "the long-term effects of historical trauma, the deliberate or amnesiac repression of historical memory, and the neurotic mechanisms developed to contain its explosiveness" (Trumpener 151). Such a history is recognizable to any reader of Sebald's novels. It is recognizable also, I would suggest, to readers of Coleridge's "Rime of the Ancient Mariner" or "Kubla Khan" (1798) with its "ancestral voices prophesying war" (30). And it is recognizable too in Cowper's *The Task*.

All of this suggests that the wartime of those first modern and global wars demands the sort of historiography suggested by Walter Benjamin's "Theses on the Philosophy of History"—also written in wartime, in a "moment of danger."[48] This earlier wartime asks the present to "take cognizance of it in order to blast a specific era"—our own, but the Romantic era as well—"out of the homogeneous course of history" (Benjamin 263). The violence of Benjamin's language should not be overlooked: he wrote even as the Nazi regime strove to blast entire peoples and their cultures out of the present (his word is *Jetztzeit*) and into an irrevocable past.[49] "*[E]ven the dead*," Benjamin famously urges, "will not be safe from the enemy if he wins" (255; emphasis original). This is what, in Scarry's account, wars do: they destroy the very "extension" of a people in time, space, and, Benjamin would add, in history. As I have said, the time of war, wartime, may contribute to the zeal for endings; putting an end to the claims of others, putting an end to feeling, to wartime's own "psychological and emotional culture."[50] But wartime can also entail a countereffect, a melee of temporal synchronies and discontinuities that results not in the end of history but its reopening. In this sense, *War at a Distance* brings into the present the experience of a distant violence, the wartime of the late eighteenth and early nineteenth centuries with all its strangeness and familiarity.

I approach wartime and its unsettling sense of chronology as forever challenging the "settlements" of history by drawing in part on its affective reservoir: the sense, for example, that current wars call up old conflicts, that old

[47] Katie Trumpener, *Bardic Nationalism: The Romantic Novel and the British Empire* (Princeton: Princeton UP, 1997), 151.

[48] Walter Benjamin, "Theses on the Philosophy of History," in *Illuminations: Essays and Reflections*, ed. and intro. Hannah Arendt, trans. Harry Zohn (New York: Schocken, 1968), 255. The "Theses" were completed in spring of 1940 (267n).

[49] "History is the subject of a structure whose site is not homogeneous, empty time," asserts Benjamin, "but time filled by the presence of the now [*Jetztzeit*]" (261).

[50] Benjamin's critique of historicism has been taken up as a critique of periodization per se. See for example Berman (325).

conflicts have not fully passed away. In place of the tunnel of empty homogeneous time through which one sort of history glides, wartime finds its history in a dangerous and unpredictable minefield. This latter view of history is particularly romantic. Wartime calls forth something similar to what Ian Baucom (also drawing on Benjamin) calls a *melancholy* or *romantic* historicism. For Baucom this romantic historicism "insists on its ability to return to the lost or absent scene, person, or thing imaginatively, fancifully, but also, crucially, *truthfully*." The "paradigmatic . . . case" of such melancholy history is "the lost news of the news of loss" (Baucom 217; emphasis original). The *melancholy* of this form of history indicates a condition Freud famously diagnosed, the repeated introjection of the lost object so that the healing work of mourning is suspended, never finished. In this way, the loss remains an open psychic wound.[51] The truthful return Baucom identifies can never effect a full recuperation: it is rather this opening or suspension, not a return *of* the lost object, but a return *to* its loss or absence—like the retracings described in "The Ruined Cottage," the compulsive turning back to the abandoned house by Margaret, the Wanderer, and his listener. What a romantic history offers in its returns is a haunted awareness that calls up powerful feelings of loss and sorrow so that they are never put to rest. Baucom's thinking derives from the history of the slave trade, and its signal moment is the lost news of fallen bodies. He follows the case of the slave ship *Zong*, where 133 slaves considered sick and unmarketable were thrown overboard in 1781 by order of the captain and drowned. The owners of the ship subsequently collected insurance money to compensate them for their "lost" merchandise. In Baucom's treatment of this story, romantic or melancholy history arises at the end of the eighteenth century in reaction to a specific historical situation: the increased role of speculative finance (in enabling the long-distance transactions of the slave trade) and correlative modes of thought: those which attempt to account for human experience "in the aggregate" or average (as "common tales"), and those which redeem an event by assigning it a compensatory meaning or value (as "interest" or a satisfactory return on your investment).

The historical situation revealed by a romantic history, however, could also be derived from the lost news and the news of loss produced by distant global warfare. The system of modern global war, like the slave trade, did not emerge all at once: certainly the Seven Years' War and the American War of Independence contributed to a new understanding, especially in Britain, of the geopolitics of warfare.[52] But by the opening of the nineteenth century, the British

[51] Sigmund Freud, "Mourning and Melancholia," in *On Metapsychology: The Theory of Psychoanalysis*, ed. Angela Richards (Harmondsworth, UK: Penguin, 1984), 11: 257–58.

[52] Recent work on this topic includes C. A. Bayly, *The Birth of the Modern World, 1780–1914: Global Connections and Comparisons* (Malden, MA: Blackwell, 2004), esp. 86–120, and *Imperial*

national economy had refined its systems of credit so as to support prolonged wars with mass armies across the globe: William Pitt not only successfully instituted income tax but in 1797 suspended specie payment by the Bank of England, promoting the use of credit almost to the point of bankruptcy in order to pay off coalition forces on the continent.[53] Finance capital, in other words, was as formative for global warfare as it was for the Atlantic slave trade; indeed the two practices were tightly implicated, one in the other. At the same time, the translation of men like Robert in "A Ruined Cottage" into the numbers needed for mass armies had become proverbial, though more slowly in Britain than on the continent (Napoleon was said to have boasted that as a military commander "A man like me does not give a shit about the lives of a million men").[54] Worldwide, the war advanced a vision of men taken in the aggregate. In a near-parody of the numbers that came increasingly to represent the war, Philip Shaw gives the statistics of the battle of Waterloo: "Within an area of land measuring just less than three miles from east to west, and less than a mile and a half from north to south, over 40,000 men"—and 15,000 horses—"were killed in a mere eight hours, "short even by modern military standards" (20). Attritional battles were now the norm. Napoleon aimed to dominate by sheer force of numbers; among his reasons for proceeding to India was the thought of the enormous reserves of conscriptable bodies there (Lefebvre 112, 163; Bayly, *Modern World*, 86). Cannon fodder was also on the mind of Charles William Pasley, whose influential *Essay on the Military Policy and Institutions of the British Empire* (1811) advocated using colonial bodies to bolster Britain's fighting strength.[55] As many as five million

Meridian: The British Empire and the World, 1780–1830 (London: Longman, 1989); J. G. A. Pocock, "Political Thought in the English-Speaking Atlantic, 1760–1790," in *The Varieties of British Political Thought, 1500–1800* (Cambridge: Cambridge UP, 1993); Dror Wahrman, *The Making of the Modern Self: Identity and Culture in Eighteenth-Century England* (New Haven: Yale UP, 2004); and Kathleen Wilson, *The Sense of the People: Politics, Culture, and Imperialism in England, 1715–1785* (New York: Cambridge UP, 1995).

[53] By 1809, the risks of Pitt's financial system had unleashed wide debate about the principles of political economy. See critiques by William Cobbett, *Paper against Gold: The History and Mystery of the Bank of England* (1810) and David Ricardo, *The High Price of Bullion a Proof of the Depreciation of Bank-notes* (1809). On the growth of the military fiscal state in eighteenth-century Britain, see John Brewer, *The Sinews of Power: War, Money and the English State, 1688–1783* (London: Routledge, 1989). On the late century more specifically, see Bayly, *Birth of the Modern World*, 92–96; Georges Lefebvre, *Napoleon* (New York: Columbia UP, 1990), 108–9; Arthur Hope-Jones, *Income Tax in the Napoleonic Wars* (Cambridge: Cambridge UP, 1939), 1–4, 72–125; and Jerome-Adolphe Blanqui, *A History of Political Economy in Europe*, trans. Emily Josephine Leonard (New York: G. P. Putman's Sons, 1885), 454–61.

[54] David A. Bell, *The First Total War: Napoleon's Europe and the Birth of Warfare as We Know It* (Boston: Houghton Mifflin, 2007), 251.

[55] Charles William Pasley, *Essay on the Military Policy and Institutions of the British Empire*, 2nd ed. (London: A. J. Valpy, 1811), 205–25.

soldiers in Europe—there are no reliable numbers for civilian deaths or deaths on other continents—died in the Napoleonic venture.[56]

More significantly, perhaps, the impulse to understand the enormity of these wars through enumeration was supported by new scientific methods for calculating war fatalities and casualties. A distinct strain in romantic writing identifies and attacks the impulse, evident in early demographical studies like Thomas Malthus's *An Essay on the Principle of Population* (1807), to convert human bodies to the abstraction and speculation promoted by numbers. Here again is Joseph Fawcett, aghast at the "arithmetical eyes" encouraged by modern, mediated war:

> There is nothing perhaps, so shocking in all the horrible perversion of nature, which the monstrous and prodigious state of war exhibits to the contemplative mind, as the coldness, with which . . . [readers] throw their eye over the sum total of the slain in battle, which the . . . [news]paper presents to them. No emotions of horror are excited in them by the largest amounts of these military murders, which the public prints can announce. They look at the sum with only arithmetical eyes. They see nothing but figures in it. They consider it with the cold, mathematical feelings of an accomptant, as if it consisted only of abstract units. They do not seem to reflect, for so much as a moment, that one of these units denotes a MAN; that it is the little summary mark of a volume of anguish and of ill. . . . (*Elegies* 10–11n)

Affective response seems a cure to the arithmetical eye: "a horror . . . should cause his [the reader's] head to swim, and strike a sickness into his heart" (*Elegies* 10–11n). More often, though, these fallen bodies were quickly exchanged as promissory notes for nation, culture, and religion.[57]

In returning to the wartime of the Revolutionary and Napoleonic wars, I am looking for signs of this persistent romantic history. An intellectual tradition since Kant and Hegel has organized its history around a singular sign or event, the French Revolution. For his part, Baucom steps away from this tradition by introducing the *Zong* as an alternative event, the unacknowledged

[56] Historians debate these numbers; the count of war dead in Europe varies from two to four million; civilian deaths may have reached one million. For a list of varying statistics and their sources, see http://users.erols.com/mwhite28/wars19c.htm.

[57] In *A History of the Modern Fact* (Chicago: U of Chicago P, 1998), Mary Poovey argues that Coleridge, Southey, Hazlitt, and others found Malthus's use of numbers could be "heartless and amoral—. . . the few who used them could inflict actual damage on the many who were powerless to resist" (294). See also Frances Ferguson, "Malthus, Godwin, Wordsworth, and the Spirit of Solitude," in *Literature and the Body: Essays on Populations and Persons*, ed. Elaine Scarry (Baltimore: Johns Hopkins UP, 1988), 106–24; and Maureen N. McLane, *Romanticism and the Human Sciences: Poetry, Population, and the Discourse of the Species* (Cambridge: Cambridge UP, 2000).

truth of what he calls "our long contemporaneity."[58] I share Baucom's desire to let something other than the French Revolution cast its light upon this ongoing, unsettled history. Since its inception, the French Revolution has appealed to intellectuals as an event that, retrospectively, has granted considerable historical agency to intellectuals great and small.[59] The Revolution—along with British counterrevolution—has also provided the primary axis for a long and familiar tradition of scholarship interpreting romantic texts. Focusing on the French Revolution in these ways has contributed to an emphasis on political discourse, ideological struggle, utopian possibilities, and the modern orientation toward an open future.[60] But such a focus has not encouraged us to attend to the response—felt and unfelt—to fallen bodies.[61]

If the modern is an era of revolution, of dramatic social and political upheaval, then it is worth remembering that the revolutions which inaugurated this modernity—in America, France, and Haiti—were accomplished through state-sponsored violence against bodies. The bloody nature of these revolutions distinguishes them from the earlier Glorious Revolution in England and inaugurates the modern meaning of the word. Thus Reinhart Koselleck ends his historiographical essay on "The Modern Concept of Revolution" by noting that, as the declarations of the American, French, and Russian revolutions all make clear, modern expressions of Revolution "all . . . spatially imply a *world revolution*" (52; emphasis original). Turning then to the example of Napoleon, Koselleck observes sadly that the notion of worldwide revolution has produced a planet where "all wars have been transformed into civil wars," "regionally limited but globally conducted"; where civil wars, "boundless" in their "awfulness," are held in check only by the prospect of total nuclear

[58] "It is now well past time," Baucom complains, "for anyone wishing to speak of the European discourses on and of modernity to have done with this monomania of historical vision [directed at the French Revolution]" (227).

[59] Roger Chartier, "Do Books Make Revolutions?" in *The Cultural Origins of the French Revolution* (Durham: Duke UP, 1991), 67–91. Chartier targets works like Robert Darnton's influential *Literary Underground of the Old Regime* (Cambridge: Harvard UP, 1982).

[60] On the "open future" of modernity, see Reinhart Koselleck, *Futures Past: On the Semantics of Historical Time*, trans. Keith Tribe (New York: Columbia UP, 2004), esp. 223–55.

[61] The shift in emphasis from revolution to war has begun. The second essay in the 1999 *An Oxford Companion to the Romantic Age*, ed. Iain McCalman (Oxford: Oxford UP, 1999), is titled "War"; the first essay is "Revolution." Other signs of change are Philip Shaw's *Waterloo and the Romantic Imagination* and his edited collection, *Romantic Wars: Studies in Culture and Conflict, 1793–1822* (Burlington, VT: Ashgate, 2000); Gillian Russell, *The Theatres of War: Performance, Politics, and Society, 1793–1815* (Oxford: Clarendon, 1995); Simon Bainbridge, *British Poetry and the Revolutionary and Napoleonic Wars: Visions of Conflict* (Oxford: Oxford UP, 2003); J. R. Watson, *Romanticism and War: A Study of British Romantic Period Writers and the Napoleonic Wars* (Basingstoke, UK: Palgrave Macmillan, 2003). More telling is the recent work by David Simpson. His essay "Remembering the Dead: An Essay upon Epitaphs," in *9/11: The Culture of Commemoration* (Chicago: U of Chicago P, 2006), reflecting on the aftermath of September 11, 2001, draws deeply on Wordsworth's "Essay on Epitaphs" (21–51).

destruction (56).[62] For Koselleck, the warlike heart of revolution is "the unspoken law of present international politics"; it is our long contemporaneity (57).
And so this work steps away from the French Revolution as the signal event of
our contemporaneity because for all its *éclaircissement* of modernity, its brightness throws into shadow crucial situations and systems: finance capital with
the increasingly speculative traffic in fallen bodies is one; the unbounded awfulness of modern warfare, paid for by finance capital and legitimated by the
discourse of revolutionary freedom, is another.

I should say as well that I step away from Revolution to distance myself
from its aesthetics of the spectacular and sublime. In taking the singular and
awful event of the *Zong* murders, Baucom very much hopes to put his readers
in the position of eyewitnesses of that spectacular horror. His chapter "The
View from the Window" imagines the scene from the perspective of an eye-
witness, watching the bodies fall past his cabin window, close enough to
count each one, and being called later to testify to this event. "The view from
the window," Baucom discovers, "is . . . the viewpoint that, indeed, *produces*
humanity *as* a testamentary effect of bearing witness to the massacre" (201;
emphasis original). Baucom's imagination wants to bypass the obstacles of
time and mediation and forge immediacy. Not unlike the war photography
Sontag discusses, or the great panoramas of the romantic period (to which
we will turn in chapter 5), Baucom's melancholy history hopes to erase distance and make the absent unflinchingly present to our minds. The wartime
perspective, by contrast, sees very little out its window—sees, if anything,
darkness, slashing sleet, or only Cowper's uncountable "downy flakes /
Descending, and with never-ceasing lapse" (IV: 326–27). This wartime view
acknowledges without overcoming obstruction and distance. What is evident
of distant massacres appears second-hand or as intimation, a fleeting apparition, a *sense*. And wartime's history, though touched with melancholy, draws
from a more vexed and varied affective store. It is not, then, the history of a
signal event illuminating a situation; it takes up instead the "not obvious"
that fascinates Paul Fussell; it takes up Hazlitt's "minute and inconsiderable
passing events." It takes up eventlessness as the very texture of the situation of
distant war.

These last remarks suggest that wartime translates war from the realm of
sublime event to an underlying situation or condition of modernity. In doing
so, the wartime perspective shares with some recent philosophers and intellectuals an understanding of war as an absent presence that infiltrates political

[62] Bayly notes that the "most potent legacy" of the so-called age of revolutions was "the creation
of yet stronger, more intrusive states, European, colonial, and extra-European" (*Birth of the Modern
World* 88).

and cultural institutions and moves through everyday life.[63] This approach, for instance, turns away from just-war theory, based as it is on a notion of war as a delimited event with identifiable decisions and actions, to investigate the preexisting conditions that lead to war and render military violence plausible or inevitable. When war is not an event but a condition, then its distinction from peace becomes harder to see; in a militarized society, in other words, it may always be wartime. Thus, speaking about the contemporary situation, Chris Cuomo makes the link between a wartime experienced by those at a distance from the fighting and (an illusory) peacetime, where military bases uphold local economies, military service provides education and social advancement, and popular culture routinely identifies masculinity with the figure of the citizen-soldier. She could be describing the late eighteenth century in Britain. "Neglecting the omnipresence of militarism allows the false belief that the absence of declared armed conflicts *is* peace. . . . It is particularly easy for those whose lives are shaped by the safety of privilege, and who do not regularly encounter the realities of militarism, to maintain this false belief" (31; emphasis original).

Authors of romantic literature, privileged as they were, did not necessarily share this negligence or false belief. Jane Austen, for instance, understood in quite specific terms the significance of the militia encamped at Meryton.[64] Both Joseph Fawcett and Mary Robinson, two of the most powerful antiwar poets of their generation, understood the emergence of something Fawcett called "inactive war" or "armed peace": the transformation of society not by warfare per se, but by a militarization of institutions, social systems, and sensibilities.[65] The absence of open fighting in their midst did not always deceive those in England that they lived in peace. I share with writers like Cuomo the desire to conceive of war beyond the limits of the (often spectacular, often distracting) event, to trace its extension throughout a culture, even to those whose lives appear "shaped by safety and [the] privilege" of distance. I look for signs of the infiltrating sense that a system of war, waged on a global scale, year

[63] War as "presence" is the thought of Robin May Schott, "Gender and 'Postmodern War,'" *Hypatia* 11.4 (1996): 19–29. Others who move war away from the realm of "event" include Chris J. Cuomo, "War Is Not Just an Event: Reflections on the Significance of Everyday Violence," *Hypatia* 11.4 (Autumn 1996): 30–45; Judith Butler, *Precarious Life: The Powers of Mourning and Violence* (London: Verso, 2004); Lucinda Peach, "An Alternative to Pacifism? Feminism and Just-War Theory," *Hypatia* 9.1 (1994): 152–72; and Manuel de Landa, *War in the Age of Intelligent Machines* (New York: Zone Books, 1991).

[64] Tim Fulford, "Sighing for a Soldier: Jane Austen and Military Pride and Prejudice." *Nineteenth-Century Literature* 57.2 (September 2002): 153–78.

[65] Fawcett's discussion will be treated below. Mary Robinson's poem "The Camp" (1800) testifies to the social transformation effected by a militarized society. On military camps, see Russell's discussion of "Camp Culture" in *Theatres of War*, 26–51.

after year, conditions the movements of your day: where you walked, what you talked about, how your mind wandered.

War as All Wars

In its permeability and temporal waywardness, in its collapsing of event into condition or situation, modern wartime risks flattening all wars into one War, standing apart from any specific occurrence. Wartime enables the word "war" to congeal into a universal and collective entity which "appear[s] to unite within itself the course of all individual" wars, to borrow again from Koselleck (50).[66] This is not an entirely new turn: ancient cultures, for instance, understood war in a transhistorical way, enjoining codes of conduct beyond all particular manifestations of its power. In modernity, however, the turn takes particular forms: in modern wartime, war becomes understood as a concept, an absolute, and ultimately as purification.

First, war "becomes a regulative principle of knowledge in addition to action and conduct" (Koselleck 50). Writing in the aftermath of these wars, Hegel would famously take War as a principle of the Idea of History. He offers a glancing analogy between the career of Napoleon—the general willing to sacrifice the lives of a million men—and the "general idea" which operates with the cunning of reason:

> It is not the general idea that is implicated in opposition and combat, and that is exposed to danger. It remains in the background, untouched, uninjured. This may be called *the cunning of reason*—that it sets the passions to work for itself, while that which develops its existence through such impulsion pays the penalty, and suffers loss. . . . The particular is for the most part of too trifling value as compared to the general: individuals are sacrificed and abandoned.[67]

Hegel's analogy relocates the terrain of warfare to the realm of the intellect, where the passional and particular, embodied and mortal, suffer in the service of a transcendent and impervious Idea. More crucially, War supplies that governing Idea. Against an Enlightenment view of war as anarchy, savagery, and confusion, Hegel posits a War that makes sense of History (even as it sacrifices specific wars).[68] This transformation, from wars to War and from specific acts

---

[66] Koselleck uses this phrase to describe the fate of the word "Revolution."

[67] G.W.F. Hegel, *The Philosophy of History* (New York: Dover, 1956), 33.

[68] Michel Foucault redirects this tendency, seeing in history, especially the writing of history, the prosecution of war "by other means," and a way of undermining the legitimacy of the state. See Foucault, *"Society Must Be Defended": Lectures at the College de France, 1975–76*, eds. Mauro Bertani and Alessandro Fontana, trans. David Macey (New York: Picador, 2003), 141–66.

of violence to a principle of knowledge, will be charted repeatedly in the pages that follow: in a history of historicism, in critiques of theories of the everyday, and in a survey of eighteenth-century definitions of the word. Indeed, one aim of this project is to call attention to our unquestioned reliance on a metahistorical War as the very substance of some of the most radical and progressive contemporary intellectual work, where it yields a fascination with strategies and tactics or a commitment to unending conflict.

Even as it promotes a malleable, heterogeneous, and indefinite sense of time, romantic wartime generates its hyperrational alternative. This is the second way by which the wartime of the late eighteenth and early nineteenth century pressed individual wars into War: not just through the conceptualization of war as universal and abstract, but through its conceptualization as total—war "to extremes."[69] Roger Chickering rehearses the reigning master narrative of Total War among military historians, which stresses its "natural" progression and inevitability over the course of the past two centuries. This narrative, he notes, "informs all the standard histories of modern warfare."

> It begins in 1792, when the armies of republican France, backed by the mobilized citizenry at home, revolutionized combat by virtue of their sheer numbers and the intensity of their commitment to the cause they were serving. The French Revolution thus foretold developments during the next two centuries.[70]

In this story, "the growth in both intensity and expanse that marked the modernization of warfare en route to totality" was further augmented in the nineteenth century by the growth of industrialization, new technologies of transportation and communication, and, finally, developments in weapons technology. Together, these forces increasingly extended the theater of operations to civilians, until in the twentieth century it culminated in the "calculated and systematic annihilation of civilians, both from the air and in the death camps" (14–15). This is a "romantic" story, by which Chickering means its plot centers on the "growth and fulfillment" of modern war, and its *Selbstbehauptung* (self-assertion) and self-transcendence in gas chambers and nuclear bombs. Sacrificing historical facts (many wars in this period were not fought "to extremes"), the common story of War becomes the story of Total War.

In *The First Total War: Napoleon's Europe and the Birth of Warfare As We Know It*, historian David A. Bell specifies some of the particular ways that this

---

[69] Carl von Clausewitz, *On War*, ed. and trans. Michael Howard and Peter Paret (New York: Oxford UP, 2007), 15.

[70] Roger Chickering, "Total War: The Use and Abuse of a Concept," in Roger Chickering and Stig Forster, eds., *Anticipating Total War: The German and American Experiences, 1871–1914* (Cambridge: Cambridge UP and Washington, DC: The German Historical Institute, 1999), 14.

totalizing impulse took shape at the end of the eighteenth century. To do so, he charts the historical conjunction of two forces: an Enlightenment philosophical tradition that sought the end of all wars, and a political reality that furnished mass armies ready to fight to extremes for ideals. Together, "the dream of perpetual peace and the nightmare of total war" gave birth to the modern understanding of war.[71] The desire to repudiate war as barbaric and outdated was joined to the desire to envision each new military conflict as a final, apocalyptic struggle "that must be fought until the complete destruction of the enemy and that might have a purifying, even redemptive effect, on the participants" (Bell 3). One result of this modern tangle is a mix of enlightened and preenlightened ideas of warfare: modern wars are at once technologically advanced and savage, secular and sacred. Another is the abstraction or generalization of war that takes it out of history: debate focuses less on the specifics of this or that conflict, or even over who has the sovereign right to declare war, than over the idea of War. Bell maps that shift in the debate in the French National Assembly in May 1790, opening his book with an apt quotation from the French General Dumouriez in 1792, as he contemplates the coming war in Europe: "This war will be the last war" (1). Eventually, this vision of war carried over the Channel to Great Britain. Twenty years after Dumouriez's pronouncement (after his defection to the Allied armies, and after his removal to London, where he advised the British War Office), the *Times of London* of 1812 announced what lay within Dumouriez's vision: that the war to end all wars also entailed a war of extermination: "We are engaged in a war—a war of no common description—a war of system against system, in which no choice is left us, but victory or extirpation" (qtd. in Shaw 8). Such rhetoric suggests a new mindset, replacing the idea of limited war with the modern idea of a war to end all wars, Clausewitz's "absolute war." As a general idea, such war admits of no subtraction or diminution: all or nothing, without remainder.

Ironically, this reorientation dissolves any war into the one War, so that the war to end all wars never, in fact, ends. The war to end all wars can be understood semantically as the subsumption of individual wars, here and there, now and then, into one universal War, everywhere and always.[72] It is an idea of war we have inherited. Even as he dates the emergence of this view of war as total, Bell reminds his reader that his description "applies equally well to two different centuries" (1). As his subtitle announces, he is interested in "the birth of

[71] Here Bell follows closely the work of Jean-Yves Guiomar, *L'invention de la guerre totale, XVIIIe–XXe siècle* (Paris: Le Félin Kiron, 2004).

[72] To his credit, Kant understood the danger of this view of perpetual peace: a "war of extermination," he maintained "would allow perpetual peace only upon the vast graveyard of the human race" (96).

warfare as we know it," which is to say, War as Idea or "regulative principle of knowledge"—as if it were something we might, finally, know.

World Wars

The idea of a last war is always the idea of a world war, a war on behalf of the world (conceived as civilization, or humanity) that nevertheless threatens the end of the world, apocalypse, or a new world. The idea of a last war legitimates the emergence of a planet where, as Koselleck says, civil wars are "regionally limited but globally conducted" (*Futures Past* 56), where, since the late eighteenth century, any war can conceivably take as its outcome the fate of the world. We might say that each last war dreams (again) of being finally the only world war. Counting (first, second, third) marks the repeated failure of this dream.

Enumerations of world wars, however, do not typically begin with the wars of the late eighteenth and early nineteenth century; those wars, in recent histories, have counted neither as world wars nor as truly modern wars. Despite the fact that they comprehended armed conflict not only in Europe, but in Africa, Asia, and the Americas; despite the fact that they worried waters from the Philippine Islands to the Indian Ocean, from the Cape of Good Hope to the Mediterranean, from the English Channel westward to the Chesapeake Bay and Gulf of Mexico: nonetheless these wars are thought not to encompass the world. And yet, unlike the earlier Seven Years' War, which could boast a comparable geographical reach, these wars from their revolutionary beginning were unequivocally addressed to the world. They took as their object not simply contested territories, dynastic feuds or imperial trade routes, but centrally, as the London *Times* asserted in 1812, world systems.

Since the end of the nineteenth century, and increasingly during the two world wars of the early twentieth century, the general wisdom has been that the Napoleonic conflict could no longer be considered "The Great War," as it had been known through most of the previous century. According to some assumed calculus of violence, and in keeping with a faith in technological progress, the sabers, bayonets, muskets, and cannons of these earlier wars could not keep up with the machine gun, the rocket-launched missile, or the increasingly destructive bombs devised in the twentieth century. Paul Fussell, in his ground-breaking *The Great War and Modern Memory*, insists repeatedly on the inadequacy of the early nineteenth-century wars or their literature (at least in the British tradition) for understanding the conflict of World War I—despite the fact that soldiers in the trenches were reading Wordsworth, Austen, and Byron; despite the fact that that war reconsecrated battlegrounds from the

Napoleonic venture (in France and the Low Counties certainly, but also in Central Europe and the Mideast). The war of 1914–18 could be understood only as an "unparalleled situation," a trauma precisely because nothing comparable had preceded it (Fussell 1975, 139). Fussell is mixing two levels here, that of individual memory and that of history and tradition, when he asserts, "The war [World War I] will not be understood in traditional terms: the machine gun alone makes it so special and unexampled that it simply can't be talked about as if it were one of the conventional wars of history" (153). To say this is to make all previous wars, no matter what their innovations, "conventional." Here Fussell seems unable to imagine that, for many participants, warfare might always be "an unparalleled situation." The desire to mark a conflict as unprecedented, new, and therefore "special" is indeed a reflex of modernity, and was abundantly expressed in the other, first "Great War." Goethe, for instance, having witnessed the first victory of French revolutionary troops at Valmy in 1792, testified to its world-historical novelty: "From this place, and from this day forth begins a new era in the history of the world, and you can all say that you were present at its birth" (qtd. in Bell 131).

Equally we find the commonplace disparagement that "back then" the home front had been insulated, as if in childlike innocence, from the horrors of war. So despite the relentless invasion scares, the economic hardships, and the thousands of widows and orphans produced by the earlier wars, Leslie Stephen could in 1896 condescend to Britain a hundred years earlier (and use "French Revolution" as a stand-in term for the twenty-year-long war):

> when we speak of the misery of a nation at the time of some great trouble—the French Revolution, for example—it is difficult to remember how small was the proportion of actual sufferers; how many thousands or millions of children were enjoying their little sports, utterly ignorant of the distant storm; how many mothers were absorbed in watching their children; and how many quiet commonplace people were going about their daily peaceful labour, pretty much as usual, and with only a vague—and possibly pleasurable—excitement at the news, which occasionally drifted to them, of the catastrophes in a different sphere.[73]

Stephen is not wrong to suggest that a wartime populace, especially the more privileged ranks, could continue in its everyday routines while the "drift" of media reporting supplied occasional, thrilling reminders of catastrophes occurring elsewhere—Sontag's "calamities taking place in another country." For Stephen this is the general condition of "the nation at the time of some great

---

[73] Leslie Stephen, "Forgotten Benefactors," in *Social Rights and Duties* (London: Swan Sonnenschein, 1896), 242.

trouble"; the state of Great Britain during the years of the Revolution and Napoleon's rise serves as only one example. A few decades later such generalization would itself look naïve and anachronistic.

For many later wartime readers, the village life of Jane Austen's novels typified this privileged insulation and her wars an outmoded possibility. An anonymous critic, writing of Austen's work in 1941, attempted to draw parallels
between her time of national trouble and his own: "Jane Austen, for example,
wrote *Pride and Prejudice* when Nelson was patrolling off Spain." But the historical comparison surfaces only to reinforce the sense of absolute difference:
"Such parallels," it seems, "fail to carry conviction":

> for there is no precedent in the national history for the present condi-
> tion of things. Jane Austen's nerves were never set on edge by the strain
> of continuously expecting sensational news from the outside world. The
> calm of her Hampshire village was broken by no radio messages of crisis.
> Even the news of Trafalgar did not reach her till many days after the
> battle. She was visited by no A.R.P. warden to fit her with a gas mask,
> nor was she instructed to make provisional arrangements for receiving
> in her home a number of children suddenly evacuated from London.[74]

A review of Jane Austen's work in the *London Observer*, near the end of World
War II, makes the quite specific and familiar charge:

> These Austen characters are the greatest escapists of all time. The year
> may be 1815, but Waterloo is as far off as Cathay, and the idea of war-
> work vexes neither strapping youngster nor potential despatcher of the
> military "comfort" and the nutritive package.[75]

If dismissing the seriousness of the earlier wartime on the basis of distance
were not enough ("as far off as Cathay"), the reviewer conjures the presumably
gamelike nature of those wars: "Campaigns were then conducted like football
tours in foreign countries." In reading Austen, "we can ourselves escape, feeling for an hour or two as remote from the flinty and steel couch of war as were
Emma and Mr. Knightley among the settees and strawberry-beds of their
tranquil Highbury" (ibid.). It seemed "a pleasant cosy war" to another English
reviewer in 1940.[76]

Denigration of the earlier wartime evinces a perverse pride in contemporary technology (our steel vs. their soft beds; our bombs vs. their cannons); but

[74] Unmarked newspaper clipping, probably 1941 English. Notebooks of Augusta Burke, Burke
Collection, Goucher College Library.

[75] Ivor Brown, Review of "Emma" [stage production], "Theatre and Life," *The London Observer*,
11 February 1945: 2.

[76] Review of Royde Smith, *Jane Fairfax*, *Times Literary Supplement*, 28 September 1940.

it also wobbles between assumptions about lived experience and interpretations of the literature of the period; one is used to explain and critique the other. Even as perceptive a reader as Virginia Woolf, updating her father, Leslie Stephen's, observations, could not find in the British novels of Napoleon's day even a trace of her own modern awareness of distant catastrophe. In a late essay, completed before the Battle of Britain, she charts her own distance from romantic literature, summarizing the common view:[77]

> In 1815 England was at war, as England is now. And it is natural to ask, how did their war—the Napoleonic war—affect them? Was that one of the influences that formed them . . . ? The answer is a very strange one. The Napoleonic wars did not affect the great majority of those writers at all. The proof of that is to be found in the work of two great novelists— Jane Austen and Walter Scott. Each lived through the Napoleonic wars; each wrote through them. But, though novelists live very close to the life of their time, neither of them in all their novels mentioned the Napoleonic wars. This shows that their model, their vision of human life, was not disturbed or agitated or changed by war. Nor were they themselves. . . . Wars were then remote; wars were carried on by soldiers and sailors, not by private people. The rumours of battle took a long time to reach England. . . . Compare that with our state today. Today we hear the gunfire in the Channel. We turn on the wireless; we hear an airman telling us how this very afternoon he shot down a raider; his machine caught fire; he plunged into the sea; the light turned green and then black; he rose to the top and was rescued by a trawler. Scott never saw sailors drowning at Trafalgar; Jane Austen never heard the cannon roar at Waterloo. Neither of them heard Napoleon's voice as we hear Hitler's voice as we sit at home of the evening.
>
> That immunity from war lasted all through the nineteenth-century.[78]

The passage suggests that the war-torn writer of the twentieth century has a more immediate, less "immune" experience of war than her counterparts from the previous century; even the "private person" cannot now escape the war. And though this will be true for Woolf and her compatriots in a few months, once the blitzkrieg begins, it is not yet true at this moment, as she writes. Look closely at how Woolf herself loses sight of the distinction between war and war mediated. Her war is brought to her by the wireless radio, by disembodied voices in the air. Except for the gunfire in the channel, it is heard secondhand

---

[77] The Battle of Britain, with its bombing campaign by the German Luftwaffe, lasted from 9 July to 31 October 1940. Woolf wrote her essay and delivered it as a speech in May of that year.

[78] Virginia Woolf, "The Leaning Tower," in *The Moment and Other Essays* (New York: Harcourt Brace, 1948), 130–31.

rather than seen. (Has she actually witnessed sailors drowning? planes crashing into the sea? And yet we have no doubt that such mediation could set "nerves on edge," as the anonymous critic in 1941 put it.) Napoleon's voice could not be heard in Britain in 1814, but it could be read aloud or silently; his speeches were frequently transcribed into print form.[79] The media for broadcasting war had changed, but did they truly offer greater immediacy? Their affective force may be markedly different from earlier modes of communication, but was that force necessarily stronger? By what measure? Do feelings, like weapons and communications technology, become more powerful and effective over the course of (a progressive) history? Woolf and her contemporary audience "sit at home in the evening"—not unlike Jane Austen and her contemporaries—and try to imagine the violence happening elsewhere.

The following pages attempt to show that many of Stephen's and Woolf's assumptions—about "distant storms" and the "drift" or force of the news, about "private persons" and the peacefulness of the everyday, about forms of absorption and utter ignorance—were in fact tested and revised by "quiet commonplace people," writers like Austen herself, who lived through those earlier catastrophes. They found themselves incapable of confining catastrophe to a different, distant "sphere"; they allowed it to invade their everyday. Precisely in these registers of the mundane and unspectacular, registers that have mistakenly been read as signs of immunity—or worse, obliviousness—British romantic writers struggled to apprehend the effects of foreign war.

Perhaps the simplest way for me to make the case for reading romantic literature as wartime literature, for understanding its continuing effect on our present world, and for taking seriously the overlooked and unspectacular conditions of wartime culture is to end with a detail from William St. Clair's *The Reading Nation in the Romantic Period*. His materialist account of the publishing business will take the reflections of this chapter and put them before your eyes and in your hands. From the library stacks, pick a book published in Britain in this period two hundred years hence. It could be almost any volume, on any topic. It could be a bound volume of the *Monthly Review* or a book of sermons; it could be the *Memoirs of the Author of the Vindication of the Rights of Women* or a chapbook for children. Hold it, touch its pages, and look at the sheets of paper, background to the printed words.

The paper was made by hand, sheet by sheet. The battlefields of Europe were picked over before the blood was dry for every scrap of cloth that could be sold in the rag fairs and on to the international markets. [In addition t]he cast-off smocks of Hungarian shepherds, the shirts of

---

[79] See, for example, ongoing reports in the *Annual Register*, as well as Napoléon Buonaparte, *An Account of the French Expedition in Egypt*, 2nd ed. (Leeds: Edward Baines, 1800).

Italian sailors, and the bonnets of Irish ladies all made their way to the booming British paper mills which were springing up along many British rivers. Boiled, bleached, and smoothed, the paper from which most English books of the romantic period were made remains white and spotless after two hundred years, shaming all subsequent books.[80]

The pages in your hands, in their hands, on which they read novels, histories, poems, treatises, and tirades; on which they scanned fashion plates and Bible verses; these pages may have traveled—but who could be certain?—from the battlefields of Europe. Not only those wartime readers but readers today can look over these "white and spotless" sheets and witness (or not) this romantic transmutation: from the ground of war to the ground of reading. The difficulty of reading and writing in wartime is made palpable.

[80] William St. Clair, *The Reading Nation in the Romantic Period* (Cambridge: Cambridge UP, 2004), 178. I am grateful to Deidre Lynch for calling this passage to my attention.

CHAPTER TWO

Telling Time in War

This chapter extends the thought that the experience of war at a distance, of a mediated war, is fundamentally dislocating, and that such dislocation expresses itself most frequently and forcefully through our sense of the movement (or stasis) of time, through temporalities. Thus the wartime poems set on a winter's evening, considered in the prelude, elaborate the simplest markers of time (winter, evening) into channels of memory and prophecy, avenues of recursivity and nodes of stillness. Wartime in modernity refers not to a single temporal mode—*the* time of war. Rather it houses many temporalities, each one, as we will see, a structure of feeling with its own affective qualities, its own expressivity, its own silences. Throughout this book, we will see wartime writers and artists handle and manipulate with intense care the forms or what we might call the instruments for telling time. This chapter treats specifically the question of how war in Romanticism became a matter of time, became wartime. And it examines four crucial instruments for telling the time of war that contributed to this conversion: clock time (the historian's code), the time of the post-boy (the coming of the news), the meantime (waiting), and prophecy (the time to come).

Wartime

Always and everywhere we have rather to do with something that happens to time; or perhaps, as space is mute and time loquacious, we are able to make an approach to spatiality only by way of what it does to time.[1]

How can you tell the time of worldwide war? By what instruments is wartime sounded?

Here is one attempt to provide what Fredric Jameson might call a "loquacious" instance of what happens to time during and because of a world war. While British soldiers and sailors fought the French and their allies across the

---

[1] Fredric Jameson, "The End of Temporality," *Critical Inquiry* 29 (Summer 2003): 706.

globe, back in England time underwent its own shocks and alterations. For the middle and upper ranks of society, the rearrangement of time was evident in the very disposition of clocks and watches. In 1796, the clock- and watch-making industry for which Britain was renowned reached its all-time height: between 120,000 and 190,000 clocks and watches were produced, the majority for export. In more ways than one, timepieces were helping to introduce the industrial revolution: even as clocks were calling out the hours of the workday, the world was buying British time. The following year, however, marked a re-direction in the movement of timekeepers. With tax revenues falling and the costs of war growing, the Pitt administration introduced a tax on clocks and watches. The ownership of a watch, the need or luxury (legislators were un-clear) of telling time, would help fund the war effort. But it was a remarkably unpopular and unsuccessful tax. "The tax was regarded as folly; as setting up a system of espionage [to ferret out who did or did not possess clocks in the home]; and as a blow against the middle class. There was a buyer's strike."[2] Eight months after its introduction, the tax was revoked. Though short-lived, the 1797–98 tax on clock time "marked a turning-point in the fortunes of the industry" from which it never recovered; competition from Swiss and French watchmakers grew (Thompson 66).[3] Continental timepieces were increasingly smuggled into the shops of British jewelers, milliners, and dressmakers, into toyshops and pawn shops, so that by 1813 the Clockmaker's Company alleged nearly 35,000 gold and silver watches from abroad had been sold in Britain on the black market.[4] Not only was Britain no longer the world's leading time-keeper, but many Britons, in the upper classes of society especially, kept time by foreign, even enemy manufacture.

This episode of timekeeping comes from the classic account of the function and meaning of clocks in this period, E. P. Thompson's essay, "Time, Work-Discipline, and Industrial Capitalism." Gathered into the corners of Thompson's larger narrative of that revolution lie hints of a complex time sense con-tingent upon the coincident war—a wartime linked but not reducible to the temporality of nascent industrial capitalism, linked but not reducible to the temporality of the modern nation.[5] Pitt's tax proposal did imagine a certain

[2] E. P. Thompson, "Time, Work-Discipline, and Industrial Capitalism," *Past and Present* 38 (December 1967): 68.

[3] Contemporaries estimated the production of silver watch cases at 185,102 in 1796, dropping to half that number by 1816. In 1798, on the heels of the failed clock tax, Pitt successfully introduced Britain's first income tax to fund Britain's war effort.

[4] Anon., *Observations on the Art and Trade of Clock and Watchmaking* (London: J. Richardson, 1812), 16–20. Qtd. in Thompson 66n34.

[5] Though Thompson does not allude to it here, wartime is also constructed along the rhythms of finance capital. See John Brewer, *The Sinews of Power: War, Money, and the English State, 1688–1783* (Cambridge: Harvard UP, 1990); Ian Baucom, *Specters of the Atlantic: Finance Capital, Slavery, and the Philosophy of History* (Durham: Duke UP, 2005).

nationalism ticking away in the heart of every British-made timepiece. The *Morning Chronicle*, not often given to endorsing Pitt's projects, blithely editorialized:

> The *half-crown* tax upon watches is appointed to be collected *quarterly*. This is grand and dignified. It gives a man an air of consequence to pay *sevenpence halfpenny* to support *religion, property,* and *social order*.[6]

Pitt predicted that the tax would bring in at least 200,000 pounds per annum, calculating that the 700,000 tax-paying households of Britain must each own a watch or clock that would, in the ensuing quarter-annums, produce the means of defeating, or at least warding off, French troops. Even as the tax measure was failing, a pamphlet loyal to the administration pushed the matter even further, making clock time itself a bulwark against the horrors of war.

> If any person can abandon the use of so valuable and almost indispensable a convenience as a watch, to avoid the payment of half a crown annually towards the protection of the Country, he or she deserves to have no other means of measuring time, than by counting the succession of miseries which would attend a successful irruption of the French into this Country."[7]

The convergence between clock time and national security in this case suggests that if you choose not to abide by clock time (and the tax it entails), you will count time instead merely as the accumulation of miseries. The watch or clock would be an instrument of vigilance; attention to it would keep at bay the woes of threatened invasion.

These timed calculations, with their rhythmic calendrical yield, all proved erroneous: a London gentleman might be inclined to order his day according to a French rather than an English timepiece and thereby circumvent the tax. The effects of war—in this case the economic effects of rising taxes, blockades, and black markets—meant that in some material way Britons were no longer telling time as they were used to, or as they had been expected to. Unmoored from experience as well as expectation, time—or at least timekeeping—was out of joint. This episode provides a brief fable of how clocks may evade the very calculations and schedules they would otherwise seem to uphold, and evade as well the ideological programs built upon such structures. Yet the episode itself depends on a telling chronometric order. The movements of each

[6] *Morning Chronicle*, 26 July 1797, emphasis original; qtd. in Thompson 68.

[7] *An appeal to the head and heart of every man and woman in Great Britain, respecting the threatened French invasion, and the importance of immediately coming forward with voluntary contributions* (London, 1798), 25. *Eighteenth Century Collections Online (ECCO)*. Gale Group. Lily Gurton-Wachter provided me with this reference and an excellent analysis of it, for which I am grateful.

clock and watch are here subsumed and contained by bigger clocks, that is, larger chronometric systems: 1797–98, eight months, 1813.

These larger clocks are the timekeeping structures of what we now recognize as historicism, itself a romantic invention. This system of timekeeping, of situating what happens within the even chronology of dating, allows us to approach what Jameson would call a broader "spatiality" (international markets and the exigencies of distant war) through a particular, dated, national occurrence (the British tax on clocks).[8] The date "1797" locates the clock tax and its effects not only within British history, but also in relation to events in the world. As James Chandler puts it in his study of romantic historicism, *England in 1819*, two temporalities intersect here at the date: one traces the movement of a society "stepwise through a series of stages sequenced in an order that is more-or-less autonomous and stable"; the other, to some extent competing order of temporality correlates the movement of different societies against each other (128). The vagaries of clocks in Britain are at once stabilized by such dating and, in a way that nicely parallels the effects of Pitt's tax, set loose into unpredictable exchanges with a volatile world; these exchanges are in turn reined in and organized by historians using the system of dating. Derived from Scottish Enlightenment historiography and developed in the romantic period in Great Britain, romantic historicism uses what Chandler (following Levi-Strauss) identifies as "the historian's code" to locate "what happened" within a certain dating or period of time, and from there to map and remap the "state of society" within "the state of the world" (126, 102, 128).

By means of the historian's code, the wayward clocks can be made to speak more clearly a story of Britain in wartime; their smuggled movements in and out of the nation can be organized within a larger world picture. Time is no longer out of joint, but rather articulated within a universalizing temporal and spatial grid. By virtue of the historian's code, the ticking of clocks can be written into historical narrative as an intelligible reminder of what was happening in and because of a contested spatiality.

Romantic historicism reveals itself as a device especially desirable and effective for telling time amid the disruptions of distant war. It is, moreover, itself a datable response, one clearly tied in time (via its preferred tool, the historian's code) to this historical period of late eighteenth- and early nineteenth-century warfare. And, because it is neatly self-descriptive—because the practices of dating can themselves be dated—it can seem to exhaust our possible conceptions of time. But as I suggested in chapter 1, it has (and had) its limitations, as well as its rivals. For, of course, to look to dates and clocks to tell the time

---

[8] On "even chronology," see James Chandler, *England in 1819: The Politics of Literary Culture and the Case of Romantic Historicism* (Chicago: U of Chicago P, 1998).

of war already rigs the response. The thought of their regular ticking reassures me that I can find and hear and follow time's utterance; it lifts time within war to this higher, impersonal and universalizing level: the sequence of dates, passing in a "more or less autonomous and stable" order, detaches itself from the instability and disorder of war. (It doesn't ask me to imagine, for instance, smashed clocks or lost clocks or clocks left unwound.) One way of telling time in war, historicism suggests, is to lift it out of war, above or beyond its reach, immune to its vicissitudes. As Reinhart Koselleck puts it, the abstraction of time into "quantified, uniform units" creates a time that appears "valid regardless of history, regardless of the historical situation in which [it was] first ascertained."[9] If and when time is out of joint, the instruments of historicism aim not to preserve its inarticulacy but rather to render it articulate. But when you turn to clocks and calendars to tell of war, what noises are left unheard or filtered out?

Before these other noises can be heard, a prior question hangs over Pitt's and historicism's weighty reliance on "quantified, uniform units" of time: why turn to timekeepers in times of war? A quick answer can be found in a combination of Jameson's and Chandler's comments above: temporality is the mediating voice of a mute spatiality; we turn to temporal structures to discover our relationship to distant spaces. This is an effect of the dating system that Chandler describes arising in the Romantic period in Great Britain. It is evident as well in the invention in the 1760s of a maritime clock, the accuracy of which could allow for longitudinal calculations. As Heather McHugh puts it, the invention provided "a way of carrying home time with you, no matter what faraway straits and passages you ply." But it also meant holding "two times" in your head at once: Greenwich Time and local time.[10] Time becomes a distinctly modern medium for apprehending activity in a world of expanding distances. It becomes too, as McHugh hints and in ways that the end of this chapter will elaborate, a tool of expanding empire.

Modes of Temporality, Structures of Feeling

"Let us return from the timepiece to the task," E. P. Thompson urges, guiding attention from the symbolic value of timekeeping instruments to the matter

<hr>

[9] Reinhart Koselleck, "Time and History," in *The Practice of Conceptual History: Timing History, Spacing Concepts*, trans. Todd Samuel Presner et al. (Stanford: Stanford UP, 2002), 104–5.

[10] Heather McHugh, "Presence and Passage: A Poet's Wordsworth," *MLQ: Modern Language Quarterly* 63.2 (June 2002): 170–71; and Tim Fulford, Debbie Lee, and Peter Kitson in *Literature, Science and Exploration in the Romantic Era: Bodies of Knowledge* (Cambridge: Cambridge UP, 2004), 22. On James Harrison's invention of the nautical clock see Dava Sobel, *Longitude: The True Story of a Lone Genius Who Solved the Greatest Scientific Problem of His Time* (New York: Walker, 1995).

of labor (70). I'd like to give that redirection a half-turn, as it were, from the timepiece to Cowper's *The Task*, introduced earlier as one of the most popular and cited poems of the late eighteenth and early nineteenth centuries. The crucial wartime value of Cowper's poem needs to be accounted for: how in *The Task* he constructs a poetic form adequate to his consciousness of modern, global warfare. In this poem, penned in 1783–84 at the end of disastrous military outings by the British in North America and southern India, the poet aims to work out his own wartime disciplines. Book II of the poem has the title "The Time-Piece," but my attention falls on Book IV, "The Winter Evening," which moves to an area of experience that lies beyond the timepiece itself, to the poet's meditations on war.[11] "The Winter Evening" is a compendium of modern modes of telling time during war, an experiment in making temporality loquacious to report, however feebly or inchoately, on the wars that were being conducted across the globe. It reports, in other words, on how time serves as a medium not just for understanding but also for unsettling understanding, for making war felt.

In subsequent years, the "terror" and "alarm," introduced yet muted in Cowper's poem, would become for Britain the trumpeted watchwords, if not the rationale, for warfare.[12] When the next generation of poets turned to Cowper they picked up not only these terms but also his devices for telling time in order to tell of distant war. By attending to what happened to time, they too registered the unseen operations of remote violence. More significantly for my argument, they helped construct a modern sense of "wartime" that exceeds or falls short of historicism and its chronometry. Without finally coordinating them into a single practice, Cowper lays out the temporal instruments that would be picked up by later writers. In addition to the clock, Cowper makes special use of the post-boy, the vacant "meantime" of war, prophecy (with its echoes), and stillness. (Stillness is a special case which I address in an interlude between this chapter and the next.) Telling time to tell of war, turning not only to clocks, but to other even more loquacious temporal instruments, Cowper made war into a temporal experience: he made war into wartime.

Cowper gives an early and well-known expression of the routine, clock-

---

[11] Adam Rounce suggests that the affecting temporal stance of Cowper's poetry "makes him a more central figure at the end of the century." "Cowper's Ends," in Tim Fulford, ed., *Romanticism and Millenarianism* (New York: Palgrave, 2002), 35.

[12] See, for instance, Samuel Taylor Coleridge, "The War and International Law," from *The Friend*, 1803, in *Collected Works*, ed. Barbara Rooke, vol. 4 (London: Routledge and Kegan Paul, 1969), 265–67; his "Fears in Solitude"; or Walter Scott's *The Antiquary*. On the rhetoric of terror and alarm in the 1790s, see John Barrell, *Imagining the King's Death: Figurative Treason, Fantasies of Regicide, 1793–1796* (Oxford: Oxford UP, 2000), 1–46.

bound organization of wartime experience—an expression we've already seen in the prelude—when he reads his newspaper on a winter's evening:

> Thus sitting, and surveying thus at ease
> The globe and its concerns, I seem advanc'd
> To some secure and more than mortal height,
> That lib'rates and exempts me from them all.
> It turns submitted to my view, turns round
> With all its generations; I behold
> The tumult, and am still . . .
> While fancy, like the finger of a clock,
> Runs the great circuit, and is still at home.[13]

Cowper converts the turning planet and its far-flung concerns, otherwise invisible to him, into a circuit he can trace at ease on a flat clock face.

But the time he describes—and that other poets of the period also describe—was not simply a medium for an increasingly far-flung spatiality. It was, more specifically, a medium for apprehending distant war. His recourse to news and clock here works to dampen, if not finally still, the noise of that violent world. We need to situate the passage above within a larger movement: the poet has been raising questions about Britain's war with the American colonies and the wars in southern India. He reads, we're told, in order

> To hear the roar she [the world] sends through all her gates
> At a safe distance, where the dying sound
> Falls a soft murmur on th' uninjur'd ear.
> Thus sitting, and surveying thus at ease,
> The globe and its concerns . . .
>   . . . I behold
> The tumult, and am still. The sound of war
> Has lost its terrors ere it reaches me;
> Grieves, but alarms me not. . . .
> [I] Hear the faint echo of those brazen throats . . .
> And sigh, but never tremble at the sound. (91–95, 99–102, 104, 106)[14]

The broader movement of Cowper's passage proceeds to the trope of the smoothly turning clock via repeated assertions of stillness. But in doing so, his verse also smuggles in a hubbub of noises: roar, tumult, alarm; murmur, echo,

---

[13] William Cowper, *The Task*, in *The Complete Poetical Works*, ed. H. S. Milford, 4th ed. (Oxford: Oxford UP, 1967), IV: 94–99, 117–18.

[14] James Sambrook notes the Miltonic echo: *P.L.* XI, 713: "The brazen throat of War had ceased to roar." *The Task and Selected Other Poems*, ed. James Sambrook (London: Longman, 1994), 144n.

sigh; mere sound, which apparently cannot fully be resolved into clock time.[15] They suggest that there are other temporalities (still) telling of distant war. Even Cowper's epic blank verse, its rhythm discontinuous and thwarting the ease he describes, voices these unsettling noises.[16] In coming years, he would use the same blank verse for his translation of *The Iliad*.

What are these muffled noises attempting to articulate? What is the wartime they express? They provide alternative structures for wartime. Though the *Oxford English Dictionary* rather unhelpfully defines "wartime" as "the time when war is being waged," its historical survey of the word's usage makes clear that, against the rationalizing, organizing impulse of clock time, a more experiential, affective understanding of "wartime" developed in the nineteenth century. The *OED* cites two historical novels that mark this development:

> **1831** SCOTT *Castle Dang[erous]*, v. if, Above all, it was war-time, and of necessity all circumstances of mere convenience were obliged to give way to a paramount sense of danger.

> **1849** C. BRONTË *Shirley*, v. ii, These war times were hard, and everything was dear.

Both examples gesture toward the intertwining of wartime and affect (a "sense of danger"). Brontë's use of the plural "these war times" and the *OED*'s third example from the nineteenth century suggest, moreover, a blurring of wartime's chronological structure:

> **1851** KINGSLEY *Yeast [A Problem]*, v., xiii, There was too much filthiness and drunkenness went on in the old war-times, not to leave a taint behind it, for many a generation.

Brontë's *Shirley*, it is worth noting, refers to the "war times" of the Napoleonic era, when the standard structure of declaration of war followed by signing of treaty was repeatedly challenged; the time of war was multiple and indeed "hard" to order. By the twentieth century, during World War I, "wartime" could be employed as an adjective, again often signaling something more than mere dating. Hence the *OED* features C. E. (Charles Edward) Montague writing in *Disenchantment* (1922), his memoir of the war years: "Men's friends at

---

[15] In *Georgic Modernity and British Romanticism: Poetry and the Mediation of History* (Cambridge: Cambridge UP, 2004), Kevis Goodman remarks, "Sound is never just sound for Cowper but has distinct epistemological consequences. Different ways of hearing are, for him, different ways of knowing" (86). Goodman's reading bears closely on my own.

[16] Northrop Frye identifies the Romantic period as the source for a "voice of feeling" in poetry, based on "essentially oracular," "discontinuous," "unpredictable," and "meditative" rhythm, a rhythm that exceeds or falls out of measured chronology and meter. *Anatomy of Criticism* (Princeton: Princeton UP, 1971), 272–73.

home would have the agonies of false alarms added to their normal wartime miseries." The coupling of "normal" and "wartime" here would be utterly devastating if "wartime" were not able to encompass the temporality of alarm as well as the temporality of the routine or everyday. This modern sense of "wartime" as a sensed and variously charged temporal experience of war, as something that includes but also supersedes dating, was raised, tested, and given voice—or at least sound—in the late eighteenth and early nineteenth century in Britain. As Cowper demonstrates with great intricacy, this sense of wartime emerged in tandem, though often at odds, with another sense of wartime, which desired to historicize war, to hand it over to the clocks (ticking or silent) in order to be "lib'rate[d] or exempt[ed]" from it.

Bearing witness to affective responses to war conducted at a distance, these complex, jarring temporalities can be understood as what Raymond Williams famously called structures of feeling; in their contrary ways, they express what Williams called a history of "the undeniable experience of the present" or, as Cowper suggests, a history of un-stilled "tumult."[17] With Cowper as one of her guides, Kevis Goodman recently and carefully develops Williams's thought about a history of the present in order to pursue "that immanent, collective sense of any moment as a seething mix of unsettled elements," where befores and afters have not yet been determined (3). Like Williams, Goodman is concerned with the felt experiences or "senses" of history, before or beyond any clear, retrospective "idea" of history. She proposes "a revised historicist method that reserves a place . . . for sensation and affect" and specifically locates that place through figures of sound: "the noise of living" and "affective dissonance" that baffle the regular ticking of history's clocks, but even more pointedly compete with the settled view they offer (Cowper's "surveying" and "beholding") (4). For my purposes—also taking my lead from Cowper—war only amplifies the turbulence of "any moment . . . of unsettled elements" (4). Indeed, we become most apt to recognize structures of feeling—they become audible or telling—when "our categories cannot accommodate the flux or excess of events," when noise refuses to settle into stillness, and when modes of telling time are in conflict (6). Emerging under these conditions, wartime houses many such structures of feeling.

Williams defended his term "structures of feeling" by claiming that it got at "all that is not fully articulated, all that comes through as disturbance, tension, blockage, emotional trouble."[18] This is not quite the same thing as purely

[17] Raymond Williams, *Marxism and Literature* (London: Oxford UP, 1977), 128. On this passage in Williams, see Goodman, 3–4 and 70–71. My understanding of Williams has also been aided by David Simpson, "Raymond Williams: Feeling for Structures, Voicing 'History,'" *Social Text* 30 (1992): 9–26.

[18] Raymond Williams, *Politics and Letters* (London: New Left Books, 1979), 168.

unmediated sense or experience, as Williams and Goodman both insist; after all, something is "coming through" structures of feeling "*as* disturbance, tension," and the like. Goodman puts the matter well:

> If the structure of the present is not available at the moment to thought [not precipitated, in Williams's language], does it nonetheless lodge, at least in part, in modes of perception and representation that elude both "idea" and direct articulation? (71)

Temporality is a just such a mode of perception and representation and, as critics such as Brian Massumi have suggested (and I will explore later in this chapter), its correspondence with affect is strong. That correspondence becomes increasingly charged in modern apprehensions of war.

My sense of the tension between clock time and other forms of temporality in wartime correlates with Williams's thought that structures of feeling can have different, even dialectally opposed effects:

> There are cases where the structure of feeling which is tangible in a particular set of works is undoubtedly an articulation of an area of experience which lies beyond them. This is especially evident at those specific and historically definable moments when very new work produces a sudden shock of *recognition*. What must be happening on these occasions is that an experience which is really very wide suddenly finds a semantic figure which articulates it. . . . On the other hand, a dominant set of forms or conventions—and in that sense structures of feeling—can represent a profound blockage. . . . In these cases, it is very dangerous to presume that an articulate structure of feeling is necessarily equivalent to inarticulate experience. . . . [T]here are historical experiences which never do find their semantic figures at all. (*Politics* 164–65)

On the one hand, structures of feeling may newly "recognize" an "area of experience which lies beyond them"; on the other hand, they may form dominant conventions or ideological dispositions that "block" access to such areas which therefore remain inarticulate. Historicism (evident in the recurrent use of the clock or of dates) is one such obstructive structure of feeling which blocks access to areas of inarticulate experience—experience which is therefore audible only as noise, if at all. Some of the writers addressed in this chapter turn to dating and the regularities of clock time to organize their experience of a war that threatens to undermine such regularities. But as Williams's remarks suggest, other structures of feeling, represented in figures other than the clock or dates, mediate these experiences more audibly and intelligibly. Such enabling structures do not always provide war with limits in time, or give clear divisions between event and affect. The telling frames of *this* war in *these* places at *this* time give way instead to a disorienting confusion where sequence and situation are undermined. "This" war could be (or become) another war; the scene or ground of fighting could shift suddenly, lose its identity, or just as probably never be located; and the present of war could be overwhelmed or forgotten or unnervingly halted in the pull of the past or posterity. Of course, such unsettling conditions bleed over into their description and analysis. In telling what happens to time in modern wartime, specifically in the late eighteenth and early nineteenth century in Britain, I have to recognize that the very form of the question—its dating—serves such obstructive ends and restricts what can be told of wartime. But, even as I demonstrate how men and women writing during this particular wartime (1793–1815) timed it, the instruments or figures they use for telling time often dodge or even refuse the security of phrases such as "this wartime," or even "modern wartime." As a result they make this task both historical and ahistorical, located and dislocated—regretfully, but also hopefully, timely.

The Post-Boy and the News

Wartime emerged in British literature in the late eighteenth century in the opening lines of Cowper's "Winter Evening," centered on the figure of the post-boy:

> Hark! 'tis the twanging horn o'er yonder bridge . . .
> He comes, the herald of a noisy world,
> With spatter'd boots, strapp'd waist, and frozen locks;
> News from all nations lumb'ring at his back.
> True to his charge, the close-pack'd load behind,
> Yet careless what he brings, his one concern
> Is to conduct it to the destin'd inn:
> And, having dropp'd th' expected bag, pass on.
> He whistles as he goes, light-hearted wretch,
> Cold and yet cheerful: messenger of grief
> Perhaps to thousands, and of joy to some;
> To him indiff'rent whether grief or joy. (IV: 1, 5–15)

The noisy arrival of the post-boy intrudes upon the "Winter Evening," where the poet hopes to cobble out of "undisturb'd retirement, and the hours / Of uninterrupted ev'ning" a rural retreat from hostile weather and imperial hostilities (IV: 142–43). Yet the arrival of the post-boy also provides entry to the poem that follows; it alerts us to unquiet. The post-boy daily disrupts Cowper's efforts to represent war retrospectively, to think of it as something in the past. If, while gathered with friends by the fireside, he reviews in "mem'ry"

> The dangers we have 'scap'd, the broken snare
> The disappointed foe, deliv'rance found
> . . . life preserv'd and peace restor'd (IV: 185–88),

his daily anticipation of the newspaper belies the security of these past participles. "Have our troops awak'd," he asks, "Or do they still . . . / Snore to the murmurs of th' Atlantic wave?" "Is India free? and does she wear her plum'd / And jewell'd turban with a smile of peace, / Or do we grind her still?" (IV: 25–30).[19] Cowper initially sets the time of his winter evening by the clock of the post-boy and the newspaper he delivers—but that device disorganizes the scene of retirement that follows.

The solitary youth with his makeshift uniform and purposive air, not a stranger but a familiar figure who arrives with trumpeting and departs whistling, performs a national service while standing in for so many absent and awaited young men gone to war. The post-boy offers the poet and reader fleeting contact—and fleeting consolation: however unexpected or disabling the burden he unloads, however unanswerable the questions he prompts, his coming and going nevertheless inscribe a secure rhythm ordering the upheaval. And whatever the effect of his news, the young man performs his duty unscathed—*pace* mud and frozen locks. He is more than a messenger; he is an impassive figure of translation, condensation, and displacement: disburdening his own body of a load of pain and grief, he converts the war into a matter of reading, its "grief perhaps to thousands" packaged for consumption while he himself remains immune to feeling, "indiff'rent." As Cowper reports later (in lines noted in my prelude), scanning the newspaper delivered from the post-boy's bag, reading for him provides the "loop-holes of retreat": "The sound of war / Has lost its terrors ere it reaches me; / Grieves, but alarms me not" (88, 100–2). For now, the post-boy tells of a war made safe, regular, and only intermittently present: part of an evening routine. The military's own trumpets, posts, columns, and charges on horseback are quietly reconfigured within the scenario of the post-boy and his daily delivery.

Cowper's post-boy was only one of many who brought home to England news of a war fought on foreign ground and distant. A 1793 poem in Betty Bennett's anthology of *British War Poetry* answers Cowper's post-boy simply

---

[19] The first question refers to the troops in North America, at the end of the failed campaign against the fledgling United States. The second refers to the notorious administration of Warren Hastings, governor-general of Bengal, who would face impeachment for prosecuting unnecessary wars in India and using unscrupulous means to finance them.

and unequivocally: "Post, after post, soon brings a heavy tale, / Though gloss'd with victory, fatal to the peace / Of fathers, mothers, children, wives, and friends."[20] But the personification of this "post after post" as post-boy provides a particularly rich figure, comprising several of the strategies for representing war which would emerge in literary production in the coming decades. The post-boy heralds the opening of Wordsworth's "Alice Fell; or, Poverty," ducks out of the door in Austen's *Sense and Sensibility*, manhandles letters in Charles Lamb's "Distant Correspondents," and marks the passage of revolution and military glory in Hazlitt's "The Letter-Bell." In a fantastic moment he expands into Thomas DeQuincey's imperial "English Mail-Coach" ("Waterloo and Re-covered Christendom!"). He mutates, in Anna Barbauld's "Dialogue in the Shades," into the divine messenger Mercury, advising Clio, the Muse of History, how to manage the unwieldy number of names of the recent war dead. In still darker mood, the post-boy collapses into his alter-ego, the long-awaited soldier or veteran—like the veteran soldier turned post-boy who haunts the finale of Charlotte Smith's *The Old Manor House*, hobbling on crutches to deliver the crucial letter; or like that solitary, nameless veteran who appears out of the blue on the "public road" in Wordsworth's *Prelude*, bearing a message the poet does not want to hear. The post-boy's ubiquity attests to his picturesque ability to arrange and soften the contours of history, but also to his contravening charge, to broadcast the disruptions of war.[21]

The appearance of the post-boy gives human form to the temporality of newspapers he brought, rendering the war routine and familiar, something to be anticipated and read about rather than fought. In Benedict Anderson's now familiar narrative, the newspapers of the later eighteenth century helped to link a nation of readers to a certain shared sense of time, the ongoing "homogeneous, empty time" of modernity. Anderson evocatively describes

> this extraordinary mass ceremony: the almost precisely simultaneous consumption ("imagining") of the newspaper-as-fiction. We know that particular morning and evening editions will overwhelmingly be consumed between this hour and that, only on this day, not that.[22]

[20] Betty T. Bennett, ed., *British War Poetry in the Age of Romanticism, 1793–1815* (New York: Garland, 1976), 96.

[21] The post-boy often appears in discussions and parodies of the picturesque: Cowper's own history of John Gilpin, Collins's depiction of Dr. Syntax, as well as Mackenzie's *Man of Feeling*, where the post-boy is continually resorted to for information and reassurance.

[22] Benedict Anderson, *Imagined Communities: Reflections on the Origins and Spread of Nationalism*, 2nd ed. (London: Verso, 1991), 35. Anderson is citing Walter Benjamin's "Theses on the Philosophy of History," *Illuminations: Essays and Reflections*, ed. and intro. Hannah Arendt, trans. Harry Zohn (New York: Schocken, 1968), 263.

In the late eighteenth century, war only increased the desire for and mass consumption of print news: there certainly was no buyers' strike on the British periodical. And, though the tax on stamps rose throughout the war years, putting a particularly heavy burden on periodicals, it was not overturned. Whereas Pitt's faith in British clocks had failed, newspapers succeeded in telling the time of and for the nation at war.[23]

John Galt's fictional *Annals of the Parish,* set in a small village in Scotland, gives glimpses of the growing culture—and timing—of the news, all framed by a clergyman's account of his rural parish in the years between the Seven Years' and the Napoleonic wars. At the time of the outbreak of war with the American colonies, "a wonderful interest was raised among us all to hear of what was going on in the world." So the Rev. Balwhidder agrees to split a subscription with his father-in-law for delivery of a twice-weekly newspaper from Edinburgh, while the local gentry get their news from London three times a week. "So that we had something fresh five times every week; and the old papers were lent out to the families who had friends in the wars."[24] By 1802, in the midst of the later wars with France, Rev. Balwhidder receives his paper daily from the metropolis, and a new local bookshop provides "Magazines, and Reviews, and other new publications" for the newly news-hungry (183). Galt's village in Scotland, where the pace of news and news consumption accelerated with war, is "but a type and index to the rest of the world" (192); the very words "type" and "index" disclose just how much this identity is indebted to the infiltration of print culture.

As Daniel O'Quinn has argued, Benedict Anderson's view of ideological consolidation at the moment of newspaper reading must be counterbalanced by an awareness of the "contradictory and often spurious accounts [that] jostle for the attention of the public"; but the *timing* of the paper, as Galt knows, remained a powerfully consolidating force.[25] As the number of newspapers and newspaper readers shot up in the war years, the British public were increasingly united in their rhythms, together experiencing their reading of news from abroad, news of the war's effects at home, and other news that—apart from the shared space on the page—perhaps bore no relation at all to the global violence. Thus Samuel Taylor Coleridge laments in his "Fears in Solitude" (1798) that "Boys and girls, / And women, . . . / . . . all read of war, / The

---

[23] American colonists had cited the Stamp Act of 1765, issued to solicit money for the Seven Years' War, as impetus for the Revolution. Later, in England, Leigh and John Hunt of the *Examiner* dubbed it a "tax on knowledge," but nevertheless paid it. Other radical publishers tried to evade the tax. With the Six Acts, enacted in the wake of Peterloo, 1819, the stamp duty sought to eliminate the cheap and radical press altogether.

[24] John Galt, *Annals of the Parish* (London: Henry Frowde, 1908), 94.

[25] Daniel O'Quinn, *Staging Governance: Theatrical Imperialism in London, 1770–1800* (Baltimore: Johns Hopkins UP, 2005), 22.

best amusement for our morning meal!"[26] And George Crabbe, in his poem "The Newspaper," published the same year as *The Task* (1785) and again in 1807, notes the "thousand starving minds" awaiting the arrival of the paper as, in fact, a substitute meal: "And such this mental food, as we may call / Something to all men, and to some men all."[27] The newspaper's rhythms, Crabbe admits, overwhelm even those of music or poetry: "A master-passion is the love of news, / Not music so commands, nor so the Muse" (279–80). Decades after the war, re-creating the time sense of that period, Thomas DeQuincey proudly recalls the regular "gatherings of gazers about a mail-coach" delivering the news of Salamanca or Trafalgar; they "had one centre, and acknowledged only one interest."[28] The arrival of news regulated the day and concentrated the interests, appetites, and movements of the reader.[29] A concise formulation of this thought appears even earlier in a poem by Christopher Anstey, carefully dated 1779, three years into Britain's war with its North American colonies:

In Promptu, written in 1779.

You say, my Friend, that every day
Your company forsaking,
In quest of news I haste away,
The Morning Post to take in:

But if nor news nor sense it boast,
Which all the world agree in,
I don't take in the Morning Post,
The Morning Post *takes me in*.[30]

Taken in by a medium that contained and regulated the otherwise impromptu nature of the world's events, and by a routine that transcended its contents,

[26] *Samuel Taylor Coleridge (The Oxford Authors)*, ed. H. J. Jackson (Oxford: Oxford UP, 1985), 104–7.

[27] George Crabbe, "The Newspaper," in *Poems* (London: J. Hatchard, 1807).

[28] Thomas DeQuincey, "The English Mail Coach," in *Confessions of an English Opium-Eater and Other Writings*, ed. Grevel Lindop (Oxford: Oxford UP, 1996), 194.

[29] Crabbe's poem sees the schedule of the news replacing, if ominously, more natural markers for the passing of time:

    For, soon as Morning dawns with roseate hue,
    The *Herald* of the morn arises too;
    Post after *Post* succeeds, and, all day long,
    Gazettes and *Ledgers* swarm, a noisy throng.
    When evening comes, she comes with all her train
    Of *Ledgers, Chronicles*, and *Posts* again;
    Like bats, appearing, when the sun goes down.
    From holes obscure and corners of the town. (51–60)

[30] Christopher Anstey, *The Poetical Works* (London: T. Cadell, 1808). English Poetry Database. http://gateway.proquest.com.

the newspaper reader hastens to his reading. As the trumpeted advent of Cowper's post-boy suggests, haste and anticipation are dictated as much by the predictable punctuality of the periodical as by the import of its contents. "All read of war" and set their clocks by the periodicals.

As these varied sources suggest—and as Jerome Christensen recently argued—periodical journalism tells not just the time of the nation but more acutely and specifically the time of the nation at war. Indeed, Christensen claims, without the structuring rhythms of daily news there would be no sense of wartime:

> [M]odern wartime, which is not an event but a condition of eventfulness—that is, the simulation of dailiness within an imposed totality—is inconceivable without journalism. Journalism . . . constituted the discursive superstructure and the material infrastructure that was the chief instrument of British time-making. (5)[31]

The compelling nature of journalism's modern wartime, its "condition of eventfulness," rests in part in its promise of intensity, of heightened affect. "By *intense*," Christensen explains, "I mean that in wartime reported incidents of conflict acquire a pronounced episodic structure that, in the reporting . . . effectively implicates the noncombatant auditor or reader in its narrative unfolding" (5). Yet the episodic nature of this structure, as we'll see in a moment, allows for and even encourages vacuity as much as eventfulness. Like the reading of a good story—"like a romance," Christensen suggests (5) or "newspaper-as-fiction," in Anderson's terms—offered daily at your breakfast table or at evening by the fire, the experience of wartime can be intense, but also circumscribed. Perhaps it would be more exact to say that this experience of wartime gains intensity because it is so circumscribed ("within an imposed totality"). Here is Cowper, settling down to deal with the "sound of war":

> Now stir the fire, and close the shutters fast,
> Let fall the curtains, wheel the sofa round, . . .
> So let us welcome peaceful ev'ning in. (IV: 36–37, 41)

Along with the adjective "peaceful," Cowper's hortatory circumscription (let us stir, wheel . . . round) is overdetermined in this scene of reading. As these circular figures suggest, narrative unfolding per se does not create the intensity. It is rather the binding of affectively potent events within a predictable, cyclical structure (every day, every morning) that "takes in" a wartime public reading about what may be otherwise (and elsewhere) overwhelming violence.

---

[31] On the theatrical aspects of war in this period in Britain, see also Gillian Russell, *The Theatres of War: Performance, Politics, and Society, 1793–1815* (Oxford: Clarendon, 1995); and Jane Moody, *Illegitimate Theatre in London, 1770–1840* (Cambridge: Cambridge UP, 2000).

The tempo of the daily newspapers could thus establish something like the "circumstance of [poetic] metre" in Wordsworth's famous description: its regularity and predictability providing a "sense of difficulty overcome," "tempering the painful feeling which will always be found intermingled with . . . the deeper passions."[32] The tempo of the news takes the edge off pain. Thus Christensen's narrative "unfolding" is not the appropriate term for the conscriptive beat of modern wartime, the wartime of the news, which announces itself each evening (or morning), fades away in subsequent hours, then resumes with tomorrow's renewing blast of eventfulness. This instrument of timekeeping rather performs an artful conversion of existential uncertainty into predictable pattern: noise into meter.

Cowper repeatedly ties his encounter with the news to figures of circling and rotation, as if to produce an illusion of the news as a smoothly operating, closed system. Not only the globe and all its concerns ("it turns submitted to my view, turns round); not only the finger on the clock face ("the great circuit"), but also evening itself ("Resplendent less [than day], but of an ampler round") with its "conversable" routine govern the poem (IV: 98, 119, 258). Through its manipulation of domesticated distance, its tropes of plenitude and prospect, and recurring images of what Book I identifies as the "revolvency [that] upholds the world," Cowper's *Task*, Julie Ellison notes, "helped craft the sensibility that allows us to think about the news as a cultural system" (I: 372)[33]—a sensibility of intensified reproduction characterized by "the flow of sensation and mood through events, reports, readings, and replies" (235). In Cowper's "The Winter Evening," poetry learns to show the news revolving and involving—moving round and through, but also making a round whole of—its readership and the world. This genial revolution in sensibility accords well with a poem set at the hearth, extolling the virtues of country retirement and domestic society, where the "bubbling and loud-hissing" tea kettle portends a generally warm circulation.[34] Within such a system, the time of domestic routine could be smoothly aligned with larger passages of time. Like the very gears of clockwork, large and small circles rotate in unison, producing a comprehensive system of times. Cowper locates his poem within this sort of coordinated system, the rotating gears of the domestic circle fitting neatly within

---

[32] William Wordsworth, Preface, in *Lyrical Ballads with other poems, in two volumes*, 2nd ed. (Bristol: T.N. Longman and O. Rees, 1802), 1: xi–xii.

[33] Julie Ellison, "News, Blues, and Cowper's Busy World," *MLQ: Modern Language Quarterly* 62.3 (2001): 219.

[34] Stuart Sherman remarks on the growing prominence in eighteenth-century Britain of more precise time mechanisms—pendulum clocks and repeater watches—which allowed for an apprehension of time as "series within series," radiating in concentric circles out from the seconds to the minutes and hours, and beyond to days and years. Stuart Sherman, *Telling Time: Clocks, Diaries and English Diurnal Form, 1660–1785* (Chicago: U of Chicago P, 1996), 5.

the rotating globe of the news, which in turn fits inside the "great circuit" of Cowper's clock face, which fits as well into the cycles of day and season.[35]

Of course, this well-constructed system, smoothly coordinating reading in retirement with the topicality of a "busy world," can also impress a deadening anesthesia. Structures of feeling can occlude experience as easily as they convey it. Even as he serves as the herald of this system, the post-boy announces its remarkable sangfroid: "light-hearted wretch, / Cold and yet cheerful: messenger of grief" (IV: 12–13). Though he "passes on" on his round of deliveries, and presumably will pass again tomorrow, there is in his disaffection something which might give pause to any happy sense of the "revolvancy" of the verse. The turning can become a mechanized task rather than conversable exchange, as when the poet's silent companions do needlework: "the threaded steel / Flies swiftly, and, unfelt, the task proceeds" (IV: 165–66). Later, Cowper's imagination wanders from the newspaper and cozy parlor to another scene of "unfelt" labor. As a wagonner trudges through the cold winter night, the lines themselves labor, and circulation slows:

> The wain goes heavily, impeded sore
> By congregated loads adhering close
> To the clogg'd wheels; and in its sluggish pace,
> Noiseless, appears a moving hill of snow. . . . (IV: 343–46)

The traveler "plods on," and the poet responds to the frozen man with oddly impeded feeling: "Oh happy; and in my account, denied / That sensibility of pain with which / Refinement is endued, thrice happy thou!" (IV: 357–59). Such a man "feels least, as more inur'd . . . / To winter" (IV: 387–88). It's as if, in this extended tableau, even as he insists that the laborer has "a friend in every feeling heart," Cowper deliberately describes the limits of circulation and with it, the waning of feeling, if not of life. The wheels within wheels are not turning at the same speed, nor to the same end.

In eerie ways, the tableau repeats the opening scenario with the post-boy. Though he moves with less fanfare, this "trav'ller," like the post-boy, carries his "congregated loads" insensibly. The news of the world "equally affect[s]" the post-boy and his horse—which is to say both are "unconscious of them all" (IV: 22); here the wagonner and his team are equally reduced to an insensate mound of snow. The finger of fancy recurs here as the "learned finger" that never felt the need to feel the man's pulse (IV: 362) and again as an ominous "cold finger's end" along which "I saw" a "taper soon extinguish'd" (IV: 392–93).

---

[35] Goodman suggests that the poem's "*intentional* strategy" may be to articulate scattered bits of the news into "well-cultivated conversation," to "construct the nation—indeed the globe—in the image of the parlor's conversable world." Yet, she adds, Cowper's verse remains threatened by "the noise of the hordes at the door" and "a terrible, isolating silence" (86–87; emphasis original).

Light, sensation, and possibly life are being drained from these images that had been associated with the delivery and reading of the news of the world. Later, at the end of the poem, the unfelt task is transferred to something that turns "faster far" in these "times": conscription to the militia. The new recruit mumbles his oath and, with this unfelt "task perform'd," he "puts off himself" and turns military, unfit now for any other line of work (IV: 629, 637). "Universal soldiership," Cowper laments, "has stabb'd / The heart of merit in the meaner class"—but not only there (IV: 617–18).[36] The constellation of figures—fancy's finger, mechanical turnings, and tasks performed without heart, insensible of the dangerous climate and others' pain—implicates as well the poet who is holding a pen in his fingers; performing his *Task* while conscious of his unfitness for any other; inscribing but also deconstructing its various turnings.

If Niklas Luhmann is right in calling the daily news an "autopoietic system" that introduces "into a determined even if unknown world an area of self-determination which can then be dealt with in the system itself," within Christensen's "imposed totality," then the smoothly turning wheels celebrated in Cowper's verses, as well as the self-determined "exemption" and "liberation" of the newspaper reader do not bring the world to this fireside circle, as Ellison suggests, but rather substitute a simulacrum of that world.[37] "A *form* develops," writes Luhmann of the daily mass media, "whose inside is characterized by reusability [recycling] and whose outside disappears from view" (37). The daily news, this is to say, is one of those "dominant sets of forms or conventions" that, in Williams's view, pose "profound blockage" to recognition of a whole world of experience (*Politics* 164). In Cowper's poem, this "form" depends upon a regular, cyclical arrangement of time, one that coordinates the close circle of home with larger turnings of the world and of history, all the while leaving the world and history elsewhere, "disappeared."

At the same time, however, in its echoes and turns of phrase, Cowper's poem takes pains to reveal the very fatal consequences—stabbings at the heart, steel flying to its target, frozen bodies, lights soon extinguished—that the journalistic cycle also occludes. And in revealing those consequences Cowper begins to suggest that there are structures of feeling in competition with those of the circle and the round, the post-boy and the news. For instance, he overtly disarticulates the time of the fireside circle and his retirement from the time of those in the social world who fill "the void of an unfurnish'd brain" by playing

---

[36] Compare to Book II, "The Timepiece," where Cowper laments the passing of the heroic age of Chatham and Wolfe: "Farewell those honours, and farewell with them / The hope of such hereafter. . . . They made us many soldiers" (239–40, 245).

[37] Niklas Luhmann, *The Reality of the Mass Media*, trans. Kathleen Cross (Stanford: Stanford UP, 1996), 27.

cards. Yet as the comparison develops, the two times take on the differences between peace and war.

> Time, as he passes us, has a dove's wing,
> Unsoil'd and swift, and of a silken sound;
> But the world's time is time in masquerade!
> Their's, should I paint him, has his pinions fledg'd
> With motley plumes; and . . .
>   is tinctur'd black and red
> With spots quadrangular of di'mond form,
> Ensanguin'd hearts, clubs typical of strife,
> And spades, the emblem of untimely graves. (IV: 209–19)

Echoes of the biblical Passover haunt this scene of card playing: one time passes like a dove over "us"; the other, with its clubs and bloodied hearts, forebodes to "them" untimely graves.[38] "Untimely" here signals a break in what had been established as the "natural" rhythm of the poem (here, too, young men "pass on," but too soon). "Untimely" also marks the incursion of biblical history into the present. (Even as he welcomes evening's "season of peace," Cowper glances in the mirrors of the parlor, where he "might have seen" the warrior Goliath "tow'ring crest and all" [IV: 270–71].) And, unmistakably, "untimely" marks the disarticulation of times so that they no longer rotate in unison. Times in these untimely times are in conflict. Even the difference between peacetime and wartime (both seeming to pass at the same time, the time of Cowper's writing) registers here as the possibility that times themselves can figure conflict, with deadly effects.

The Meantime

Beginning with the arrival of the post-boy, "The Winter Evening" finds Cowper winding and rewinding his figures for time as a way of telling of war. As often as these windings assume the form of an autopoietic system, ensuring "undisturb'd retirement" via temporal regularity, they also reveal more untimely turnings, figures of violence that suggest other temporalities within wartime. Of these other wartimes, the one that presses Cowper most closely is a sort of lulled, untasked time, time that itself encourages what might be called

---

[38] From the *King James Bible*, Exodus 12: 27–29: "It is the sacrifice of the **Lord's** Passover, who passed over the houses of the children of Israel in Egypt, when he smote the Egyptians, and delivered our houses. And the people bowed the head, and worshipped. And the children of Israel went away, and did as the **Lord** had commanded Moses and Aaron, so did they. And it came to pass, that at midnight the **Lord** smote all the first borne in the land of Egypt."

time-killing. Cowper charges the social world with an "idleness" that seeks to kill time, to "fill the void of an unfurnish'd brain." Filling the void by playing cards—as in the passage quoted at the end of the previous section—leads through metaphor from black spades to untimely graves: so the empty hole gets filled. Such voids open throughout the poem. At one point, the poet himself is caught in "indolent vacuity of thought": "I lose an hour," he admits, then recuperates it; the untasked vacuity becomes as if a "man / Were *task'd* to his full strength, absorb'd and lost" (IV: 297, 302, 300–1; emphasis added). Several lines later, emptiness opens out again: he stares through his window at the snow, falling in "never-ceasing lapses" (IV: 327). The challenge of "never-ceasing lapses" runs throughout the "Winter Evening," revealing the gaps, vacancies, and failings forever falling outside seamless cycles of time.

To Coleridge's speaker in "Fears in Solitude," a public reading about, but not immediately suffering war appears to have the luxury of experiencing wartime as recreation or morning ritual rather than incessant ticking.

> We, this whole people, have been clamorous
> For war and bloodshed; animating sports,
> The which we pay for as a thing to talk of,
> Spectators and not combatants! . . .
>   Boys and girls,
> And women, that would groan to see a child
> Pull off an insect's leg, all read of war,
> The best amusement for our morning meal! (93–96, 104–7)

The rest of their day seems available to temporalities dissociated from the ongoing war. Yet the time spent not consuming news of war has its own dialectical bearing on modern wartime. Here is Crabbe, describing the response of a news-hungry public caught out of the rhythm of the news when the paper fails to arrive on time:

> . . . no welcome post appears,
> But the dull morn a sullen aspect wears:
> We meet, but ah! without our wonted smile,
> To talk of headaches, and complain of bile;
> Sullen we ponder o'er a dull repast,
> Nor feast the body while the mind must fast. (273–78)

His description upends the thought that for a public distant from warfare, time away from the news might prove independent of the beat of news consumption. A missed meal, as much as a full feast, can affect your very body—and the rest of your day. There are other dissatisfactions as well: "Newspapers always excite curiosity," Charles Lamb notices in "Detached Thoughts on

Books" (1833), yet "[n]o one ever lays one down without a feeling of disappointment."[39] If the modern wartime experienced by most romantic readers was, as Christensen claims, determined by the "chief" time-making instrument of the daily news, other instruments were smuggled in to tell the time of these misalignments and disappointments, the lapse between one installment of eventfulness and another, and the gap between what news does and does not account for. Wordsworth's Margaret, from the wartime of "The Ruined Cottage" gives, as we've seen, one version: "I wander," she says, "knowing this / Only, that what I seek I cannot find."[40] Wartime also includes this wayward meantime, the "lost hours" or "dull morn" between one delivery of the news and the next. And this meantime brings with it affective and epistemological effects that fall out of or away from the reassurances of chronological time.

"I know nothing but what I learn from the General Evening [Post]" Cowper writes in a letter to his friend Joseph Hill.[41] But what about the time spent outside of news reading? Cowper records this structure of wartime feeling, this meantime as well. Having feasted upon the newspaper ("a rich repast"), and just seen Goliath make his brief invasion into the parlor, the poet of "The Winter Evening" falls into that "lost hour" and "indolent vacuity of thought" which, in his Argument to Book IV, he names a "brown study." The most frequently excerpted portion of *The Task* and still, as demonstrated by the poems discussed in the prelude, a vital influence on wartime poetry, the "brown study" is Cowper's concentrated analysis of a pause in eventfulness:

> Not undelightful is an hour to me
> So spent in the parlour twilight; such a gloom
> Suits well the thoughtfull or unthinking mind,
> The mind contemplative, with some new theme
> Pregnant, or indipos'd alike to all.
> Laugh ye . . .
> That never feel a stupor, know no pause,
> Nor need one; I am conscious, and confess,
> Fearless, a soul that does not always think.
> Me oft has fancy, ludicrous and wild,
> Sooth'd with a waking dream of houses, tow'rs,
> Trees, churches, and strange visages, express'd
> In the red cinders, while with poring eye
> I gaz'd, myself creating what I saw.

[39] Charles Lamb, *The Life and Works of Charles Lamb*, ed. Alfred Ainger, 2 vols. (London: Macmillan, 1899), 2: 26.

[40] See chapter 1.

[41] Cowper, *The Letters and Prose Writings of William Cowper*, ed. James King and Charles Ryskamp, 3 vols. (Oxford: Clarendon, 1979–86), 1: 247. Cited in Ellison 224.

Nor less amus'd have I quiescent watch'd
The sooty films that play upon the bars,
Pendulous, and foreboding, in the view
Of superstition, prophesying still
Though still deceiv'd, some stranger's near approach.
'Tis thus the understanding takes repose
In indolent vacuity of thought,
And sleeps and is refresh'd. . . .
      . . . I lose an hour
At ev'ning, till at length the freezing blast,
That sweeps the bolted shutter, summons home
The recollected pow'rs, and . . .
      . . . restores me to myself. (IV: 277–98, 302–5, 307)

Goodman finds Cowper wrestling in this passage with a Lockean notion of consciousness, the poet exploring "those conscious gaps or syncopes of thought" that Locke introduces but leaves aside (90). The poet's vacuity of thought, according to Goodman, is (perhaps like the card game) "acutely open to context." In the lapse of thinking, the meantime pictured here holds open the possibility of the "stranger's near approach" and with it, a world outside or beyond the cycle of news and its intelligence. "It is as if," Goodman explains, "not only the newspaper itself but foreign intelligence has entered the home," though foreignness enters only after the newspaper has been put aside (90, 92).

For Goodman, the scene underscores how Cowper surrenders the privileged view of the spectator ("surveying thus at ease / The globe and its concerns") for that of historically "dispossessed and vagrant subjects," those associated with "the risks, gains, and culpabilities of transoceanic conquest" (92). Her account attends to the "poring eye" of this scene, linking it with other figures in *The Task*, notably the Tahitian Omai, brought to England by Capt. Cook and later returned to his home.[42] In Book I, Cowper had presented Omai back in Tahiti, scanning the ocean for some sign of his now-distant European friends:

      . . . with eager eye
Exploring far and wide the wat'ry waste
For sight of ship from England. Ev'ry speck
Seen in the dim horizon turns thee pale
With conflict of contending hopes and fears. (I: 664–68)

Goodman's account illustrates how the semantic figure of Cowper's "peering, poring, scanning eye" (197)—on either side of the globe's surface—strains to

---

[42] See also Fulford, Lee, and Kitson's account of Cowper's response to Omai, 62–68.

collapse the space of a world that does not submit easily to view. In a sense, the emptiness or vacuity of the scene is filled affectively, with "conflict of contending hopes and fears." It promises even as it forebodes the stranger's "near approach," all the while marking the limits of human knowledge and perception: near but not in fact here. Cowper's "teeming vacuity of thought" actually responds to a nearly overwhelming, "information-laden present," Goodman argues (105). It responds, I would add, with this welter of conflicting feelings— promise and dread, hope and fear—that itself hollows out the here and now.

I want to reinforce Goodman's sense of Cowper's accomplishment, extending her argument to consider how the mediation of distant warfare by such regular events as the coming of the post-boy generates spaces of apparent emptiness in the meantime: in the long stretches between the post-boy's appearances. Cowper's "brown study" offers a self-conscious model of poetry's— especially poetic fancy's—own mediation of distant violence. Goodman's reading focuses on the "sooty films" that the poet sees in the fire, which she takes as a synecdoche of the larger passage (90). Yet just preceding the films as object of the poet's "poring eye" is this "waking dream":

> . . . a waking dream of houses, tow'rs,
> Trees, churches, and strange visages express'd
> In the red cinders. . . . (IV: 287–89)

Presented as "soothing" and "amusing," this image of a built world populated with strange faces and then reduced to "red cinders" hints at devastation even as it attests to the poet "creating what I saw." This flickering image, like the fleeting presence of Goliath in the parlor mirrors twenty lines earlier, colors the more neutral flickering image of the "sooty films." It is as if the poet's fancy is called upon here to supply what his representation of the newspapers has not: images of war's threat and destructiveness. In doing so, the poet's powerful if indolent imagination participates quietly in the unseen warfare waged out of view in strange and foreign lands: creating, it also destroys. Poetry becomes another medium for bringing home war, as Simon Bainbridge argues, and as Goodman's analysis implies. Furthermore, in mediating it cannot exempt itself from war.[43]

My second extension of Goodman's reading returns to the question of telling time to tell of war. The stranger whose approach is anticipated and feared is associated with Omai, the victim of imperial expansion; but the stranger also combines the figure of the feared enemy, Goliath, with that of the anticipated herald of British militarism, the post-boy. Connecting all these objects

---

[43] See Simon Bainbridge, *British Poetry and the Revolutionary and Napoleonic Wars: Visions of Conflict* (Oxford: Oxford UP, 2003), esp. 17–31, 133–39.

of the poet's view is that curious, flickering temporality, caught between something not quite present and yet passing. It is temporality captured within a "conflict of contending" feelings: anticipation and dread. The temporal and affective unease—crucially distinct, in Cowper's meditation, from "thought" or "thinking," but associated all the more with a layered poetic figuration—emerges as the immeasurable measure of the meantime of war.

The punctuated eventfulness within dailiness which organized the public's experience of distant war created simultaneously a sense of living in the meantime, waiting for news of events which happened at a distance both geographical and temporal.[44] There were for instance long gaps when no news arrived. But when the news did arrive it often brought with it another sort of gap—an epistemological gap between news and event—and therefore another experience of the meantime. News could not yet travel by rail or telegraph or satellite hook-up; its tidings often arrived months "late."[45] The story of Nelson's victory at Aboukir and the destruction of the French fleet there took three months to travel to and be verified by the British papers. "The long awaited news is come at last," announced the *Times*; and its account repeatedly elides the event of victory with the end of waiting for news of the event.[46] Confronting such reports, even British readers who received the newspaper in a timely fashion absorbed an awareness of its belatedness. Joined to this awareness was a sense of their ignorance of what might have happened in the meantime and off the page. As the newspapers made manifest, by the time a crucial victory had been reported in England, the British navy or army could, in the meantime, have suffered shattering defeat. The Navy List could tell you that your son had not died as of a month ago, but they could not reassure you about time since. Therefore, though the reported events of war had always already happened, they were also open to revision. "[W]hat security can I have," Charles Lamb would ask, "that what I right now send you for truth shall not, before you get it, unaccountably turn into a lie?"[47] Or, as a poem in the *Morning Chronicle* mocked in 1804, news of victory could spread like wildfire, but

[44] The flat pages of the newspaper might have, as Donald Lowe puts it, "contracted time to the instantaneous and the sensational, expanding space to include anything from everywhere," but poring and scanning readers could sense the temporal lags and epistemological holes occluded by this two-dimensional picture. Donald Lowe, *History of Bourgeois Perception* (Chicago: U of Chicago P, 1982), 38.

[45] In his discussion of empty homogeneous time, Anderson points to the coordinating "meanwhile," or sense of simultaneity that spreads laterally across the imagined space of the nation: "marked . . . by temporal coincidence, and measured by clock and calendar" (24). So firmly constitutive is this sense of "meanwhile" that, according to Anderson, "one could argue that every essential modern conception is based on the conception of 'meanwhile'"—including presumably modern wartime ("meanwhile, back at the front . . .") (24n.).

[46] *Times of London* (2 October 1798): 2.

[47] "Distant Correspondents," *The Life and Works*, 1: 204.

"lo! What a change will a day or two show / For Truth now declares, we've scarce injur'd the foe."[48]

The lag time built into reports of war promoted a deeply unsettled sense of chronology. This feeling was only exacerbated for those living through these Revolutionary and Napoleonic wars, riddled as they were with starts and stops, failed treaties, foiled victories, and a cataclysmic Hundred Days poised to reverse history. The sense of living "in the meantime" gave birth to an anxiety that both history and future could be obliterated, and time left drifting in the nearly present (but never present enough) wartime. Temporal vacancy could then plausibly characterize a person, as Cowper suggests, "task'd to his full strength, absorb'd and lost."

From an earlier generation of distant warfare, David Hume gave a model of fear that serves as well for a model of this sense of the meantime of war. Hume tells of a man who learns that his son has been killed on the battlefield. But the news is inadequate, for he has two sons and is not told which one has fallen. Aristotle's leading example of fear—the soldier on the battlefield, facing a death-dealing opponent—is thoroughly rewritten by Hume for a wartime audience. Here, contrary to the conventions of moral philosophy, fear is oriented to what has happened, rather than to what approaches—but only at first glance. The temporal vectors are rerouted by a father contemplating the fate of his progeny and by a situation where full knowledge of what has befallen is yet to come.[49] In glossing this passage from Hume's *Treatise*, Philip Fisher explains the dilemma concisely: "[T]here is nothing the father can do. His uncertainty requires him to wait, nothing more. He can have no strategy or forward-looking choice of plans."[50] At the same time, Fisher goes on to say, Hume's wartime father is also denied what Aristotle's model emphasized: a retrospective judgment on the case. The object of his grief remains unidentified; nor does Hume tell when the not-knowing will end (when the father learns of the other son's death? or of his return home?). On the one hand, living "in the meantime" of war means living in constant anticipation and dread; simultaneously, and on the other hand, it means living belatedly. Caught out of alignment with chronology, feeling itself would become intense, and intensely unmoored. "That passion" of the waiting wartime parent, Hume explains, "cannot settle" (445).

Waiting: the meantime marks out a hole in history, a sense evacuating the lived present. For psychiatrist Adam Phillips, the vacuity of such waiting presents a "sprawl of absent possibilities" and promotes feelings of "dreary agita-

[48] Anon. "A New Song to an Old Tune," in Bennett 329, first published in the *Morning Chronicle*, October 1804.

[49] David Hume, *A Treatise on Human Nature* (London: John Noon, 1739–40). The passage is found in, bk. 2, pt. 3, sect. 9, p. 445.

[50] Philip Fisher, *The Vehement Passions* (Princeton: Princeton UP, 2002), 129.

tion" rather than the clarity of distinct expectation.[51] Military historians remind us that for infantrymen and cavalrymen, the conduct of warfare in the age of Napoleon consisted primarily of waiting. Both Napoleon and Wellington figured out the strategic advantage of keeping troops busily in abeyance; in the Peninsular campaign of 1812, for example, "only a minority of the [British] army as a whole would have smelt the smoke of battle in their nostrils in that, or any other year of the long war."[52] The majority of the men were themselves waiting, oddly, for war to take shape. The home front discovered its own versions of waiting in wartime and filled them with affective potency. Nina Auerbach makes the case for "dreary agitation" as such a wartime structure when she attends to a passage from *Pride and Prejudice* (1813): "In presenting these drawing rooms full of women watching the door and watching each other," Auerbach observes, "Jane Austen tells us what an observant, genteel woman has to tell about the Napoleonic Wars: she writes novels about waiting," waiting especially for a man—even a post-boy—to arrive.[53] Auerbach provides a way of recognizing that intensely felt eventlessness, that meantime of Austen's novels, as itself a measure of the war. The reader too is recruited into the position of waiting with great concentration for something decisive— or simply distracting—to arrive. This insight could be extended to a novel such as Ann Radcliffe's *The Mysteries of Udolpho* (1794), where the agonized waiting, rimmed round with threats of violence, is less restrained than in Austen and approaches more nearly the soldier's predicament. Carted through the very terrain of the war in southern Europe, *Udolpho*'s heroine yearns to find something decisive while imagining she sees corpses.

The heroes of Walter Scott's fiction, sustained by their author's confident historicism, invert this logic of agonized waiting. Like Darsie Latimer in *Redgauntlet* (1824), they learn the value of "temporizing": not committing themselves to a definite position, but cautiously waiting out the violence of military encounter.[54] Their temporizing position is echoed by Robert Southey, speaking of military policy in 1811, where he argues for "prudence" and "forbearance" over "rashness" in waiting out the response of the continental powers to Bonaparte's incursions. "To his [Napoleon's] oppression there must be a period: a day of retribution and freedom will at last arrive; . . . till [Prussia, Austria, Holland, and Germany] shall be prepared to strike, at once and in

---

[51] Adam Phillips, "On Being Bored," in *On Kissing, Tickling and Being Bored: Psychoanalytic Essays on the Unexamined Life* (Cambridge, MA: Harvard UP, 1993), 74. Phillips pursues the thought that boredom could be associated with melancholia.

[52] Rory Muir, *Tactics and the Experience of Battle in the Age of Napoleon* (New Haven: Yale UP, 1998), 9. See also his ch. 5 and 6.

[53] Nina Auerbach, *Communities of Women: An Idea in Fiction* (Cambridge: Harvard UP, 1978), 39.

[54] Sir Walter Scott, *Redgauntlet* (1824), ed. Kathryn Sutherland (Oxford: Oxford UP, 1985), 342.

concert, . . . For that hour England will anxiously watch; at that hour she will be prepared to put forth all her strength."[55] Waiting out the periodicity of history—"there must be a period"—provides Southey and Scott with a meantime wartime strategy.[56] But not everyone had such confidence. And this "anxious watching" has the feel of warding off a more unsettling feeling of loss— specifically the loss of "something to do."[57]

For they wait, yet wait belatedly. As Scott's historical romances, Austen's own *Persuasion*, and the newspapers themselves make clear, expectation can hardly be extricated from a conviction that the meaningful events had already occurred. Thus the agony of waiting often lived alongside profound anomie. For Wordsworth, writing a string of sonnets in October of 1803, the anticipated threat of invasion coincides with the fear that nothing will happen because everything has already happened. In "October, 1803," he fears that time itself has been evacuated: "The great events with which old story rings / Seem vain and hollow"; "such emptiness . . . / Seems at the heart of all things."[58] When Wordsworth depicts war, he habitually locates it at a great temporal remove, as in his "Poems Dedicated to National Independence and Liberty," the Salisbury Plain poems, or "Yew Trees": "Not loth to furnish weapons for the bands / Of . . . those that crossed the sea / And drew the sounding bows at Azincour . . ." (622). Nor is he alone in trying to pull his experience of war into alignment with a select, but distant past: Scott, Southey, Felicia Hemans, Byron, and many lesser known poets would gravitate to past and foreign battles in order to mine some affective relationship to the current war, in part from the sense that feeling had been drained from "the present face of things" when, at least for Keats's belated knight-at-arms, "no birds sing." The familiar turn to the past by romantic writers thus allows for an expression of feeling that otherwise might remain inarticulate, drifting lost in the present. For Byron, picking through the rubble of chivalry in *Childe Harold's Pilgrimage*, the question of belatedness suffuses his response to the Peninsular campaign: Harold's very identity is cultivated from the charged affective limbo accompanying this sense of being adrift from history. As Matthew Arnold would recognize years later, Byron's work offered the image of a "passionate and dauntless soldier of a forlorn hope."[59]

[55] Robert Southey, "Review of Pasley's *Essay on the Military Policy and Institutions of the British Empire*," *Quarterly Review* 5 (May 1811): 432–33.

[56] Fisher associates the "strategy" of "playing for time" with a "modern" as opposed to a "traditional" attitude toward fear, based on economic rather than ethical models. See *The Vehement Passions*, 111–12 and 124–25.

[57] The phrasing is from Phillips, "On Being Bored," 71–72.

[58] William Wordsworth, *The Poems*, ed. John O. Hayden, 2 vol 5. (Harmondsworth: Penguin, 1977), 1: 597–98. All other citations of Wordsworth are from this text.

[59] Matthew Arnold, *Essays in Criticism, Second Series*, ed. S. R. Littlewood (London: Macmillan, 1958), 119.

"Forlorn hope" is not simply a projection of Arnold's own Victorian belatedness. The term was used by Wellington's forces in the Peninsular campaigns to
designate the advance guard, especially of a besieging army: the *avant garde* was
simultaneously the forlorn hope.[60] The limbo of the poet echoed at some remove the soldier's quandary.

It is difficult to give scale or scope to this temporal and affective limbo, except perhaps by reckoning the vivid desire it produced in some readers and
writers to close the gap of the meantime. Readers at home clearly lapped up
poetry that told of bygone warfare, and this thirst was felt even by soldiers on
the front. Simon Bainbridge reports that in the Peninsular campaign, Captain
Adam Ferguson read aloud to his men the battle scene from Canto VI of
Scott's best-selling poem, *The Lady of the Lake* (1811), even as they were being
shelled by French guns. The recited episode thrilled the troops: they cheered
and begged for more recitations. Ferguson wrote to London for popular illustrations and music written for stage adaptations of the poem (Bainbridge 1–2).
Their distance from Scott's pointedly premodern (sixteenth-century) battle
does not appear to have dampened their enthusiasm. Indeed, their enthusiasm
must have responded to the mediated, explicitly belated character of Scott's
account: even in the narrative, the battle is over and told only in retrospect.
Highland chieftain Roderick Dhu, in prison, asks his bard to recount the combat he has missed. Dhu wants the bard's singing to carry him from his prison
and back in time: "I'll listen, till my fancy hears / The clang of swords, the
clash of spears."[61] Presumably, though on the front and presently engaged in
fighting, Ferguson's men reactivated Dhu's keen (if ancient) desire not to miss
out on a battle long finished. Bainbridge comments that Scott's poem provides
"a set of instructions to the reader on how to imagine war," which must mean
in part imagining it anachronistically, in another time and place, as if already
past (17). If this appears a game of "fancy" or displacement, the stakes are
nonetheless high. Bainbridge does not mention that, having experienced the
battle belatedly and at a distance (listening to the bard), Dhu himself falls
dead. "[H]is fading eye / . . . sternly fix'd on vacancy," Roderick Dhu draws his
last breath (VI: 21). What living present can there be in such vacancy?[62]

The conflicted position of a wartime that falls between expectation and belatedness is frequently assigned to the exile or wanderer—as we saw in discussing

[60] In his account of the siege of Badajoz, Sergeant William Lawrence refers to himself three times
as one of the "forlorn hope." In John Keegan, ed., *The Book of War* (New York: Viking, 1999),
142–49.

[61] Scott, *The Poetical Works of Sir Walter Scott*. The Oxford Complete Edition, ed. J. Logie Robertson (London: Henry Frowde, 1908): canto VI, stanza 14.

[62] Dhu's death interrupts the bard's account of the battle. Ironically, the battle recounted to Dhu
should not have been: King James V had sent out a flag of truce to prevent the violence, but his
messenger arrived too late.

Wordsworth's "The Ruined Cottage" in chapter 1. Charlotte Smith exploits this purgatorial position in her long critique of the effects of war, "*The Emigrants*" (1793), dedicated to Cowper and occasioned by the French exiles, primarily widows, then wandering the English countryside. Pacing the downs above the sea in Sussex, the poet identifies her own position with that of the exiles, as if absorbing their war-torn situation into her own: "They, like me, / From fairer hopes and happier prospects driven, / Shrink from the future, and regret the past" (II: 14–16).[63] A contemporaneous poem by Smith, "The Female Exile," features a Frenchwoman who, like Omai, scans the horizon for a ship bringing news from overseas; when a speck appears, she is nearly undone by contending emotion:

> But the sea-boat, her hopes and terrors renewing,
>   O'er the dim grey horizon now faintly appears;
> She flies to the quay, dreading tidings of ruin,
>   All breathless with haste, half-expiring with fears.[64]

Smith's exiles are lost between past and future; rushing and wandering, they live between hope and dread. Taking her cue from Cowper's "brown study," where the poet wanders from himself and "home" to encounter strange visages and the stranger's near approach, Smith ventures repeatedly into scenes of wartime homelessness. Here times—and wits—are deranged: "when Nature seem'd to lose / Her course in wild distemperature, and aid, / With seasons all revers'd, destructive War" ("*The Emigrants*," II: 156).[65]

Not knowing how to mark the temporal vectors of the events of war, writers in wartime also did not know how to direct their emotions. Some of the most evocative writing during wartime dramatizes this difficulty. Wordsworth's statement of his own "Anticipation: October 1803" illustrates the dilemma. He finds himself hoping for invasion so that he can in fact experience a finished event.

> SHOUT, for a mighty Victory is won!
>   On British ground the Invaders are laid low;
>   The breath of Heaven has drifted them like snow,

[63] Charlotte Smith, *The Poems of Charlotte Smith*, ed. Stuart Curran (New York: Oxford UP, 1993), 131–63. The poem was written in two parts that fall just before and after England's declaration of war with Revolutionary France. On this passage of "The Emigrants," see Bainbridge 61, and Stuart Curran, "The 'I' Altered," in Anne Mellor, ed., *Romanticism and Feminism* (Bloomington: Indiana UP, 1988), 199.

[64] Smith, "The Female Exile: Written at Brighthelmstone in November 1792," in *The Poems of Charlotte Smith*, 98.

[65] The figure of derangement in response to war news reappears notably in Smith's "The forest boy," in *The Poems of Charlotte Smith*, 111. In her note to the poem, Smith quotes at length from Cowper's *The Task*.

And left them lying in the silent sun,
Never to rise again!—*the work is done.*
Come forth, ye old men, now in peaceful show
And greet your sons! drums beat and trumpets blow!
Make merry, wives! ye little children, stun
Your grandames' ears with pleasure of your noise!
Clap, infants, clap your hands! . . . (1–10 emphasis added;)

Throughout the series of sonnets written during the 1803 invasion scare, the poet begs for an end to the waiting. "England! the time is come," begins one; "Now is the time," he repeats in "To the Men of Kent." Yet the same series finds him mourning an "emptiness . . . at the heart of all things" and even as he turns in one poem to an imagined future, he looks to victories from the past: "O for a single hour of that Dundee, / Who on that day the word of onset gave!" ("In the Pass of Killicranky"). The invasion sonnets recognize that war "approaches near" but not near or soon enough. "Anticipation, October 1803" echoes the noisy joy of biblical psalms in (proleptically) welcoming the soldiers home. Yet the final lines falter from the anticipated assurance of happy retrospection when they imagine the dead and wounded:

Divine must be
That triumph, when the very worst, the pain
And even the prospect of our brethren slain,
Hath something in it which the heart enjoys: —
In glory will they sleep and endless sanctity. (10–14)

Like Cowper imagining the frozen wagonner, the speaker here is happy to project those injured by violence into a realm beyond feeling. Yet the sonnet's own emotional aims are as elusive as its tenses. What exactly does the speaker want: War here and now? The possibility of retrospection? The "prospect" of brethren slain? Or an "endless"-ness that overwhelms even his anticipation? The temporal ambivalence—Smith's "distemperature"—demonstrates that Wordsworth's wartime "Anticipation" cannot tell where it stands in time or when (or how) to feel.

Why would the vacancy, the eventlessness of a meantime emerging in the interstices of the news, create such affective dissonance—not just contending emotions of hope and fear, but also the oscillations between intensity and anomie? It is not just that this "conflict of contending" in the affective realm, as Cowper names it, simply mirrors on the level of individual psychology a contentious, war-torn world "out there." (As Goodman's account suggests, the division between individual and context disintegrates in the "lost hour": Cowper's brown study—like Smith's exile—un-houses the self altogether, opening it to strange or foreign sensibilities.) The dissonance seems instead a structural matter, a product of the peculiar nature of wartime and the meantime vested in it. Recent scholarship on affect, borrowing in part from cognitive psychology, can clarify that dissonance and its sources. Though situated in the body and thus responsive to what we might call context, affect remains in excess of consciousness, and thus of recognized event. Brian Massumi associates affect with the virtual; it designates "something happening out of mind," something "passing too quickly to be perceived, too quickly, actually, to have happened"—like the flickering moments glimpsed in Cowper's poem (29–30). Affect, Massumi continues, is a realm with "a different temporal structure, in which past and future brush shoulders with no mediating present"[66]—where the present, we might say, is vacant, or filled only with the past and future. In this passing present, then, affect comprises a welter of unsorted feelings and sensations, often contradictory and contending. These are the entities that David Hume, writing in his own idiom, identified as "passions" per se. They arise, Hume says, "originally in the soul, or body, whichever you please to call it, without any preceding thought or perception." It is therefore "impossible we can ever, by a multitude of words, give a just definition of them" (270–71). As a result affect is assigned meaning only retroactively and reductively after it has, in Hume's terms, "settled" into an identifiable emotion—say fear or hope. In fact, to follow Massumi's characterization of this dynamic, it becomes clear that affect is identifiable only as it enters (is "dampened" down into) what he calls linearization, causal explanation, or accounts of before and after: the chronology of clock time (30). Until assigned a place in narrative sequence, until given a temporal/emotional vector (hope or dread), affect exists rather as undifferentiated intensity. To write, then, a history of the meantime—where the present is empty and where historical meaning cannot yet be assigned—is to conjure temporal *and* emotional confusion. As a sort of emotional hiatus, or a feeling not yet recognized as such, anomie—no less than derangement—serves as emblem and acknowledgment of the excessiveness of dwelling in a time with no mediating present. Wartime is (also) this unmediating present writ large, a historiographical meantime—where past and future brush shoulders, where promise cannot separate from a sense of being too late.

The post-boy may be the unfeeling instrument of historicity—a sort of anthropomorphized clock, "indiff'rent," in Cowper's words, or, "regardless," as Koselleck puts it, "of [its] historical situation" (205). If so, he is thus and also the ideal soldier of a media culture, announcing with fanfare—but not feeling—the passing of each eventful day. In Cowper's hands he represents the

---

[66] Brian Massumi, *Parables for the Virtual: Movement, Affect, Sensation* (Durham: Duke UP, 2002), 31. Massumi explicitly paraphrases Henri Bergson, *Matter and Memory*.

conversion of the experience of war into the wartime of the news. The post-boy is the possibility of dating and episode; with him it's as if beginnings and ends and passings-away are all accounted for. His is an unfelt war, accompanied nonetheless (and all the more) by a surge of eventfulness. Cowper's poem puts the post-boy in the spotlight, but this focus has the effect of conjuring as well the darkness and confusion—not to mention the burden of news, all that it does not tell—that follow in the post-boy's wake. Around him pools the meantime of war, a temporality of eventlessness and as-yet-unacknowledge-able feeling. It yawns there in the darkness at the edge of the day, making it hard to differentiate one day from another, this winter from others, this war from those. Here definition, location, identity blur. The meantime is this other, nearly unreadable version of war. In the shadows of the cozy parlor, in unaccounted noises and echoes, in glimpses and flickers of hardly recognized figures, the meantime abides. It unsettles the distance separating a poet by the fireside from a world outside, from unsheltered night and suffering.

Prophecy

When speech becomes prophetic, it is not the future that is given, it is the present that is taken away, and with it any possibility of a firm, stable, lasting presence.[67]

And [I] heard . . .
A loud prophetic blast of harmony,
An Ode, in passion uttered, which foretold
Destruction to the children of the earth,
By deluge, now at hand. . . . (Wordsworth, *The Prelude* 5: 93–98)

For all its affective dissonance, the unknowing meantime can be remarkably soundless. The lost nature of Cowper's lost hour is signaled by the absence of noise: unlike other crucial moments in "The Winter's Evening," the "brown study" passage does not refer to the aural register, not even to quiet or silence. Cowper seems here to imagine a poetry that will not be vocalized, as if the words on the page will remain mute. As Goodman notes, attention in this passage rests with visualization and the "poring eye." It's as if "the noise of living," which Goodman otherwise associates with a history of the present, has shut down: this is living with held breath. It is finally punctured by the sudden return of noise to the poem when, as in Hazlitt's "Letter-Bell," a "freezing blast, / . . . sweeps the bolted shutter," summoning the poet back to himself,

---

[67] Maurice Blanchot, "Prophetic Speech," in *The Book to Come* , trans. Charlotte Mandell (Stanford: Stanford UP, 2003), 79.

even as the winter beyond his parlor sweeps in (303–4). With the inrush of noise the poet takes up an alternative mode for telling the time of war, one that turns its untimeliness not to wayward vacancy but to fullness and conviction—though not necessarily to a viable present. Cowper calls upon the voice of prophecy.

In his "Winter's Evening," Cowper introduces prophetic time first dismissively: his "brown study" imagines the films on the grate "foreboding, in the view / Of superstition, prophesying still, / Though still deceiv'd" (IV: 293–94). But the blast of winter that shakes him from his indolent vacuity inspires the poet himself cautiously to venture prophecy. He looks out his window and foretells a strangeness to come:

> To-morrow brings a change, a total change!
> Which even now, though silently perform'd
> And slowly, and by most unfelt, the face
> Of universal nature undergoes.
> Fast falls a fleecy show'r: The downy flakes,
> Descending, and with never-ceasing lapses
> Softly alighting upon all below,
> Assimilate all objects. (IV: 322–29)

The never-ceasing lapses of time are perhaps welcome, convincing signs of a world-to-be-changed. But they are also signs of a world erased.

In the later war years, Cowper himself was read as prophetic: Charlotte Smith invoked *The Task* in her dedicatory epistle to *The Emigrants* (1793), suggesting that Cowper's poem "seemed to foretell" subsequent events in France. She noted that Charles James Fox, objecting in Parliament to a counterrevolutionary war against France, also turned to the prophetic authority of *The Task*.[68] Anna Barbauld drew extensively from Cowper's poem in her *Eighteen-Hundred and Eleven*, an antiwar jeremiad. In her prophetic mode, Barbauld borrowed from Book II of *The Task*, "The Time-Piece," where Cowper himself borrows from the Hebrew prophets Daniel and Jeremiah to produce lines, as he noted, "intended to strike the hour that gives notice of approaching judgment . . . dealing pretty largely in the *signs* of the *times*": earthquakes, storms, diseases, and "unsuccessful or successful war" (Sambrook, *The Task* 83n; II: 4). "A Winter's Evening," by contrast, deals more with the *times* of the times. A prophetic undercurrent persists, though it too has undergone change. Here, in the never-ceasing lapses of falling snow, the future appears muted and nearly illegible: like and unlike the newspaper, it is a blank page that "assimilates all

---

[68] Smith 134 and 134n. Smith (following Charles Fox) refers to a passage in *The Task*, V: 380–95.

objects" into a vast sameness. It could be a figure of time redeemed, a new time, or, in its frozen stillness, the end of time.[69]

What interests me is the possibility of total change or new time in Cowper's poem, and the accompanying effort to convert the changing time from something "unfelt," as he says, to something deeply, if disturbingly, moving. It is not news that the period of the late eighteenth and early nineteenth century in Britain saw a tremendous upsurge in popular prophets and prophecy, and that several of the poets most associated with Romanticism (Blake and Wordsworth most explicitly) identified their vocation with prophecy.[70] Nor is it news that the appeal of prophecy was closely allied with the turbulence of war. Prophets emerged to give guidance in what they saw as a profoundly unsettled present. A believer in 1795 put it this way: "This being a time the most momentous, that the history of nations affords, some prophets may be naturally expected to arise for the guidance of man through this maze of awful, impending fatality."[71] The prophetic mode aimed, in fact, to "repair time," as Geoffrey Hartman suggests; or, as Paul Fussell proposes, it fills in at a time (wartime) "when clear explanations of purpose and significance seem especially unavailable."[72] The utterance of prophecy, like the telling of the meantime, stood against the cycle of news and its regular installments of time, to urge a different

[69] It is instructive to contrast Cowper's prophetic urge here with Coleridge's fifteen years later in "Frost at Midnight," a poem written during the 1798 threat of invasion. Cowper's looks forward to a "total" if illegible "change" in the "face of universal nature"; Coleridge's wartime conviction is more modest, substituting for Cowper's glimpse of redeemed time a cautious "loop" that holds his past and his son's future in what Jon Mee characterizes as "a comforting unity of time and place that never ventures out into the crowded social world." Jon Mee, *Romanticism, Enthusiasm, and Regulation: Poetics and the Policing of Culture in the Romantic Period* (Oxford: Oxford UP, 2005), 160.

[70] Recent books on this matter include those by Morton D. Paley, *The Traveller in the Evening: The Last Works of William Blake* (Oxford: Oxford UP, 2003); Ian Balfour, *The Rhetoric of Romantic Prophecy* (Stanford: Stanford UP, 2002); Jon Mee, *Dangerous Enthusiasm: William Blake and the Culture of Radicalism in the 1790s* (Oxford: Clarendon Press, 1992) and *Romanticism, Enthusiasm*; and Tim Fulford, ed., *Romanticism and Millenarianism* (New York; Palgraven 2002). They respond to and extend earlier work by Northrop Frye, *Fearful Symmetry* (Princeton: Princeton UP, 1947); David Erdman, *William Blake: Prophet against Empire* (Princeton: Princeton UP, 1977); and M. H. Abrams, *Natural Supernaturalism* (New York: Norton, 1973). See also Geoffrey Hartman, "Poetics of Prophecy," in *High Romantic Argument: Essays for M. H. Abrams*, ed. Lawrence Lipking (Ithaca: Cornell UP, 1981), 15–40.

[71] Richard Brothers, *Wonderful prophecies. Being a dissertation on the existence, nature, and extent of the prophetic powers in the human mind . . .* , 3rd ed. (London: B. Crosby, 1795), 16.

[72] Hartman, "Poetics of Prophecy," 25–26, 26n; Paul Fussell, *Wartime: Understanding and Behavior in the Second World War* (New York: Oxford UP, 1989), 35. Reading Wordsworth, Hartman suggests that prophecy seeks to turn the "lesion in the fabric of time" into "time for thought," to be able to say there is (still) time (23, 25–27). Thus Hartman separates prophecy from apocalyptic rhetoric (and grants it an "anxious hope"). It is not clear that this distinction holds, even for Wordsworth, who, like many of his contemporaries, feels the desire for and fear of the end of time press heavily. See Mee, *Romanticism, Enthusiasm*, 83–128; and J.F.C. Harrison, *The Second Coming: Popular Millenarianism, 1780–1850* (New Brunswick, NJ: Rutgers UP, 1979).

account of the time of global war. In some instances, prophecy told of time to move the people of England to a feeling of wandering or exile; alternately, prophecy told of time to move them to imperial ambition.

Similarities between the time of waiting, or meantime, and the time of prophecy are easy to spot. Prophecy appears to share with the meantime a strong association with affect, and thus a distance from rational chronology. In the eighteenth century especially, popular forms of prophecy, often tied to religious enthusiasm and radical politics, were viewed with suspicion by the established church and government, in part because of their emotional volatility and irrationality. Prophetic proclamations reformulating the prophets of the Hebrew Testament and the Christian Book of Revelation depended on a rhetoric that seemed to provoke "delirium" or "illapses of the spirit"; this delirium in turn suggested a rending of the temporal order (Mee, *Romanticism, Enthusiasm* 160). A more obvious similarity between these two modes of time-telling is their general air of expectation, which in the meantime is beset with doubts, but is attended with conviction by prophecy. Despite this orientation toward what approaches, however, both wartime prophecy and wartime waiting share a counterinclination toward the past. In the unsettled time of war, prophecy looks to the past not to restore the settled narrative of national history, but to change and perhaps fulfill it. "To prophesy the present," suggests Ian Balfour in *The Rhetoric of Romantic Prophecy*, "is, typically, to cite the past"; it is "turning one's back from one's own time to the past" in order to redirect the future (16).

In this last regard, its play of before and after gives prophecy a political force and direction that redeems the anxieties of the meantime—redeems in particular the experience of being belated that comes with the meantime. Walter Benjamin, the twentieth century's best-known philosopher of prophecy, turns to the eighteenth-century economist and philosopher Anne-Robert Jacques Turgot to make this point. "'Before we can inform ourselves about a given state of affairs,'" Walter Benjamin quotes Turgot, "'it has already changed many times. So we already experience too late what has taken place. And thus one can say of politics that it is directed, as it were, to foretelling the present.'" Benjamin continues: "It is precisely this concept on which the relevance of genuine historiography is based"; it works with and beyond the belatedness of the meantime.[73] The prophet is thus engaged in a mode of telling time that rejects the present (or the semblance of the present) offered by the news, the chief time-telling instrument of the nation; the prophet deals in rival synchronies and anachronism.

With prophecy the stakes of telling time in war, of making loquacious what happens at a distance, can be quite high. This chapter concludes, then, by

[73] Walter Benjamin, "Theses on the Philosophy of History," qd. in Balfour 16.

pulling away from the hushed prophecy with which Cowper fends off war's eventlessness to take up more extreme utterances. Two bolder prophets loudly proclaim to the nation how to tell time in war, and the nation listened attentively, though it responded differently to each. My first example comes from the milieu of radical politics and millenarian religious practices, though it is worthwhile to mention that it was written by a former naval lieutenant, discharged after the war in America: Robert Brothers's *A Revealed Knowledge of the Prophecies and Times* (1794). My second example comes from the military establishment and was circulated not in pamphlet or book form but in the newspaper itself: Charles William Pasley's curious "Letter to the *Times of London*" (1813). Both prophecies effectively move the register of timekeeping away from the time of the nation in order to introduce the end of time and with it the end—in one sense the dissolution, in another the unfurling project—of empire.

The uncertainties of fear and alarm stand paradoxically as the source of conviction for both these wartime prophets. In Pasley's words, which echo Brothers's,

> if I could flatter myself that my voice would rouse the nation to an earnest view of this most alarming part of the dangers to which we are exposed . . . I shall be consoled against any clamour [of criticism] by the consciousness of having discharged a duty of the most sacred . . . nature to my country.[74]

To a degree, their predictions mirror, magnify, and restructure what had become, by the mid-1790s, the government's own policy of issuing "alarms"— predictions first of treason at home, then increasingly of invasion from abroad. "Alarmism" was itself a recognized form of prophecy by 1796, attributed to and practiced primarily by government supporters, both sincere and cynical. A pamphlet titled *The Alarmist* tried to define and defend the term, and in doing so showed the connections between Brothers, Pasley, and Pitt's wartime administration: "Alarmist" describes "One whose understanding is for ever disturbed by visions of imaginary public dangers, One, who labours to instill into the minds of the People the same vain terrors which infest his own."[75] More often than not, as Mark Rawlinson shows, the alarms spreading through

[74] Charles William Pasley, *Essay on the Military Policy and Institutions of the British Empire*, 2nd ed. (London: A. J. Valpy, 1811), 5.

[75] *The Alarmist, No. 1* (London: J. Owen, 1796), vi; cited in Barrell 15. See Mark Rawlinson, "Invasion! Coleridge, The Defence of Britain and the Cultivation of the Public's Fear," in Philip Shaw, ed., *Romantic Wars: Studies in Culture and Conflict, 1793–1822* (Aldershot, UK: Ashgate, 2000), 110–37, on the cultivation of alarm see John Barrell's helpful discussion of alarms and alarmism (*Imagining* 15–18). See also Scott's gentle parody—and political defusing—of alarmism in *The Antiquary* (1816).

the print culture of "garrison Britain" between 1795 and 1805 aimed to anchor fear by projecting it onto past history. Alarmism tied a temporal and emotional knot: the alarmist conjured threats in the future that recalled threats from the past, sometimes dating back before the Battle of Hastings to Caesar's invasion.[76] If he succeeded in persuading the public that such fears were not imagined but real, not fleeting but grounded in what had been, and yet not past but still to come, the alarmist would then be hailed as prophet.

In 1794, having been repeatedly repulsed in his attempts to convince the King, the Queen, the Prime Minister, Parliament, and various foreign ambassadors of approaching disasters, Richard Brothers took his message to the public, issuing *A revealed knowledge of the prophecies & times. Book the first. Wrote under the direction of the Lord God* and its companion, *A revealed knowledge of the prophecies and times. Particularly of the present time, the present war, and the prophecy now fulfilling . . . Book the second.*[77] Editions of the two volumes proliferated rapidly and were greeted with amazement, fear, and ridicule, not least because of the never-ceasing lapses, or fallings, forecast in the second volume: "the sudden and perpetual FALL of the TURKISH, GERMAN, and RUSSIAN EMPIRES" as well as "the general fall of *European Monarchy*" as a consequence of the current war with France (2: title page, 19; emphasis original). God had moreover given to Brothers a vision of Britain, once "Queen among the nations," now a woman "without a covering on her head, worn thread-bare,— and rent in many places"—a judgment on her entry into the war (19). In fact the present "delusive war," Brothers explained, was "designed" by the divinity to "throw down for ever the English Monarchy, and from the confusion it will make throughout the country, involve almost every family of wealth in beggary and death!" The evils befalling from her "*Colonial Conquest*" will be "the cause of [Britain's] death" and war will be death's instrument. Britain will "retire . . . under that falling blow, which will break the Empire into pieces, and throw herself down on the ground; from whence she is never to rise up any more" (20–21).[78]

[76] Rawlinson, "Invasion!" 116–17.

[77] Richard Brothers, *A revealed knowledge of the prophecies & times. Book the first. Wrote under the direction of the Lord God, . . . it being the first sign of warning for the benefit of all nations; containing, with other great and remarkable things, not revealed to any other person on earth, the restoration of the Hebrews to Jerusalem, by the year 1798* (London, 1794) and *A revealed knowledge of the prophecies and times. Particularly of the present time, the present war, and the prophecy now fulfilling. . . . Book the second. Containing, with other great and remarkable things, not revealed to any other person on earth, the sudden and perpetual fall of the Turkish, German, and Russian empires* (London, 1794). Both texts from *ECCO*. Gale Group. http://galenet.galegroup.com/servlet/ECCO.

[78] The most thorough account of Brothers's case appears in John Barrell, *Imagining* 504–47. See also Morton D. Paley, "William Blake, the Prince of the Hebrews, and the Woman Clothed with the Sun," in *William Blake: Essays in Honour of Sir Geoffrey Keynes*, ed. Morton D. Paley and Michael Phillips (Oxford: Oxford UP, 1973), 260–93; and Mee, *Romanticism, Enthusiasm*, 94–99, 108–9.

Brothers's prophetic writings held forth the promise of an absolute end: not simply to monarchy and empire, but to "the present War" and "the present Time of the World." War, empire and what he would elsewhere call the "present form of time" were interlocking and coterminal; the end of one would be the end of the others. Thus his readers were living in "the latter days of the world: THE PRESENT IS IT," after which the end would come (1: 33). The single hope was for George III to cede his crown to the unlikely Brothers, now disclosed by God's command as the Prince of the Hebrews. Brothers announced that he had been called to lead the scattered Jews of every nation—those known to be Jews as well as "invisible" or unknowing Jews newly revealed to the prophet, such as William Pitt himself, Charles James Fox, the King and his family, and John Luke, "a poor Quaker"—to "repair" to the land of Israel, where they would restore the ancient temple, rebuild Jerusalem, and inaugurate a new age:

Then shall there be no more war, no more want, no more wickedness; but all shall be peace, plenty, and virtue.
Surely all these things will be, and that soon.[79]

Brothers quickly attracted a large and fairly distinguished group of followers in Britain. His appeal lay partly in this radical unraveling of national destiny. He invited his countrymen and women to end their identification with a colonial empire and embrace instead the role of a victimized people—the ancient Israelites—dispersed, enslaved, and exiled, yet beloved of their God. His account of the Israelites, offered now as destiny to their unwitting descendents, tells of the survival, "even under . . . constraints and oppressions of a learned and civilized people, sent to cultivate the earth not through conquest but through defeat."[80] Even in the 1790s, critics noted the anachronism of Brothers's prophecies: the echoes of seventeenth-century fanaticism chimed awkwardly with much radical thought, which saw itself as enlightened and liberal.[81]

[79] Richard Brothers, *Brothers's prophecy of all the remarkable and wonderful events which will come to pass in the present year: foretelling, . . . the downfall of the Pope; a revolution in Spain, Portugal, and Germany; . . . Also, a dreadful famine, pestilence, and earthquake* (London: [1795?]), 8. *ECCO*. Gale Group. http://galenet.galegroup.com/servlet/ECCO. See Hartman's note on "repairing time" which he associates with both the verb *repatriare* (to return to one's country or home) and *reparare* (to restore or mend) (26n).

[80] Richard Brothers, *An exposition of the Trinity: with a further elucidation of the twelfth chapter of Daniel; one letter to the King, and two to Mr. Pitt, &c. by Richard Brothers. The descendant of David, King of Israel, &c.* (London, 1795), 25–30. *ECCO*. Gale Group. http://galenet.galegroup.com/servlet/ECCO. Brothers understands the threat from France in the light of the necessary and fortunate defeat of Israel by Nebuchadnezzar. As Barrell points out, Nebuchadnezzar is a mobile figure in the 1790s, often linked with George III (*Imagining* 544–47), but here Brothers clearly associates Nebuchadnezzar with an external threat.

[81] Mee, *Romanticism, Enthusiasm* 94–97; Barrell, *Imagining* 513–18.

Yet Brothers's anachronism clearly spoke to an embattled present, desperate to extract itself from its own narratives of commercial and imperial progress and to inhabit time differently. He offered a different time, the end of time.[82]

For Brothers, the prophecy of a radical temporality was intimately connected with the "GREAT WAR" of "all nations," a war unlike all previous wars (30).[83] What Cowper intimates, Brothers makes explicit: along with the perpetual fall of kings and nations occurs "the present war of *Time, Times*, and the *dividing of Time*" (*Revealed Knowledge* 2: 25; emphasis original).[84] Time becomes the very medium of war. The knowledge of "times" presented in *A Revealed Knowledge* and in Brothers's later works runs deliberately counter to modern chronologies. He argues that "the figurative denominations of fixed time have . . . operated in the minds of people as a stumbling block" which his "revealed knowledge" hopes to remove.[85] With delicacy, Brothers dates most of his writing "in the month called . . . ," signaling his distance from the accepted temporal order. His writings are full of reminders that to God's post-boys—the angels with whom he converses and Brothers himself—days are not days, months not months. There is in Brothers's work a bewildering fluidity of years, hours, and days, as if to insist they are mere figures: for instance, the year "comprehending from June 1795 to June 1796, figuratively expressed by St. John under the denomination of *Hour*" (*Trinity* 43). To the Lord God, Brothers explains, "the whole of three years and a half . . . [is] but comparatively as an *hour*" (as in the "hour of judgment is at hand").[86] One angel is fond of repeating enigmatic lines from the book of Daniel: "it [the latter time] shall be for a time—times—and half an half [*sic*]" (*Trinity* 17)[87] "Days are mentioned by the Angel [in Daniel] instead of years," Brothers explains, to conceal until "the proper time" the true dating (*Revealed Knowledge* 1: 7). Another angel

[82] A full discussion of several types of anachronism is provided in Srinivas Aravamudan, "The Return of Anachronism," *MLQ: Modern Language Quarterly* 62 (2001): 331–53.

[83] Though Brothers refers to the Book of Revelation for warrant, his description of the present "GREAT WAR" is tinged with consciousness of a distinctly modern turn. This is a new sort of war, where a prince can no longer "sit down at his leisure, and calculate from his success how long to carry it on, or by his defeats how soon he must leave it off." Rather, the Judgment of God "has rendered it so entirely different" that, once fighting had begun, all monarchs would find themselves in escalating and unabating conflict, as if "unexpectedly caught in a large Trap on forbidden ground" (*Revealed Knowledge* II: 38–39).

[84] See also *Revealed Knowledge* II: 36.

[85] Richard Brothers, *A letter from Mr. Brothers to Miss Cott, the recorded daughter of David, and future Queen of the Hebrews. With an address to the members of His Britannic Majesty's Council* (Edinburgh, 1798), iv. ECCO. Gale Group. http://galenet.galegroup.com/servlet/ECCO.

[86] Brothers, *A Letter . . . to Miss Cott*, v. Emphasis original.

[87] This is Brothers's own emendation of the text of Daniel, where the angel refers to "three years and a half." Through revelation, Brothers learns what the angel could not tell Daniel: "and a half an [*sic*] half." He explains this change several times in his work; it is crucial to his dating of events (*A Letter* v). See also *Revealed Knowledge* I: 7.

cites Revelation, "that there should be time no longer," to which Brothers responds: "'Time no longer.' It means no longer in its present form than this year" (*Trinity* 38–39)—but then, what or how long is this year?

In the present "war of *Time, Times,* and the *dividing of Time*," the world needs, and Brothers provides, a "Chronology of the World," calculated by him from the evidence of Scripture and divine communication: "After it was done, the Lord God said to me in a Vision at Night,—That is the true Age of the World, and the general computed One is erroneous" (*Revealed Knowledge* 1: 2). The chronology was subsequently elaborated and published in pamphlet form. In it, Brothers is guilty of almost exponential anachronism: even as it looks to scripture for its dating, his chronology is itself a throwback to the seventeenth century and earlier, when the art and science of calculating chronology—coordinating various ancient calendars, written texts, and languages—attracted the most learned men of Europe.[88] Armed with the light of revelation, Brothers is ready to refute the "invention and ingenuity" of such learned men.[89] His "true chronology" refutes more directly the contemporary timeline of universal history, first introduced by Jacques Barbeu-Duborg in 1753, then refined and popularized by Joseph Priestley in 1765.[90] Against Priestley's visualization of time moving unidirectionally along a horizontal axis, Brothers offers a table of computations, its years ascending and descending in columns simultaneously, its eras overlapping and repeating. Here the clocks of "time, Times and the divisions of times" are indeed rewound, but also and finally bound, according to "three calculations":

FROM THE CREATION 1795,

FROM THENCE RETROSPECTIVELY to the CREATION

AND THE AGE OF THE WORLD BEFORE CHRIST

IN the YEAR of CHRIST 1795.[91]

In its version of a recursive, yet mathematically calculable time, the chronology moves up and down, falling, but also rising, rather than moving forward like an arrow. It synchronizes events in scripture with events since, up until the

---

[88] Anthony Grafton studies the chronologists in *Joseph Scaliger: A Study in the History of Classical Scholarship, Vol. 2: Historical Chronology* (Oxford: Clarendon, 1993), esp. 1–51. See also Sasha Archibald and Daniel Rosenberg, "A Timeline of Timelines," *Cabinet Magazine* 13 (Spring 2004). http://www.cabinetmagazine.org/issues/13/timelines.php.

[89] Brothers, *A corroborating proof from the holy scriptures, of the truth of the chronology of the world, as given by revelation to Richard Brothers* (London, 1795), 3. *ECCO.* Gale Group. http://galenet.galegroup.com/servlet/ECCO.

[90] On the significance of Priestley's timeline, see Daniel Rosenberg, "Joseph Priestley and the Graphic Invention of Modern Time," *Studies in Eighteenth-Century Culture* 36.1 (2007): 55–103, and "The Trouble with Timelines," *Cabinet Magazine* 13 (Spring 2004). http://www.cabinetmagazine.org/issues/13/timelineIntro.php.

[91] Taken from the title page of *Corroborating Proof.*

present times.[92] Displayed in parallel columns, some portions of the Time of
the World read from top to bottom, others from bottom to top. Creation
marks the beginning and the end of various computations: year 0 and year
3729. Year 1794 is both the year "answering to 1794" and year 5913 since the
Creation. Along the bottom of the chart, the year "answering to 1794" is syn-
chronized with generation 50 (the present era) on the one side, and with the
birth of Christ and the prophecy of Daniel 9: 25 on the other. Nothing, presumably, falls off the page or out of the table. Only the present year, 1795, does
not appear in this reckoning.[93]

Rather than an exemption from or evacuation of the present, Brothers's
version of wartime finds a present filled to the breaking point, the simultaneous concentration and explosion of all time. "THE PRESENT IS IT": it comprehends all the Time in the World, even as it completes it. Brothers calls up the
voices of nearly all the prophets of the Hebrew scriptures. Like Cowper, he fa-
vors Daniel and Jeremiah, but Isaiah, Hosea, Micah, Joel, Haggai, Zachariah
also serve; he demonstrates how the present moment will respond to them all,
even as the present war will recapitulate the fall of Jerusalem, the fall of Baby-
lon, the fall of Rome. The temporal and vocal accumulation is distinct from
the displacement of the present by poets and propagandists who hear in the
abyss of the meantime echoes of bygone battles. Brothers's prophetic mode
rather freights the present beyond reason: other times are not analogies for the
present, they clamor for fulfillment *now*. These synchronies with the past
are not given in order to allow distance or perspective on current events: distance collapses into an all-consuming, urgent momentousness. The "*Fall* of
CITIES, the *Fall* of THRONES, the *Fall* of PRINCES, the *Death* of MILLIONS, the
Desolation of KINGDOMS" are imminent (*Revealed Knowledge* 2: 31). The time
of waiting is over; no time is left.[94]

In the end, Brothers's timing of the end, his end of time, was defeated by
dates. The earthquake Brothers had forecast for 1795 did not occur; though he
recalculated the dates, the ground upon which Britain stood refused to give
way. Nor had he been able to persuade the dispersed Jews to move to Jerusalem under his guidance in 1798, the year ordained to put an end to the present

[92] Though given by God, the Chronology is proved by numbers: "[Y]es, I reassert it, even to the
comprehension of a youth that has just passed through his first academic degrees of arithmetic."
(*Trinity* I: 23).

[93] The pamphlet goes further, doubling the chronology over on itself in a condensed "summary"
version. The left-hand column (of four columns) proceeds from Creation to Solomon's reign and
the construction of the temple; the second column (of four columns) from the reign of Rehoboam
to the birth of Christ (and the present era) (*Corroborating Proof* 5–7).

[94] On this sense of "no time" or the inability to "take time," see David Simpson, *9/11: The Culture
of Commemoration* (Chicago: U of Chicago P, 2006), 6–15. Compare also Hartman's more hopeful
comments on time in prophecy in "Poetics of Prophecy," esp. 25–28.

form of time. Though some did, not all nations and all thrones fell in those years. By the end of the war, of course, millions *had* died, kingdoms *had* suffered desolation, and it was apparent that war had changed forever. Yet Brothers had, pathetically, relied too much on dating—the historian's but not the prophet's code—to be able to claim these as verification of his revelation. Instead, the war of times was won by the state, with its unyielding system of days, months, and years. In the aftermath of spectacularly unsuccessful treason trials, and with disastrous news from allied forces on the continent, Pitt's administration could not tolerate Brothers's view of a diasporic people poised at the end of time. On March 4, 1795, Brothers was arrested and later tried for treason. Though the treason charge did not hold, he was ruled insane and locked up in Dr. Samuel Simmons's madhouse, from which, though chastened, he continued to publish pamphlets and letters. The imprisonment and rude treatment accorded to him, Brothers explained in a public letter to the Prime Minister, were intended by the Lord God to cure him of his "predilection in favour of this place [England], and likewise of all compassionate motives to hereafter befriend a falling people" (*Trinity* 44). But Brothers was never able to leave England. He lingered in confinement for eleven years until he was released—though still deemed a "lunatic." He died in London in 1824.

In November 1813, the *Times of London*, which had characterized Brothers as a "tool of a faction, employed to seduce the people, and to spread fears and alarms," printed with approval a long letter from Captain Charles W. Pasley, proposing his own repertoire of fears and alarms.[95] The *Times*'s editor grouped Pasley, a central figure in the military reforms of the day and head of the newly established school of military engineering at Chatham, with "Walsh, Wordsworth, and Coleridge" as a man "whose views appear to me comprehensive and important . . . [and of] the true English spirit."[96] The renowned author of an *Essay on the Military Policy and Institutions of the British Empire*, Pasley had argued—successfully it turns out—for Britain to switch its attentions from its navies to its armies, to take up a more "manly" and "vigorous" approach to the

---

[95] *Times of London*, 5 March 1795; cited in Barrell, *Imagining* 515.

[96] Cited in "Introduction" to C. W. Pasley, *The Military Policy and Institutions of the British Empire*, ed. and intro. B. R. Ward, 5th ed. (London: W. Clowes and Sons, 1914), 10. A leading advocate for the science of military engineering, Pasley was also the author of the standard textbooks on *Military Instruction* (1814–17), *Practical Architecture*, and *The Practical Operations of a Siege* (1829–32), among other works. He invented a new type of cement, new explosives, a pontoon boat for military expeditions, and an early telegraph system. He is also credited as the "world's first military diver," for his work raising sunken ships from the Thames. His extraordinary career is given in the *Oxford Dictionary of National Biography*, vol. 43 (Oxford: Oxford UP, 2006), 439; and C. R. Wilson at http://www.remuseum.org.uk/biography/rem_bio_pasley.htm. "Walsh" probably refers to Edward Walsh, M.D. (1756–1832), the author of *The Progress of Despotism: A Poem on the French Revolution*, (1792), a collection entitled *Bagatelles* (1793), and several reports from the campaigns in Europe. See *Dictionary of National Biography*.

war with Napoleon, to expand its troops with bodies recruited from its colonies, and, acting as a "Military Nation," to adopt a system of conquest and aggrandizement that would secure both its empire and the respect of posterity. First published in the bleak latter months of 1810, just after Wellington's dispiriting retreat from Talavera, Pasley's *Essay* had seen four editions by 1812, its success mirroring the rising fortunes of the allied armies in those years. Policies that Pasley had recommended had been put to work effectively on the Iberian peninsula, and British victories followed swiftly. By 1813, moreover, Napoleon's armies no longer looked invincible, having barely escaped the Moscow campaign and the wars in Germany. Pasley, who had in 1810 dared to imagine the vulnerability of French forces, was hailed as a prophet. This was an identification the author had quietly courted: "I could not help speaking," he confessed, "and I have spoken what I fully believed to be the truth" (*Essay* 11). During this last stage of the fighting, his *Essay* was arguably one of the most talked-about pieces of writing in Britain and was considered, as the author himself acknowledged in later years, to have contributed "in a comparatively humble degree, to the success of the war." [97] When the *Times* published his letter in 1813, then, Pasley could speak in a voice of confidence and strength, his opinions and principles tightly woven into the newly revived martial spirit in Britain.[98]

Yet at this moment of cresting optimism, Pasley addresses the *Times*'s readership with curiously unwavering fears, explicitly deflecting the assurances of recent news reports. Tapping near and distant pasts and invoking the far future, Pasley seems hardly able to countenance the present tense; his wartime letter plays extravagantly with its own temporal position. The various time frames placed upon and within the letter might remind some readers of Coleridge's framing of "Kubla Khan," with its jarring succession of early modern travelogue, dream, everyday incident, and "ancient voices prophesying war" in an interrupted and unfinished poem. At the outset, Pasley informs the *Times*'s editor that there is a letter within his letter, an unfinished piece written four years earlier and originally intended for his *Essay*; he calls upon the witness of several friends to verify that it was indeed written "before . . . the late glorious public events [presumably allied victories at Vittoria, in Spain, and Leipzig]." [99] This verification contributes to the prophetic stance Pasley adopts. Because of the lag in publication, his letter-within-a-letter can "place in the strongest light the wonderful change for the better, which under Providence,

---

[97] Ward, "Introduction," in Pasley, *Military Policy*, 6.

[98] For an account of Pasley's impact among the contemporary literati, see Tim Fulford, "Romanticizing the Empire: The Naval Heroes of Southey, Coleridge, Austen, and Marryat," *MLQ: Modern Language Quarterly* 60.2 (June 1999): 161–96.

[99] "Letter to *The Times*," 12. In Ward, "Introduction," in Pasley, *Military Policy*, 12–17.

has been effected in our National affairs," and it can do so by benefit of a sort of historical chiaroscuro, "since it calls to mind the former gloomy impressions which had resulted from the former unenterprising . . . military operations . . . during the first years of this memorable war" ("Letter" 12). Reaching back to an unpublished fragment he had written four years previously would seem to allow Pasley to demonstrate his accurate foretelling of the present situation. Yet the fragment foretells disaster and disgrace for the British forces—the exact contrary of the eventual outcome. Because Britain heeded Pasley's warnings, the allies had achieved victory. These warnings are now being issued after the event, their truth or power verified by the fact that what they foresaw did not come to pass.[100] This is apophatic prophecy, the creation of a counter-story, an if-then-not of history whose bent is less to verify what has come to pass than open these finished events to reconsideration, to doubt. The counterfactual prophecy leapfrogs over the assurances of the present to suggest an unsettled future derived from past fears: this may yet be. The counterfactuality repeats in a new vein his rationale from the *Essay on Military Policy*: "true courage, and true wisdom, consist alone in calculating danger in its utmost extent, in foreseeing and preparing for the worst that may happen" (*Essay* 5). The prophecy persists years after the event as warning, thereby eroding any sense of security.[101]

The enclosed fragment complicates and extends the circuit of prediction (not yet) fulfilled: not unlike Brothers's, Pasley's prophetic history reaches to the ancient past, blasting open the narrative of the previous four years. The fragment letter-within-a-letter is in fact a speculative conversation with Hannibal, the great Carthaginian warrior of the second and third century BCE, whose advice Pasley solicits on the global situation in 1809, then delivers to the public in 1813. As the Hebrew prophets served Brothers, so for Pasley Hannibal provides an ancient voice prophesying the current war. A great martial strategist and leader, Hannibal had helped Carthage, a maritime power, increase its land forces and nearly (but only nearly) defeat the armies of the Roman Empire. The fragment does not assume the temporal immediacy of an actual conversation; it reads more like a constructed interview, where the questioner sends the interviewee questions in advance, to which he then replies at leisure—presumably, in Hannibal's case, with all the time the world. The sense

----

[100] Brothers had used the opposite and more conventional tactic, reporting in 1795 that he had earlier predicted the deaths of the Kings of Sweden (1792) and France (1793). See Barrell, *Imagining* 509n17.

[101] Both Southey and Wordsworth, though well-disposed toward Pasley's work, bristled at its rhetoric of fear and "despondency"; they found such fear unnecessary and argued against Pasley's arrangement of the facts. Southey, "Review of Pasley's *Essay on the Military Policy and Institutions of the British Empire*; and Wordsworth's letter to Pasley, qd. in Ward, "Preface to the Fifth Edition" in Pasley, *Military Policy*, 54–61.

of an encounter in the present is replaced moreover by the conditional tense: the inner letter generally follows the format, "if it were explained to Hannibal that X, . . . Hannibal would then reply Y . . ." Where Brothers had preached the dated finitude of time ("THE PRESENT IS IT") Pasley adopts the more open, conditional tense; it not only serves his counterfactual strategy (*if* he had had a conversation with Hannibal, Hannibal *would have* said . . .) but places the anxieties of war within the frame of all the time in the world: not now, perhaps, but at any time.[102]

Hannibal's words thus resonate in a sort of echo chamber for British readers. "I . . . would have destroyed the Romans [read: the French] had not the Senate [read: Parliament] of my country, blinded by commercial notions and distracted by factions withheld the necessary supplies of men and money from me" ("Letter" 14).[103] Parliament's parsimony and divisiveness in wartime had exasperated Pasley and other members of the military, who preferred that military concerns alone drive British policy. The larger lesson Hannibal has to give, however, concerns time itself. The British, he warns, cannot see beyond the present moment, what he calls "the news of the day."

> You tell me that instead of acting on a wise and vigorous system of policy, these people are guided in their military operations by the news of the day, that they will embark one of their ridiculous little armies because there happens to be good news from Spain; stop its sailing because a rumour of bad news arrives; and send it after all on some other change of news; reinforce it, recall it, in short give it a thousand contradictory orders because of the news of the day. Now a nation that acts in this way like a miserable stock-jobber, fluctuating and speculating on the news of the day, cannot possibly prosper in war. ("Letter" 16)

In his anachronistic understanding of modern media (and stock markets), Hannibal insists that what happens in the now, in the daily coming of the newsboy, matters little: wartime demands a different temporal vision, oriented toward the lessons of the past, but also simultaneously toward the future. Sound military policy, Hannibal warns, echoing (or anticipating?) Turgot, should not read the present so much as shape the future; not react to news but "create good news" ("Letter" 16). In his anachronistic format, moreover, Pasley does not separate the classical past from an ever-receding end of time or, as he calls it, posterity. Hannibal's advice in the case of Britain's present situation,

[102] In the *Essay*, Pasley based his argument primarily upon reasoned probability, resorting to such phrases as "probable operations," and "admitting the probability which has just been stated, . . ." (7, 13). The rhetoric of probability is less strong in the "Letter," where it is supplanted by the counterfactual and the conditional tense.

[103] A recurrent complaint in Pasley's *Essay*.

based as it is on his experience two thousand years previously, is identical, Pasley insists, to "the sentence that will be passed upon it by an impartial posterity, when we shall come in review before the great tribunal of History, on a par with Rome and Carthage" ("Letter" 16). History does not happen in discrete sequential periods of time, the news of today following the news of yesterday. Rather, History stands as one transcendent, simultaneous military review, with all the peoples of the ancient and modern worlds arrayed and judged together. In the judgment of History, the British are competing not against France alone, but against Carthage and Rome as well; and they are losing there too:

> [W]e shall . . . be judged by men, who will despise our Parliamentary parties, . . . they will judge of us, not by our speeches in our Senate, or the paragraphs in our newspapers, but by our public measures and actions, and by the events which result from them. ("Letter" 16–17)

The British must adopt a position beyond the contemporaneous: a universalizing and transhistorical view of their role in the world. In its embrace of all the time in the world, Pasley's prophecy thus inclines toward the temporality of Empire, which Michael Hardt and Antonio Negri characterize as "present[ing] its rule not as a transitory moment in the movement of history, but as a regime with no temporal borders and in the sense outside of history or at the end of history."[104] Empire, in this instance, shares some of the characteristics of prophecy.

There is something perverse about sending to a leading daily newspaper a letter denigrating "the paragraphs in our newspapers" and denouncing the nation's subservience to "the news of the day." Pasley's insistent shattering of sequential time into anachronistic expanses defies the very topicality of journalism, as well as a view of History marching, to cite Chandler again, "stepwise through a series of stages sequenced in an order that is more-or-less autonomous and stable" (128). The autonomous and stable movement of societies and nations must submit, in Pasley's view, to the reach of imperial ambition. Pasley asks his readers to think no longer in the temporality of the nation, but rather in the temporality of empire where, in the end and in the beginning, empires forever compete with empires. There is also something perverse in sending forth prophecy as if to say: you ought to have been more afraid of the

---

[104] Michael Hardt and Antonio Negri, *Empire* (Cambridge: Harvard UP, 2000), xiv–xv. Compare Pasley's hope, in his preface to the first edition of the *Essay*: "[I]f I have succeeded in the inquiry something will be found applicable to all times and circumstances," with regard to what he calls the "military system" (x). Pasley has not given up the idea of a distinctly British empire, what Hardt and Negri call the "modern" as opposed to "postmodern" empire. Yet in his view of time, Pasley does tend more to the postmodern view described by Hardt and Negri; or perhaps he shows how that view inheres already in the "military system" of modern imperialism.

future, even if that future, wrapped in the gloomy prospects of memory and history, did not or has not come to pass. Any sense of self-congratulation or security that had been won in recent years would be overturned and cast back by this retrospective prophecy into the realm of threat and alarm. In the conditional and counterfactual tense that governs Pasley's logic, disaster *could* or *would* occur any time. Despite its blasting open of the present then, Pasley's forecasting does not share Benjamin's view of Messianic time; tied to a seemingly outdated sense of history, Pasley's prophecy is both secular and imperial. It is a temporality which the "military system," to adopt Pasley's own term, seems to demand.

For these prophets, time serves not only as a medium but as an instrument of war, a system alternately of dispersal or inevitability, replacing the role of Providence. Brothers's answer to the uncertainty of the meantime is to call an end to waiting, to have disaster unmediated, immanent. Pasley responds less to waiting than belatedness. His counterfactual, retrospective prophecy suggests that defeat could have occurred and might yet: it entails eternal vigilance, which in turn entails belligerence. According to these prophecies, the thought of disaster (as well as the anxieties of waiting and belatedness) can be mobilizing: either to repentance and mass emigration or to invigoration and military movement. Both prophecies aim to move their readers out of chronological time, out of the narrative of the nation and beyond the limited borders of England. Instead of uprooting its people to the Holy Land, the end point of Brothers's time, the British state adopted Pasley's temporal vision and consolidated a world empire.[105] The question these prophets have bequeathed to the future, then, is whether or not wartime has become all the time in the world.

Postscript:

I can see vast changes coming . . . ; great upheavals, terrible struggles; wars such as one cannot imagine; and I tell you London will be in danger— London will be attacked and I shall be very prominent in the defense of London. . . . I see further ahead than you do. I see into the future. This country will be subjected somehow to a tremendous invasion, . . . but I tell you I shall be in command of the defenses of London and I shall save

---

[105] An updated version of Pasley's prophetic mode appears in Niall Ferguson's recent *Empire: The Rise and Demise of the British World Order and the Lessons for Global Power* (New York: Basic Books, 2004), a review of (and apology for) the British Empire, framed by an appeal to the United States to "bear the burden" of a liberal empire imposing order on the world. Ferguson too employs a potent counterfactual rhetoric ("the counterfactual of a world without the British Empire" [xxi]). He understands the fate of the British Empire ultimately as a contest with other empires and as a model against which the United States will be judged.

London and the Empire from disaster. (Winston Churchill, age 16, qtd. in Ferguson 245)

Post-postscript:

You need to watch Jerusalem as never before. We are going to see one half of that city fall very soon. IT COULD HAPPEN THIS YEAR—2006!... "Behold, the day of the Lord cometh, and thy spoil shall be divided in the midst of thee" (Zechariah 14:1).... The verse starts with Christ conquering the European and Asian powers.... The city shall be taken, houses rifled and women ravished. This is when a superpower comprised o[f] European nations conquers the whole city of Jerusalem, as several other biblical prophecies explain (also America and Britain—Jerusalem is also a type of all the nations of Israel today, particularly the U.S. and Britain, as our free book proves), shortly after he conquers an Iran-led Middle Eastern coalition. (Gerald Flurry, "East Jerusalem to Palestinians in 2006?" *The Trumpet,* January 13, 2006)

Still Winter Falls

Meantime, in sable cincture, shadows vast,
Deep-tinged and damp, and congregated clouds,
And all the vapoury turbulence of heaven,
Involve the face of things. Thus Winter falls . . .
—James Thomson[1]

Wartime summons winter. It would perhaps be best for this interlude to be read as it was written—at the darkest time of the year, in weather able to chill the blood, numb the body, and halt the movement of clocks. Were it presently December in London, or William Cowper's Olney, the sun would not rise before 8:00 a.m.; it would illuminate the sky for fewer than eight hours. Imagine the length of the cold night before electricity. Imagine your dependence on the fire you built, before which you now sit, reading about a world at war. What makes you put down your reading, step away from the hearth where "strange visages [are] express'd / In the red cinders," and look out the window at snow falling in the night?

> To-morrow brings a change, a total change!
> Which even now, though silently perform'd
> And slowly, and by most unfelt, the face
> Of universal nature undergoes.
> Fast falls a fleecy show'r: the downy flakes,
> Descending, and with never-ceasing lapse,
> Softly alighting upon all below,
> Assimilate all objects.[2]

When Cowper inserts these lines into "The Winter Evening," he testifies not only to the night weather, but also to a tradition of writing about winter and

---

[1] James Thomson, "Winter," in *The Seasons* (New York: A. S. Barnes, 1860), 54–57.
[2] William Cowper, *The Task*, in *The Complete Poetical Works*, ed. H. S. Milford, 4th ed. (Oxford: Oxford UP, 1967), IV: 322–29.

war. He has in mind, here as elsewhere in *The Task*, James Thomson's *The Seasons*, with its famous description of Winter, part of which I cite as epigraph. In Thomson's "Winter," shadows, clouds, and turbulence "Involve the face of things" such that "things," or what Cowper calls "objects," all wear the same inscrutable face. This is how "Winter falls"—a lowering opacity.

Cowper moves from falling Winter to an image of Winter having fallen, a landscape transformed. Thomson's rendition similarly turns from the event and stages of snowfall to the very condition—the ground, as it were—of Winter.

> Through the hush'd air the whitening shower descends,
> At first thin wavering; till at last the flakes
> Fall broad and wide and fast, dimming the day
> With a continual flow. The cherish'd fields
> Put on their winter robe of purest white.
> 'Tis brightness all; save where the new snow melts
> Along the mazy current. Low the woods
> Bow their hoar head; and ere the languid sun
> Faint from the west emits his evening ray,
> *Earth's universal face, deep hid, and chill,*
> *Is one wild dazzling waste, that buries wide*
> *The works of man.* (229–40; emphasis added)

As with Cowper's view out the window, the promise of redemption in Thomson's verse (the robes of "purest white" and the hint of a *felix culpa*) opens onto obliteration: "one wild dazzling waste."

It is reasonable to read Thomson's image as a frozen repetition of the biblical deluge or wintry intimation of apocalypse, not necessarily linked to man's prosecution of war. But Thomson recapitulates Homer's *Iliad* in this passage, suggesting that the scene of snowfall and snow fallen is intimately linked with a classical history of imagining warfare as well. Here is Alexander Pope's 1715 translation of a famous extended simile from Book XII of the *Iliad*, when the Trojans attack the Greek camps with a barrage of stones:

> Their Ardour kindles all the *Grecian* Pow'rs;
> And now the Stones descend in heavier Show'rs.
> As when high *Jove* his sharp Artill'ry forms,
> And opes his cloudy Magazine of Storms;
> In Winter's bleak, uncomfortable Reign,
> A Snowy Inundation hides the Plain;
> He stills the Winds, and bids the Skies to sleep;
> Then pours the silent Tempest, thick, and deep:
> And first the Mountain Tops are cover'd o'er,

Then the green Fields, and then the sandy Shore;
Bent with the Weight the nodding Woods are seen,
And one bright Waste hides all the Works of Men:
The circling Seas alone absorbing all,
Drink the dissolving Fleeces as they fall.
So from each side increas'd the stony Rain,
And the white Ruin rises o'er the Plain.[3]

Hector's army may attack in summer, but still winter falls.

What Thomson—or Cowper after him—hears in the fall of winter are the muffled sounds of this distant battle, which he echoes closely. The stones that initiated Homer's description have been erased from the scene, as have the fighting armies and the specific circumstances of ancient warfare raging on the shores of Ilium. But in erasing these details the latter poets are only following Homer's lead. The work of the simile tends toward assimilation and annihilation: differences, feelings, motives, bodies, structures, landmarks all fall away while "white ruin" rises.

Homer, Pope, Thomson, or Cowper could not have known of absolute or total war, or of nuclear winter. Yet the modern understanding of these terms, our conception of what war can come to, its prospects, owes something to these older poets and their vision of winter. For in addition to the mobilization of mass armies, domestic populations, and state economies to its ends, total war is distinguished by its tendency to limitlessness in scale and intensity, and by its thorough lack of discrimination. Roger Chickering provides the definition accepted by most military historians:

> Total war is distinguished by its unprecedented intensity and extent. Theaters of operations span the globe; the scale of battle is practically limitless. Total war is fought heedless of the restraints of morality, custom, or international law.[4]

A more chilling if curiously poetic rendering of total war comes from the American general Philip Sheridan who, after his successes in the U.S. Civil War, advised the Prussians during the Franco-Prussian war of 1870–71. "The people must be left nothing," Sheridan instructed, "but their eyes to weep

---

[3] Alexander Pope, *The Iliad of Homer: Translated by Mr. Pope* (London: Bernard Lintot, 1715–20), XII: 329–44; emphasis added. Cowper himself translated the *Iliad* later in the century but downplayed the absolutism of the "waste" in this passage. William Cowper, *The Iliad and Odyssey of Homer, translated into English Blank Verse* (London: J. Johnson, 1791), XII: 335–49. Both texts from *Eighteenth Century Collections Online* (*ECCO*). Gale Group. http://galenet.galegroup.com/servlet/ECCO.

[4] Roger Chickering, "Total War; The Use and Abuse of a Concept," in Roger Chickering and Stig Forster, eds., *Anticipating Total War: The German and American Experiences, 1871–1914* (Cambridge: Cambridge UP and Washington, DC: The German Historical Institute, 1999), 16.

with over the war."[5] In a sense, the poets offer a more dire vision to the eyes. In Winter, as we will see, even the ability to weep can be taken away.

Such devastation has a temporal aspect as well. In holding together the past and the future of warfare, and at the same time erasing nearly all but war's capacity for erasure, Thomson's imagery in "Winter" suggests an appropriate freeze or collapse of historical narrative; it even blocks one's sense of any particular historical situation. In his lines, the anthropological or cultural (the works of Man) lies buried, along with—almost—the literary allusion to the Trojan War. If the snowy field provides a figure for the field of war, it also serves as a figure for disfiguration, the effacement of what Cowper calls the "face of universal nature" and Thomson, "Earth's universal face." Such burial leaves the field of history unmarked, inscrutable, and illegible: a white sheet.[6] It recalls what William St. Clair told us of the "white and spotless" pages of romantic-era books, manufactured from the rag scraps of battlefields (see Chapter 1). There looms in the view out Cowper's window something that Susan Stewart identifies as the "third and anonymous possibility" of point of view, the view of "blindness, [or] the end of writing."[7] Yet in dazzling but not quite blinding one's sense of what remains, the winter scene resists even as it accomplishes this blankness. Not only does Thomson's poem (following Pope, following Homer) carefully itemize what now appears lost to sight; but the alliteration of the verses, the laboring hexameter ("Fall broad, and wide, and fast . . ."), the epic echoes all insist on an aural sense that survives the blanked, blanketed field.[8] There are, if one listens or reads carefully, many layers to the snowy ground; not one final blankness, but a sonic archeology of "things," "objects," and even "faces" otherwise assimilated, covered over. The snow hasn't fallen; it is still falling.

[5] Qtd. in Joseph R. Stromberg, "Strategies of Annihilation: Total War in U.S. History." *LewRockwell.com.* http://www.lewrockwell.com/stromberg/stromberg22.html.

[6] Milton had taken this erasure one step further, suggesting in his characterization of the uncharted regions of Hell that the "frozen Continent" will swallow up the traces of war itself:

Beyond this flood a frozen Continent
Lies dark and wilde, beat with perpetual storms
Of Whirlwind and dire Hail,
　　. . . or else deep snow and ice,
A gulf profound as that *Serbonian* Bog
. . .
Where Armies whole have sunk. (*PL* II: 587–89, 91–92, 94)

Milton ties this "profound" epistemological gulf to a particular geographical site: the region near Mt. Cassius between Egypt and Jerusalem, on the coast of Sinai.

[7] Susan Stewart, *On Longing: Narratives of the Miniature, the Gigantic, the Souvenir, the Collection* (Durham: Duke UP, 1992), 3.

[8] The tactile register is also operative here, as if in defiance of the numbing cold: "fleece" and "down" and the "weight" of bowing, bending, and burial.

In her fine essay "Unspeakable Weather," Anne-Lise François takes up simple reports on the weather, such as "it is snowing" or "the snow falls," discerning in them "the sense of a claim that hardly makes a claim," that is, a constative statement that appears "impervious to the desires and actions of human agents." For François, the object of such statements is "something with which one can do little except precisely mention, state or consign it to writing."[9] In these wartime poems, however, reports on the weather are never so simple or bare. Something more urgent presses its claims, acknowledging even as it protests such imperviousness. The poets' scenes of winter fallen or falling suggest that writing about war in wintertime or about winter in wartime might be understood as the poets' desperate act against obliteration, against laying waste to the work of human hands, against what Hannah Arendt identifies as the absolute silence of violence.

> Where violence rules absolutely, . . . everything and everybody must fall silent. . . . The point here is that violence itself is incapable of speech, and not merely that speech is helpless when confronted with violence.[10]

Layer 1: A History of Snow

"[N]othing so much as language supplies our memory of things that came before," writes David Bromwich. He raises this claim in the face of the "totalitarian presumption" of rhetoric post-9/11, rhetoric which argues that "history begins today," that what has been can be erased from memory.[11] In Bromwich's view, such presumptious rhetoric supports military violence. Taking my cue from Bromwich and these poets, I turn to the past that language remembers.

Among the words used by Indo-European languages to designate the seasons, words for winter have shown "the greatest stability and the largest extension," according to Emile Benveniste, making winter a uniquely suggestive element of the common "Indo-European cultural lexicon."[12] What makes winter's provenance particularly interesting to the linguist is an ambivalence built into the term from its most ancient appearance. From the first, Benveniste explains, "at the interior of this great lexical unit" two related meanings or "themes" emerged: the radical terms for both winter and snow. Though the association

---

[9] Anne-Lise François, "Unspeakable Weather, or the Rain Romantic Constatives Know," in *Phantom Sentences: Essays in Linguistics and Literature Presented to Ann Banfield*, ed. Robert S. Kawashima et al. (Bern: Peter Lang, 2008), 148.

[10] Hannah Arendt, *On Revolution* (Westport, CT: Greenwood, 1982), 18–19.

[11] David Bromwich, "Euphemism and American Violence," *New York Review of Books* 55.5 (April 3, 2008).

[12] Emile Benveniste, "'Hiver' et 'Neige' en Indo-Européen," in *Gedenkschrift Paul Kretschmer*, eds. Mnhmhs Xapin and Heinz Kronasser (Gottingen: Hubert & Co., 1956), 31; my translation.

has been phonetically buried in English, it remained close and audible in many other languages of this group. In ancient Greek, for instance, the root split between *xeimon* and *xion*; in Latin between *hibernus* and *hiems*; similar pairings occur in ancient Armenian, Indian, and Iranian (31–32). The two meanings evidently parted ways to express related but distinct themes: one became a division of time, the cold part of the year, and thus a state or condition that could be used for marking time. The other theme, Benveniste reports, comprehends "everything else"; you might say it carries winter's figural and emotional baggage. It is "charged with qualifications and evocative of imagery"; it can be described as "rude," as "destructive"; it falls "like a calamity"; it is "created by demons." It lends itself to anthropomorphism and allegory. In brief, from ancient times, this "face" or figure of winter, the one aligned with snow, signifies less a portion of the calendar than "a time of cold and suffering" (34). It is clear, though, that Benveniste's two winters readily fall back into their ancient congruity, as in the opening lines of Wordsworth's "Tintern Abbey," which marks the years since Britain entered into war with Revolutionary France: "Five years have past: five summers, with the length / Of five long winters!" This doubling at the heart of winter (a time of the year but also a time of suffering) may be one reason it has served for so long as a marker—temporal but also affective— for war. And yet this part of the linguistic genealogy offered by Benveniste does not account for what appears, in the poems already reviewed, as a virtual anesthesia, where, along with other powerful feelings, as well as the built world of humankind, suffering is obliterated by snow. "On every nerve," Thomson remarks, imagining a man caught without shelter,

> The deadly Winter seizes; shuts up sense;
> And o'er his inmost vitals creeping cold,
> Lays him along the snows, a stiffen'd corse,
> Stretch'd out, and bleaching in the northern blast. ("Winter" 317–21)

In the ancient Greek of Homer's *Iliad*, the semantic ground of *snow* discloses a further ambivalence. Homer makes use of two separate radicals: *xion*, the term for snowy matter, the stuff itself; and *niphas*, which refers to "the atmospheric phenomenon," the sensation or felt experience of falling precipitation.[13] Thomas Rosenmeyer has surveyed the recurrent equation in classical literature of snow with warfare, and in his "inventory of the frozen wastes," he attends especially to the latter term, *niphas*, the sensation of falling snow (222). In its variants he finds persistent connotations of "impetus, violence, and disturbance"; *niphas* is "snow as movement, or experience of movement,"

---

[13] Thomas G. Rosenmeyer, "On Snow and Stones," *California Studies in Classical Antiquity* 11 (1979): 221.

which is at the same time "cruel" and "injurious" (221–22). The *Iliad*'s several uses of wintry snowfalls emphasize the "density, swiftness, and sheer energy" of snow as "bombarding atoms" (215, 219). The equation of wintry snows with military attack thus operates, at least in part, on the level of psycho-physiological sensation. And yet in his analysis of the extended simile from Book XII of the *Iliad*, the attack of the Trojans, Rosenmeyer observes something different: not the dynamism of violent motion, but rather an "ominous calm, [a] seeming motionlessness, [a] muffling of all other sensations." In Homer's simile, snow brings with it a "violence . . . held in suspense while nothing *seems* to move" (emphasis original). Rosenmeyer continues: "But of course . . . [t]he violence persists, and is effective, in spite of the momentary delusion of motionlessness." This is a "pseudo-calm . . . produced by the dovetailing of contrary motions" (212). Despite the semblance of stillness (despite the dovetailing concord), violence still prevails.

If there is an explanation for this paradox of violent movement yoked to suspension or "ominous calm," it might be found in a return to the materiality or stuff of snow, *xion* rather than *niphas*. Both Benveniste and Rosenmeyer note that words for *snow* (including *xion*) descended from the Indo-European morpheme *sneigh-*, which connotes adhesion or coagulation, stuff stuck together in a way that does not allow for movement or differentiation. It could be (and once was) used to refer to a warrior fallen to the ground: instead of saying he got himself killed, you could say in Attic Greek, "the stupid fool got himself . . . stuck [*snowed*] to the landscape": it suggests a sort of ontological collapse (Rosenmeyer 221). When Thomson finds his poor man lain "along the snows" inert and ultimately "bleaching," he maintains this archaic meaning: the poor man has been rendered snow. Individual bodily integrity as well as feeling are laid waste. To be *snowed* in this sense is to suffer the violence of unfeeling; to become an object assimilated, to become silently *snow*. Two sorts of violence, then, seem to be at work in Homer's simile of battle as snow. On the one hand is the violence of hurled weapons, an injurious motion that the human body can feel, and is meant to feel acutely. On the other hand is a violence of nearly molecular surrender, where all difference is subsumed or coagulated into this blanket of smooth white stuff. With the latter, nothing seems to move or change, because everything has been changed totally—assimilated. Insofar as it effects similitude or eases difference and distinction, the work of simile appears as (is like) the terrible work of war.

The linguists insist that the meanings built into the ancient words for snow are not distinguishable temporally as snow falling and (then) snow having fallen; rather the two coexist along the hard-to-distinguish lines of physical force and one's (simultaneous) experience of that force; or perhaps the experience of force *as* cancellation of that experience: ominous, calm.

Winter fallen and falling tells one kind of history of war: war as something that you experience, the experience of which deprives you of the capacity to experience it; war as sensory violence, felt and thereby unfelt; war as the disabling of these distinctions. So William Cowper searches in his newspaper for news of distant war, then looks out his window, sees the snow falling out there beyond his reach. In echoing the language of Thomson and Pope and Homer, he offers the prospect (but also the history) of some unfelt, total change.

Layer 2: Still and Still

In the wartime reflections of *The Waste Land* T.S. Eliot suggests something like the equation of winter snow and forgetting: "Winter kept us warm, covering / Earth in forgetful snow" (5–6).[14] Eliot's is winter conjured in retrospect; the snow may be forgetful but the speaker certainly remembers something now gone. The poets I have been considering are not interested in winters past and over; rather, they anticipate that more winter, not spring, follows winter. Still winter falls. For Cowper, looking out the window on a winter's night and imagining a snowy prospect, stillness itself, the very word *still* forestalls forgetfulness. Its unsettled temporality finds a topographical equivalent in the snowy scene. Consequently, the word "still" also raises questions about the supposedly settled matter of winter. "[H]ave our troops awak'd?" the poet asks at the outset of his evening, with the arrival of the newspaper; "[o]r do they still . . . / Snore to the murmurs of th' Atlantic wave?" And again: "Is India free? . . . / Or do we grind her still?" (IV: 25–30). If the distant warfare of *The Iliad* lies buried beneath snow outside, it still emerges as these questions about distant imperial warfare hang in the air.[15] A sense of temporal irresolution, of uneasy persistence, works in tension with the other use of stillness that does settle, like a snowy blanket, elsewhere in Book IV of *The Task*. Recall Cowper as he reads the newspaper:

> I behold
> The tumult, and am still. The sound of war
> Has lost its terrors ere it reaches me;
> Grieves, but alarms me not. (IV: 99–102)

and as he imagines himself, as reader, traveling the globe:

> While fancy, like the finger of a clock,
> Runs the great circuit, and *is still* at home. (IV: 118–19)

---

[14] T. S. Eliot, *The Waste Land*, ed. Frank Kermode (Harmondsworth, UK: Penguin, 2003), 5.

[15] By the time *The Task* appeared in print (1785), the answers to these questions should have been settled. But they hang nevertheless unanswered in the text.

These latter uses of "still" suggest unmoved movements, changes without change; sounds silenced. When Cowper insists that amid the tumult "I . . . am still," he invites both the adverbial meaning (even now, yet, persistently, and enduringly) and the adjectival meaning of the word still (quiet, calm, inert, perhaps dead). In "The Winter Evening," stillness thus forms a troubled pivot for the poet, on matters both temporal and geopolitical: "Oh Winter, ruler of th' inverted year," the poet muses, "Thou hold'st the sun / A pris'ner in the yet undawning east, / . . . [B]ut kindly *still* / Compensating his loss with added hours / Of social converse and instructive ease" (IV: 120, 129–30, 133–35). Later in the evening, a lyre accompanies a singer and together, "in the charming strife triumphant *still* / [They] Beguile the night" (IV: 163–64). When the poet gazes upon the "sooty films" hovering on the hearth, he imagines them "prophesying *still*, / Though *still* deceiv'd, some stranger's near approach" (IV: 294–95). Situated at the end of a line, "still" serves as the hinge or turning point of his thought. Thus, even as irresolution marks Cowper's use of the word, elsewhere it inclines to a trade-off (compensation) between loss (or triumph) and ease (or strife). For Cowper, "still" often presses to the far side of its synonym "yet," where it shades into "nevertheless": less a temporal marker than a hesitation in what otherwise might seem settled, a doubt or counterthought. In either case—in temporal or ideological irresolution—the stillness of Cowper's winter evening does not readily fall into peaceful complacency.[16]

Cowper is not alone in appreciating the peculiar charge of "still." In a review of Wordsworth's reliance on the word, Heather McHugh shows how "still" permits a singular form of historical perception, one that teeters between the adjectival and the adverbial, between what she calls "the natural life of events" (understood as past, finished, and fixed) and their "relationship to eventuality" (their ongoing-ness or persistence).[17] The poet's "still" thus holds together what would otherwise be two separate temporal levels in historical representation: the level of event and the level of preconditions or underlying circumstances. "Still" discloses a knotted temporality lying within historiography. Reinhart Koselleck, for instance, identifies the level of preconditions or ground as "a matter of structures '*in eventu*' . . . that . . . will only '*post eventum*' become semantically comprehensible."[18] The eventual tendency of a situation is realized

---

[16] Compare François's sense of weather reporting in Romantic poetry which, she suggests, has its its own tense. "'[R]ain,' like snow, may be allergic both to the simple present tense and the aorist historical past of completed action, preferring instead progressive, iterative tenses . . . which keep vivid and open-ended the relation to what has just been and is about to be" ("Unspeakable Weather" 149).

[17] Heather McHugh, "Presence and Passage: A Poet's Wordsworth," *MLQ: Modern Language Quarterly* 63.2 (2002): 174.

[18] Reinhart Koselleck, *Futures Past: On the Semantics of Historical Time*, trans. Keith Tribe (New York: Columbia UP, 2004), 109. Koselleck elaborates on the interrelationship of these two levels, their mutual work in the writing of history. For, as he says, in order to obtain meaning, events need

only in retrospect, after the event which that situation makes possible. To see what McHugh and Koselleck are driving at, we can take a typical image from Wordsworth such as "black tempests bursting, blacker still in view." McHugh notices in these lines the sort of knotted temporality I have located in the earlier poets' depictions of snowfall: "a balance between what bursts and what remains motionless; between what happens merely to pass and what is held fast in the mind." She elaborates: "its image [is] taken into memory; and [yet lingers] between what is happening now and what is about to happen (since 'still in view' can mean 'yet ahead')"—Koselleck's *in eventu* (174). For McHugh, the value of stillness lies in this "act of lovely equilibration" which provides a "literary restoration to time, of the all-at-onceness" even as it removes motion "from its perishing ways" (174–75). McHugh's is, needless to say, an optimistic, even therapeutic view of stillness, not knotted but resolved. It emphasizes balance over conflict and, in the end, discovers in stillness a host to feeling, perception, and memory. In a deft reading of the famous ice-skating episode from Book I of Wordsworth's *Prelude*, McHugh follows the movement of stillness ("flying still," "spinning still") to its culmination in finite verbs (and a simile): "Yet still the solitary cliffs / Wheeled by me—even as if the earth had rolled" (I: 451, 455, 458–59). In this winter scene stillness works to introduce a phenomenological "intertransitivity," an affecting movement back and forth between the figure of the perceiving subject and what would otherwise remain background, the perceived world, the earth itself. If the experience seems earthshaking, McHugh notes, "it's because the skater's shaken; if the moment is moving, it's because the man is moved" (177). The event and the phenomenological ground of the event, its preconditions or eventuality, are whirled into one.[19]

---

to be placed within these larger structures. Since his example for this relationship is a battle, it is worth citing at length:

> That a battle can be executed in the simple rhythm "*veni, vidi, vici,*" presupposes specific forms of domination, technical disposal over natural conditions, a comprehensible relation of friend and foe, etc.; that is structures belonging to the event of this battle, which enter into it by determining it. The history of this one battle, therefore, has dimensions of different temporal extensions contained in the narration or description long "before" the effect which lends "meaning" to the event of the battle is reflected. This is a matter of structures "*in eventu*" . . . notwithstanding the hermeneutical reassurance that they will only "*post eventum*" become semantically comprehensible. (109)

[19] Like Cowper, Wordsworth is following the lead of Milton here. Near the end of "The Winter Evening," Cowper in fact plays tribute to Milton, echoing the very intertransitive (and intergenerational) use of the word that McHugh finds in Wordsworth:

> As twice sev'n years, his [Milton's] beauties had then first
> Engag'd my wonder; and admiring still
> And still admiring, with regret suppos'd
> The joy half lost because not sooner found. (*Task* IV: 714–17)

Here, too, however, Cowper sneaks in with his double "still" the question of loss and recompense.

Wordsworth aligns stillness here with the emotionally momentous: he delivers a fleeting image or event into the hold of memory where it can work upon and be reworked by feeling. Then what do we make of the anaesthetizing impulse of Cowper's stillness, linked as it is with the blank whiteness threatening to cancel poetic figuration? What happens when "the balance between what bursts and what remains motionless" is enlisted in the representation of a war that itself hovers between violent events and their relationship to eventuality? Who dares be moved along with this movement?

Unlike the Wordsworth McHugh reads, Cowper catches the stillness of violence itself, of seemingly "dovetailed" yet ominous calm. In the irresolution that Cowper maintains, stillness can at best hesitate before the prospect of such all-at-once-ness as well as its all-at-one-ness, before the assimilation of all objects into what offers to be an absolute intertransitivity. (Recall the phenomenal intertransitivity, that union of subject and object experienced by the fallen Greek soldier, "snowed" along with the snowy world.) In Cowper's lines, stillness does not collapse the difference between two temporal levels, but rather sets them in jarring contrast, unsettling historical representation. If, in his rendering of a winter episode, Wordsworth achieves a sort of comprehension of the movement of the world, Cowper does not share that comprehension. His repeated invocation of the word "still" in "The Winter Evening" is less a reparative strategy than a way of summoning alternatives (nevertheless) to the lowering stillness and its silence. In Cowper's "I . . . am still" we can hear the risk of being unmoved—frozen?—by the movements of the world. But we can also hear in its ambivalence (still prophesying/still deceived) something that nevertheless keeps it from falling into absolute, earth-shaken stillness, keeps it from being snowed. "Is India free? Or do we grind her still?"

Layer 3: Inactive War

It was evening all afternoon.
It was snowing
And it was going to snow.[20]

Nearly twenty years later, anticipating the Peace of Amiens, Joseph Fawcett published his poetry collection *War Elegies* (1801) in which he, perhaps following Cowper's 1783 prospect of a snowy world, addresses a "stillness in the military tempest."[21] This stillness signals no end to war.

---

[20] Wallace Stevens, "Thirteen Ways of Looking at a Blackbird," *The Collected Poems of Wallace Stevens* (New York: Vintage, 1982), 95; cited in François 149.

[21] Joseph Fawcett, *War Elegies* (London: J. Johnson, 1801), i.

Fawcett's collection contains poems on "The Battle," "The Siege," and "Famine," but also on popular sentimental topics like "The Despairing Mother," and "The Mournful Maid." In this wartime litany, his poem "To Winter" seems an anomaly, for here Fawcett praises the season for putting a halt to warfare: winter appears to offer a climatological peace treaty. Yet his figuration of a pacific Winter covers now familiar ground: blank waste and the cessation of feeling:

To Winter

Hail, Winter, hail! Thy horrors glad my soul!
Welcome thy bulkiest mass of rigid snow!
Thy blasts, that roar as loud as thunders roll,
And stern arrest, that stops the water's flow!

Tho' thy white scene, one blank, unfigur'd waste,
Nature's green charm and varied beauty veil,
And thro' thy groves unloitering footsteps haste,
Staid by no soothing note, nor balmy gale;

Tho' shivering millions, while thy fury reigns,
Feel thy cold empire o'er their idle blood;
Who need alike, to shoot it thro' their veins,
The hearth's kind sunshine, and life-gladdening food;

Tho' many a traveler lose his viewless way,
Till thou have time on all his frame to steal
The sleep, that bids his pulse give o'er its play,
And his check'd heart for ever cease to feel, . . .

Yet, Winter, hail! Thy frowns my bosom cheer!
I hear the voice of Mercy in thy wind;
It calms inclemencies far more severe—
It stills the wilder tempest of mankind!

Thy blasts suspend the cannon's direr war:
Thine edged cold the keener sword restrains:
And, drench'd howe'er thy fields, no flood of gore
Thy guiltless plain with human crimson stains. (1–16, 25–32; emphasis
            added)

Fawcett is writing before Napoleon's disastrous winter encounter in Russia following the Siege of Moscow. The poem alludes to an earlier practice, common in Europe throughout the eighteenth century, where armies would retreat for the season to winter quarters to await weather more conducive to fighting.[22] Yet the hardship of the 1777–78 winter camp at Valley Forge, widely reported in the British press and soon worked into the mythology of the American War of Independence, had already complicated accounts of Winter's inclement clemency.[23] Poorly clothed (one man in four had no shoes) and housed for much of December and January in tents and temporary "huts" without any heat, the American troops saw with despair the snow relentlessly fall. Starvation and exposure pushed the rate of disease and death higher than anyone anticipated. In his report to Congress at the end of 1777, Gen. Washington famously wrote that "unless some great and capital change takes place, . . . this Army must inevitably . . . starve, dissolve, or disperse."[24] The American Joel Barlow, in his popular *The History of England, from the Year 1765, to the Year 1795*, contributed to the contemporary myth by making the frozen waste of that Pennsylvania winter starkly legible—and newly modern:

> The American army might have been tracked by the blood of their feet, in marching without shoes or stockings over the hard frozen ground between Whitemarsh and Valley Forge. Some hundreds of them were without blankets. Under the circumstances they had to sit down in a wood, in the latter end of December, and to build huts for their accommodation. This mode of procuring winter-quarters, if not entirely novel, has been rarely, if ever, practiced in modern war. (385)

In Barlow's account, and in the contemporary accounts of others, Valley Forge is the army's submission to Winter in the name of liberty.[25]

---

[22] A late-century "Treatise on Winter Posts," written in the wake of the Seven Years' War, explains the logic of this hibernation: "When the setting in of severe winter weather makes it probable that the end of the campaign is approaching, . . . the army moves into quarters of cantonment, and remains ready to assemble in order of battle at the shortest notice, until reports of the separation of the enemy's forces are confirmed by the most indubitable intelligence." George Friedrich von Tempelhoffe, *Extracts from Colonel Tempelhoffe's History of the Seven Years War*, trans. Colin Lindsay, vol. 2 (London: T. Cadell, 1793), 269.

[23] The first winter of that war found both armies holed up in winter quarters, with relatively comfortable shelter. During the second winter, the British quartered in the city of Philadelphia, and the revolutionary troops constructed temporary shelter at Valley Forge.

[24] John C. Fitzpatrick, ed., *The Writings of George Washington from the Original Manuscript Sources* (Washington, DC: U.S. Government Printing Office, 1933), 10: 192; qtd. in John B. B. Trussell Jr., *Birthplace of an Army: A Study of the Valley Forge Encampment* (Harrisburg: Commonwealth of Pennsylvania, Pennsylvania Historical and Museum Commission, 1976), 17. For contemporary accounts, see the 1777 and 1778 *Annual Registers*; John Aikin, *General biography; or lives, critical and historical, of the most eminent persons of all ages . . .* (London: G.G. and J. Robinson, 1799–1815); John Andrews, *History of the War with America, France, Spain, and Holland*, vol. 2 (London: John Fielding, 1785–86); and Joel Barlow, *The History of England, from the Year 1765, to the Year 1795*, vol. 2 (London: J. Parsons, 1795). The eighteenth-century accounts all found on *ECCO*.

[25] In both the United States and England the periodicals took the Americans' willingness to submit to "the extremities of the season" as a sign that they would not submit to a tyrant: the

Fawcett's poem "To Winter" proposes a different sort of submission, similarly dangerous, but unredeemed by an ideology of patriotism or by a distinct (that is, completed) historical narrative. His Winter and its devastations are, therefore, harder to read. Indeed, even as he calls Winter merciful, Fawcett lists the familiar "horrors" by which Winter has laid waste to the freedom and feeling of "millions." In bypassing the historical for the allegorical, Fawcett borrows extensively from the tradition of a warlike Winter passed down from Homer to Pope to Thomson and Cowper. The epigraphs for his poem cite Horace: "*Informes hyemes reducit / Jupiter*" (Jupiter calls back deforming/shapeless winter snows); and Thomson: "Wintry blasts / Deform the year delightless," lines which echo in Fawcett's Advertisement to *War Elegies*, where he calls attention to the "undisguised deformity of War" (iv). If winter is the only alternative to war, he seems to say, it is no less devastating. Here allegory serves as the very form for deformation: consequently, the difference posited between war and winter is itself blurred.

Fawcett nevertheless places his poem of Winter-as-war-suspended in a particularly telling historical context: he locates it in the "stillness of the military tempest" associated with the anticipated peace treaty, a stillness he also characterizes as "armed peace" or "inactive war." The "stillness of the military tempest," in other words, rests in the fact that the military tempest is still present, "blacker still in view." In the Advertisement to his *War Elegies*, Fawcett offers perhaps the most incisive contemporary analysis of this season of ominous calm:

> . . . inactive war; [is] an armed though a quiet scene; a season of calm, in a system of society containing all the materials of tempest and principles of storm; a motley picture, at variance with itself . . . of steel wiped of its sanguinous stain, but retaining its dangerous shape; of arms, put off by the wearers only to be reposited in arsenals; of forts, whose thunder is hushed, but that still threaten in silence with frowning battlements; of fleets and armies ceasing from murderous action, but maintained in proud existence; and having the venerable name of ESTABLISHMENTS; and of garments, though no longer "rolled in blood," continuing to be worn, with undiminished ornament, as the gay badge of barbarous occupation. (iii–iv)

Americans were determined, observed the *Annual Register*, "to suffer all things rather than submit to force." *AR 1777*, "History of Europe" (1778), 140. Exposure to the freezing weather indicated by an inverted logic the "warmth . . . of their attachment, both to their General and to the[ir] cause" (Andrews 380). Not by fighting, but by suffering winter, the Americans could be read as passionately resisting their opponents.

The suspension of hostilities takes a decided leap from the dovetailed calm of Homer's battle scene outside the walls of Troy and from Thomson's "dazzling waste." It jumps to the institutions of the modern militarized state. These are war's "disguised forms" as opposed to its "undisguised deformations." It's as if the deformations found in the form of poetic allegory, in the Winter of the poems, tell what the established forms of this historical moment would otherwise obscure; Winter displays the truth of the decreed "stillness." Even at peace, Fawcett understands, Britain is still at war; which is to say, war has *established* itself on the landscape, assimilating everything it touches into one "system of society." At the same time, war as winter has shifted from unique event to exigent precondition or underlying structure: war quieted (stilled) and cleaned up (wiped of its bloody stain), but nevertheless and all the more *in eventu*, an eventuality.[26]

"Hail, all the rigours of thy tyrant's reign!" cries the poet in submission to this Winter. The speaker of "The Mournful Maid," a later poem in Fawcett' s collection, understands the situation even more intimately. "'Alike to me if lowers or smiles the day,'" says the maid, whose lover has died in battle;

"If snows deface or flowers adorn the plain;
My frozen breast admits no genial ray;
There winter, everlasting winter reigns!" (36)

Submission to winter is submission to a loss of distinctions, to everlasting unfeeling, to war by other means.

Layer 4: The Faces of Winter

Thus far my archeology of war/winter has yielded two crucial formal features, two aspects or faces that seem to recur in every layer of snow. And indeed, their recurrence makes distinguishing one layer, one shade of whiteness, from another difficult. The first is a sort of catachresis, where two separate levels of representation—falling and fallen, events and their eventuality, figure and ground—collapse into each other in ways that undermine historical narrative and thwart epistemology; critical differences become hard to see; allegory supplants history. One way to register this is to say that the figure that takes war

[26] William Godwin, in a similar vein, protests the need for military training in peacetime: "It cannot be a matter of indifference, for the human mind to be systematically familiarized to thoughts of murder and desolation. The disciple of mere reason would not fail at the sight of a musket or a sword to be impressed with sentiments of abhorrence. Why expel these sentiments?" William Godwin, *An Enquiry Concerning Political Justice*, 2 vols. (London: G. G. J. Robinson, 1796), 2: 89. *ECCO.*

for winter (or winter for war) resists being differentiated into this or that war, one winter and not another, indeed one set of verses and not another; its totalizing impulse resists, in other words, an archeology like mine. The second, related formal feature occurs at the level of sensation and motion, where violent activity is assimilated to blank unfeeling, so that violence—specifically the violence of war—is not conceived as the actions of unfeeling persons so much as an unfelt state. A quiet scene, a season of calm. The collapse of the event into *in eventu*, figure into ground, coincides with a numbing or cancellation of the senses; no sentient being is left to feel the violence. The prospect offered is profoundly disturbing: if the world were to go blank, who would feel it? Or perhaps, when you can no longer feel, will the world go blank? [27]

It seems worthwhile, confronted with this bleached and bleaching prospect, to recognize that the poetry that brings together war and winter to create scenes of absolute effacement is itself elaborately figured. If Homer sees Jupiter as the agent of winter's onslaught, Homer's successors move from myth per se to personification. "For, see! . . . Winter comes, himself" calls Thomson, "Striding the gloomy Blast." The poets call out to "him," to Winter, as if challenging his silence. "Oh Winter, ruler of th' inverted year," sings Cowper in his "The Winter Evening." Fawcett concludes his poem "Hail, all the rigours of thy tyrant's reign!" "Hail! Tyrant of the gloomy season, hail! . . . Lord of the freezing hour!" echoes Mary Robinson, in the taunting notes of her "Ode to Winter" (1806).[28] William Blake, in his early "To Winter," calls out with supplication to the conquering figure: "O Winter!" And when Blake's apostrophe, like those of his contemporaries, falls on unhearing ears, his efforts to personify Winter—to clothe it with skin and bones and put a scepter in its hand—only intensify, even as Winter "unclothes" creation:

> He hears me not, but o'er the yawning deep
> Rides heavy; . . .
>   I dare not lift mine eyes,
> For he hath rear'd his sceptre o'er the world.

---

[27] Cicero, whose writings on war were consulted frequently during the eighteenth century, distinguishes between human mortality and the destruction of the *civitas*, recapitulating this question of who is left to feel the loss of a world:

> For a man death is not only inevitable but very often even desirable, whereas when a *civitas* is destroyed, wiped out, extinguished, it is (to compare small with great) as if the whole of this world should collapse and perish.

Qtd. in Richard Tuck, *The Rights of War and Peace: Political Thought and the International Order from Grotius to Kant* (Oxford: Oxford UP, 1999), 22.

[28] Mary Robinson, "Ode to Winter," in *The Poetical Works . . . In Three Volumes* (London: Richard Phillips, 1806), 1: 197–98; ll. 1, 25.

Lo! now the direful monster, whose skin clings
To his strong bones, strides o'er the groaning rocks:
He withers all in silence, and in his hand
Unclothes the earth, and freezes up frail life. (5–8, 9–12)[29]

Blake's poem does not give Winter a face ("I dare not lift my eyes," he writes, as if abased by the figure before him), but his contemporaries press further. Fawcett insists that he can discern the tyrant's face: "Thy frowns my bosom cheer!" And Robinson, in her "Ode to Winter," accosts this "Tyrant" and "Intolerable Despot," insisting on meeting "him" face-to-face:

I greet thine hoary brow and visage pale:
I greet thy grey and solemn eye,
Thy bosom deathly cold,
Thy breath, that breathes to petrify. (2–5)

The animating force of such verses is relentless and intense. Winter's silent violence and violent silence are all the more cruel *because* Winter is personified; prior to such imagining, Winter is simply voiceless, without eyes or ears, without in fact any human feature or feeling. So even as they turn to a long tradition, a culture of writing about winter and war in order to fend off the negation of history and culture, the poets also cry out, desperately creating personifications in the face of this depersonalizing force.

In his preface to *Lyrical Ballads*, Wordsworth famously rejects the poetic figure of personification for not dwelling, as he puts it, "in the company of flesh and blood." Personification characterizes poems with less human feeling than the kind Wordsworth proposes; it sheds "no natural and human tears." Perhaps, these poems about winter and war suggest, this is precisely the point: to indicate a sort of personhood evacuated of "flesh and blood," bereft of "human tears." Stephen Knapp has argued that debates over allegorical personification throughout the eighteenth century turned on the issue of poetry's relationship to *im*-personal power. If poetry could endow metaphors or abstract concepts "with the agency of literal persons," poetry also suggested that the process could be reversed, that literal persons could be metaphorized or turned into abstractions.[30] Literary personification, it was understood, illuminated the vulnerability to sublime violence of individual personhood, what Knapp calls "literal persons" with "empirical consciousness" (2, 4).[31] By this

---

[29] William Blake, "To Winter," in *Blake: Complete Writings*, ed. Geoffrey Keynes (London: Oxford UP, 1971), 2–3.

[30] Stephen Knapp, *Personification and the Sublime: Milton to Coleridge* (Cambridge: Harvard UP, 1985), 2.

[31] Knapp's larger aim is an investigation of the dynamics of the sublime, which he finds typified by the "personified abstraction" (4).

logic, war seems to literalize, even epitomize the figurative threat of personification: war converts flesh and blood into the sublime abstraction of the nation, into sacrificial metaphors. Fallen bodies can be made signs of, say, un-
daunted purpose. Blood on the frozen wastes can become legible as the figures
of liberty. When these poets persist in giving War a face, animating Winter as
conqueror, they emphasize not that warfare is the activity of persons, but just
the opposite: that War, like the snow of Winter, saps real persons of feeling,
features, and agency. In this way personification, as a form of animation, discloses the surrogation of life, the transfer of life from persons (and in these instances, from the natural world) to impersonal force.[32]

Susan Stewart observes that "a ready animation of all things results in a
widespread amnesia regarding death."[33] She is speaking not about personification per se but about the animating powers of postmodern media. And it's
possible to imagine the personification of Winter in these romantic poems as
forerunner to the abstracting force of our contemporary media, where the
pain and suffering of individual bodies are forgotten, discounted, or rendered
spectacular; and where animation lodges not in bodies but in technologies.
But whatever technologies are at work in the medium of print poetry, I want
to distinguish (not assimilate) them, insisting that they do not in this case
provide the same "ready animation of all things." Rather they demonstrate
that the animation of one thing—call it Winter—requires the desolation of
"all [other] things": the abjection of the poet ("Hail! Tyrant"); the rapacious
"unclothing of creation"; the annihilation of a felt, sensual world. The destruction of life, the erasure of "the face of universal nature" is not forgotten by
such animation, but starkly attested. The poetic responses bear witness—like
Cowper's stillness—to both possibilities: to a blank sheet and a densely layered
field of felt experience. Or, to put it in a temporal register, the poems evoke simultaneously what has happened and what is happening. A great deal is at
stake here for the poets, for they understand that the work of their hands is
uniquely threatened by the winter of war. They acknowledge the danger, as I
hope my archeology has shown, that war will only literalize what poetry shows
as figural; that war will anesthetize what art has made felt; that simile, allegory,
personification will all be changed utterly into a new, senseless reality. This
danger these poems feel intensely. "To-morrow brings a change, a total
change!" Cowper muses, as he looks out the window in Olney at the falling

---

[32] In "A Winter's Day" (1790) Joanna Baillie works extensively to counter this dynamic by having a human figure emerge out of the winter storm and elicit feeling from a group of people sitting
around the fireside. He appears first as personified Winter ("His hair white as the snow on which
he treads" [l. 187]) then as the sentimental type of the veteran. Joanna Baillie, *Poetical and Dramatic
Works* (London: Longman, Brown, Green and Longmans, 1851), 772–74.

[33] Susan Stewart, *Poetry and the Fate of the Senses* (Chicago: U of Chicago P, 2002), 333.

snow (IV: 322). And Stewart, poet and critic, having finished writing a section entitled "War and the Alienation of the Senses," looks out her window in 2002 and wonders, "Perhaps I am writing at the end of a world" (333). And C. K. Williams, on an evening in February 2003, turns off the TV with its news of impending war in Iraq and writes a poem that opens with the "bitter," "slashing" winter weather outside and ends, as I will end too, thinking about feeling:

> I was thinking,
> as I often do these days, of war;
> I was thinking of my children, and their children,
> of the more than fear I feel for them,
>
> and then of radar, rockets, shrapnel,
> cities razed, soil poisoned
> for a thousand generations; of suffering
> so vast it nullifies everything else.[34]

The poem does *not* end there, with nullification. None of the poems actually ends there. Another line follows, another stanza, and another; the poet is still writing.

---

[34] C. K. Williams, "The Hearth," in *The Singing* (New York: Farrar, Strauss and Giroux, 2003), 37–44.

PART II

Invasions

CHAPTER THREE

War in the Air

[B]ut doth war never produce any good? A fair comparison may possibly make it doubtful, whether war, like the weather, ought not to be resigned to the conduct of Providence: seldom are we in the right, when we repine at its dispensations.
—Lord Kames[1]

A battle won or lost may decide the fate of an empire: but a battle may be won or lost by a shower of snow being blown to the east or the west. . . .
—Anna Letitia Barbauld[2]

Historiography has to test its presence of mind in grasping fleeting images.
—Walter Benjamin[3]

Poets of the late eighteenth century ask us to see in the snows of winter a history of warfare, with its anesthetizing threat to both history and writing. They conjure prospect poems where the view looks out upon total annihilation. Yet in their mining of the literary tradition and the resources of figuration, they disrupt that prospect, insisting that beneath and within the snow we recognize something still surviving. So much is written into the snow that these poems suggest the value of, indeed the need for a wartime rereading of that most romantic trope, the weather. To the precise degree that weather situates a concern about feeling and nonfeeling—about conditions suffered or merely

---

[1] Henry Home (Lord Kames), "War and Peace Compared," in *Sketches of the History of Man* (Edinburgh, 1788), 2: 294–95. *Eighteenth Century Collections Online* (*ECCO*). Gale Group. http://galenet.galegroup.com/servlet/ECCO

[2] Anna Letitia Barbauld, "On the Uses of History," in *A Legacy for Young Ladies*, ed. Lucy Aikin, 2nd ed. (London: Longman, Rees, Orme, Brown, and Green, 1826), 125.

[3] Walter Benjamin, *Gesammelte Schriften*, qtd. in Kevis Goodman, *Georgic Modernity and British Romanticism: Poetry and the Mediation of History* (Cambridge: Cambridge UP, 2004), 99.

observed, measured, and reported—so it becomes a crucial structure of modern wartime.

It is by now a critical commonplace to see in romantic images of weather, such as the cloud, a metaphor of transcendence and evanescence. A wartime reading, on the other hand, finds in the clouds and winds of romantic literature elements of a global system of communication, bearing if not news then pulses of feeling, currents from abroad. "What tell'st thou now about?" Coleridge asks the howling wind, as his "Dejection: An Ode" (1802) reaches its crescendo (110). And the wind, a "mighty Poet" but also a mighty journalist, reports:

> 'Tis of the rushing of an host in rout,
> With groans, of trampled men, with smarting wounds—
> At once they groan with pain, and shudder with the cold! (111–13)[4]

Coleridge had good reason to make the wind serve as medium for a world at war. And this wartime report, inserted into his famous ode, offers just one example of a much larger cultural phenomenon. This chapter moves then, from questions of temporality and history per se to attend to how a new weather science provided forms for mediating distant war. In the changing metaphorics of weather, writers and readers discovered ways that distant warfare might invade, inform, and reshape daily life.

Live Air

> No soldiers in the scenery,
> No thoughts of people now dead,
> As they were fifty years ago,
> Young and living in a live air,
> Young and walking in the sunshine,
> Bending in blue dresses to touch something,
> Today the mind is not part of the weather.
> Today the air is clear of everything.

When Wallace Stevens looks back over the first fifty years of the twentieth century and announces, "Today the mind is not part of the weather," he reiterates the modernist dismissal of romantic poetics: nature no longer provides a sentient echo of human thought or feeling. When the mind was part of the weather, the poem suggests, the air was full of touching memories of "some-

---

[4] Samuel Taylor Coleridge, *Samuel Taylor Coleridge (The Oxford Authors)*, ed. H. J. Jackson (Oxford: Oxford UP, 1985), 116.

thing": it was "live air." Now, in this newly purified element, not just memory but meaning falls away, and we are cast adrift of place and time:

> Today the air is clear of everything.
> It has no knowledge except of nothingness
> And it flows over us without meanings,
> As if none of us had ever been here before
> And are not now. . . .[5]

The promise of clear air and no memories carries with it a daunting recognition of all the meaning, the lost history, a mind-filled weather had once borne. But why, clearing the modern air "of everything" having to do with human subjectivity and distancing himself from the poetics of romantic precursors like Coleridge, does Stevens turn also from warfare and grief?

This chapter aims to fill Stevens's empty sky up again with the traces of warfare and grief evident in romantic poetry through metaphors of the weather. We have seen the complex set of motifs—of obliteration and endurance, stillness and hesitation, pain and numbness—that winter afforded to poets of wartime. But weather more generally afforded a yet broader set of motifs, as it allowed not just the equation of war with winter, but the coordination of warfare with tempests, storms, winds, and other climatological occurrences. The richness of these associations, their semantic serviceability, has meant that weather and war have been associated for ages. But, for a variety of reasons—scientific, poetic, and geopolitical—this metaphorical association took a specific turn in the late eighteenth and early nineteenth century, especially in England. Reversing Walter Benjamin's comment about the Great War, when "nothing remained unchanged but the clouds," we might say that in the era of the Revolutionary and Napoleonic wars the clouds themselves changed.[6] This change emphasized, but also put pressure on metaphor's ability to communicate across established borders, to bear or transfer change (from the Greek *meta-ferein*). That changeable weather was perhaps the crucial metaphor of the period is a familiar claim; we are used to reading the appearance of weather in romantic writing as picturesque effect or emblem of transcendence.[7]

[5] Wallace Stevens, *Opus Posthumous*, ed. Milton J. Bates, rev. ed. (New York: Alfred A. Knopf, 1989), 138–39, ll. 8–12. On Stevens's rejection of romantic metaphor, see John Dolan, "'Today the Mind Is Not Part of the Weather': Cognitive and Rhetorical Perspectives on the Construction of Poetic Metaphor," *Qui Parle* 7.2 (Spring/Summer 1994): 57–77.

[6] Benjamin, "The Storyteller," in *Illuminations: Essays and Reflections*, ed. and intro. Hannah Arendt, trans. Harry Zohn (New York: Shocken, 1968), 84.

[7] Arden Reed's book *Romantic Weather: The Climates of Coleridge and Baudelaire* (Hanover: UP of New England, 1983) makes this claim implicitly. His book owes a debt to Paul de Man's essay "The Intentional Structure of the Romantic Image," which concludes with a long meditation on weather imagery. Alan Liu's many considerations of weather imagery and metaphor in Wordsworth's

More surprising, then, is the thought that metaphors of weather participated in mediating history: as in Coleridge's "Dejection," they provided one of the primary means of imagining and bringing home the effects of distant war.[8] At first glance, metaphor (like Luhmann's version of mass media) may appear to efface the given world and refer only to itself; but in fact, as Paul Ricoeur reminds us, metaphor provides "the negative condition for freeing a more radical power of reference to those aspects of our being-in-the-world that cannot be talked about [or apprehended] directly" (qtd. in Liu 47). Metaphor—and here weather as metaphor becomes exemplary—can refer to what is elsewhere, beyond our ken.

As I have stressed, for those who then remained on the home front in England, military conflict took place almost constantly, but elsewhere, at a great remove. The twenty-year-long war they lived through was a global war, difficult to apprehend directly. Its disruptions had to be borne to them—mediated. Conventional media played a significant role, then as now: clocks, the post-boy, and the newspaper collectively established a regular structure of feeling which both enabled and obscured diverse responses to the fact of distant war. In drawing out the responses obscured by the clockwork regularity of this structure—in attending to the noises and lapses, the untimeliness and empty present of wartime—I have underscored the affective power of these more elusive experiences. The metaphoric connections between weather and war provide yet another, competing structure of feeling: never quite articulated into "clear" knowledge of war, metaphors of weather offered instead a history of affect, even perhaps the "climate" we call modern wartime.

One reason for the central role of weather as metaphor in the period was, in fact, its unrivaled appropriateness to the experience of global warfare. Contemporary developments in the science of meteorology offered new ways to coordinate the working of weather with the movement of geopolitical forces. As we will see, scientists and poets together produced a recognizable *georgics* of the sky, fusing the *work* of war and weather to highlight questions of mediation, especially between bodies and events located at great removes from each other. Such georgic impulses within meteorology brought together the representation of transcendent and terrestrial powers, global movements and local climate, devastating event and minor fluctuation. "A few drops of water . . . an unseasonable cloud crossing the sky sufficed for the overthrow of the world," wrote Victor Hugo of the battle of Waterloo.[9] Or, as Anna Barbauld remarks

---

poetry take de Man's conclusions in a different direction, seeing them as obstacles to history. *Wordsworth: The Sense of History* (Stanford: Stanford UP, 1989).

[8] This thought lies at the core of Eduardo Cadava's excellent *Emerson and the Climates of History* (Stanford: Stanford UP, 1997).

[9] Victor Hugo, *Les Misérables*, trans. Charles E. Wilbour (New York: Modern Library, 1992) 271.

in the epigraph above, "a shower of snow being blown to the east or the west" can destroy an empire. Yet even as it aspired to systematize what seemed so radically contingent, to comprehend the aerial movement of global forces, weather science unleashed a free-floating anxiety, an affective surplus: Stevens's "live air."

Like other structures of feeling, the not quite "precipitated" network of beliefs and feelings about war and weather is perhaps detectable only in hindsight—Stevens's fifty years, for instance, or perhaps our own two hundred years from the age of the first modern and worldwide war.[10] We can delineate stages in the historical movement toward this particular precipitation: the incorporation, for instance, of the United States Weather Bureau as a branch of the War Department in 1870. Today we have SCUD missiles, named after the low-flying clouds mariners used to call "messengers"; we have airborne agents of destruction, weapons that travel as toxic clouds or haze.[11] For Stevens and subsequent generations, though, the final precipitation or realization of that structure of feeling, that which makes hindsight possible, occurred when the fusion of weather and war was accomplished—if not exhausted—in the mushroom cloud and the forecast of eternal nuclear winter.

Beyond Control

> Our task remains . . . to show how historical agency is transformed through the signifying process; how the historical event is represented in a discourse that is *somehow beyond control.*[12]

Anna Barbauld's ferocious "Eighteen Hundred and Eleven, a Poem" (1812) opens with a blandly conventional couplet:

> Still the loud death drum, thundering from afar,
> O'er the vext nations pours the storm of war. (1–2)[13]

The predictability of such an image of weather breeds neglect, if not contempt. Barbauld has, however, set us up: several lines later she chastises her

---

[10] In his explanation of "structures of feeling" Raymond Williams uses "precipitation" in its chemical sense: structures of feeling are not-yet-precipitated entities, "social experiences *in solution*"; they become detectable only after precipitation. Raymond Williams, *Marxism and Literature* (New York: Oxford UP, 1977), 133–34; emphasis original. On structures of feeling, see chapter 2 above.

[11] Andrew Ross, "The Work of Nature in the Age of Electronic Emission," *Social Text* 18 (Winter 1987/88): 116–28; Richard Hamblyn, *The Invention of Clouds: How an Amateur Meteorologist Forged the Language of the Skies* (New York: Farrar, Straus and Giroux, 2001), 11–18.

[12] Homi K. Bhabha, *The Location of Culture* (London: Routledge, 2004), 18; emphasis original.

[13] Anna Letitia Barbauld, *Selected Poetry and Prose*, ed. William McCarthy and Elizabeth Kraft (Toronto: Broadview P, 2002), 161.

country (and readers) for living in climate-controlled ignorance, not heeding the weather:

> And think'st thou, Britain, still to sit at ease,
> An island Queen amidst thy subject seas,
> While the vext billows, in their distant roar,
> But soothe thy slumbers, and but kiss thy shore?
> To sport in wars, while danger keeps aloof . . . ? (39–43)

"Ruin, as with an earthquake shock, is here," the poet announces to the unwary. If neither storm nor earthquake will rouse England, perhaps the country will attend to the less sublime effects of evaporation, learning through misfortune to read the skies:

> Thy baseless wealth dissolves in air away,
> Like mists that melt before the morning ray: . . .
> Sad, on the ground thy princely merchants bend
> Their altered looks, and evil days portend,
> And fold their arms, and watch with anxious breast
> The tempest blackening in the distant West. (53–60)[14]

Barbauld depicts the climate of war—its political, economic, and emotional consequences—through a catalogue of meteorological metaphors. For her, and for many contemporary artists, war becomes a vast impersonal system whose agents include clouds, mists, thunder, drought, and snow. Urging on Polish patriots, for instance, Amelia Alderson (later Opie) invokes Homeric similes to imagine their "force" moving "like a storm that swells the troubled gale / Rolls down the hill, and sweeps the vale."[15] Warfare, despite all its strategies and tactics, is thus placed outside human agency. Thomas Campbell's "On the Battle of Hohenlinden [1800]" (published in 1803) similarly translates weaponry into meteorological effect:

> Then shook the hills with thunder riven,
> Then rush'd the steeds to battle driven,
> And vollying, like the bolts of heaven,
> Far flash'd the red artillery. . . .

---

[14] Due to continental blockades on British goods as well as exorbitant taxation to fund the wars, Britain in 1810 was near economic collapse. In 1811, the Orders of Council halted British trade with the United States, now French allies, and exports fell severely. The hardship which ensued, together with the threat of another war front opening in North America, would certainly make merchants look anxiously across the Atlantic.

[15] Amelia Alderson, "Lines, Written on the Capture of Gen. Kosciusko," in *British War Poetry in the Age of Romanticism, 1793–1815*, ed. Betty T. Bennett (New York: Garland, 1976), 139–40.

'Tis morn; but scarce yon level sun
Can pierce the war-cloud rolling dun,
Where furious Frank and fiery Hun
Shout, mid' their sulphurous canopy.[16]

In these poems and countless others, distant violence is effortlessly and conventionally naturalized. More surprisingly, other texts use weather to bring the war home as an immediate physiological—even political—experience:

Pavement slip'ry; People sneezing;
Lords in ermine, beggars freezing;
Nobles, scarce the Wretched heeding;
Gallant Soldiers—fighting!—bleeding![17]

Perhaps most curiously, popular poetry uses weather as Barbauld—or Coleridge—does, to bear messages or prophecies associated with the war, making palpable otherwise unseen or unknowable effects. A quick scan of periodical poetry collected in Betty T. Bennett's *British War Poetry in the Age of Romanticism, 1793–1815* discovers a wealth of such weather reporting, delivered in a range of moods: wary optimism, gothic fear, hortatory nationalism, apocalyptic awe. Regardless of their sense of the climate, such poems all employ the weather as a messenger, a voice floating on the air. In one instance, a storm-borne specter announces a lover's death in battle; in another, cloud-borne shades urge patriots to avenge their death; in a third, militant songs and shouts roil the heavens. Like the poems themselves, weather speaks, or at least sounds, in an echo of classical and biblical precedent; but this weather most often conveys not divine instruction—as in the convention of *liber naturae*—but the news of war. If instruction is offered, it usually advises the reader not to expel the foe or follow the call or even mend her ways, but to attend to shifts in the air.

To have a sense of what was happening in wartime, then, it seems one was expected to practice meteorological prognostication: reading the skies was itself a civic duty. Yet difficulties of interpretation immediately register themselves. While the weather occasionally speaks with a clear voice, it more frequently provides only the expressive inarticulacy of winds howling or people sneezing or "hoarse thunders" thundering. And as the redundancy of thunders thundering reveals, divining war through weather often founders on the very metaphor that binds the two. Indeed, as Robinson's parataxes demonstrate, it is hard to know how metaphorical the relationship between war and weather is, or in

---

[16] Thomas Campbell, "On the Battle of Hohenlinden [1800]," in Bennett 292–93. For similar uses see "The Orphan Sailor-Boy" and "On a Late Victory at Sea" in Bennett 307–10 and 130–32.
[17] Mary Robinson, "January, 1795," in Bennett 142.

which direction it moves: the hardships of the winter of 1795 were felt to be the result of both brutal weather and the state's brutal policies for financing an unpopular war. Famine, like plague, had conventionally been considered a meteorological event, but in 1795 and subsequent years of famine in England, the public suspected a political cause. In the rhetorical association of war and weather, the coordinates of metaphor, like the weather itself, could change location, reverse direction, veer toward literalization, or fade away completely.

"[W]hen two Englishmen meet," Samuel Johnson famously wrote, "their first talk is of the weather; they are in haste to tell each other, what each must already know." [18] But for Barbauld's wartime contemporaries, weather provided a language both unfamiliar and somehow beyond control. In Barbauld's own verse, for example, citing the weather exceeds logic: in the mixing of metaphor and forecast, death-drums somehow "pour" out war; tempest and earthquake evaporate into morning mist, which then yields a tempest; clouds on the continent veer round to become clouds in the distant West; and, in her most confusing image, merchants stare at the ground while with "anxious breasts" they watch the sky. Are weather and the war it betokens grounded or metaphorical, felt or imagined, cataclysmic event or daily operation, earthly fact or dissolving mist? In "Eighteen Hundred and Eleven," Barbauld struggles to get a fix on the weather of war.

To understand the fugitive movements of weather and war, we must simultaneously situate them within the history of meteorology, where, by the Romantic period, the nature and location of weather were vexed; and within a history of wartime communication, where again, location, temporality, and responsibility were problems. The need to conceptualize a war in which Britain was vitally engaged but geographically removed contributed to an expanded interest in the weather, which only in the late eighteenth century could be understood as a global system. As we see in the poetry of Robinson and Barbauld, the desire to represent wartime as a climate of politics and affect weighed heavily. But the spaces and places assigned to weather made that subject, like the war itself, increasingly hard to pin down.

Early Weather Science: Grounding the Weather

When Barbauld's merchants find themselves looking down and up simultaneously, perhaps regarding the wreckage of an earthquake while attending to the clouds, they act out a fundamental shift in meteorological understanding. Two

---

[18] Samuel Johnson, *The Idler, No. 11. The Yale Edition of the Works of Samuel Johnson*, ed. Walter J. Bate, J. M. Bullitt, and L. F. Powell (New Haven: Yale UP, 1963), 2: 36.

questions shaped weather science as it developed through the eighteenth century, approaching the "meteorology" we now recognize: Did weather originate from the earth or the sky? And was it a local or global phenomenon? The struggles over these questions altered the public sense of what counted as weather and consequently changed what weather—in theory and in poetry—could communicate.

Well past midcentury, scientists drawing on Aristotle, Ovid, and other ancient sources reckoned that the *earth* provided the source of all atmospheric change. The "exhalation theory," propounded by John Woodward in 1726 and influential for decades, imagined that vapors exhaled from a source within the earth carried mineral deposits into the atmosphere, which, in reaction with the heat of the sun, initiated all sorts of meteorological events: volcanic eruptions were a favorite, but also thunderstorms, changes in air pressure, and fogs. These precipitations were then reabsorbed into the earth.[19] Meteor, it should be noted, was a general term for a range of sublunary phenomena: it comprehended rainfall as well as comets, dew as well as the northern lights.[20] For Woodward and contemporary philosophers of science, meteorology was an essentially chemical, even mineral, study. Despite its apparent empirical emphasis, though, the exhalation theory traced the vagaries of weather back to a hypothetical geological origin (Woodward calls it a "*Collection of waters* inclosed in the *Bowels of the Earth*, ... which *Moses* calls the *Great Deep*, or *Abyss*") and explained them in terms of a hypothetical historical origin, the biblical flood (117; emphasis original).

In his excellent *Reading the Skies: A Cultural History of English Weather, 1650–1820*, Vladimir Janković argues that because it relied so heavily on inference and analogy, weather science in the eighteenth century lagged behind other physical sciences, resisting the prescriptions of a Newtonian universe (126–29). Echoing generations of skeptics, for instance, William Jones, a late disciple of Woodward, warned that in observing the weather we have no "certain rules and principles to direct us, as in other sciences."[21] Anchored to a volatile earth, weather happened in and to a temperamental body: it issued forth from the "pores," "crevices," and "bowels" of the earth in the form of "gases," "vapours," "effluvia," or, indeed, "affections." As such, it correlated closely with a view of human nature as erratic, hysterical, and even tragic.

[19] John Woodward, *An Essay toward a Natural History of the Earth: And Terrestrial Bodies, Especially Minerals: As also of the Sea, Rivers,* and *Springs. With an Account of the Universal Deluge: And of the Effects that it had upon the Earth* (London: R. Wilkin, 1695), 117–18; emphasis original.

[20] See Vladimir Janković, *Reading the Skies: A Cultural History of English Weather, 1650–1820* (Chicago: U of Chicago P, 2001); Reed 9–12; and Hamblyn 21–46.

[21] William Jones, "On the Appearances, Causes, and Prognostic Signs of the Weather," in *The Theological, Philosophical and Miscellaneous Works of the Rev. William Jones* (London: F. and C. Rivington, 1801), 395; also 399.

Meteorology in this neoclassical outlook took as its main subject what William Cowper called "[p]ortentous, unexampled, and unexplain'd" events in the sublunary realm: volcanoes, earthquakes, tornadoes (*The Task* II: 58). By positing an unseen "abyss" beneath the earth that unified all meteorological phenomena, weather observation seemed to require no other coordinating principle; weather was determined to be wildly idiosyncratic. Until 1791, for instance, the *Transactions of the Royal Society* gave extensive coverage to reports of unprecedented frosts, meteor sightings, or unusually destructive storms. These reports, often from curates and scholarly gentry, remind us that the oddity that counted as weather was also resolutely local. For much of the century, even in later reports such as Gilbert White's *Natural History of Selborne* (1788), weather sported as *genius loci*, a defining spirit of the place, a topographical feature which often suggested—and naturalized—political character.

Taken as a local (and given) characteristic, weather could be incorporated into the Aristotelian tradition of climatology, revived by Montesquieu and later Buffon, that is, the study of peoples and cultures through the features of their climate.[22] By coordinating unpredictable variation with the fixity of place, climatology lent itself to ethnography and, later, race theory: one could organize the features of a people—physique, sexuality, intelligence, governmental organization, even language—by noting the climate in which they lived.[23] The British developed their own brand of climatology in the eighteenth century, tying it closely to political identity and extolling the virtues of the island climate for fostering liberty. Any unruly changeableness in the island weather could serve as objective correlative for a national character understood as idiosyncratic and defiantly independent. Cowper makes his own tribute to the nation's quirky climate:

> Though thy clime
> Be fickle, and thy year most part deform'd
> With dripping rains, or wither'd by a frost,
> I would not yet exchange thy sullen skies
> And fields without a flow'r, for warmer France,
> With all her vines; nor for Ausonia's groves. (*The Task* II: 209–14)

In eighteenth-century Britain, where localism and exceptionalism were increasingly tied to national identity, an interest in the local weather and espe-

[22] On the evolution of climatology and its influence, see Leo Spitzer, "Milieu and Ambiance," in *Essays in Historical Semantics* (New York: S. F. Vanni, 1948), 203; and J. W. Johnson, "On Differing Ages and Climes," *Journal of the History of Ideas* 21 (October–December 1960): 465–80.

[23] Johnson provides a helpful history and credits the earliest extant geographer, Strabo, for initiating "our own theory of *climata*" (Johnson, *Dictionary* 470).

cially its marvels was almost a national occupation. Though variable and even freakish, weather was thus tethered to a piece of earth and a political identity.

As stabilizing as the neoclassical view of climate might appear, the exhalation theory and the climatology it fostered rested nonetheless on unstable ground. For all its cooperation with ideas of a natural political order, the exhalation theory relied on an analogy that imagined constant disruption, even warfare, both on the earth and in the skies. According to Janković,

> Woodward's *Essay* reiterated the peristatic [exhalation] theory with an enticing metaphor: when the nitrous and sulphurous vapors saturated the air to a critical level, he claimed that they constituted a kind of "Aerial Gunpowder," the cause of "dismal and terrible Thunder and Lightning which commonly, if not always, attend Earthquakes." (27)

Empirical evidence for this explanation was, as Janković demonstrates, "a moot issue": the exhalation theory lived by the force of this explosive analogy (29).[24] An extraordinary example of its imaginative reach appears in a natural history written in 1696, detailing a battle in the sky fought with "sulph-nitrous ammunition":

> The Battel by this time growing very hot, the Main Bodies engage, and then nothing is to be heard but a Thundering Noise, with continual Flashes of Lightning, and dreadful showers of Rain, falling down from the broken Clouds. And sometimes random shots flie [*sic*] about, kill Both Men and Beasts. . . . If the fiery Exhalations keep the Field, the east Wind blows still hot and sulphureous. If the Vapors get the Victory, the West Wind blows cold and moist, the Sky is clear, the Air is cold, the Battel is over and the Earth buries the Dead and gets the Spoil. (qtd. in Janković 27)

Here we can hardly distinguish the aerial battle from an account of battle on the ground. The vehicle for understanding the weather is war—not vice versa; war is apparently familiar enough to explain the otherwise inexplicable or unknown. Destructive, volatile, and unpredictable in outcome, war and its gunpowder somehow humanize the weather—or at least keep it tied to earth.

If, along with this sulfuric combustion, we recall the other guiding analogy of this early weather science, the radically porous human body, their shared kinship with warfare, with what Elaine Scarry has called the mutual injuring or "opening up" of bodies, becomes even easier to recognize.[25] For instance,

---

[24] See Barbara Maria Stafford's comment on "flashy" analogical thinking in *Visual Analogy: Consciousness as the Art of Connection* (Cambridge: MIT P, 1999), 63.

[25] Elaine Scarry, *The Body in Pain: The Making and Unmaking of the World* (New York: Oxford UP, 1985), 124–33.

the plausibility of warfare as a metaphor for weather relied on the invasive power of smell: the smell of gunpowder. Janković notes that the "smell [of sulfur] was by far the most frequently cited observation in meteorological reports prior to the 1750s" (30). To apprehend the workings of weather, it seemed, you had to recognize or recall the smell of exploding shot.[26]

This conception of weather requires what Wallace Stevens rejects in "A Clear Day and No Memories"—that is, an orientation toward the past. The early eighteenth century had a powerful, memory-filled weather. Natural science early in the century understood weather less as a matter of prognostication than of recollection; its analogies drew on what was known, felt, and remembered (the human body's effusions, warfare, biblical deluge) in a way that situated meteorology in the abysmal reservoirs of a past seen as violent and erratic. Later scientists of weather would criticize the "Puritan enthusiasm and political millenarianism" inherent in the exhalation theory (Janković 11). Nested in the obvious rationalism of this criticism is a desire to refute the notion, popular in the wake of the civil wars, that warfare and violent commotion are unpredictable and yet always possible phenomena, emanating from the ground beneath our feet.

To make precise what weather of this sort could represent about war, I offer three observations. First, neoclassical weather seemed capable of conveying either fixed states (the organized and familiar climate of a place) or total upheaval (an otherwise invisible "commotion" of all things)—nothing in between, nothing in transition or undergoing orderly change. It was, in this sense, static. Second, conceived as irregular disturbance, weather offered a view of war itself as *unsystematic*, as disorganized as it was violent. Finally, weather presented itself as isolated or *local*, rooted in a fixed place. Extreme, unsystematic, and local, neoclassical weather—and the warfare it figured—was thus incomparable and untranslatable. It happened here and only here.[27] Vestiges of this conception of weather survived into the next century, but by the latter decades of the eighteenth century, an alternative and emergent science of meteorology worked to rewrite all these associations. This new science articulated instead the dominant modern view of war: mobile rather than static, predictable and systematic rather than erratic; and above all, global in its reach.

---

[26] We might assume that familiarity with the smell of gunpowder would conjure up images of hunting more often than warfare. This was not the case. Evidently the unrestrained violence of battle had a more powerful analogical hold.

[27] The current method of reading weather by tracking the movement of air masses over large geographical areas and watching the pseudo-military *fronts* forming between them was not devised until the First World War.

A Georgics of the Sky

Frustration with the intransitivity of early conceptions of the weather helped spur the new weather science of the latter half of the century. In the 1750s and 1760s, discoveries in electricity and chemistry not only discredited the exhalation theory and with it the claim that weather was a grounded, if erratic, affair; they also offered a system of comparability and translation. The coordinated efforts of scientists and amateurs across the globe contributed to a newly integrated understanding of the earth's weather. What emerged was a vision of weather as a global system of exchange, something that passed from one region to another, moving over local and national borders. This dramatic change in what counted as weather in turn transformed what weather might bear across such borders, what it could metaphorize.

With the discovery of the role electricity played in evaporation, cloud formation, and storms, weather was lifted into a truly universal idea. Joseph Priestley explains in his *History of the Present State of Electricity* (1765) that the "electrical fluid is no local, or occasional agent in the theatre of the world. . . . [I]ts presence and effects are every where. . . . [I]t acts a principle part in the grandest and most interesting scenes of nature." [28] For Priestley, an early advocate, electricity made the study of weather a matter of "internal structure" as opposed to "sensible properties"—the sights, smells, and sounds which had occupied previous generations of weather observers (Priestley xv). Winds and clouds served, appropriately, as the emblems of this newly uplifted science, and were awarded their own chapters in works devoted to natural philosophy and weather. John Dalton's *Meteorological Observations and Essays* (1793) was well-known and typical, turning to the skies to demonstrate the "well regulated system, or whole" of the weather.[29] As the tether between ground and climate began to fray, weather science was freed for the skies of full-fledged theory. This was a system no one individual could perceive; it demanded an aerial, global, and theoretical stance.

It was the scientist's job to model that detached stance through experimentation. Priestley reports that the Italian philosopher and reformer Cesare Beccaria designed an experiment that simulated cloud movement across the surface of the earth. Beccaria

> insulat[ed] himself between the rubber and conductor of his electrical machine, and with one hand dropping *colophonia* into a spoon fastened

[28] Joseph Priestley, *History of the Present State of Electricity, with Original Experiments*, 2 vols. (London: C. Bathurst and T. Lowndes, 1775), 1: xiv.

[29] John Dalton, *Meteorological Observations and Essays* (London: W. Richardson, 1793), 94–95.

to the conductor, [he held] a burning coal, while his other hand com-
municated with the rubber. In these circumstances the smoke spread
across his arm, and, by degrees, all over his body. . . . The lower surface
of this smoke was every where parallel to his cloaths, and the upper surface was swelled and arched like clouds replete with thunder and rain. In
this manner, . . . the clouds that bring rain diffuse themselves from over
those parts of the earth which abound with electric fire, to those parts
that are exhausted of it; and, by letting fall their rain, restore the equilibrium between them. (429–30)

Beccaria's project realizes the idea of coordinated, global weather; it also situates the individual no longer "as a local or occasional agent" but, like electricity itself, "every where": an impersonal global subject. In a striking reversal of
earlier analogies for the weather, the human body is now the untouched
(clothed and closed) surface over and around which electrical currents, and
the clouds they help generate, travel. The translation of weather from ground
to air, from isolated phenomena to imagined system, made it the work of genius itself. Thus Barbauld, a close friend and student of Priestley, would in
1793 celebrate "man, the great magician, who controuls / Fire, earth and air,
and genii of the storm"—an idea to which she returns in "Eighteen Hundred
and Eleven," as we shall see.[30]

Priestley's account of Beccaria's genius also demonstrates how the weather
science developing at late century merged easily both with nascent finance capitalism (discussed in Ian Baucom's work) and with natural theology. His experiment creates a visible whole of global weather changes, allowing the scientist to
speculate about their economy: electricity works here as an invisible hand to
achieve "equilibrium."[31] Indeed, the scientists' special attention to clouds and
winds suggests an impulse to show the system at work in the most irregular and
idiosyncratic phenomena. "[A]midst perpetual fluctuations, and occasional
tremendous perturbations [in the atmosphere]," writes Luke Howard in his
The Climate of London (1818–20), "the balance of the great machine is preserved, and its parts still move in harmony: each returning season verifying the
assurance given to mankind after the deluge" (2: vi). The new weather science
posed as a latter-day version of the rainbow of Genesis, guaranteeing climatic
consistency while freeing mankind from Woodward's abysmal waters.

These scientific developments, then, produced a distinctive sense of climate
in late-century Britain. More surprisingly, however, those developments were
underwritten by what has been called the "georgic revolution" in the century's

[30] Barbauld, "Inscription for an Ice-House," in *Selected Poetry and Prose* 140.
[31] For examples, look to Luke Howard, *The Climate of London*, 2 vols (London: W. Phillips,
1818–1820), 2: vi–vii; and Dalton 120 and 145ff. See also Janković 129.

intellectual culture.[32] In fact, as fully as any scientific development, what we might call a georgic disposition facilitated the passage midcentury from the old weather science to the new. Paired with the emerging awareness of a global, speculative weather, georgic weather would create a new sense of climate which, in turn, offered new ways to anticipate and worry over a world at war.

Translated into English and promoted by John Dryden in 1697, Virgil's *Georgics* offered a poetic "middle way" between the epic concerns of the *Aeneid* and the pastoral ease of his *Eclogues*. Its middle-ness replaced the heroics of war and the pleasures of leisure with the practical and everyday work of cultivation, broadly construed. Like the old weather science, the georgic mode generally inclined toward a grounded, rather than a theoretical perspective; a traditional, rather than an inventive approach to natural phenomena (hence its reliance on classical authorities). But several features of the georgic did align with a less backward-looking meteorology. While the georgic imagined weather as patterned change, it also promoted an interest in prognostication, which in turn accentuated weather's role in mediation and communication, especially of an affective climate.

With its faith in regulable change, the georgic mode enabled the new meteorology to become a science of anticipation rather than recollection. Weather prognostication, the art of divining change through observation of natural "signs" (e.g., insect activity or the appearance of the sky), provides the content and dramatic finale for the first book of Virgil's *Georgics*. This forecasting impulse flourished in weather reporting in later eighteenth-century England. The thought that change itself could be both naturalized and anticipated had its attractions: farmer's almanacs and shepherd's calendars experienced a real vogue.[33] "Some are weatherwise," notes Benjamin Franklin in a characteristic aphorism from his *Poor Richard's Almanac*, "some are otherwise" (qtd. in Hamblyn 250). Paradigmatically, Franklin himself would help convert weather wisdom into the reassurances of scientific experimentation.

The consolations of regulation and prediction built into the new georgic weather nevertheless disclosed deep anxiety, especially about the state of the

---

[32] Janković 131–42, passim. Helpful studies of the georgic mode in the eighteenth century include Anthony Low, *The Georgic Revolution* (Princeton: Princeton UP, 1985); John Barrell, *The Dark Side of the Landscape: The Rural Poor in English Painting, 1730–1840* (Cambridge: Cambridge UP, 1980) and *English Literature in History, 1730–1780* (London: Hutchinson, 1983); Clifford Siskin, *The Work of Writing: Literature and Social Change in Britain, 1700–1830* (Baltimore: Johns Hopkins UP, 1998), chap. 4; Rachel Crawford, "English Georgic and British Nationhood," *ELH: English Literary History* 65.1 (1998): 123–58; and Kurt Heinzelman, "Roman Georgic in the Georgian Age: A Theory of Romantic Genre," *Texas Studies in Literature and Language* 33 (1991): 182–214.

[33] For this I have relied heavily on Janković, as well as the various meteorology works already mentioned (Howard, Jones, Dalton, Priestley).

world. As her title suggests, in *Georgic Modernity and British Romanticism: Poetry and the Mediation of History*, Kevis Goodman associates mediation with the georgic mode; and she stresses the powers of the georgic to mediate affect in particular. Drawing on Virgil's own characterization of his *via media* as a recognition of the poem's work as medium, and turning to central poetic texts of the Georgian era (by Thomson, Cowper, and Wordsworth), Goodman charts the development and technologies of georgic mediation in eighteenth-century England (8–22). Her argument helps us see in the logic of Virgil's *Georgics* that God or Jupiter had ordained weather signs as one mode of communication and had attuned animate nature to receive his messages. Thus Thomas Short, a Sheffield physician interested in meteorology, could claim that Providence had given the inhabitants of the earth "Presages, Marks, and Signs of Weather, especially when a total Incapacity to prepare for . . . extraordinary Changes might be of the worst Consequence" (qtd. in Janković 137). What the georgic mode gave to weather science was the potential to operate as a media technology, a communicative device that worked on the body as well as the intelligence. As we've noted, in the old weather science weather operated on a local level; farmers and mariners were responsive to particular impulses taken from the animals, plants, and skies of their own location. But by late century the weather could be imagined much more broadly through the movements of forces circulating through the earth's atmosphere. Intimations of change over time and at a distance could be transmitted, felt, through the weather. More often than not, they were intimations of trouble, and it was unclear exactly what sort of response—besides anxiety itself—they demanded.

We should differentiate, then, between the sort of mediation presented by an earlier georgic tradition and the revised version practiced by the new science of meteorology. In the classical tradition, the practice of weather prognostication developed by ancient Greeks and Romans was taken to have universal applicability. No matter the locale or period of history, the signs of classical weather were secure: an unchanging diagnostic of change. In the new meteorology, weather was a dynamic, overarching system of forces, which linked one land to another through the movement of (usually electrical) forces.[34] The sort of prognostication available in this new orientation was less interested in uniformity or local characteristics than in metamorphoses over space and time. In other words, their weather was not merely *comparable* to our weather; in time, and with some translation, their weather *became* our weather—and our weather would soon become someone else's. Modern georgic weather thus offered a physics of global communication.

---

[34] Thus Dalton's "general circulation of air," his trade winds and currents, depend upon the rotation of the earth; without that change, the system would prove "stagnant" (91).

Luke Howard, the man who gave clouds a nomenclature as well as systematic predictability, was one of the early, influential practitioners of the new
meteorology and his work exemplifies the integration of the georgic mode
with a science of worldwide weather, while signaling a concern with worldwide war. In his seminal essay on cloud formation, "On the Modifications of
Clouds" (1803), Howard insisted on using Latin terminology to coin a language for clouds, the now familiar *cumulus, cirrus, nimbus,* and *stratus.* Against
repeated attempts to anglicize his nomenclature, he argued that clouds had
no nationality: there were no *English* clouds. "[T]he principal objection to
English, or any other local terms," he writes, is that they offer no "universal
Language, by means of which the intelligent of every country may convey to
each other their ideas without the necessity of translation" (*Climate* 1: xxxiii).[35]
Beyond this taxonomy, however, Howard offered a way of studying clouds
that understood them as structures constantly *in* translation. His insight was
to read the future of clouds in their present, that is, to anticipate what a given
cloud might become: its "anacoluthic changeability" (Hamblyn 174). Clouds
are no longer simply here and then gone; they become harbingers of their
own transformation.[36] In Howard's description of a stratus cloud, for instance, a sheet of enveloping mist lifts from the ground, meets the sun, then
"ascends and evaporates, or passes off with the appearance of a nascent cumulus [cloud]."[37] To recognize a stratus cloud is to anticipate its translation into
something else. Howard tracks the various cloud forms through their many
modifications (in fact, he refers to each form as itself a "modification"). Like
Priestley, he aims less to pin down this phenomenon of the weather than to
apprehend its internal or theoretical structure. Universal yet transitive signs
of hidden and constant translation, Howard's clouds epitomized the new
weather.

Thus in his meticulous study of London's weather from 1806 to 1817,
Howard was forced to survey global weather as well. When he recorded the
rainfall in London, for example, he also recorded that of France and Iceland,
as well as Barbados, Martinique, St. Petersburg, Calcutta, Edinburgh, and
Hong Kong. *The Climate of London* is studded with notes of "Inundations
Abroad," "Weather Abroad," and "Heat Abroad," as if to remind its reader not
to isolate local and metropolitan climate from fluctuations across the globe.

[35] Hamblyn records the dispute over Latin versus vernacular terminology (201–15).
[36] In this regard, his work had a great influence on the painter John Constable, especially his
well-known cloud studies; and on Wilhelm Goethe, who composed a poem in Howard's honor. See
John E. Thornes, *John Constable's Skies: A Fusion of Art and Science* (Birmingham: U of Birmingham
P, 1999); Edward Morris, *Constable's Clouds: Paintings and Cloud Studies by John Constable* (Edinburgh: National Galleries of Scotland, 2000); and Hamblyn 281–320.
[37] Luke Howard, *On the Modifications of Clouds, and on the Principles of their Production, Suspension and Destruction, etc.* (London: J. Taylor, 1803), 8.

When Howard paused to explain contemporary theories of rain, his specula-
tions took a flight unimaginable even a few decades before:

> Vapour brought to us by such a [southeasterly] wind must have been
> generated in countries lying to the South and East of our island. It is
> therefore probably in the extensive vallies by the Meuse, the Moselle and
> the Rhine, if not from the more distant Elbe, with the Oder and Weser,
> that the water rises, in the midst of sunshine, which is soon afterwards
> to form *our* clouds, and pour down in *our* Thunder-showers. And this
> island, in all probability, does the same office for Ireland: nay, the East-
> ern for the Western counties. (2: 218; emphasis added)

Whereas his Latin terms need "no translation," international weather is an office of translation and exchange: their sunshine, our storms; our sunshine,
their rain.

Beneath these assurances, however, lurk hints of a troubled climate. In
reading the rain during wartime, Howard, a devout Quaker and ardent cam-
paigner for the relief of war victims, also intimated a new geopolitical map for
Britain at the start of the nineteenth century. His account alights uncannily on
the hot spots: the most contested region of the recent Napoleonic wars, and
the nearby colony of Ireland where, in 1798, rebellion had been violently
quelled. One might say his account of the weather both condenses and evaporates the subject of war. Alert to messages from abroad, georgic weather has its
receptors tuned to distant warfare.

It might seem that weather simply communicates weather. But when the
scientists borrowed Virgil's authority, they borrowed a semantic and affective
supplement as well, for the poet's own discussion of weather forecasting places
itself within the climate of war. In verse that would reverberate for disciples of
natural theology and prognostication, the *Georgics* assures mankind that "[I]f
you mark the scorching sun and mark / The moon's successive phases, then
tomorrow / Never will catch you by surprise."[38] Yet the *Georgics* has something
more to communicate about the climate of the first century BCE. "[T]he Sun
will give you signs," but of what?

> Who dares call Sun a liar? He it is
> Who often warns of dark revolts afoot,
> Conspiracy and cancerous growth of war. (I: 463–66)

For all its invocation of a benevolent order, for all its apparent plowing under
of history, the georgic turns here to warn against imminent violence. Like
Barbauld later, Virgil warns the unwary to be attentive to distant rumblings:

[38] Virgil, *The Georgics*, trans. L. P. Wilkinson (Harmondsworth, UK: Penguin, 1982), I: 424–26.

"[T]hroughout the world / Impious War is raging" (I: 510–11). For Virgil, a sense of the weather is inseparable from a proper sense of history; it provides the felt sensation of history.

A nervous vigilance thus informs the new work of the georgic: poets as well as scientists performed their civic duty by means of weather anxiety. Two years after Britain's loss of its North American colonies, Cowper borrowed the weather prognostics of the *Georgics* and worked them into a full-blown weather obsession in Book II of *The Task*. To communicate the precarious state of the Empire, Cowper assembled reports of freakish weather across the globe—hurricane in Jamaica, dismal fog over Europe and Asia, and, most dramatically, earthquake in Sicily—all portending a total overthrow of established order.[39] The poet prays for peace "in a world that seems / To toll the death-bell of its own decease, / And by the voice of all its elements / To preach the gen'ral doom" (II: 50–53). Like Virgil, like Barbauld, Cowper agonized that his compatriots were not paying due attention to the weather. "What then!" worries the poet,

> . . . were they [elsewhere] the wicked above all,
> And we the righteous, whose fast anchor'd isle
> Mov'd not, while their's was rock'd, like a light skiff,
> The sport of ev'ry wave? No: none are clear. (II: 150–53)

The georgic emphasis is clear: the island's climate—physical, political, moral, emotional—cannot be isolated from and must be understood alongside weather elsewhere.[40]

Civic unease accompanies man's receptivity to weather signs; prognostication becomes a science of history-in-the-making as much as a science of the weather, and it is an anxious science. "Although the georgic is often written in the past and present tenses," Susan Stewart observes, georgic poetry has "its entire orientation . . . toward the future; what it records is meant to be taken up by future generations."[41] Whether or not it will be taken up, whether or not there will be a future, are questions agitating the genre, especially as it contemplates war. Goodman understands this anxiety another way, when she examines the flashes of affect which, like Virgil's flashes of lightning, dart out from georgic writing. These "clashes" or "intensifications," she writes, "seem to mark the genre's engagement with what we would now identify with history

---

[39] Hamblyn gives details of the unusual weather of 1783 (66–82).

[40] Cowper's and Barbauld's concern over climate makes palpable the more abstract advice offered in Barbauld's 'The Uses of History.' To attain "clear ideas on the subjects of history," Barbauld insists, one must keep in mind "the relative situations of other countries at the time of any event recorded in one of them" (*Legacy* 161). On this essay, see James K. Chandler, *England in 1819: The Politics of Literary Culture and the Case of Romantic Historicism* (Chicago: U of Chicago P, 1998), 114–20.

[41] Susan Stewart, *Poetry and the Fate of the Senses* (Chicago: U of Chicago P, 2002), 367n32.

but which are more often registered as discomfort or resistance" (10, 12). The complacency that would seem to govern the georgic mode and infiltrate a georgic-inflected science and literature breaks apart precisely as it receives these disruptive sensations of weather from abroad. What the georgic transmits, particularly through an aerial weather, is the unease, the disturbance, the emotional static accompanying transmission itself.

Voices in the Air

> What is . . . important is the metaphoricity of . . . those subjects of the narrative that mutter or mumble . . . or keep a still silence.[42]

In order to communicate something otherwise ineffable about wars beyond their ken, British artists of the late eighteenth and early nineteenth centuries became intimate with the sky, making news of weather. Participating in the changes that created a new meteorology, with detailed knowledge of and attention to the weather, they could impute to its shifting nature a profound responsiveness to distant events as well as intimations of an otherwise unforeseeable future.

Among the consequences of these changing conceptions of the weather was a newly unsettled sense of human agency. On the one hand, human beings were understood to suffer—often in sympathy, as we will see—the effects of an inexorable, even mechanical weather operating now on a global scale. On the other hand, human genius was understood to be capable of harnessing and mastering this weather, that is to say, translating it into something else: if "our sunshine" could become "their rain," perhaps their pain could be systematically smoothed into our gain.

In poetry, the tension between these competing options revealed itself most dramatically in the weather's communicative function, in the topos of its voice. One strain of poetry in the Napoleonic era heard inchoate but affecting voices in the weather, echoing Cowper's lines where "the voice of all [earth's] elements" might "preach the gen'ral doom." Such voices conveyed to their listeners a wartime beyond control emotionally and epistemologically. Almost in repudiation of that helplessness, however, an alternate strain of poetry translated the waywardness of weather into the clear pronouncements of elevated genius and human potency—as with Franklin's lightning rod or Beccaria's experiment, where the storms of the world circled by command over the surface of his brilliant self. Of course, if genius could tame storms, it could also promulgate them: by 1800 the question of who controlled the course of the

42 Bhabha 18.

world's weather, and by extension the medium of wartime, became an urgent political, military, and poetic concern.

Amelia Alderson was particularly sensitive to the international climate of wartime, casting several of her poems about the war as addresses to weather conditions. For Alderson, war often figures as eternal winter, as in her "Ode, Written on the Opening of the Campaign" (1795), where the coming of war denaturalizes the seasons, turning back the advent of spring. In "Ode on the Present Times, 27th January 1795," she constructs a more elaborate version of the distempered climate of war, coupling it with a distinctive, if not distinct, aurality:

> But Winter! not to thee alone
>   Their heart-appalling sway they owe,
> For they to war's despotic throne
>   As tributary subjects bow;
> War, who bids trembling Europe gasp,
> With wild convulsions in his bloody grasp.
>   Whence yonder groans? O wretched land!
>   Poland, from thee, alas! they came. . . . (Bennett 140)

Like Robinson's contemporaneous "January 1795," Alderson's "Ode" mixes war with winter weather so the border between natural and man-made is blurred. The very lines on the page seem blown by gusting winds. With those gusts comes the intimation that wintry desolation is making its way from Poland to Great Britain. Having ravaged central Europe, the offspring of war, Famine, Poverty, and Want, will fly cloud-borne to England.[43]

Mediating war fought at a distance through the weather, conceiving of the weather as bearing that war, allowed poets to present the effects of war as if immediate, readily felt and absorbed. The weather can brush up against your skin, soak into your pores, and sound in your ears. Alderson and some of her contemporaries recognize weather especially as the audible news of war: they discern international voices, moans and groans which, like radio transmissions of sheer emotion, move with and in the weather.[44] In describing the conditions of the war's grievous and unnatural climate, Alderson's "Ode" relays to readers groans from Poland, laments from France, and "the song of victory" mingled with "despair's appalling tone" from Belgium, as if these affecting cries too are carried from east to west on the icy blast, as if war-as-weather comes with a

---

[43] Both poets echo and redirect Thomson's famous depiction of the winter, where the violence of a snowstorm results in the chilling brightness of a new, absolutist state. See "Still Winter Falls," above.

[44] For a similar use of the audible pains of war, see the anonymous poem "Effects of War" (1794), in Bennett 108–10.

warning and moaning, if not fully articulate voice. Not all meteorological noise conveyed dismal news; in the poem "On the Peace" (1802), for example, clouds and winds are transformed into singing "angels in the listening sky, / The widow's bosom to relieve," offering the consoling image of a sky responsive to human cries (Bennett 275). More frequently, though, weather broadcasts wartime suffering: "The din begins, the thunder shakes the deep, / From thousand mouths now hear the fatal doom / That summons mortals to eternal sleep."[45] In the book of Genesis, Abel's blood calls out from the ground; here it calls from the skies. If such weather has a theological and supernatural cast, associated as it is with the voices of spirits, fiends, and angels, it is also resolutely tied to inordinate and unanswerable mortal pain. The helplessness extends to the listener as well as the crier. The almost occult nature of these voices insists, moreover, that such weather is outlandish, unnatural, hardly to be borne.

The outcry of these poems thus harkens back to the old weather science, which imagined weather phenomena as the "effusions," "eruptions" and "affections" of a vulnerable human body. The wailing sound also offers a sensory equivalent for the old weather's signature smell of gunpowder; less precise, perhaps, but still affecting in a way that exceeds empirical fact.[46] While clinging to aspects of the old weather science, these poems nonetheless understand the more global reach of the new. And even as it exceeds the contemporary structure of the news, such sound-filled weather often arises from specific moments of violence: hence the insistent dating of many of these poems, which appeared in periodicals alongside more conventional news items. Indeed, poets of this wartime seem to be writing in advance of later technologies of broadcasting. The word "broadcast," we might note, had its origins in eighteenth-century agricultural innovations (referring to grain sown "over the whole surface" of the field, rather than in specific rows), which reveal its georgic inclination. According to the *OED*, its first use in the contemporary sense of the mass dissemination of information occurred in 1922, when the *Times of London* reported a request that the postmaster-general include "weather forecasts in any broadcast distribution of information by wireless telephony."[47] We now take for granted that you can hardly broadcast news without also broadcasting the weather, but we can see in romantic poems the prehistory of that conjunction. One might argue that in fusing the weather with the news, broadcasting invites the sort of response Andrew Ross identifies in his essay on

[45] T. O., "On a Late Victory at Sea" (1794), in Bennett 130.

[46] On affecting sound, see Geoffrey Hartman, "Words and Wounds," in *Saving the Text: Literature, Derrida, Philosophy* (Baltimore: Johns Hopkins UP, 1981); Stewart, chap. 2; and Goodman's account in the case of Wordsworth, *Georgic Modernity*, chap. 4.

[47] See the *Oxford English Dictionary*, 2nd ed. (1989), s.v. "broadcast," A.3. The first use of the word, as an adjective, is listed as 1767.

the Weather Channel, where weather becomes the only news, and news is thus naturalized. The agricultural origin of the word, however, indicates that broadcasting has a less direct or predictable yield.[48] In these poems especially, the broadcast voices are still too freakish and unsettling—traces of that georgic unease—to resolve into anything like the natural course of things.

These representations of listeners suffering the weather, and sympathizing with the sounds that it carried, were not the only sort of representation encouraged by the new, georgic science of weather. Other poets found in that science a remarkable engine of translation and control. In their poems, weather and war are drained of affecting, pain-filled voices and become, instead, the terrain of the Mind. On the one hand we have, for instance, the wind of Coleridge's "Dejection: An Ode," which bears the groaning and shuddering of fallen soldiers; on the other the weather of his "Frost at Midnight," which famously provides a medium of pure communication, an "eternal language." I have already located Coleridge's "Frost at Midnight" in wartime, and in the tradition of wartime poetry; this conversation poem also reveals the affinity of his poetic genius with the new, speculative meteorology of the day. At the outset of the poem, Coleridge has hushed the weather: the freezing cold outside is windless, and "'Tis calm indeed! So calm, that it disturbs / And vexes meditation with its strange / And extreme silentness" (8–10).[49] The poem proceeds in this near vacuum of external noise or motion, as if in a scientist's experimental chamber. At the end of the mental experiment conducted there—one is tempted to say on the basis of the experiment—the poet elevates his son ("thou shalt wander like a breeze"), produces imaginary clouds, and with these transformations, introduces an alternative weather. The remediated climate, generated from the internal movements of the poet's mind (his memories, anticipations, and associative leaps), and structured as a move from earth to sky, allows him to predict a peaceful future for his infant son: "Therefore all seasons shall be sweet to thee" (66). Coleridge's verse mirrors Luke Howard's vision of an intelligible, translateable weather:

> [the clouds] image in their bulk both lake and shores
> And mountain crags: so shalt thou see and hear
> The lovely shapes and sounds intelligible
> Of that eternal language, which Thy God
> Utters, who from eternity doth teach
> Himself in all, and all things in himself. (57–62)

---

[48] Ross himself avoids the equation of an "advanced form of weather consciousness" with sheer "false weather consciousness," adding, "it is difficult, if not impossible, to say what kind of weather consciousness is generated" by the media (125–26).

[49] Coleridge, *Samuel Taylor Coleridge*, 87–89.

Breeze and cloud serve as emblems and guarantors of an imagination that will no longer languish in the dim cloisters, in the waiting and doubt that haunted earlier passages of the poem. Such a mind—mobile, and in translation between father and son—will survive the threat of war-as-winter.[50]

Barbauld's "Eighteen Hundred and Eleven" makes the movement of such a mind even more impersonal and political, crucial not to the future of the individual but to the future of civilization. Though the poem begins with the dramatic concatenation of weather and worldwide warfare beyond control, the unruly state of the weather is gradually converted to an easy-to-follow spirit. Compare the opening lines of the poem, "Still the loud death drum, thundering from afar, / O'er the vext nations pours the storm of war," with its conclusion:

> For see,—to other climes the Genius soars. . . .
> And lo, even now, midst mountains wrapt in storm,
> On Andes' heights he shrouds his awful form; . . .
> Sudden he calls:—"'Tis now the hour!" he cries,
> Spreads his broad hand, and bids the nations rise. . . .
> Ardent, the Genius fans the noble strife,
> And pours through feeble souls a higher life,
> Shouts to the mingled tribes from sea to sea,
> And swears,—Thy world, Columbus, shall be free. (321, 323–24, 327–28,
>   331–34)

Weather here functions as mere clothing for an allegorical Genius, who has assumed the role of mobile global agent. Genius "calls" and "cries"; it "Shouts . . . And swears" in distinct, phatic language. Instead of storms of war poured from death-drums, we have an ethereal "higher life" poured from the fonts of Genius. Barbauld seems to agree with Alderson that the weather of war is not altogether natural, but she counters it less with the voice of suffering bodies than with an improved climate. In a departure from her initial georgic warning to heed the weather, Barbauld insists late in the poem that "Science and Art [can] . . . / New mould a climate and create the soil, / Subdue the rigour of the northern Bear, / O'er polar climes shed aromatic air" (299–302). From the climate of war, we turn to another, better, man-made climate, where winter is wisely under control and unthreatening.

Barbauld eventually translates weather into a heady experience even less tethered than in Beccaria's experiment; for her it becomes the accomplice to a

---

[50] For a more ambivalent meditation on weather and the power of poetic imagination, which is at the same time a more explicit consideration of weather as war, see Wordsworth's "To the Clouds" (1808).

soaring, fanning, pouring, shouting Genius. In the culminating movement of the poem, when the agitations of global weather are replaced by the figure of disembodied Genius soaring from east to west, Barbauld appears to subsume the dangers of war into the conventional question about the proper climate for genius—and its partner in climatological lore, liberty.[51] In short, when the impending storm clouds we are asked to watch in the opening of "Eighteen Hundred and Eleven" convert into the "mighty impulse" of Genius floating from continent to continent, Barbauld's poem demonstrates one consequence of a meteorology veering toward theories of electricity: that "mighty impulse" wanders lonely as a cloud but somehow independent of clouds. If weather has turned to charged atmosphere, what has happened to war in the poem? Has it too become a function of "Genius"—a vaguely "noble strife"?

Barbauld's conversion of weather into the effects of a commanding genius betrays a desire we have seen before: to organize the war as if from outside wartime, to make it submit to human intelligence in a way that would guarantee a peaceful future. This would seem to be the promise of the new weather science, which indeed imagined its knowledge as standing above and organizing cataclysmic change and irregularity into a perceptible and ultimately benevolent pattern. But the coordination of genius with weather remains a troubled affair, not entirely mastered by scientists or poets. Genius could not be easily dislocated from war, as these poems themselves demonstrate. Geoffrey Hartman warns that an alliance between the genius of poetry and the English Character remained "precarious" in late eighteenth-century poetry, since "[a] demonic agent . . . [was] never far away" ("Genius" 333). For Hartman the demonic genius is conventionally "oriental" and averse to Enlightenment reason; but for Barbauld and her contemporaries, the more obvious candidate threatening to blow in from the east was Napoleon Bonaparte.

Napoleon figured as the uncanny double of the weather scientist, the supernatural supplement of a rational, benevolent system. As "meteor," "comet," or fiendishly flashing "genius" of liberty, he appeared in British popular literature to command the world's weather. In his "Meteorological Register" (1802–3), a retired naval officer and amateur meteorologist played heavily on the association:

> The most remarkable [occurrence] this year, is a threatened appearance of an infernal and transitory meteor, which with its diabolical Satellites have already laid waste a great part of Europe; and now in its northern course of devastation, threatens the destruction of this happy Island by storm and fire. . . . (qtd. in Hamblyn 149)

[51] Geoffrey H. Hartman, "Romantic Poetry and the Genius Loci," *Beyond Formalism: Literary Essays 1958–1970* (New Haven: Yale UP, 1970), 318.

Wordsworth famously pays Bonaparte tribute in the "unfather'd vapour" of the Simplon Pass; less famously, in the poetry of the periodicals, he is a "Meteor" whose "baleful rays" wilt France; his warriors are "like the Desart's burning breath, / Where'er they rush'd they scatter'd death" (Bennett 277–78).[52] The personification of his own global weather-and-war science, Napoleon changed the climate irrevocably. Thus Barbauld's soaring Genius, with his promise of climatic and political greenhouses, could be read as a corrective to Napoleon's wayward comet. As erratic meteor, Napoleon operated according to an outdated yet ominous meteorology, but he also appeared as the commanding genius of the new weather science. In the rhetoric of popular poetry, he was like Beccaria, the mastermind amid the storms of global war, but his machinations were unpredictable, malevolent. If the new weather science moved toward an impersonalizing of global forces, moving above and beyond individual bodies, Napoleon was the name given to the demonic, inflated, repersonalization of such forces for readers in Great Britain. Unlike the affective supplement offered by the moaning voices in the air, Napoleon kept intact the new emphasis on war and weather as a struggle of mental forces.

Even the speculative abstraction of weather in the figure of genius, even that urge toward an air-borne weather, demonstrates its connection to a particular wartime climate. In the often tense negotiations over control of the weather—whether it will remain in the domain of the creative artist or the political leader, whether it will carry the sound of pain or the voice of ideology, whether it will progress in a wayward or intelligible fashion—these poems echo the concerns of the weather scientist while pointing to something "somehow beyond control." What continue to seep out are those inarticulate moans and groans, "those subjects of the narrative that mutter or mumble . . . or keep a still silence," troubling historical mediation, troubling too the easy translation of any metaphor. These poems then register, perhaps more subtly, a new valuation of war. In Barbauld's version of the weather, in Coleridge's clouds, and in the imagined figure of Napoleon's genius, war had the potential to become something you watched, read, and perhaps feared rather than something you suffered. Unattached to specific pieces of ground, war sustained itself through the forces of an impersonal mind. It could become an intellectual rather than a physical contest, a shifting system conducted outside of and beyond bodies via prosthetic techniques. Moving ceaselessly on a global scale, according to charted patterns, war had the potential to become an all-enveloping system, indeed, the regular and recognizable fluctuations of the everyday. The first modern war thus took place, for many readers and writers, in the skyscape of this new weather.

[52] See also the satiric poem "Buonaparte," in Anon., *The Meteors* (London: A. and J. Black, and H. D. Symonds, 1799), 17–25.

CHAPTER FOUR

Everyday War

Perhaps, these lyric poems propose, the weather can serve as a forceful wartime medium, broadcasting the voices or at least the sounds of distant violence, carrying in its currents an audible, palpable sense of suffering elsewhere. This was one way war at a distance could invade—affectively and effectively—the home front. An air-borne sense of suffering, however, escaped like involuntary sighs or moans from a growing, more rationalized understanding of global weather and global war. The new meteorology aimed to regularize violent extremes into an intelligible system, less felt than observed, and predicated on a predictable and continuous nature. The ambivalence of wartime that has been traced throughout this study—here or there, felt or unfelt, strange or known, aberrant event or ongoing condition—extends itself into the circumambient air, the atmosphere.

There remain other ways for distant warfare to return to the body and be brought back down to earth. They can be found even in the rejection of the affecting, lyric voice, the voice Anne Elliot, in Jane Austen's *Persuasion*, cautions a young naval officer to resist because it seems to communicate vulnerability: it could not, she argues, be "safely enjoyed by those who enjoyed it completely"; it does not "rouse and fortify the mind."[1] The heroine of the novel has something important to share with the sailor. In bringing her military men home, and in fashioning a wide-ranging conversation between Anne's situation and the situation of these sailors, Austen explores an alternative but no less risky grounding for wartime: the everyday. Through her novelistic construction of the everyday, she composes a negative history of wartime—built less of rousing fortification than of rejection, unspoken pains, and unaccountable failings and fallings. This chapter takes up the everyday, our legacy from Romanticism, as another structure of modern wartime, indeed as a structure of feeling akin to trauma, conveying in its gaps and silences an unrecoverable, absent sense of suffering.

[1] Jane Austen, *Persuasion*, *The Novels of Jane Austen*, vol. 5, 3rd ed. (Oxford: Oxford UP, 1933, 1988), 100–1. All references to this text will be cited parenthetically by page number and abbreviated *P*.

A History of Suffering

> The traumatized, we might say, carry an impossible history within them, or they become themselves the symptom of a history that they cannot entirely possess.[2]

In her novel *Persuasion*, Jane Austen offers up symptoms of a history not entirely possessed. The past presented in the novel is incomplete, interrupted. Over the narrative hangs the unaccountable weight of "eight years and a half ago," a period of romance which the novel conjures only to dismiss in a few paragraphs. "A short period of exquisite felicity . . . and but a short one.— Troubles soon arose" (26). The narrator emphasizes the brevity of a lost love which, now in the form of enduring pain, possesses her heroine, Anne Elliot. "A few months had seen the beginning and the end of their acquaintance"— already the narrator diminishes the affair:

> but, not with a few months ended Anne's share of suffering from it. Her attachment and regrets had, for a long time, clouded every enjoyment of youth; and an early loss of bloom and spirits had been their lasting effect. (*P* 28)

Loss of bloom, loss of spirits, loss of money, loss of status: characters in *Persuasion* are variously in danger of having the present slip away. "Tell me not that I am too late, that such precious feelings are gone for ever," Captain Wentworth writes desperately, and he too uses the language of pain to underscore his own share of suffering: "You pierce my soul. I am half agony, half hope" (*P* 237). In the end the novel, like Shakespeare's *A Winter's Tale*, reassures us that love can, magically, come back to life. But even that resuscitation remains tenuous, and not without the threat of further pain. The narrator closes the novel by reminding us that the moment of happiness may not last and troubles may arise again. United with her love, Anne Elliot "gloried in being a Sailor's wife," but had to "pay the tax of quick alarm"—dread of his being called back to war (*P* 252). What does endure, filling most of the narrative and more than eight years, testifying to love and loss, is suffering. One name for that history of suffering is the everyday, a term often invoked to characterize the world of Austen's novels. Another name for that history, which cannot be possessed but possesses the novel, is war.

Like others versions of the everyday constructed in the Romantic period, Austen's in *Persuasion* emerges from the reality of worldwide war. Reading these unaccountable histories of pain and loss confirms the thought that the everyday is another form of wartime. This chapter thus extends claims made

---

[2] Cathy Caruth, *Trauma: Explorations in Memory* (Baltimore: Johns Hopkins UP, 1995), 5.

at the end of the previous chapter: in tracking the itinerary of pain and suffering into the realm of Austen's novel, it tracks anew the mediation of distant war, this time not through lyric poetry but rather through the narrative structures of domestic realism. Sending my argument about modern wartime into what might be called the romantic home of everydayness, the chapter also pursues a distinct strand of thinking about the everyday, from its philosophical and aesthetic roots in Romanticism into twentieth-century critical theory. Throughout I find the everyday informed by the language, the features, and the affective resonance of wartime. Austen and her contemporaries allow us to see with specificity how modern war—with its national armies, its tendency to erase the line between combatants and noncombatants, its global reach—is the history that possesses, perhaps determines our own current thinking about the everyday. At moments when war appears to have no horizon, it seems appropriate to acknowledge, as Austen's *Persuasion* does, this marriage of war and the everyday, but also to call into question, as the best romances do, the inevitability of this marriage.

For Austen, the everyday is the elastic form in which she tries to hold the recent history of the Napoleonic wars; by understanding the everyday as a record of pain and alienation, as Anne's story, Austen makes it permeable to the suffering of war. The everyday, with its rhythms of routine and accident, of endless waiting and unforeseen returns, provides a chronotope for Austen's novels; in *Persuasion* it reveals itself to be as well the register, the telling surface, on which to read traces of nearly ineffable loss. Distressed, anxious, and punctuated by confusion and pain, the everyday Austen creates for *Persuasion* is, I want to argue, another form of wartime; more and less than a container, it is the medium through which she evokes the costs of prolonged war.

Like the wartime of Cowper's influential poem, Austen's everyday composes itself of uncertainties and gaps of time; his lost hour grows into her lost years, increasing the historical burden of Cowper's "unceasing lapses." Shadowing Anne's history, and even more sketchy in its details, is Frederick Wentworth's naval service in Britain's wars with Napoleon. Much of the drama of the novel depends on the reader—and Anne—not having access to Wentworth's "share of suffering" during those years. Even the Musgrove sisters' eager reading about his ships and postings in the Navy List merely points to the scarcity of information. With danger apparently behind him, Wentworth can now affect a nonchalance, who knows how hard-won, and joke about the less than seaworthy ship that was his first command. The satisfaction later afforded by his love letter to Anne, which arrives at the climax of the novel, rests in part in its revelation of how much pain he has borne. Here Austen seems to eclipse the sufferings of warfare with the trials of love, and wipe away both with the romance of her ending. But why then does she leave the novel with the "dread of a future war" and that nagging tax of quick alarm? And why does she set her novel so carefully in 1814, the year known as the False Peace, after which "troubles soon arose" and Europe found itself again at war?

When the Duke of Wellington wrote that "The history of the battle [Waterloo] is not unlike the history of a ball," he was not being flippant: both, he went on to insist, are histories impossible to grasp.[3] Despite their seeming punctuality (one can usually assign them a date), both ball and battle are composed as much of eventlessness (a fraught waiting-for-something-to-happen, or meantime) or unfelt, mechanical behavior (repeated recourse to one's equipment) as distinct event. Beyond these similarities stretches the ineffable affect of each occasion, which leaves its representation open to the seemingly disaffected modes of formality, mockery, or understatement. Thus a British sailor, recording in his diary the "dreadful massacre" of his companions that took place in November 1803, provides a characteristic account of how much cannot be told:

> Wilkinson [the captain] makes his appearance at the entrance of the gangway and salutes his bleeding[,] partly exhausted first lieutenant in this manner[:] "Well, Pridham, you have had a fine night's diversion. What the devil were you all about to let the damn'd Croppoes [the French] give you such an infernal drubbing? Why you must have been all asleep along side her." "Capt. Wilkinson," answered Mr. Pridham, "Sir, had you been there perhaps you might have done some great exploit, and as for sleeping we are all convinced you would not have found much opportunity to sleep, there was quite the contrary sort of employment."[4]

When, in her last complete novel, Jane Austen, that great historian of the ballroom, attempts something "not unlike" a history of war, she does so precisely by calling the reader's attention to a negative sort of history, a lost history, a history of what seems unable to be told. Through this untold and nearly eventless history—so laden with silence, litotes, and negation that her first draft of the final chapter had at its heart a series of pronounced "No's"—she demonstrates another crucial way modernity binds together the structures of military

[3] Qtd. in John Keegan, *The Face of Battle* (Harmondsworth, UK: Penguin, 1976), 117. Compare Walt Whitman, writing fifty years later, during the American Civil War:

> Such was the war. It was not a quadrille in a ball-room. Its interior history will not only never be written—its practicality, minutiae of deeds and passions, will never be even suggested. The actual soldier of 1862–'65, North and South, with all his ways, . . . will never be written—perhaps must not and should not be.

"The Real War Will Never Get in the Books," in *Prose Works 1892, Vol. 1: Specimen Days*, ed. Floyd Stovall (New York: New York UP, 2007).

[4] John Wetherell, *The Adventures of John Wetherell*, ed. C. S. Forester (London: Michael Joseph, 1994), 78. All references to this text will be cited parenthetically by page number and abbreviated *W*.

violence and the everyday.[5] In following William Galperin's recent suggestion that Austen writes as a conscious historian of the fate of the everyday during those tumultuous years in Great Britain and drawing out, as he advises, the possible histories "that are always close at hand" if left unwritten in her novels, I hope to call forth Austen's history of everyday war along with the everydayness of modern war.[6]

In doing so, I will also draw out a barely submerged preoccupation with the troubling but enduring marriage of the everyday with war shared by twentieth-century theory. The everyday emerges as an object of significant historical and theoretical interest in the wake of the Second World War. Signaling the shift from wartime to its aftermath, attention to the everyday appears to demonstrate an ability to situate oneself at a distance from wartime itself; it takes the survivor's perspective. And yet twentieth-century theorists of the everyday seem eager to hold on to or perpetuate war, to realize in the everyday what Michel Foucault calls "the continuation of war by other means" a reformulation of what Joseph Fawcett, as seen above, had identified in 1803 as "inactive war."[7] From this point of view, the postwar everyday maintains under the veneer of peace the work of war even after its formal end.

As a philosophical pivot point, however, the everyday had emerged earlier, during those world wars preceding and concurrent with the Napoleonic period, where reflection back upon war was barely imaginable. "Long months of peace . . . / Are mine in prospect," Wordsworth writes tentatively at the outset of the 1805 *Prelude*; but he has to admit the fantasy of this view, inserting the parenthetical, "(if such bold word [peace] accord / With any promises of human life)."[8] This earlier everyday understood itself from within wartime, absorbing, if not embracing, war and its pains. Comparing romantic representations with twentieth-century discussions of everyday war calls into question not the operations of war, which are in both cases almost always assumed; rather it calls into question peace. Romantic writers found it nearly impossible

---

[5] The canceled chapters 10 and 11 of an earlier draft of *Persuasion* are reprinted in Appendix A of Bree's edition. In a remarkable passage, Austen finally reunites her lovers precisely through a negative truth: "'No Sir. . . . There is no message. . . .—There is no Truth in any such report.' 'No Truth in any *part* of it?'—'None.'" The two subsequently share "a silent, but a very powerful Dialogue" (263). The entire chapter 10 abounds in negatives, double negatives, and silences. Austen, *Persuasion*, ed. Linda Bree (Peterborough, Ont.: Broadview, 1998).

[6] William Galperin, *The Historical Jane Austen* (Philadelphia: U of Pennsylvania P, 2003), 12. See esp. chap. 1 and 8.

[7] Michel Foucault, *"Society Must Be Defended": Lectures at the College de France, 1975–76*, ed. Mauro Bertani and Alessandro Fontana, trans. David Macey (New York: Picador, 2003), 48 and following. On these issues, I have profited from Chris J. Cuomo, "War Is Not Just an Event: Reflections on the Significance of Everyday Violence," *Hypatia* 11.4 (Autumn 1996): 30–45.

[8] William Wordsworth, *The Prelude, 1799, 1805, 1850*, ed. Jonathan Wordsworth, M. H. Abrams, and Stephen Gill (New York: Norton, 1979), I: 26–29.

to imagine any space or time free from the pains—Austen's "tax"—of warfare. Many twentieth-century theorists, by contrast, find it not impossible, but rather undesirable or disadvantageous, to conjure peace. The twenty-first century, with its promise of enduring global warfare, invites us to review the romantic position and reconsider our subscription to a critical practice that relies upon, elaborates, and promotes the logic of war.

After sketching a history of the marriage of war and the everyday in contemporary thought, I will return to *Persuasion* to show how this marriage infiltrates and transforms not only any understanding of peace, but understanding itself—especially (and again) historical understanding. My method prompts me to arrange another improbable marriage, this time between two contemporaneous versions of everyday war: Austen's novel and the aforementioned diary of a navy sailor, John Wetherell. Military historians have commented on the unprecedented number of journals and diaries by "ordinary" military men that found their way into print in England during and after the Napoleonic wars. The archive of written materials for Waterloo, for instance, exceeds that of any battle fought before the twentieth century.[9] Accounts of the war in participants' personal letters or published memoirs brought home the fighting precisely as ordinary experience, thus publicizing a new terrain for the everyday.[10] Wetherell's diary shadows and rearranges my sense of Austen's novel, just as the untold war experience of Captain Wentworth haunts the novel's account of its heroine's experience. Begun in 1803 (after the failure of the Treaty of Amiens) and interrupted in 1814 (the year that frames *Persuasion*), the *Adventures of John Wetherell* provides one way of imagining the nearly lost eight years around and over which the novel is constructed, and it broadens our sense of that wartime everyday while echoing *Persuasion* in unpredictable ways.[11] Joining these two texts may yield some satisfaction, but nevertheless,

---

[9] See Keegan 119; and Rory Muir, *Tactics and the Experience of Battle in the Age of Napoleon* (New Haven: Yale UP, 1998). Muir notes the "extraordinarily rich collection of first-hand British accounts of combat, which appears to be unmatched in any other language" (viii).

[10] Keegan emphasizes the "dramatic" and almost "surreal" approach taken by Romantic painters in their depictions of Napoleonic battles and notes that the major historians of the nineteenth century followed their lead (188–89). However, as Keegan's own reconstruction makes clear, the versions of battle given by participants include partial and very circumstantial descriptions, more aligned with an aesthetic of the everyday.

[11] Forester's edition of Wetherell's journal is an abridged version of the original manuscript, written and reconstructed by Wetherell after he left the king's service. He eventually settled in New York City; there he made fair copy of whatever notes remained with him (he had been shipwrecked many times) and illustrated the text with his own watercolors. Forester argues that the manuscript, though authentic, is not a reliable account, written as it is mostly after the fact. For the purposes of this book, however, Wetherell's accuracy is not significant: what his personal history provides is another mode of recollecting and representing the everyday of those wartime years.

like the union of Anne Elliot and Captain Wentworth, it allows neither closure nor security. Rather, it extends the enigmatic and disturbing qualities of both works, telling all the more of suffering that cannot or has not been told. Reading Austen's *Persuasion* in consort with the diary of an ordinary sailor, we find that the two everyday worlds given to us—domestic and military—cannot be held at a distance from each other. Like more recent conceptions of everyday war, but in a different tonal register, they insist there is no separate peace or, more bluntly, no separation between the structures of everyday and war and thus no ground for peace.

No Peace

For all its spectacular trappings, modern warfare rarely escapes intimacy with the prosaic everyday. Historians have argued that the concept of the everyday arose when the military enterprise of the early modern nation-state "faded as the preeminent activity of elites" and court life replaced camp life as a social and political ground.[12] The ideal of military heroism, so much at odds with the everyday, yielded to the ideal of leisurely gentlemanliness. "There was a 'place' now . . . to notice how pleasant ordinary occupations might be" (Kinser 79). The everyday became charming—witness the paintings of Chardin or Greuze—when warfare was put aside; indeed, it suggested that warfare could be put aside. For the now genteel, no longer warrior classes, the everyday could be cultivated as a reward for such putting aside, a transition repeatedly inscribed in Scott's *Waverley* novels. But by the time of the Revolutionary and Napoleonic wars, when ordinary men rather than battle-trained elites assembled on ship and in camp, the quotidian redefined itself both as the goal of warfare, what one was fighting for; and as the very practice of waging war, the daily routine of ordinary men.[13]

We saw in the first chapter how subsequent wartime readers such as Virginia Woolf appeared almost to blame Austen's contemporaries for sustaining the belief that war could be held separate from everydayness. A conventional

---

[12] Samuel Kinser, "Everyday Ordinary," *diacritics* 22.2 (Summer 1992): 79. For a parallel thought about the historiographical shift from accounts of battles to accounts of social interaction and everyday experience, see Mark Salber Phillips, *Society and Sentiment: Genres of Historical Writing in Britain, 1740–1820* (Princeton: Princeton UP, 2000).

[13] Austen stages set pieces of a national everyday in her other novels: Henry Tilney's outraged (or facetious?) speech to Catherine Morland in *Northanger Abbey*; Emma's relieved reflection upon Donwell Abbey's "Englishness"—different tonal shading, but a similarly nationalized frame for the everyday. See Kinser and Deidre Lynch's helpful insights in "Homes and Haunts: Austen's and Mitford's English Idylls," *PMLA* 115.5 (October. 2000): 1103–8.

reading recalls that Romanticism, at least in the familiar English version, consecrates

> . . . the life
> In common things, the endless store of things
> Rare, or at least so seeming, every day
> Found all about me in one neighborhood. (*Prelude* I: 117–20)

So writes Wordsworth, in a near echo of Austen herself. Wordsworth's task in *Lyrical Ballads* (1798), reports his collaborator Samuel Taylor Coleridge, was to re-create the "charm" of the everyday by "awakening the mind's attention from the lethargy of custom, and directing it to the loveliness and the wonders of the world before us."[14] Such charm, loveliness, and wonder seem a far cry from the violence of war, perhaps deliberately so: Coleridge and Wordsworth write *Lyrical Ballads* at a particularly inauspicious moment in England's global struggle with Napoleon's armies. In the context of this creation of the everyday, we can see how Coleridge's version of Wordsworth's project borrows from Cowper's strategy, developed fifteen years before *Lyrical Ballads*, for celebrating present, everyday charms as therapy for a mind troubled by a world at war. We can turn again to that passage in Cowper's "Winter Evening," where he reads a newspaper filled with the noise of a world at war while quietly carving his "loop-hole of retreat":

> 'Tis pleasant through the loop-holes of retreat
> To peep at such a world; to see the stir
> Of the great Babel, and not feel the crowd;
> To hear the roar she sends through all her gates
> At a safe distance, where the dying sound
> Falls a soft murmur on th' uninjur'd ear. . . .
>
>   I behold
> The tumult, and am still. The sound of war
> Has lost its terrors ere it reaches me;
> Grieves, but alarms me not.[15]

Cowper's speaker would like to pretend—or so it seems at first glance—that war is a mere peep show, a noisy spectacle performed at some distance. Indeed he moves from this announcement to contrast the joys and "intimate delights" of the fireside with the pomp and fuss of a theatrical world, a world of masquerade and "strife." For him, and perhaps still for us, the everyday is not only

[14] Samuel Taylor Coleridge, *Biographia Literaria*, in *Samuel Taylor Coleridge (The Oxford Authors)*, ed. H. J. Jackson (Oxford: Oxford UP, 1985), 314.

[15] William Cowper, *The Task*, in *Poetical Works*, ed. H. S. Milford, 4th ed. (London: Oxford UP, 1967), IV: 88–93, 99–102.

far from the spectacle of war; it is also and by contrast true or real in the face of war's unreality. This truth, too, appears to be the fragile product—and privilege—of distance.

The everyday seemed to serve as the antithesis to warfare, then, the quiet bedrock against which the pageantry of war exploded fitfully, but to which all would return in peace.[16] Bolstered by the cessation of war marked by the Treaty of Amiens in early May 1802, Wordsworth weighed the spectacular genius of Napoleon against the secure power of the everyday in his sonnet "I grieved for Buonaparté":

> Wisdom doth live with children round her knees:
>   Books, leisure, perfect freedom, and the talk
>   Man holds with week-day man in the hourly walk
>   Of the mind's business: these are the degrees
> By which true Sway doth mount; this is the stalk
> True Power doth grow on; and her rights are these.[17]

The poet's grief for the upstart, "battle-trained" emperor gives way to this embrace of a leisure-filled "week-day" routine where manly intercourse about the "mind's business" is sandwiched between proof and promise of reproductivity ("children round her knees," and "the stalk / True Power doth grow on"). The assurances of this scene, its happy repeatability, work to silence the poet's questions about the spectacular man of war.

This insistent splitting of wartime into the powerful and real safety of the everyday versus the dangerous, but distanced and slightly unreal spectacle of military aggression is compelling and widespread in the Romantic period and after. Yet the everyday in this period of imperial expansion was itself simultaneously wedded to an awareness of war: in many cases the everyday emerged as the temporal and experiential structure for wartime, reiterating on home turf a sense, however distant and haunting, of combat. After all, *Lyrical Ballads*, that locus of everyday "charm," is famously populated by the residue of a violent age: vagrants and paupers, thoughtless murder and untimely deaths. A careful reading of Cowper, too, as I have tried to demonstrate elsewhere, exposes the threat of war ever-present within his celebration of fireside pursuits, even as his poem on the Sofa calls forth echoes of the *Iliad* and *Aeneid*.

---

[16] In *The Theatres of War: Performance, Politics and Society, 1793–1815* (Oxford: Clarendon, 1995), Gillian Russell finds the military in these years making itself visible to the English public through a calculated exhibitionism: on parade in ceremonial reviews, staged reenactments of battles, and theater performances starring officers, not to mention the flash on the street of a military uniform. See also Jerome Christensen, *Romanticism at the End of History* (Baltimore: Johns Hopkins UP, 2000), who argues that with Romanticism "[w]artime becomes modern as it becomes spectacle" (4).

[17] Wordsworth, "1801 [I Grieved for Buonaparte]," in *The Poems*, ed. John O. Hayden, vol. 1 (Harmondsworth: Penguin, 1977), 558–59.

Yes, "dying sounds" of violence fall softly on the "uninjur'd ear," but they cannot do so without hinting at other dying, other falls, and ears that can be, have been, injured. Similarly, the innocent pleasures of the evening cannot fully escape the world outside Cowper's retreat: a "clear voice" sings "in the charming strife triumphant still"; a needle, a "threaded steel" flies swiftly to its target; scripture reading recalls "[t]he dangers we have 'scap'd . . . / The disappointed foe, . . . / . . . life preserv'd and peace restor'd."[18] The distance of war is itself a constructed illusion: whatever promise of refuge they offer, Cowper knows that both "loop-hole" and "retreat" are fundamentally military terms. Intimations of warfare seep in throughout Cowper's "Winter's Evening"; they shape his "season of peace" and do so unspectacularly. In such moments, the literature of the Romantic period reveals the everyday not as a zone of peace in contrast to a distant war, but as the unspectacular register or medium of wartime.[19] This revelation Austen, like so many others of her generation, inherits from Cowper, her favorite poet.

The coincidence of war and the everyday is perhaps more familiar to us in twentieth-century theories of the everyday. Though these theories do not usually align themselves with Romanticism, indeed might understand themselves at odds with matters romantic, they offer hints that the roots of everyday war lie in the Napoleonic era, during those earlier world wars. Romantic meditations on everyday war are shrouded with irony, negation, and resignation, written as they were amid a decades-long military struggle. Written, for the most part, in that extended period known as the Cold War, postwar and subsequently poststructuralist theories tend rather to celebrate the coincidence of the everyday and war. Romantic texts do not share poststructuralism's investment in never-ending, ubiquitous conflict, though both traditions begin from the same premise: the absence of peace.

Much of the theorizing about the everyday since World War II in fact trumpets its dissatisfaction with the pleasures—or maybe illusions—of peace. Consider Henri Lefebvre, who in 1945 came down from the Pyrenees, where he had been hiding as a Resistance officer, and brought to the press his seminal work, *Critique of Everyday Life*. Rather than an alternative to war, Lefebvre found in the everyday both truth and a recasting of war: "We fail to see [the human facts] where they are, namely in humble, familiar, everyday objects . . . we seek [human truth] in the clouds or in mysteries, whereas it is waiting for

---

[18] Cowper IV: 162–63, 165, 185–87.

[19] On this passage in *The Task*, see Kevis Goodman's "The Loophole in the Retreat: The Culture of News and the Early Life of Romantic Self-Consciousness," *South Atlantic Quarterly* 102.1 (Winter 2003): 25–52. Goodman prefers to read the "loophole" primarily as a passage or conduit for information, veering away from its first definition as "a narrow vertical opening . . . to allow of the passage of missiles" (*OED*).

us, besieging us on all sides."[20] There is an echo, grown aggressive, of Coleridge's description of Wordsworth's project: "awakening the mind's attention . . . and directing it to the loveliness and the wonders of the world before us." That Lefebvre imagines truth besieging us—rather than, say, attacking us—is telling, for a siege is where warfare hits home most dramatically, obliterating any dream of distance. The charm and wonder of the everyday surrender to what Lefebvre can now claim as the cachet of a war surrounding us "on all sides."

Lefebvre's influence on thinking about the everyday was profound, informing the work of his younger compatriots even as they shed his Marxist underpinnings and residual psychoanalytic bent. Michel Foucault's work in *Discipline and Punish*, for instance, argues that the military practices of the eighteenth century were the spawning ground of a new type of everydayness, of "disciplinary tactics" which allow "both the characterization of the individual as individual and the ordering of a given multiplicity."[21] In Foucault's account, beginning in Prussia in the eighteenth century and culminating in the armies of Napoleon, the European military helped organize the ordinary individual within a system of rules, routines, and practices, thereby fashioning both a disciplined individual and the concept of ordinary life as an affair of daily timetables, charted motions, performed duties (hence the echoing terms ordinary, ordinance, ordnance, *ordonnance*). An ordinary was the lowest rank of sailor in the British navy, the equivalent of a private in the army: the terms only reinforce Foucault's larger argument. His understanding of discipline shows how the everyday can be aligned smoothly with not only the modern army but also the clock time of historicism and the mass media, discussed above in chapter 2. Here he extends and transforms Lefebvre's vision of a besieging everyday into a disciplined, internalized ordinary. Whereas Lefebvre would have us awaken and presumably surrender to the everyday truths besieging us, Foucault would have us admit we have already surrendered, and war is the everyday truth to which we have been conscripted.

The implications of this intercourse between war and the everyday escalate in Michel de Certeau's *The Practice of Everyday Life* (1984), which takes the violence of the everyday Foucault has internalized, routinized, and historicized and opens it back up to surprise—and glamour. For de Certeau and the cultural critics who follow in his wake, the practice of everyday life *is* the practice of "the everyday art of war," not in terms of its military orderliness, but rather in its "battles, or games between the strong and the weak," its ceaseless

---

[20] Henri Lefebvre, *Critique of Everyday Life*, trans. John Moore, pref. Michel Trebitsch (London: Verso, 1991), 132.

[21] Michel Foucault, *Discipline and Punish: The Birth of the Prison*, trans. Alan Sheridan, 2nd ed. (New York: Vintage, 1995), 149.

strategies, tactics, maneuvers, deployments.[22] In de Certeau's vision of life during wartime—that is, everyday experience—war designates an exuberant and bloodless resistance to the disciplinary order:

> Dwelling, moving about, speaking, reading, shopping, and cooking are activities that seem to correspond to the characteristics of tactical ruses and surprises: clever tricks of the "weak" within the order established by the "strong," . . . hunter's tricks, maneuverable, polymorph mobilities, jubilant, poetic, and warlike discoveries. (40)

War punctuates and infiltrates daily life, but without obvious suffering or pain. De Certeau's optimism and excitement for this project contrast strongly with Foucault's more somber pronouncements. In *The Practice of Everyday Life*, an energizing discovery of the war*like*, a realization of war's open possibilities within the everyday has the potential for revolution. But the dynamic between war and the everyday moves in only one direction. De Certeau does not correlate his generalized view of everyday war with any of the ongoing wars being fought at the time—most notoriously in Vietnam, Cambodia, and Lebanon. How does a population at war experience "jubilant, poetic, warlike discoveries"? For whom and where is the everyday a war and for whom is it warlike? The uses of everyday war by De Certeau and Foucault lead to different views of the modern subject: one trained within an ever-elaborating military regime; the other discovering warlike openings or ruptures in that regime. Neither has time or space for peace. At the same time, neither really imagines the modern subject, with its discipline or ruses, suffering the carnage of modern war.

Subsequent critics have absorbed and elaborated this line of French postwar, poststructuralist thought.[23] In a helpful 1992 essay on the value of the everyday to the work of cultural studies, Laurie Langbauer positions feminist theorists Gayatri Spivak and Meghan Morris against the likes of Raymond Williams and Stuart Hall, using the war-or-peace of the everyday as faultline. For Langbauer, the British wing of cultural studies threatens to draft the everyday into the service of a congratulatory consensus, into an equation with "the people" or "the popular" or "culture" itself. This communal view of the everyday as those things "we English" all do in common (like Pierre Nora's study of shared French "*lieux de mémoire*") effectively flattens differences,

---

[22] Michel de Certeau, *The Practice of Everyday Life*, trans. Steven Rendall (Berkeley: U of California P, 1984), 39, 34.

[23] Hannah Arendt draws a similar line celebrating violence from Franz Fanon's *The Wretched of the Earth* through Jean-Paul Sartre and the New Left, noting that when Sartre declares that "irrepressible violence . . . is man recreating himself," he also signals his departure from Marxist thought. See Hannah Arendt, *On Violence* (New York: Harcourt, Brace & World, 1970), 11–25. She quotes Sartre on 12.

offering the illusion—Morris will call it the banality—of peace.[24] Unlike Hall or Williams, these feminists profess no queasy "discomfort with real conflict"; they reject peace to embrace "the dilemma of the everyday," hailing it as "a site of irresolvable . . . conflict whose resolution is not simply delayed, but theoretically impossible."[25] Though this version of the everyday may lack the surprise of Lefebvre's "siege" or the excitement of de Certeau's "war-like discoveries," it shares with them an unqualified investment in "irresolvable" conflict.

An inclination toward "irresolvable conflict" commensurate with poststructuralist thought more generally is, as I have said, familiar to us. Yet even in the writings of philosopher Stanley Cavell, who is driving at the everyday from a different route altogether (via American transcendentalism and ordinary language philosophy), we find again the insistent framing of the everyday within the language of war. What interests me about Cavell's treatment is its announced debt to British romantic literature, evident not only in the texts he treats but also in the sobriety of his considerations. If Foucault draws his insights from the institutions of the military at the turn of the eighteenth century, Cavell draws his from the poems of Wordsworth and Coleridge, writing at the same moment. In his 1988 book *In Quest of the Ordinary*, Cavell elaborates his intuition that "ordinary language philosophy is not *a defense* of . . . certain fundamental, cherished beliefs we hold about the world . . . but . . . *a contesting* of that presentation, for, as it were, the prize of the ordinary."[26] Here he chimes, however distantly, with the fundamentally Marxist notion of the belligerent everyday laid out by Lefebvre and de Certeau; ordinary language philosophy is engaged in an everyday contesting. At the same time Cavell positions the ordinary as the goal (ideal perhaps) of a conflict—internalized as a discipline?—which appears to have no end (at least no end in language). Cavell's initial metaphors are only remotely military (defense, contest), yet as his argument moves closer to the texts of Romanticism, the metaphors build in intensity. Especially in the essay "Texts of Recovery: Coleridge, Wordsworth, Heidegger," the prize of the contest is, in Cavell's words, not simply the ordinary but an entire "world." In this essay littered with casual killings, dead bodies, and extinguished worlds, and where it is not clear "how . . . to bring philosophy peace, . . . how to tell whose life is found and whose lost by philosophy," Cavell reads "The Rime of the Ancient Mariner" and the broader

[24] Pierre Nora, *Les Lieux de Mémoire*, 7 vols. (Paris: Gallimard, 1984–92).

[25] Laurie Langbauer, "Cultural Studies and the Politics of the Everyday," *diacritics* 22.1 (Spring 1992), 47, 63, 48. Alan Liu offers an extended meditation on this loss of the "sensus communis" in "Remembering the Spruce Goose: Historicism, Postmodernism, Romanticism," *South Atlantic Quarterly* 102.1 (Winter 2003): 263–75.

[26] Stanley Cavell, *In Quest of the Ordinary: Lines of Skepticism and Romanticism* (Chicago: U of Chicago P, 1988), 4; emphasis added. All subsequent references to this text will be cited parenthetically by page number and abbreviated Q.

project of Romanticism as if they emerged from a world desolated by violence (*Q* 52).[27] "Romanticism's work," he writes,

> here interprets itself . . . as the task of bringing the world back, as to life. This may, in turn, present itself as the quest for a return to the ordinary, or of [the ordinary], a new creation of our habitat; or . . . for the creation of a new inhabitation. (*Q* 52–53)

The echo of Coleridge's desire to renew "the things of every day" by "awakening the mind's attention . . . to the loveliness and the wonders of the world before us" has been considerably dampened. For Cavell that world is *before* us only in the sense that its loveliness is yet to come: indeed, the known world with its familiar rhythms has died or been destroyed. I find it uncanny that in an essay devoted equally to philosophical "lines of skepticism and romanticism" and to the "ordinariness or everydayness of language," Cavell's own language repeatedly recreates the geopolitical situation of England at the turn of the nineteenth century (*Q* 4–8). Coleridge's ancient mariner returns from foreign parts to be "a disturber of [the] peace, which is no peace" at home (*Q* 62). Wordsworth's "Intimations" ode betrays the peculiar "vengefulness" of grief, where one "is always pitching one's battles on alien ground" (*Q* 75). But perhaps Cavell is just painting a picture of the United States at the end of the twentieth century. If he traces one line of twentieth-century philosophy's quest for the ordinary back to the romantics, he is also tracing it back to a world at war, and the consciousness (by his account radically alienated) produced by and responding to such war.[28] I wonder why scholars of Romanticism have taken so long to follow Cavell's lead here, to read Romanticism's preoccupation with the everyday—as well as its embrace of the language of ordinary life—as the mark of a literature saturated by the awareness, conscious or unconscious, of a world lost to war.

Cavell's account of Romanticism alerts us to the historical and theoretical implications of dismissing romantic—or any other—everydayness as simply a false peace. His reading understands a commitment to the everyday—or to the ordinary—as something forged in the face of but also through war's disasters. Here the everyday provides a profoundly wartime registration, internal to the experience of distant war by a population consciously living a "peace which is no peace." Unlike de Certeau's model, where the everyday appears almost as

[27] "To bring philosophy peace" is a phrase Cavell borrows from Ludwig Wittgenstein, who had served with distinction in the First World War.

[28] In the acknowledgments of *Disowning Knowledge: In Six Plays of Shakespeare* (Cambridge: Cambridge UP, 1987), Cavell notes that his first essay on literature—on *King Lear*—bears the scars of the war in Vietnam. For a thoughtful critique of Cavell's reading, see Rei Terada, "Phenomenolality and Dissatisfaction in Coleridge's Notebooks," *Studies in Romanticism* 43.2 (Summer 2004), 259.

a dream of endless and redemptive warfare, an attempt to get back to war, and unlike Foucault's model, which codes everyday or ordinary experience as participation in a regime of (effectively military) violence, as disciplined assent to war, the romantic everyday glimpsed in Cavell's work marks the affective alienation produced in wartime, the pained effort to bind what is present and familiar with another reality, absent and destructive. Tone, as much as content, speaks most distinctly: the romantic everyday, steeped as it is in the consciousness of living in a world at war, registers ruefulness, compulsion, pain, emptiness, futility, loss—all those feelings for which a term like conflict, however elaborated into strategies and tactics, is never adequate.

We might then locate a bridge between theories of the everyday and the history of war in the work of Sigmund Freud, who himself stands between the romantic tradition and a poststructuralist disposition, contemplating a world lost to war. For Freud, writing in the aftermath of World War I, the everyday and war bind themselves together through the mechanism of trauma. In *Beyond the Pleasure Principle*, published in 1920, Freud describes "the organism," indeed sentient life itself, as continually besieged by experience.

> This little fragment of living substance is suspended in the middle of an external world charged with the most powerful energies; and it would be killed by the stimulation . . . if it were not provided with a protective shield against stimuli.[29]

Because the external world is essentially belligerent and life-threatening, we must remain on high alert (Austen's "quick alarm"): "*[p]rotection against* stimuli is an almost more important function . . . than *reception of* stimuli," Freud insists (21; emphasis original). Even though he will go on to theorize trauma as an event for which we have no preparation, Freud's discussion of the organism is itself always on the alert for the traumatic. Insofar as we are constantly (and futilely) defending ourselves against its possibility, trauma, understood here as a warlike incursion or invasion, becomes constituent of the everyday. "We describe as 'traumatic,'" Freud goes on to say, "any excitations from outside which are powerful enough to break through the protective shield"; it is "a breach in an otherwise efficacious barrier" (23). The conditions and threat of war and invasion are repeatedly invoked throughout this crucial passage: "every possible defensive measure" is set in motion while the pleasure principle is "put out of action" (23). Mass "invasions" of stimuli cause other systems in the organism to be "impoverished," "paralysed," and "reduced" (24). By the end, Freud has successfully translated the violence of war in the external world

---

[29] Sigmund Freud, *Beyond the Pleasure Principle*, ed. and trans. Lytton Strachey, intro. Gregory Zilboorg (New York: Norton, 1961), 21.

into the domain of the psyche, an internal world. A history of the recent worldwide devastation gets written in the form of a theory of experience per se. Yet, as with Cowper's loop-hole of retreat, traces of a violent history are not lost in translation but remain written across the surface of Freud's version of the everyday.[30]

It should come as no surprise, then, that later theories of the everyday, derived in response to Freud, often share features with theories of trauma. Like the temporalities of the meantime and prophecy discussed in chapter 2, the everyday and trauma pose a challenge to conventional historicizing. For instance, Cathy Caruth's conception of trauma as the unassimilable, unnarrateable trace of history destined to self-repetition is remarkably close to the conception of the everyday developed in postwar criticism: that is, as routine practices, repeated habitually (perhaps compulsively) and the desires which surround them (Caruth 10–24). The study of the everyday requires an ability to map "a conjunction of habit, desire and accident,"[31] but admits that its object is "practically untellable," and "eludes the grip of forms."[32] The un-meaning of the everyday, Lefebvre writes in *Everyday Life in the Modern World*, "can only become meaningful when transformed into something other than everyday life" (98). Like trauma, in other words, the everyday can never know or tell itself.

In the tradition I have been tracing, the everyday has come to suggest, in fact, a collective or social version, however contested, of an experience Freud assigned to his barely defended "fragment of living substance," that is, trauma. But to call it an experience is already to misname it, for trauma, like the everyday, resides in the area of eventlessness and repetition, of dense if unarticulated affect that, like the meantime of war from chapter 2, or the voices in the air from chapter 3, or indeed like Wellington's ball and battle, defies historical record. Both the everyday and trauma, as we have inherited them through the last two centuries, continually disclose themselves as wartime structures, telling but not telling histories of war.

Even as we see how trauma and the everyday emerge in Freud's theorizing from the backdrop of war, it's important nonetheless to hesitate before making these terms equivalent. The everyday absorbs and is constituted by distant war, but at a different rate, a different tempo from the exceptional cases that for Freud identify trauma (e.g., a train accident). Unlike the shattering event

---

[30] In maintaining these traces, Freud's conversion of the historical trauma of war into his understanding of individual experience avoids the problem identified by Dominick LaCapra when theories substitute a universalizing ahistorical "absence" for a specific, historical "loss." See his "Trauma, Absence, Loss," *Critical Inquiry* 25.4 (1999): 696–727.

[31] Alice Kaplan and Kristin Ross, "Introduction," *Yale French Studies: Special Issue on Everyday Life* 73:9 (1987): 3.

[32] Henri Lefebvre, *Everyday Life in the Modern World*, trans. Sacha Rabinovitch (Piscataway, NJ: Transaction, 1984), 24, 182.

announced by trauma, the everyday structures a shadowing eventlessness. Freud argues, for example, that the sudden influx which he calls trauma occurs where there is a "lack of preparedness for anxiety"; his sense of everyday experience, on the other hand, assumes a stance of preparedness. As illustrated in instances throughout this book, that preparedness may assume the aspect of waiting and anxiety or, as we will see in the case of *Persuasion*, the ethos of caring. In distinguishing between these two states, trauma and the everyday, then, it may be helpful to invoke what Dominick La Capra has called "structural trauma," that is, "not an event but an anxiety-producing condition of possibility related to the potential for historical traumatization" (725). Insofar as the wartime subject (like Freud's organism) attends to the possibility of a violent invasion, and positions itself in relation to violence elsewhere, my understanding of everyday war fits closely with LaCapra's model. It is formed not from a specific loss, but rather from a fundamental absence—perhaps, for our purposes, the absence of peace. Unlike historical trauma, that is, the trauma of event as theorized by Freud, structural trauma does not call for a "working through" but rather a "living with":

> One may well argue that structural trauma related to absence or a gap in existence—with the anxiety, ambivalence, and elation it evokes—may not be cured but only lived with in various ways. Nor may it be reduced to a dated historical event or derived from one; its status is more like that of a condition of possibility of historicity. (727)

LaCapra continues, in language that will resonate for Austen's Anne Elliot: "One may even argue that it is ethically and politically dubious to believe that one can overcome or transcend structural trauma or constitutive absence to achieve full intactness, wholeness, or communal identity" (727). Indeed, in his elaboration of this thing called structural trauma, LaCapra himself builds a bridge, it seems to me, from Freud's more general understanding of besieged experience to his theorizing of (historical) trauma in *Beyond the Pleasure Principle*.

Diverting Away the Time

Persuasion is Austen's most dated novel, carefully located during the False Peace of 1814, which, like the 1803 Peace of Amiens, would prove to be merely another "meantime" or suspension within war. To say, as Joseph Fawcett did in his 1803 *War Elegies*, that the announced peace is not at all peaceful is to identify the historical but also the emotional outline of this postwar novel (written in 1817). As Adela Pinch and others note, there is often a noise or "buzz" in the air around Anne Elliot which, like the stir and roar Cowper aims to keep at a distance from the "uninjur'd ear," nevertheless infiltrates the insular consciousness Austen constructed for her heroine. In *Persuasion*, "noises are frequently the means by which other presences make themselves felt" suggests Pinch, and here she echoes Goodman's reading of the noises in Cowper's "Winter's Evening." The "buzz" in the air, in her ear, serves as a counter to the heroine's— and the reader's—otherwise "soundless absorption in the text."[33] Like the weather's voices in the air, invasive noise is just one medium for the entry of historicity, of the felt experience of wartime, within the novel. Accident, injury, Anne's dizziness and various knocks to various heads—the hammering away at otherwise impervious defenses—all introduce the historical substance of *Persuasion*.

Try as she might, Anne Elliot cannot find peace in peacetime; the peace she thinks she has achieved during her nearly eight years of limbo is too fragile, too easily broken, and, as events in the novel prove, too illusory to count as true peace. Thus, following her first meeting with Wentworth after his return from the navy, Anne Elliot aims to flee the turbulence.

> [S]he began to reason with herself, and try to be feeling less. Eight years, almost eight years had passed, since all had been given up. How absurd to be resuming the agitation which such an interval had banished to distance and indistinctness! What might not eight years do? Events of every description, changes, alienations, removals,—all, all must be comprised in it; and oblivion of the past—how natural, and how certain too! It included nearly a third part of her own life. (*P* 60)

Like Anne's sense of peace, the clock time of historicism, with its clear divisions and oblivions, falls apart through the uncertain chronology of affect: "Alas! with all her reasonings, she found, that to retentive feelings eight years may be little more than nothing" (*P* 60). Anne's love for Wentworth, in fact, has to break through such false peace and tidy chronology into the stir and roar of a messier, potentially traumatic history. If we recall Walter Scott's 1816 assessment of Austen's accomplishment in the novel, we might hear the agitation of that history in his very description of the novel of "ordinary life" with its "*striking* representation of that which is daily taking place around [one]" (emphasis added).[34] What is daily taking place all around *Persuasion*, prior to

---

[33] Adela Pinch, *Strange Fits of Passion: Epistemologies of Emotion, Hume to Austen* (Stanford: Stanford UP, 1996), 159. Pinch characterizes the "absorption" and "autonomy of mind" produced by reading (and visible in Anne Elliot) as "a kind of imperviousness to the outside world," a state "which renders one simply incapable of attending to the outside world" (160, 162).

[34] [Walter Scott], "Unsigned Review of *Emma*," *Quarterly Review*, 14 March 1816. Rpt. in *Jane Austen: Critical Assessments*, ed. Ian Littlewood, vol. 1 (Mountfield, UK: Helm Information, 1998), 290–91.

1814 and afterward, is not at all peaceful; the pains of war overflow into the supposed idyll that is 1814 as they flow into the domestic novel.

Designed to register precisely that overflow are Anne Elliot's consciousness, her affective state of simultaneous belatedness and anticipation (another instance of the "meantime" state discussed in chapter 2), and her refined sensibility. Locked within Anne is the history of a war no one around her seems to acknowledge. Indeed, after keeping her heroine silent for the opening two chapters, while detailing her thoughts, Austen makes these nearly the first words that Anne utters, nearly despite herself: "He [Admiral Croft] is rear admiral of the white. He was in the Trafalgar action. . ." (her very first utterance is "The Navy, I think. . . ")(P 21–22). The repeated bouts of vertigo and dislocation Anne suffers in Wentworth's presence can be read, then, as a record of the sort of profound *vertige* Paul de Man diagnoses as the sign of self-alienation within history.[35] For de Man, such *vertige* discloses "a truly temporal predicament" or "temporal void" (222) that collapses the sequence and priorities of chronological time so that, in this case, the temporality of the past (the wartime of 1806 and after) and the present (the peacetime of 1814) are not at all given or distinct; and, as Anne recognizes, "eight years may be little more than nothing" (P 60). In this sense, the novelist situates Anne and *Persuasion* within history, suffering history in ways that recall the wayward temporalities, the porous wartime of chapter 2. Even after Waterloo, Austen refuses to let the noise and dust of wartime settle into a clear structure of before and after, now and then. What James Chandler says about vertiginous states and the history of war in W. G. Sebald's novel *Vertigo* (1990) applies directly to Anne's predicament: in the flux of powerful emotions, "[i]t is seldom an easy matter . . . to tell whether one is moving in the direction of remembering or of forgetting."[36]

To elaborate my sense of this novel as an everyday record of the felt if not acknowledged experience of war, I read Austen's last novel alongside the diary of John Wetherell. Wetherell does not quite provide the hard evidence to prove my reading of Austen, any more than Austen supplements Wetherell's account with a home-front perspective. Rather, to a reader alert to the porousness of wartime and peacetime, of everyday domesticity and physical danger, each work sustains and elaborates the other like a conversation—or a marriage. In both texts, war and the everyday fall for each other. Wetherell's account does adumbrate a possibility within the novel: more even than suggesting the contours of Wentworth's life during the lost eight years, Wetherell's

[35] Paul de Man, "The Rhetoric of Temporality," *Blindness and Insight*, intro. Wlad Godzich, 2nd ed. (Minneapolis: U of Minnesota P, 1983).

[36] James Chandler, "About Loss: W. G. Sebald's Romantic Art of Memory," *South Atlantic Quarterly* 102.1 (Winter 2003): 245.

account hints at one of the truly lost lives of the novel, introduced only fleetingly: the dead seaman and nearly forgotten son of the Musgrave family, Dick Musgrave.[37]

In the broad outline of the text currently in print, we follow Wetherell from his empressment at Harwich in 1803, through various military exploits in the North Sea and North Atlantic, to his shipwreck near Brest and his long journey to the prison at Givet, where Wetherell and his comrades spend many years as prisoners of war. Though I will refer primarily to his years on ship, half the account deals with the prison years where the sailor adopts a new career as interpreter and nurse. After the prisoners' release in 1814, subsequent to Napoleon's initial defeat, they travel through France (playing everywhere on their fiddles, a skill honed in prison) until their eventual arrival at the seacoast, where they await return to England. Throughout, it's worth mentioning, there is a continual promise and deferral of marriage: Wetherell is engaged before he meets the press gang, then engaged again before leaving France: one marriage is blocked by the war, the other by the declaration of peace. The penultimate entry finds him comforting himself about this second, halted union and—like Wentworth he writes a letter—promising his second fiancée "to write every opportunity" (W 274).[38] Wetherell is clearly proud of his literacy and his command of the English (and later French) language. Austen herself would have appreciated the strenuous manner in which, for example, the sailor parses and ironizes the word "duty." His routine use of the word "tyrant" to denominate the British commanding officers and his unflinching description of their brutality indicate no small ambivalence about the political aims of the war England is waging against Napoleon's tyranny. Wetherell is a resourceful writer, taking advantage of a range of genres—biblical lament, gothic tale, sentimental romance, even parodic verse—to craft his account of the war years. The literariness of his diary resists any attempt to affirm the priority of the immediate over the mediated, or the authentic over the invented. One feature of his work stands out though, and marks him as a possible companion for Austen. This is his predilection, throughout the years on ship as well as those in prison, to record everyday detail and routine. Together with his attention to small conversations, these registrations convey a novelistic rather than

---

[37] A typical affluent family would have sent the younger son to the navy to give him a career; he would have served among those midshipmen who persecuted the likes of Wetherell, an unwilling recruit. Donald Gray has suggested to me that *Persuasion*, for its part, sheds light on an untold part of Wetherell's account: the story of the fiancée he left behind when he went to war. But again, not only class considerations make the fit inexact.

[38] Forester informs us that Wetherell engages himself a third time, in New York, and finally marries there.

an epic sense of warfare. They evoke powerfully the felt pains and consolations of an everyday war. Thus, in a witty description of how his fellow prisoners keep busy, Wetherell sketches the man who

> quite busy at his occupation [could] Jump up, take his fiddle, scrape away for some time, then down with it and to work at his book half an hour, then take a walk round the yard, back again, eat a Mouthful if he has any left, and down again to his employment. Then he could hammer or stitch away and settle all the affairs of the two contending Nations. In this manner we diverted away the time. (*W* 141)

Glimpsed in the brief reference to "his book" is Wetherell's characteristic allegorizing of his own work as writer which, like Austen's novel, might be said in its attention to the everyday to divert away while recording a time framed by the conflict of two contending nations.

A Broken Story

> *December 22–30 [1803]. O, England, . . . [D]id thou but know their cruel treatment to thy brave Seaman on the Ocean, thou would'st Shudder at the verry [sic] name of it. And almost be perswaded to say this cannot be true.* (*W* 85)

Again: Austen's *Persuasion* is set in motion by the return home of British navy men in 1814 after the apparent defeat of Napoleon, a peace which proves no peace. In its own way *Persuasion* meditates on war and the everyday to see if, like Austen's heroines and heroes, they could remake each other. But in so doing *Persuasion* upsets—or forgoes—peace. I take my cue, then, from Cavell's proposition that the Ancient Mariner "is a disturber of [the] peace, which is no peace" (*Q* 62). *Persuasion*'s Captain Wentworth, too, is a mariner with some connection to the past (whether a distant past or not is partly at stake here); and he too disturbs a peace which is no peace, that is to say, Anne Elliot's day-to-day existence. Unlike Coleridge's "Rime," however, here disruption of peace and movement toward a wedding are not mutually exclusive. One way to approach this topic is to suggest that, ever since Wentworth's release from fighting, ever since the cessation of war, Anne Elliot has quite privately been "paying the tax of quick alarm" for having him near.[39] Another

---

[39] For example: "[S]he could not hear that Captain Wentworth's sister was likely to live at Kellynch, without a revival of former pain; and many a stroll and many a sigh were necessary to dispel the agitation of the idea" (*P* 30).

way is to show how Anne Elliot comes to represent the cultivation of war—or a wartime routine—within the everyday.

> *May 25, 26, 27 [1803]. A smart gale at N. W. In a little while we joined the Commodore in the bay and made sail to the eastward . . . , where we passed away two days Exerciseing. This was Exerciseing Officers . . . Men . . . Ships . . . Sails . . . Guns . . . Yards Washing . . . holystoning . . . Small arms . . . Mustering bags. Reefing in two minutes . . . punishment. . . . Up and down hammocks. . . . Stow them. . . . Scrub hammocks. Up all chests and bags. . . . Sprinkle and scrub. . . . Serve out pursers Slops and tobacco. . . . Serve grog . . . . Turn all hands up to skylarking. . . . Set the Watch. All those little changes were transacted in the course of two days cruise in the North Sea. (W 46)*

It has become a commonplace to note in *Persuasion* Austen's esteem for the navy, registered each time the navy appears as the realm of domestic order as well as real affection. Mrs. Croft proclaims twice, underlining the pun, that she knows "nothing superior to the accommodations of a man of war" (*P* 69). Anne Elliot admires "all the ingenious contrivances and nice arrangements" of Captain Harville's house. "[C]onnected as it all was with his profession," she finds it "the picture of repose and domestic happiness" otherwise foreign to her (*P* 98). The affection and loyalty between the brother officers also contrasts sharply with what Anne has known within her family. As several critics have argued, the novel offers the navy as a more congenial model for living than what Anne Elliot has yet experienced.[40]

Austen is at pains to inform us that life at sea in wartime has its everyday component: the officers mock the young ladies' surprise at learning that meals, prepared by a cook, are served on board.

> [Wentworth] was very much questioned . . . as to the manner of living on board, daily regulations, food, hours, etc., and their surprise at his accounts, at learning the degree of accommodation and arrangement which was practicable, drew from him some pleasant ridicule, which reminded Anne of the early days, when she too had been ignorant, and . . . accused of supposing sailors to be living on board without anything to eat, or any cook to dress it if there were, or any servant to wait, or any knife and fork to use. (*P* 64)

But what happens to our understanding of warfare, of these men's profession, when we—or Anne—choose it as a happier version of the everyday? An entry

[40] Recent examples include Anne Mellor, *Mothers of the Nation* (Bloomington: Indiana UP, 2000), 121–41; and, with qualifications, Monica Cohen, "Persuading the Navy Home: Austen and Married Women's Professional Property," *Novel* 29.3 (Spring 1996): 346–66.

from Wetherell's diaries gives an account of dinner aboard a man-of-war that moves beyond what was served and who served it, to record the deep misery of the men expected to eat it. As much as anything, the routine of eating could be a test of the sailors' stoicism.

> *December 22–30 [1803]. By this time it was near six bells in the Afternoon; went to dinner and a poor dinner it was to many, some thro' pain and others thro' their feelings at such unheard of cruelties. . . . We then Stood out to Sea and on Christmass day had a good Plumb Pudding, and a good piece of beef for dinner, but all this was nothing where contentment was fled; however like true old Philosophers we bore all as patient as possible and of our bad bargain made the best.* (W 85–86)

What spoils the meal for the sailors, especially the ordinary sailors not mentioned in the dinner conversation at Uppercross, is the everyday brutality of their commanders. In this instance, they had just witnessed the "Savage torture" of a dozen of their crew, whipped till "the deck with human gore was dy'd" (W 85). Physical punishment was routine in the British navy during this period; with parliamentary hearings into the practice of flogging, no literate person could have been unaware of the prevalence of this practice, though they may have remained persuadable that it could not be true, or truly cruel.[41] When we think about the everydayness of the navy introduced into the novel, we might also recall the quite ordinary version of the everyday available in Wetherell's diary. Like Catherine Morland with her "alarms" in *Northanger Abbey*, perhaps the ignorant young ladies who question the "degree of accommodation and arrangement" on board a warship are not absolutely risible.

A more easeful way of bringing together the everydayness of the navy with the world at Uppercross would be to recognize the ethos of care and survival at work in the novel. John Wiltshire calls *Persuasion* the story of "broken bones, broken heads and broken hearts," not quite differentiating between Anne Elliot's suffering and that of say, Captain Hayter with his wounded leg.[42] Such a broken-down story calls forth the practice of nursing—think not only of Anne tending her nephew, or Benwick tending Lydia, but of Nurse Ragg and the Musgroves' old nursery maid, Sara, who had been "living in her deserted nursery to mend stockings, and dress all the blains and bruises she could get near her" (P 122), as well as Wentworth himself, who spends a week watching over the distraught Captain Benwick—and calls it forth in such a

[41] For more on the navy and *Persuasion*, see Cohen and Jill Heydt-Stevenson, "'Unbecoming Conjunctions': Mourning the Loss of Landscape and Love in *Persuasion*," *Eighteenth-Century Fiction* 8.1 (October 1995): 51–71.

[42] John Wiltshire, "*Persuasion*: The Pathology of Everyday Life," in *Jane Austen and the Body: "The Picture of Health"* (Cambridge: Cambridge UP, 1992), 165.

way that care, a responsiveness to hurt bodies and souls, supplies the ethos of this novel. With this emphasis on care, Austen recognizes the innovations of the "new navy" promoted by Sir John Jervis (later Lord St. Vincent) during the wars with Napoleon. As Monica Cohen notes, Jervis reorganized the navy along the lines of specialization and professionalization, thus undermining the former hierarchy of class. More immediately, he "attended to the quotidian life of a naval fleet. He bickered with doctors over whether his men should wear warm flannel or a cotton weave that could be kept cleaner" (350). Jervis scheduled regular ventilation and fumigation on board; he bothered to order soap for his fleet. And he revised medical procedures so that each fleet was accompanied by a hospital ship. Commenting on Jervis's known attention to hygiene and caring for his men, Cohen notes, "there is a touch of the [domestic] heroine about Jervis" (352). One could also say, in noting her sense of service and care, that there is a touch of the officer in Anne Elliot. Though the Portsmouth episode in *Mansfield Park* may be a better text for demonstrating the intersection of Austen's focus on hygiene and diet with her knowledge of the navy, *Persuasion* shows the coordination of the domestic and the wartime everyday through acts of practical nursing.

Yet, when we hail the navy's everyday as a solution to Anne's situation, or note the interpenetration of the practices of navy and home under the ethos of care, we also need to account for the converse intrusion of alarm and accident into the surface of the peacetime everyday.

> *April 27 [1803]. [The boy's] resolution was fixed and some time in the night he made his escape overboard. . . . May 12. I made my obedience and retired in a most horrid state of mind being nearly on the brink of leaping overboard to terminate my cruel treatment. . . . August 25. "What shall it be said that Jim Burchel would suffer this from a brat of a boy? No I will die first! . . ." [H]e sprung up, took the Midshipman in his Arms, and overboard plunges head foremost, determin'd to die with him in his* ARMS. *. . . August 28. We had a very pleasant run out to the Cape, where we had the misfortune to loose [sic] one of our messenger boys named Tilford. The night being hot he got into the Mizn chains, fell asleep, and roll'd overboard; was not heard nor missed until next morning. . . . November 10. Those who had gained hold of the Nettings were all either Shot or run thro' with pikes or sabres and fell back into the Boats or the Sea. (W 37, 44, 64, 67, 77)*

We never learn what killed "poor Richard" Musgrove in *Persuasion*. We simply know "that the Musgroves had had the ill fortune of a very troublesome, hopeless son; and the good fortune to lose him before he reached his twentieth year" (*P* 50). It is one of the few moments in Austen's fiction at

which a reader might flinch. Indeed, the Johnsonian balance of this outra-
geous sentence later topples over when the narrator expresses distaste over the
mother's "large fat sighings over the destiny of a son, whom alive nobody had
cared for" (*P* 68). As D. A. Miller showed, this moment marks a more than
stylistic lapse on the narrator's part: something refuses to fit or be accommodated in this passage about the lost sailor.[43] "Stupid and unmanageable on
shore," Dick Musgrove had been shipped off to war where, sometime after
serving under Captain Wentworth, he died unaccountably. It just happened.

The narrator grudgingly grants us "this pathetic piece of family history" on
the way to revealing to Anne Elliot that Captain Wentworth is back in town
(*P* 50). I imagine that Dick's death involved some sort of fall, because falls—to
boys and young women—just happen throughout this novel. Captain Wentworth's reentry to Anne Elliot's world (he is instantly on "an intimate footing"
there) is curiously marked not just by the suddenly upending recollection of
Dick Musgrove's death, but by further injuries involving boys (*P* 84). Anne and
the reader first "escape" the possibility of encountering Wentworth when young
Charles Musgrove inexplicably falls, dislocating his collarbone and perhaps
damaging his spine. Amid the "alarming ideas" raised up by this falling down,
"Anne had everything to do at once": our first glimpse at her effectiveness in an
emergency (*P* 53). Captain Wentworth's appearance is deferred by this sudden
accident, and deferred again when Anne agrees to stay home to nurse the boy
while the rest of the family dines at Uppercross. Finally, in Lyme, when we and
Anne come closest to the fellowship of the navy and all its tidy domesticity, another body falls, this time almost—but crucially not quite—in Captain Wentworth's arms. It is as if this figure of the falling body were straining to attach itself to him—but cannot quite make contact. What Cathy Caruth said about
falling bodies in Paul de Man's writings makes sense as well of *Persuasion*: "In
naming a befalling"—or a series of falls that just happen—the "text no longer
simply knows what it says, but indeed does more than it knows."[44]

Looking at the socially fallen and invalid Mrs. Smith, Wiltshire argues that,
along with care, *Persuasion* promotes "strategies of survival" (186). He finds
these strategies epitomized by Mrs. Smith, but also honored in Anne Elliot's
resilience after eight years of suffering, which, like Wetherell's "old Philosophers," she has "born as patient as possible and of [her] bad bargain made the

[43] D. A. Miller, "Austen's Attitude," *Yale Journal of Criticism* 8.1 (Spring 1995): 1–5.

[44] Cathy Caruth, "The Falling Body and the Impact of Reference," in *Unclaimed Experience:
Trauma, Narrative, and History* (Baltimore: Johns Hopkins UP, 1996), 89–90. Caruth reads the repeated figure of the falling body in de Man's work as the "reassertion" of a "referential weight" which
cannot otherwise be accommodated or "known" within the "system" of a text (83). The figure of the
falling body also introduces de Man's discussion of the structure of irony (see "The Rhetoric of
Temporality" 213 ff.). As such it is deeply implicated in the interrogation of temporality and history
that concerns me in this book.

best." But why not assign this survival to Wentworth as well, or to any of the other men we meet who happen to come home from war? The major accident of this novel, the falling bodies seem to suggest, is that Wentworth returns at all. Put another way, the presence of this military man catalyzes the everyday into a zone of quick alarm and harmful accidents demanding both care and the strength to survive. In this sense, and in response to his presence, Anne Elliot cultivates a mode of living every day as if she were at war. In that mode of living, it seems, Austen gives an uncanny anticipation of the words of Jacques Derrida, who, in his last interview, trained his thoughts on the word "survival," even as he declared "I am at war against myself. . . . I sometimes see this war as terrifying and painful, but at the same time, I know that it's life [c'est la vie]."[45] As Sara Guyer notes, Derrida's attention to survival demonstrates a particular, and I would argue modern apprehension of war that Wiltshire also glimpses but does not pursue. When living equals living at war, as Derrida and Austen suggest, then survival becomes, Guyer tells us, "not . . . something that surpasses or comes after life and death, but the very structure of living. Survival . . . indicates a state of non-closure . . . and . . . a state of suffering, even conflict, that is living" (251). As Derrida goes on to say, survival becomes "the most intense life possible" (Derrida 54; qtd. in Guyer 251).

By the intensifying light of survival, Wiltshire's essay "*Persuasion*: The Pathology of Everyday Life" focuses our attention on the centrality of accident and injury in this novel. He argues that their everydayness resists "the moral sense which discovers a narrative rationality in events" (188). Accidents are the fruit of chance and time, simple attributes of mortality, he proposes: they just happen. But an uncanny, unclaimed sense of war rests beneath these accidents, particularly the otherwise avoided sense of war as violent injury. Rather than providing a firm ground or referent for the novel, it undermines any "easy footing" for the everyday. The tendency in *Persuasion* is to transfer not only the security and familiarity of the everyday to the "man of war," but also the violence and injury of warfare to the space of the everyday, to boys and young women, thereby making them accidental, unaccountable, the natural "miscarriages of life," to use Wiltshire's language (192). As if the need to cultivate "strategies of survival," like the word "strategies" itself, bore no trace of a circumambient war.

How much weight can be put on the vertigo-inspiring presence of Capt. Wentworth, the falling bodies, and Anne's intensely felt but thwarted desire to

---

[45] Jacques Derrida, *Apprendre à vivre enfin: Entretien avec Jean Birnbaum* (Paris: Galilee, 2005). The interview first appeared as "Je suis en guerre contre moi-même," *Le Monde*, 19 August 2004. Quoted and translated in Sara Guyer's analysis of the interview, "The Rhetoric of Survival and the Possibility of Romanticism," *Studies in Romanticism* 46. 2 (2007): 249. Guyer argues that despite Derrida's "late-modern political context" his thoughts on survival reach "all the way [back] to Romanticism" (252).

find "peace"? Her friend Mrs. Smith, presuming that Anne will marry the smooth Mr. Elliot, proclaims confidently that now Anne's "peace will not be shipwrecked . . . [she will be] safe in all worldly matters." But the evening before, when Anne met Wentworth at the concert, her "peace" had been quietly blown to the winds (*P* 196, 189). Later, after she—and the reader—undergoes the "revolution" of reading Wentworth's love letter, Anne is so dazed that Mrs. Musgrove fears her distraction may be the result of her having "at any time lately, slipped down, and got a blow on her head." The older woman must be reassured that "there had been no fall in the case" (*P* 238). In fact, the narrator describes Anne's nearly shipwrecked state and her supposed blow to the head as approaching the "perfection of her felicity" (*P* 239). *Persuasion* rewrites the opportunities of war and the so-called pleasures of peace even as it dismisses peace of mind.

> *November 10 [1804]. . . . as we were endeavoring to bear our boat*
> *astern . . . something come in contact with my head. Putting up my hand,*
> *I found the muzel of a Frenchman's Musket [,] push'd it on one side just as*
> *he fired, saved my own life and nearly shot our first lieut. near enough to*
> *graze his skull by the flash of the gun. I saw the man in the head that fired*
> *it and drawing my Pistol from my belt gave him the contents thro his*
> *noodle. (W 77)*

In the end, the head seems the body part most susceptible to the accidents of everyday war in *Persuasion*, and rightly so, if we understand persuasion as the act of getting through to, penetrating, someone's noodle. Austen's response to war may appear more material and personified, but not unlike Freud's tale about "the fragment of living substance," also written in the wake of war: both writers were trying to narrate the way war invades the mind. Walton Litz praised Austen's development in *Persuasion* of "a rapid and nervous syntax designed to imitate the bombardment of impressions upon the mind," specifically Anne's mind.[46] Litz's language—the bombardment of impressions upon the mind— intuits the conclusion of my argument: Austen has brought war home not only to everyday bodies, but also to the rhythms of everyday minds—including that of the reader. *Persuasion* demonstrates one way that the structures of feeling demanded by war—its peculiar blend of self-alienation, selfless caring for others, alarm, survival, even a felicity hard to distinguish from pain—migrate into everyday life, becoming so well understood, standing under everything one does, that one hardly knows how or when to account for them.

> *June [1810]. Bonapart's Marriage was celebrated in Paris. On the 8th of*
> *June Mr. Peytavin the Commandant and Mr. Wolfe the British Agent sent*

---

[46] Qtd. in Wiltshire 164.

for me and they requested me to leave the Commissary and go to the Hospi-
tal in order to assist Tho. Stevens attending on the sick. Several of the
French and English nurses were dead and the sickness spread such terror
thro' the town and prison that every person was afraid to undertake the
unwelcome office of Nurse and interpreter. I obey'd the call and went and
rendered all the assistance in my power. (W 159)

A Brief History of the Meaning of War

Understanding war. This book has been asking what war meant to a population whose experience and memory were shaped by warfare, a population whose armies and navies were almost constantly engaged in military conflict across the globe, though rarely, if ever, on home ground. It has asked how war was understood by those who were, at least as subjects of a sovereign state, often at war, though never actually in battle. But it has not yet asked what it meant to make war an object of understanding.

What if war is and was meaningless? A trip to the *Oxford English Dictionary* reveals the *mise en abyme* from which the English word *war* emerges. It derives from the medieval Latin *werra*, also spelled *guerra*; a word shared with Old High German. The noun *werra* signified "confusion, discord, strife"; and the verb form stressed this anti-epistemological bent: "to bring into confusion"; "to confuse, perplex." The editors of the *OED*, feeling obliged to alleviate the reader's own perplexity, understandably add a brief note:

> It is a curious fact that no Germanic nation in early historic times had in living use any word properly meaning "war," though several words with that meaning survived in poetry, in proverbial phrases, and in compound personal names.

No war proper; only improper, figurative versions "surviving"—like a traumatic memory—in poetry and proverb. Romance languages, the editors speculate, avoided the Latin word *bellum* "on account of its formal coincidence with bello- [or] beautiful," but they found no better substitute in Teutonic than the perplexing *werra*, an index of the semantic as well as aesthetic confusion reigning in the wake of the Roman empire. "The continental Teutonic languages," the *OED* continues, "later developed separate words for 'war'": the German *Krieg*, or the Dutch *oorlog*. Icelandic uses *ófriðr*, literally "un-peace." Yet the English language has stuck by war, pulling it over the centuries from its root in perplexity and confusion into some semblance of linguistic consensus—as if we all now understand what war means.

More recent centuries have resituated the question of war's definition, so that the issue is less trying to settle war into consensus, and more trying to circumscribe war, define its boundaries. Certainly, in the era of total war, war brooks no limits, resisting even the limits of a definition. "To introduce the principle of moderation into the theory of war itself would always lead to logical absurdity," insists Carl von Clausewitz.[1] "[W]ar is an act of force," he writes in *On War*, and theoretically, "there is no limit to the application of that force" (77). War obviously has a purpose (for Clausewitz, it is "to compel our enemy to do our will" [75]) but is that enough to secure meaning? War's purpose, in Clausewitz's formulation, tends toward the dismantling of meaning, to the demolition of the institutional and symbolic guarantees that allow a people to make meaning—their laws, language, customs, and religion; their buildings, streets, and villages; and of course, their bodies. War attacks Scarry's "realms of sentience and self-extension."[2] War does violence to meaning. The obsolete meaning of *werra*, "to bring into confusion," appears starkly up to date.

And there we might just end our brief history of the meaning of war, anointing our own perplexity with what appears, even in the etymologies, as war's sublime effects. But a less sublime, more historically circumscribed approach to the question of war's meaning can be told. Citing Clausewitz merely begs the historical question: what at that time was the definition of war? And citing Clausewitz alongside the *OED* begs a more hermeneutical question: what does it mean to define war? when and why do we give war meaning? I attempt to answer these questions with recourse to the most powerful technologies of definition available in the eighteenth century: the dictionary and its partner, the encyclopedia. The impact of these technologies should not be minimized for, as Michel Foucault argues in *The Order of Things*, they testify to a "profoundly nominalist" or "Classical" order of language and knowledge.[3] In the seventeenth and eighteenth centuries, "language occupied a fundamental situation in relation to all knowledge; it was only by the medium of language," insists Foucault, "that the things of the world could be known." Hence the soaring demand for dictionaries. By the nineteenth century, language would become only "one object of knowledge among others" (296), but in the prior age, to know the word was to know the thing it represented. The word for "war," once satisfactorily defined, offered the primary ground for understanding the thing itself.

---

[1] Carl von Clausewitz, *On War*, ed. and trans. Michael Howard and Peter Paret (New York: Oxford UP, 2007), 76.

[2] See chapter 1.

[3] Michel Foucault, *The Order of Things: An Archaeology of the Human Sciences* (New York: Vintage, 1973), 295–96.

Before we grapple with the definitions, however, it might be instructive to admit a few of the limits of these sources, despite their own claims to be "universal" or "complete"; and to outline the peculiar historical relationship between these technologies of definition and the meaning—or confusion—of war.

Though dictionaries began to be available in the seventeenth century, it was not until the eighteenth century that they took the form we now recognize. The first dictionaries, so-called, offered themselves as tools for translation (English–French or English–Latin dictionaries were common) or as tools for social assimilation (compilations of so-called hard words). In fact, those early "hard word dictionaries" had two purposes. The first was to train the uneducated in "our refined English Tongue"—a pedagogical effort aimed at standardization as well as assimilation. The second purpose was to organize the many "foreign words" which had entered the language as a result of commerce, world travel, and a glut of literary translations, but also as a result, as the lexicographers would say, of "conquests and invasions." By the beginning of the eighteenth century, evidently, there was a growing sense of a "New English" which included words deemed difficult or unfamiliar to even the most literate classes. Hence the appearance of a *New English Dictionary* in 1702, the first attempt to hold together words of everyday usage and "hard words," the words imported by commerce and warfare. The *New English Dictionary* was matched in its aspirations by *The New World of Words* (1706); together they proposed that language itself would register a new world order; that in one's very speech, in the practice of reading and writing, the routines of everyday experience would be coordinated with the movements of global capital and the cataclysms of military violence. Via the technology of the dictionary, a new English could establish a system out of what might otherwise appear random or violent phenomena; it could wrest meaning out of confusion.

How then does one understand the glaring omission of the word "war" from the earliest dictionaries? In *The New World of Words*, despite its mission to unite everyday with hard words, nothing appears between the entries for "wapp" and "warble."[4] Similarly, in the *Glossographia Anglicum Nova* (1707), you can find "warble" but no "war"—and no "wound" either. John Kersey's *Dictionarium Anglo-Brittannicum, or a General English Dictionary* (1708) inserts between "wapp" and "warble" the expression "war and war," a Middle English leftover meaning "worse and worse," not unrelated to that Old High German *werra*. But war itself is absent in this and most other dictionaries of

[4] "Wapp" is defined as "(in a Ship) a Rope with which the *Shrowds* are set stiff with Waleknots; . . . ." Edward Phillips, *The New World of Words, or, Universal English Dictionary* (London: J. Phillips, 1706). All the dictionaries and encyclopedias consulted were found on *Eighteenth Century Collections Online* (*ECCO*). Gale Group. http://galenet.galegroup.com/servlet/ECCO.

the day. When "war" does show up, as in Kersey's *A New English Dictionary* (1713), we are given a series outlining proper usage rather than a definition: "War, as a Civil or a Foreign War. . . . To War or War against, to make War."[5] War, it seems, does not qualify as hard or difficult, certainly not as new, but also not as an everyday word. Though to an increasingly urban population the word "warble" may require a quick gloss, the word "war" requires none. Too well-known or not worth knowing, war operated, you might say, outside the technology of definition.

Yet you would be mistaken to say that war did not matter to the construction and organization of knowledge in this period; language around and about war proved vitally new and worth knowing. At the very end of the seventeenth century, and continuing at a rapid pace into the early eighteenth century, you discover the remarkable popularity of specialized military dictionaries, often compiled by unnamed "Officers who serv'd several years at Land and Sea."[6] With "improved" editions arriving almost every other year, the elaboration of the so-called martial discipline into a bound volume of words accompanied by diagrams and definitions must have answered a profound desire in the reading public to know something, maybe everything, that is, *all the words* about war. Most of these military dictionaries understood themselves to address domestic readers, not warriors: they advertised their use-value "to all persons that read the Publick News . . . for Understanding the Accounts of *Sieges*, *Battles*, and other Warlike . . . *Expeditions*, which daily occur in this Time of Action" (Officers title page). The advertisements carry an assumption that any person who kept up with the news would also want to keep up with this ever-changing technical language: "several of [these terms]," notes one work, "[are] newly invented, and which few or none have yet taken notice of in Print."[7] In this respect, military language plays a special role in the "newness" of the "new English" that motivates dictionaries in the first place. Military dictionaries assume that the average reader requires a linguistic bridge to this new, foreign world of experience. The language of military matters is thus privileged, but also exempted, set apart from the more general use of English. Finally, military dictionaries assume that readers will agree on the characterization of theirs as "a Time of Action," that action consisting of "war-like . . . expeditions." Or, as another preface put it, "in this Warlike Age," one wants to consult a dictionary. Warlike: an age that is somehow, and on a daily basis, like war while it is at war; or, as we might say nowadays, an age rapidly producing facsimiles of war in print, precisely because the "action" of this time of action makes itself

[5] John Kersey, *A New English Dictionary* (London: Robert Knaplock, 1713). *ECCO*.

[6] See Officers, *A Military and Sea Dictionary, Explaining All Difficult Terms in the Martial Discipline*, 4th ed. (London: J. Morphew, 1711). *ECCO*.

[7] Edward Cocker, *Cocker's English Dictionary* (London: Back and Bettesworth, 1704). *ECCO*.

available only in mediated form. Though their lists of defined terms continue to grow, the military dictionaries never define the word "war."

Toward the middle of the eighteenth century, however, this technology of meaning starts to comprehend war itself. When definitions for war emerge in dictionaries of the English language, their appearance seems tied to a new feature: etymologies. Once dictionaries become more than a technology of the new and changing, fashioning themselves instead as a repository of the history of a national language, a formerly unplaceable word like "war" can be included in all its ancient glory, trailing an etymology that includes up to a dozen forebears. Quickly, though, a distinct shift occurs in the dictionary definitions, one that echoes the military dictionaries' elaboration of war into war-likeness.

Indeed, almost as soon as war is defined and given a history, its definitions proliferate. Here is a definition of war often repeated in midcentury: "War (s.): A fighting; a state of hostility between nations, states, provinces or parties." (Remarkable here is the omission of any role by "princes" or "sovereigns," which appear in other definitions; one can track the political affiliations of the lexicographer through changes in definitions of sovereignty.) It should be noted that the words "fighting" and "hostility" were similarly defined in ways that resisted figurative use: they were understood to signal a strict relationship to warfare. In less than a decade, though, dictionaries began to incorporate more figurative definitions for war. Thus by the 1770s, you regularly find: "War (s.): A state of open hostility between two or more people or nations; the exercise of violence against opposers by sovereign command; a state of opposition, an act of opposition; the instruments of hostility, forces, armies; the profession of arms."[8] This definition of war would remain dominant into the nineteenth century.

If we agree that there is more than a simple movement from the literal to the figurative here, we can delineate two curious dynamics in war's developing meanings. The first, most apparent in the midst of the definition, is a vertiginous substitution of parts for wholes. We'll see that this synecdochic movement threatens the very boundaries and divisions that construct definition. The second movement, a narrative that takes war from "a state of open hostility" and "the exercise of violence" to a bona fide profession, itself offers a telling if telescoped history of war. In doing so, this second definitional movement drives war away from the body and into the mind. Odd, but not thoroughly obsolete, these definitional dynamics continue to haunt the meaning of war.

The first movement defines war by select details, or parts, each of which aims to fix something that would otherwise threaten to obliterate fixity. War is somehow a "state" between two or more states; it is both a "state" and an

---

[8] John Ash, ed., *The New and Complete Dictionary of the English Language*, vol. 2 (London: E. and C. Dilly, 1775). *ECCO.*

"exercise," a "state" and an "act" effecting that "state" (presumably, by opposing another "state"). The word "war" can also refer to the instruments of war; "war" can mean an army or, more abstractly, the force embodied by that army. A plausible sentence could then be "General Wolfe surveyed his war, arrayed with all its war, as it prepared a war that would initiate war." Such extensive synecdoche, the substitution of part for whole, induces a dizziness, the semantic field having collapsed, its boundaries inner and outer dissolved. At one moment, war appears neatly contained and manipulable—instrumental; on second glance it appears a pervasive state or condition of things.

Faced with the collapsing field of meaning in this movement of eighteenth-century definitions of war, one is tempted to suspect that the science of definition had not yet been perfected and that as dictionaries became standardized, war would be better defined. Yet even Johnson's dictionary, the standard for a century, follows this arrangement, from the exercise of violence through instruments, armies, and profession; though he rearranges the series, positioning the arena of abstraction—"state of opposition, act of opposition"—as his last term, following "profession of arms."[9] If we take these substitutive chains of meaning seriously, we may understand them as a system that in fact mirrors war. Like war itself, the act of representing war as a system throws cause and effect into disarray, dissolves the boundaries between inner and outer, and substitutes parts for wholes, wholes for parts. In other words, the definition of war shows as much as it tells: it mimics in the realm of language and meaning what, on other terrain, war itself performs.

Perhaps an anomalous definition, an extreme if parodic version of war's figurative maneuvers will make more visible the logic of parts and wholes in this first definitional movement. Nathan Bailey's *Universal Etymological Dictionary of the English Language* went through thirty editions between the 1730s and the beginning of the new century; it had no successful rival until the appearance of Samuel Johnson's masterwork in 1756, and even after Bailey's death, editions continued to be updated and marketed. Most of Bailey's dictionaries propose a conventional definition of war, similar to ones already discussed, changing as they change. But two rogue editions published in London in 1775 and 1776 substitute this entry:

> War: The *French* are said to be like a flea, quickly skipping into a country, and soon leaping out again. The *Spaniard* like a crab, creeping into a place slowly, and not to be expelled without great violence. The *German* like a louse, slowly mastering, and as slowly driven out.[10]

[9] Samuel Johnson, *Dictionary of the English Language*, vol. 2 (London, 1756). *ECCO*.
[10] Nathan Bailey, *The New Universal Etymological English Dictionary*, 5th ed. (London: Cavell, 1775). *ECCO*.

The scurrilous nationalistic humor of the passage of course exempts the British while comparing its continental opponents to noxious parasites. While the joke substitutes a part of the world (the continental powers) for all warriors, it also reduces their armies to the singular national type, then reduces further that type to the atomized flea, crab, and louse, naturalizing war in the process. But what is most intriguing about this joke is that it is the closest any definition of the eighteenth-century war comes to biology, physiology, to the human body.

This definition points to the invasion by a smaller body of a larger body which, though irritated and annoyed, nevertheless accommodates or "hosts" the insinuating invader for an undetermined amount of time. The parasite may live within the host organism unnoticed; but presumably it is always there feeding off its host, the new part supported by a now reorganized whole. If pushed to violence, the host body must hurt itself in order to drive out the intruder because the two bodies have become so closely integrated. War in this instance is defined as a system of organisms in relation; war infiltrates and restructures its hosts in uncomfortable, perhaps lethal or fatal ways. Here war seems synonymous, as the dictionaries have taught us, with state armies; it also hints at the larger projects of colonization. Yet war is parasitical in another sense, as it seeks to collapse the boundaries of parts and wholes by substituting individual bodies for the whole nation. In *The Body in Pain*, Elaine Scarry makes visible the sacrificial logic of war, which generates and confirms meaning—in this case the meaning of the nation—from the injuring or "opening up" of individual bodies.[11] War comes into the soldier's body, invades it, and changes it irrevocably. What otherwise might appear a devastating swirl of whole and part and whole, a state of confusion and perplexity, is organized and explained in these anomalous dictionaries through the figure of the parasite. In their turn to the body, these rogue definitions themselves function as parasites, intruding into the space of the dictionary to configure an alternative meaning for eighteenth-century war.

In *The Parasite*, Michel Serres helps to explain the coordinated meanings of this word in French: parasite, guest (which also flips into host), and noise.[12] For Serres, the parasite is one "who produces disorder and who generates a different order" (3). For him, the parasite is a model for the very modality through which "the rare exists, exceptions come about, novelty appears" and "the improbable miracle" of change enters the world (122). As powerful and creative as that sounds, the parasite has another aspect as well. As one scholar commenting on Serres's work puts it, the parasite also introduces "negative,

[11] Elaine Scarry, *The Body in Pain: The Making and Unmaking of the World* (New York: Oxford UP, 1985), 81.
[12] Michel Serres, *The Parasite*, trans. Lawrence R. Schehr (Baltimore: Johns Hopkins UP, 1982).

murderous, entropic, epidemic mediations."[13] Serres himself characterizes this parasitical effect in language evocative of war:

> Everything has changed; nothing is constant; the chain has been muti-
> lated beyond all possible recognition of the message. Victory is in the
> hands of the powers of noise. . . . History in general as it is written or
> told is a network of bifurcations where parasites move about. (235–36)

The parasite figures mediation as mutilation, as destruction of meaning.

The second definitional movement at work in late-century dictionaries takes a less interactive, more progressive direction. The oft-repeated definition of war, as I have mentioned, moves from "the exercise of violence" to the "profession of arms," or, in a more philosophical and psychological vein, from State violence to the "state of opposition," as if each stage of the entry bore witness to a broadening and abstracting of the general understanding of war. In fact, distance from fighting, together with the nearly everyday awareness of being at war through reading, listening, talking about war, allowed the British to understand war as, in part, an activity of the mind.

This claim might seem contrary to the evidence. Johnson, for example, writing his *Plan for a Dictionary of the English Language* midcentury, plays on the notion of the lexicographer willingly rejecting the codes—as well as the glories—of the warrior to perform his quiescent mission. Writing to his patron, a man whose attention, he notes, is usually "with treaties and with wars," Johnson admits, in only half-apology, that his own employment "would awaken no passion, engage me in no contention, nor throw in my way any temptation to disturb the quiet of others."[14] "[O]n this province," so Johnson defines the linguistic terrain he will conquer, "I entered with the pleasing hope, that as it was low, it likewise would be safe" (1). The writer is self-consciously a man of peace. Yet the comparison between the man of war and the man of words only points out a parallelism in the vocations. In Johnson's plan, the dictionary will organize, purify, and eradicate undesirable "alien" or "foreign" words "which . . . have made no approaches towards assimilation" (6–7). In his *Plan for a Dictionary*, Johnson fights a "safe" or facsimile war against these linguistic invaders, employing his dictionary rather than conventional instruments of war.[15]

---

[13] Steven Connor, "Michel Serres's Milieux," a paper given at ABRALIC (Brazilian Association for Comparative Literature) conference, Belo Horizonte, July 23–26, 2002. Available at http://www.bbk.ac.uk/english/skc/milieux/.

[14] Samuel Johnson, *The Plan for a Dictionary of the English Language* (London: J. and P. Knapton, T. Longman and T. Shewell, C. Hitch, A. Millar, and R. Dodsley, 1747), 2–4.

[15] For more on Johnson's project, see Janet Sorensen's excellent *The Grammar of Empire in Eighteenth-Century British Writing* (Cambridge: Cambridge UP, 2000).

Johnson explains the principles of his dictionary in a manner that illuminates the common practice of combining "hard words" with the words of everyday use, but at the same time he resituates the language of war:

> It seems necessary to the completion of a dictionary designed not merely for critics but for popular use, that it should comprise, . . . the peculiar words of every profession; that [for instance] the terms of war and navigation should be inserted so far as they can be required by readers of travels, and of history; and those of law, merchandise and mechanical trades, so far as they can be supposed useful in the occurrences of common life. (7–8)

Johnson's rationale is startling: whereas the average reader will have a practical need for the jargon of law and commerce, the terms of warfare remain helpful "so far as they can be required by readers of travels, and of history." Warfare has moved, in other words, not only into distant places and times, but also and thereby into the realm of literature, the province of the man of letters. The next generation would provide several major writers—Southey and Scott come to mind—who, having never witnessed a battle, nevertheless revel in the jargon of distant warfare, establishing themselves as authorities on war. Yet Johnson demonstrates that even by the mid-eighteenth century, when Great Britain was consolidating its military preeminence in the Seven Years' War, war was moving into the language of elsewhere and other days.[16]

Displaced temporally and geographically, and into the realm of literature, the meaning of war would require only one more twist to become a function of mind, rather than of bodies and weapons. Certainly, a growing awareness of war as a profession, for which one could be trained and about which one could study, added to its intellectualization, its conversion into science. But the coup de grace arrived with the phenomenon named Napoleon, who definitively translated the wrath of Achilles into the operations of Genius. One version of this transition is already evident, as we have seen, in the representations of war and weather; one last example will illustrate this transformation in the broader realm of knowledge.

The *Encyclopedia Britannica*, published in Edinburgh in 1771, was the project of Alexander Bell and C. MacFarquhar, an attempt to offer a systematic account of human knowledge. Good sons of the Scottish Enlightenment, not yet identified with the British commercial and imperial mission, Bell and MacFarquhar pointedly elevate the man of learning over the man of war. A volume that grants thirty-eight pages to moral philosophy and forty to the science of midwifery accords a mere sentence to the ancient art of war, and that

---

[16] In 1747, when Johnson composed his *Plan*, Great Britain was ending its six-year war with Spain in the Americas, and was fully involved in the War of Austrian Succession (1740–48).

sentence treats warfare as human failure. "War. A contest or difference between princes, states, or large bodies of people; which not being determined
by the ordinary measures of equity and justice, is referred to the decision of
the sword."[17] (Another complicated rhetorical figure, mixing metonymy and
personfication.) The entries for "military" and "soldier" each receive barely a
half sentence, "militia" only slightly more. The entry on "arms" opens with
"arms of courtesy, or parade," which were "lances not shod, swords without
edge or point, etc. used in ancient tournaments" and it continues to itemize
ancient or heraldic uses of the term, ending with "Arms, in falconry, the legs
of a hawk from the thigh to the foot." "Army" gets slightly more attention, two
paragraphs, but the entry there is mostly concerned with measuring the com-
position and length of each line of battle. On the other hand, a seven-page
essay is devoted to "Fortifications," the "art" of defending a city from the
threat of such an army. This prestige is explained by the writer's desire to ally
fortification more with trade than warfare: the essay ends with specific remarks about fortifications "for the safety of commerce." In fact, it asserts, fortifications "should never be built any where else but near rivers, lakes, or near
the sea" to protect and promote commerce, "excepting in extraordinary cases,
where it cannot be avoided"—war thus becomes the exceptional case for fortification.[18] One other military term burdens the scholars' project: "Stratagem,
in the art of war, any device for the deceiving and surprising an enemy." It's
one of the very few instances in the *Encyclopedia* where the work of intellect or
"art" is granted to war, but only in this scanting fashion.[19]

The denigration of warfare, its demotion in the work of the *Encyclopedia*
from the arts and sciences of civilized societies, probably speaks for itself. But
an entry from the third edition of the *Encyclopedia Britannica* twenty-sex years
later demonstrates how dramatically the definition of war, the organization of
knowledge about war, and about war as knowledge, had changed by the end
of the century, so that men of letters writing encyclopedias could now claim
common ground with men of war. A 1798 entry, an eighty-eight-page essay on
"War," is typical of the Napoleonic and post-Napoleonic era.[20] The essay opens
by announcing "War is a great evil; but it is inevitable, and often-times neces-

[17] Alexander Bell and Colin MacFarquhar, *Encyclopedia Britannica*, 3 vols. (Edinburgh: A. Bell
and C. MacFarquhar, 1771). *ECCO.*

[18] As the source for their essay on fortifications the editors cite John Muller, *A Treatise Containing the Elementary Part of Fortification, Regular and Irregular* (London: J. Nourse, 1746). Muller's
treatise was reprinted throughout the eighteenth century. *ECCO.*

[19] The phrase "art of war" is used ten times in the 1771 edition, acknowledging, for instance, that
a cadet is interested in learning the "art of war." But War itself is not granted the sort of long entry
accorded to other sciences and arts in the *Encyclopedia*.

[20] The Consulate in France would be formed in 1799; but in 1798 Napoleon was already chief of
the French army and conqueror/liberator of Italy.

sary"; if the warrior's intention is "the defense of persecuted virtue, or the punishment of successful wickedness, to curb ambition, or to oppose the unjust claims of superior power, mankind ought to erect altars to his memory." The moralizing, vaguely chivalric framework is new to the philosophical men compiling knowledge of arts and science. Even more startling, however, especially in contrast to the earlier edition, is the emphasis here on the comprehensive genius of the man of war. The essay continues:

> War . . . is the most necessary and useful of all the sciences: the various kinds of knowledge which ought to furnish the mind of a soldier are not without great difficulty to be attained. . . . [T]he science of war branches out into so many particulars; it takes in so many different parts; there are so many reflections necessary to be made, so many circumstances and cases to be brought together; that it is only by a continual application . . . that any man can attain it.[21]

Any man may learn philosophy or mathematics or architecture, the essay explains, but war is the science of sciences, its branches and paths comprehending these others; the science of war has become itself encyclopedic.[22] The qualities of the soldier, moreover (and the soldier is always presented here as singular and as a commanding officer) "have the[ir] original source in genius;" the warrior's "[a]bility . . . is the effect of his genius" (704). This new evaluation of the man of war and his place in the realm of knowledge is confirmed elsewhere, outside the Anglophone world, by the German *Elements of Physiophilosophy* (1810–11; trans. 1847), a compendium of physiology, cosmology, zoology, and other comprehensive systems by the polymath Lorenz Oken. His multivolume masterwork concludes with this comparison:

> As in the art of poetry all arts have been blended, so in the art of war have all sciences and all arts. The art of War is the highest, most exalted art; the art of freedom and of right, of the blessed condition of Man and of humanity—the Principle of Peace.[23]

---

[21] *Encyclopedia; or, A dictionary of arts, sciences, and miscellaneous literature . . . Compiled from the writings of the best authors, in several languages . . .*, 1st American ed., vol. 18 (Philadelphia, 1798), 703. ECCO. The first twelve volumes of the third edition of the *Encyclopedia Britannica* were supervised by Macfarquhar, but the project was completed after his death by Rev. Dr. Gleig. The American publishers claim to have added and improved the entries given them by the "European editors," but neither version identifies the author of the article on war. See the Preface 1: x–xiv. A slightly abbreviated version of this essay is repeated in the 1818 edition of the *London Encyclopedia*, and likely in others around that period.

[22] The science of war, moreover, can be learned only through war itself. Peacetime—or reading the *Encyclopedia*—cannot adequately educate a man of war.

[23] Lorenz Oken, *Elements of Physiophilosophy*, trans. Alfred Tulk (London: Ray Society, 1847), 665. I thank Jonathan Sheehan for this reference.

We are a far cry from the thought that war brings confusion and perplexity; on the contrary, war has become the highest operation of intellect. The invasive parasite, infiltrating and irritating that whole which is the globe and that whole which is the human body, has been left forgotten by history, while war, as the formidable attainment of all-comprehensive knowledge, identifies the whole circumference of the human mind.

PART III

War in the World

CHAPTER FIVE

Viewing War at a Distance

When Henri Lefebvre looks at the everyday and finds there a truth "waiting for us, besieging us on all sides"; when Sigmund Freud imagines the frail organism "suspended in the middle of an external world" that attacks it with "stimuli," they demonstrate the figurative power of the siege well into the twentieth century.[1] The siege concentrates warfare, bringing it home in the most immediate and violent way. The siege marks therefore the end of war at a distance. It is thus appropriate to conclude with a meditation on sieges, or at least on the representational work sieges may perform. Even a cursory look at Lefebvre's and Freud's usage alerts us to the fact that the figure of the siege, which ought to be all about fixed location, is remarkably mobile; it travels increasingly inward, from a geographic to a phenomenological landscape. For Lefebvre it happens to a presumably human "us," regardless of where we live and whether or not we notice; the siege occurs through the agency of "familiar, everyday objects." For Freud it occurs constantly to "sentient life" itself, an assumed internal world "suspended in the middle of an external world." The siege in this instance recalls the ways modern wartime takes place at the juncture of internal and external worlds (as described in chapter 1) and how it serves as the very form of experience (as shown in chapter 4). At the same time that the figurative siege helps to locate a psychic interiority, it does so on behalf of an external world—as if, through this military figure, the force of all the world is brought to bear upon the most isolated, fragile arena of sentient life. All distance has collapsed; the world as war is made immediate.

Yet to find in the siege a model for modern experience, as Lefebvre and Freud do, remains quite strange by historical reckoning: the siege is another archaic figure invading contemporary life. Even in the late eighteenth century, the military siege describes an outdated mode of warfare. Together with the imagining of an intimate, psychic embattlement, sieges also and simultaneously signal warfare elsewhere and back then. Despite its persistent appearance

---

[1] Henri Lefebvre, *Critique of Everyday Life*, trans. John Moore, pref. Michel Trebitsch (London: Verso, 1991), 132, and Sigmund Freud, *Beyond the Pleasure Principle*, ed. and trans. Lytton Strachey, intro. Gregory Zilboorg (New York: Norton, 1961), 30. See a fuller discussion in chapter 4.

in the wars of the Napoleonic era (the sieges of Saragossa and Moscow were famous, as was, we will see, the siege of Seringapatam) the siege more generally characterized premodern warfare, as any reader of Scott's *Ivanhoe* or Felicia Hemans's *Siege of Valencia* understood.[2] The sciences of military architecture and siegecraft that flourished in Europe through most of the eighteenth century, and were celebrated in the early encyclopedias, soon grew obsolete.

Laurence Sterne's treatment of the siege of Namur (during the War of Spanish Succession) in *Tristram Shandy* (1750–67) appears prescient in the way it converts the siege into something at first distant and then quaint, ludicrous, and finally quotidian. Uncle Toby Shandy was wounded at Namur when a piece of broken parapet hit him in the groin and crushed his hip bone. In an attempt to explain this awful injury, Toby turns first to the sort of technical terminology abounding in the age of dictionaries; but "distinctions between the scarp and the counterscarp,—the glacis and covered way,—the half-moon and ravelin" fall apart and only confound his effort (I: 85). In this failure of language, Toby turns to the visual: maps and battle diagrams seem to offer him both a distant perspective on his experience and an orderly defense against its senselessness. Finally, in a move that testifies to the link between trauma and everyday routine, the siege comes home to Toby through his "hobbyhorse," the miniature reenactments of war he habitually performs on the bowling green with his friend Corporal Trim.[3]

W. G. Sebald's aptly titled novel *Austerlitz* (2001) echoes Sterne in a more sober key when the title character offers his analysis of the slow waning of siegecraft in Europe. His language too suggests the shift away from the world of warfare depicted in eighteenth-century dictionaries:

> No one today, said Austerlitz, has the faintest idea of . . . the inflated excesses of the professional vocabulary of fortification and siegecraft, no one now understands its simplest terms, *escarpe* and *courtine*, *faussebraie*, *reduit*, and *glacis*. . . .[4]

In the nineteenth century especially, cities rapidly outgrew the massive, encircling fortifications that once marked their limits; and growing armies realized they would be trapped if they remained within such defensive armature. More

[2] Robert Southey's influential "The Siege of Zaragossa" celebrates the archaic nature of the fight, which elicits from the citizens a valor and religious fervor reminiscent of its medieval past. "History of the Peninsular Wars," in *Select Prose of Robert Southey*, ed. with intro. Jacob Zeitlin (New York: Macmillan, 1916).

[3] My reading has been aided by Peter Stevick, "Miniaturization in Eighteenth-Century Literature," *University of Toronto Quarterly* 38 (1969): 173, and David McNeil, "*Tristram Shandy*: The Grotesque View of War and the Military Character," *Studies in the Age of Voltaire and the Eighteenth Century* 266 (1989): 411–32.

[4] W. G. Sebald, *Austerlitz*, trans. Anthea Bell (New York: Random House, 2001), 15.

mobile forces had the strategic advantage. Both Wellington and Napoleon capitalized on developments in weaponry and strategic planning to reorient activity away from the defensive fortification of town or city, toward the mobile deployment of massive armies over large territories (as in the battle of Austerlitz). Indeed, Napoleon's disastrous Russian campaign seemed to prove the point that the capture of the capital city mattered less than whether troops could move successfully across large tracts of land.

As Sebald's Austerlitz points out, European fortresses, built as monuments to the "insanity" of retrenchment and defense, were later refashioned by the Germans during World War II as detention centers and penal camps. What was built to repel sieges served subsequently to enclose the miserable routines of detainees and prisoners of war. A bit like Uncle Toby, Austerlitz also consults (and includes) diagrams of fortresses, models of geometrical symmetry and godlike perspective. Their distancing power collapses, however, when the protagonist approaches an actual fortress and is compelled to imagine the daily existence of its prisoners. From outside the fortress of Breendonk in Belgium, "I could not," Austerlitz reports, "despite its . . . evident rational structure, recognize anything designed by the human mind but saw it, rather, as the anatomical blueprint of some alien, crab-like creature" (22). In contrast to the perfect diagrams, these vestiges of siege warfare are alien, primordial; they appall him. Inside the fortress, the trope of inexpressibility takes over: "I could not imagine how the prisoners . . . could push [the heavy, giant wheel]barrows"; "it was impossible to picture them bracing themselves against the weight"; Austerlitz "could not envisage the drudgery performed day after day, year after year, at Breendock and all the other main and branch camps" (22–23). For Sebald's Austerlitz, brooding over the history of European warfare from the eighteenth to the late twentieth century, siege warfare is succeeded by an awful, unaccountable discipline.

Certainly in the twentieth century, but even in the wartime of the early nineteenth century, the siege was a troubling, romantic figure. I say this to emphasize its kinship with other romantic figures in this book—the post-boy, the winter snow, the passing cloud, the everyday accident—all of which hover in a similar mediatory way between portraying some felt or sentient experience of war and allowing a distant and abstracted, unfelt view of violence. The siege offered a way to imagine a world at war coming home in the most intimate ways. But it also allowed a way to frame war as a distant reality, made remote by the movements of history. One of my goals in keeping the figure of the siege present in romantic wartime is to question the too-easy distinction between the military campaigns in Europe and those elsewhere in the world—notably India, which was central to the larger geopolitics of the wars, and where siege warfare still dominated. I am interested in how this fighting too, conducted at a very great distance, came home to Britain in wartime.

This last chapter takes up the siege in order to push forward into our familiar modernity, as Sebald does, the lingering strangeness of romantic wartime and its mediatory figures. But the material form of mediation shifts here, turning from printed text to images from a burgeoning visual culture. The discussion pauses, in this passage from printed word to image, to look at engraved images of distant sieges which were often paired with printed accounts. The mixed media (not unlike the inclusion of diagrams and photographs in Sebald's novel) offer a sort of midpoint in the historical development of the depiction of war in mass media, from verbal text to photograph and film. In the visual depiction of distant war, many of the specifically temporal concerns raised earlier in this study—of belatedness and anticipation, of stillness and its historical complexity—are recast, reinterpreted via the spatial dimensions of the image. In addition, the questions of mediation I have been pursuing, with its trade-offs between information and affection, now disclose themselves through the operation of visual perspective, through manipulations of close and far, and through the visual protocols of the picturesque and sublime. The porous borders of internal and external worlds are made visible in new ways: geopolitical movements can be seen in the aesthetics of landscape.

The visual depiction of sieges in India, brought home to a viewing audience in Britain, provides an almost overdetermined means for considering what is familiar and what alien in wartime. Foreign but intimate, distant but visibly present here before you, the image of the siege provides as well a means to reconsider the claims of the wartime stranger, whose flickering presence in romantic poetry (at your hearth, on a winter's evening) returns in the visual realm as a barely distinguishable human figure. The chapter ends, then, by reflecting on another unsettling romantic image of strangers, this time positioned on a fragile bridge, fleeing a siege in a distant land.

War in Pictures

War was and still is the most irresistible—and picturesque—news.[5]

In what follows I want simultaneously to introduce a pair of British artists in India and one of their paintings especially, and to conclude my reflections on the relations among distance, temporality, and affect. Introducing and concluding, beginning and ending, what follows is also, and almost without trying, an allegory about distant wars, lines of communication, and suspense.

The artists are the Daniells, Thomas (1749–1840) and William (1769–1837), uncle and nephew, considered the finest and probably most influential land-

---

[5] Susan Sontag, *Regarding the Pain of Others* (New York: Farrar, Straus, and Giroux, 2003), 49.

Figure 1   "View from Sankry-Droog, [Sankaridrug]" by Thomas and William Daniell.
From *Oriental scenery. One hundred and fifty views of the architecture, antiquities, and landscape scenery of Hindoo-stan* (London: The authors, 1812–16). Courtesy of the University of Chicago Special Collections.

scape painters of colonial India. Their series of published aquatint engravings, *Views in Hindoostan* and later *Oriental Scenery* (1796–1805), followed in the wake of and extended William Hodges's important work in his *Select Views in India* (1788) and *Travels in India* (1793). The Daniells' engravings served for decades as an authoritative resource in England for images of Indian landscape and architecture. But they are also images of a land at war: from the late 1780s through the first two decades of the nineteenth century, the British East India Company escalated its aggressive military policy in India in the south, central, and northernmost regions of Hindustan, in the several Mysore and Maratha wars, and later in the Anglo-Ghurka war. These were the regions conscientiously recorded in the Daniells' work, and these were the years during which they traveled, drew, painted, engraved, and sold their images in India and Great Britain. In their attentiveness to hill forts and fortifications more generally, one might suspect a sort of military picturesque at work, carefully framing and commodifying the terrain of recent bloody sieges so that its outcome appears cleanly resolved—almost inevitable (figs.1 and 2).

However, I want to claim the presence of something more unsettling because more tentative in these images: call it suspense, a sort of hanging in time and space that, like the distant puffs of smoke in these images, defies the rocky solidity of the terrain. Of the view from Sankaridrug (fig. 1), the usually laconic

Figure 2   "View of Part of Rotas Ghur, in Bahar" by Thomas and William Daniell. From *Oriental scenery. One hundred and fifty views of the architecture, antiquities, and landscape scenery of Hindoo-stan* (London: The authors, 1812–16). Courtesy of the University of Chicago Special Collections.

William Daniell wrote to his mother: "the whole Expanse is one scene of unextinguishable warfare, where, urged by hunger, lust or cruelty[,] mutual destruction rages without intermission."[6] Unextinguishable warfare is not what the viewer is given in this image; instead, and partly as a function of the distance it inscribes, the engraving seems to grant an otherwise impossible—and yet suspenseful—sense of intermission, a visual "meantime" in the very landscape of war.

My claim about suspense or intermission will require attention to recent work on the picturesque and, ultimately, on cosmopolitanism. It will also demand a peeling away of current assumptions about the picturesqueness of war, about the familiar ways pictures frame the experience of distant war. A leading preoccupation, however, will be one painting's unsettling recalibration of distance—distances within the landscape and our distance from that landscape. This painting, the title of which reads "The Rope Bridge at Serinagur . . . , taken in the year 1789 during the evacuation of the city in consequence of the approach of a large army from Almorah" (fig. 12), has for several years guided and haunted my thoughts about war—and especially the threat of siege—viewed at a distance.

[6] Qtd. in Thomas Sutton, *The Daniells: Artists and Travellers* (London: Bodley Head, 1954), 73.

We saw Susan Sontag remark, in her study of war photography, that "being a spectator of calamities taking place in another country is a quintessential modern experience" (18). This quintessentially modern experience is for Sontag mediated and enabled primarily through photographic images. For all the moral and political problems associated with such spectatorship, it remains an experience worth contemplating: as Charles Simic notes in his review of Sontag's book, "A war without pictures . . . is a frightening prospect."[7] Simic's use of the words "pictures" and especially "prospect"—that favorite term of eighteenth-century landscape art—hints at the fact that not all war pictures have been photographs. War before photography was not necessarily war without pictures, but it was envisioned through what must now appear obsolete temporalities and prospects. We have grown accustomed to the photojournaled war collapsing protracted fighting into captured instants of horror, reinforcing the urgency of shooting, and shooting repeatedly. The late eighteenth- and early nineteenth-century pictures (paintings, engravings, panoramas) with which this chapter is concerned collectively offer one of the first concerted efforts to represent visually for the general public a distant, ongoing war. They represent warfare not necessarily as history but as current event, or as some complex combination of the two. In reporting on war, these images also give Great Britain some of its first views of India, coordinating those views with the surrounding prospect, in the years 1793–1815 especially, of a world at war. Instead of immediacy and urgency, however, these images more often than not offer landscapes of prolonged *durée* and vacancy. Rather than eliminating distance, they seem to insist upon it, thereby suggesting an unfamiliar, perhaps less complicit relationship to the violence of war. Of course, theirs was not the only visual medium by means of which such relationships were negotiated. We will see, for instance, that they stand in great and varied contrast to the popular panoramas, which were calculated to repudiate distance by means of a precinematic technology for viewing war. But the very contrast between these modes of picturing available to the public at the turn of the nineteenth century offers broad hints of how much contemporary culture has inherited—and lost—from romantic views of war.

In excavating the experience of the spectator of distant calamities in the era before photography, Sontag's account proves helpful, if only for her attachment (like Sebald's) to the period of the Napoleonic wars and for her symptomatic ambivalence on the question of distance. Before she considers early war photographs (Roger Fenton's 1855 photographs from the Crimean War), she pauses over the prephotographic documentation of war provided by Francisco Goya's

---

[7] Charles Simic, "Archives of Horror," review of *Regarding the Pain of Others*, by Susan Sontag, *New York Review of Books*, May 1, 2003, 9.

nightmarish *Disasters of War* (1810–20), his visual record of the atrocities triggered when Napoleon's troops invaded Spain in 1808. Goya's series of more than eighty etchings, Sontag remarks, "move[s] the viewer close to the horror," eliminating "the trappings of spectacle" as well as the buffer or frame of distance (44).

Rendering proximity to horror, albeit at the distance of many years (the etchings were not made available until 1863, when they would have competed with photography), Goya's images represent, in Sontag's account, a crucial aesthetic development. They also offer the implicit rationale for her book: a plate from the *Disasters* (plate 36) decorates its cover.

> Goya's art . . . seems a turning point in the history of moral feelings and of sorrow. . . . With Goya, a new standard of responsiveness to suffering enters art. . . . The account of war's cruelties is fashioned as an assault on the sensibility of the viewer. . . . A voice, presumably the artist's, badgers the viewer: can you bear to look at this? (44–45)

Photography only escalates the force of such up-close, in-your-face assaults on the viewer's sensibility. Sontag cites a newspaper review of the 1862 photographic exhibit "The Dead of Antietam," shown at Mathew Brady's New York gallery. While endorsing the shock these images offer to indifferent city-dwellers, the reviewer remains queasy about the exhibit's "'terrible distinctness'": "'If he [Brady] has not brought bodies and laid them in our dooryards and along the streets, he has done something very like it'" (fig. 3). Proximity brings unbearable detail: "'By the aid of the magnifying glass, the very features of the slain may be distinguished'" (63). At their best, Sontag suggests, images of distant war insist on the violence of proximity with its gift of "unnecessary, indecent"—even magnified—"information" (63).[8]

The use of short-range weapons like Goya's etchings or Brady's photographs may, then, be of value in battling the complacency or numbness wrought by modern, long-range warfare. But Sontag's strong endorsement of visual proximity and its shocking information wavers and fades as *Regarding the Pain of Others* concludes. Sontag gives an extended history of such salutary "assaults" on viewers' indifference, but finally acknowledges that assault might have an unfavorable outcome or no outcome at all; the moral and political effects of sensational or enhanced images of war are not necessarily predictable. Horrific images of war may, for instance, as easily incite as deter violence. Furthermore—though Sontag is silent on this front—up-close imaging may also facilitate the prosecution of long-distance warfare. The very violence you see

---

[8] International human rights law now forbids publishing photographs that feature the face of the dead.

Figure 3   "Dead Confederate Soldier, Petersburg, Va." by Mathew Brady (1865). Courtesy of the United States Library of Congress.

unfolding on a screen may be performed by "smart" weapon technology that, like communications technology and in concert with it, uses long-range satellite imaging to overcome geophysical distance. As it eliminates the distance of faraway warfare, the prosecution of war via computer screen makes up-close imaging our contemporary mode of warfare. In other words, the "assault by images" holding Sontag's attention takes a perverse turn in contemporary warfare, where much of the fighting is in fact conducted via imaging. Twenty-first-century warfare tightens the complicity of image and war such that there is virtually no distance between them.

The advent of real-time reporting is the logical extension of the history Sontag explores. Real-time photojournalism collapses the distance of both time and space, bringing images—horrific images—of war to your home even as the violence occurs. "The observation of events," observes Niklas Luhmann, "occurs almost at the same time as the events themselves."[9] This real-time version of visual assault, Paul Virilio argues, reflecting on the first Gulf War, "leav[es] no time or space for decision-making or reflection, and thus no time

[9] Niklas Luhmann, *The Reality of the Mass Media*, trans. Kathleen Cross (Stanford: Stanford UP, 2000), 26.

or space for politics." [10] The technology of our media replicates, moreover, the technology of warfare itself, overcoming the limits of the mortal body. Indeed, another contemporary critic notes in the development of autonomous weapons systems an effort "to get the human eye out of the loop" in implementing "smart bombs"; vision in war will be the province of machines. [11] We return in new ways to the threat, seen two centuries earlier in figurations of war as winter, that there will be no eyes left to see the devastation.

Consciously or not, Sontag seems to register this development when she shifts ground at the end of her book. In the course of her argument for the "ethical value of an assault by images," Sontag turns full-face to advocate not the visceral immediacy of images of war but rather a hope in their ability to affect a distancing (116). Unwilling to follow through to the instantaneity of real time, she comes to the conclusion—*pace* Goya—that pictures can provide a framed, "abstracted" version of reality. I take her use of "abstracted" here as demanding a rather literal meaning, as in "drawn-away" or distanced, rather than as opposite to the concrete or real:

> It is felt that there is something morally wrong with the abstract of reality offered by photography; that one has no right to experience the suffering of others at a distance, denuded of its raw power; that we pay too high a human (or moral) price for those hitherto admired qualities of vision—the standing back from the aggressiveness of the world which frees us for observation and for elective attention. . . .
>
> There's nothing wrong with standing back and thinking. To paraphrase several sages, "Nobody can think and hit someone at the same time." (118)

Finally, for Sontag, even viewing photographic images of war is only ever viewing war mediated and at a distance; bodies never actually bleed in her dooryard. Thus she herself pulls back, dropping her logic of visual assault. Despite its dangers—callousness, rejection, aestheticization—the distancing effect Sontag now assigns to images of war remains fundamental to thought. There are reasons to stand apart from the violence of war, and though they cannot guarantee, pictures allow that possibility.

Though this distinction between representation and reality is no great revelation, Sontag nevertheless keys her response to the question of distance per se. In an age where even distant calamity plays out right before our eyes, the ethical value of distance demands reconsideration. As I have suggested, her book symptomatically elaborates this insight. Moreover, in the troubled ambivalence

[10] Paul Virilio, *Desert Screen: War at the Speed of Light* (London: Continuum, 2002), 51 and passim. See also his interviews in *Pure War* (New York: Semiotexte, 1997).

[11] Manuel de Landa, *War in the Age of Intelligent Machines* (New York: Zone Books, 1991), 128.

that marks her discussion as well as her prose ("There's nothing wrong . . ."), Sontag seems to suggest here more than a simple stance of philosophical detachment: an ongoing struggle within her argument registers her affective response to the question of viewing pain at a distance.

Misgivings about proximity—and, with it, speed—in the representation of war invite a reassessment of detachment, and, counterintuitively, detachment's affective pull.[12] When Virilio wonders how to bring back into current understanding of war the felt, physical ground and span of time (*durée*) eliminated by current military and communications technology (what happens on the ground, he says, has been usurped by what happens on the screen), he suggests that landscape painting with its dated prospects may have a view and feel fit for the present. The pictures of Indian landscapes to which I now turn elaborate, even thematize, the distance of the viewer from war-torn terrain. They contemplate the literal, physical ground in a way contemporary mediation of warfare asks us to forget. In most cases the suggestion of siege warfare is itself kept at a distance, requiring real attentiveness and work on the part of the viewer if it is to be recognized, almost as if it were a painful memory or barely acknowledged threat.[13] If, as Sontag and others have suggested, visual documentation of war has driven toward immediacy and ubiquity, conflating the role of the camera with weapon technology, then images from the end of the eighteenth century will appear woefully inadequate to twenty-first-century eyes. They answer to the "landscape imperative" characterized by W.J.T. Mitchell as "the mandate to withdraw, to draw out, by drawing back from a site"; but instead of producing a purely "aestheticizing distance, a kind of resistance to whatever practical or moral claim the scene might make on us," these pictures of India do make demands. They contribute to what Mitchell otherwise acknowledges is eighteenth-century landscape's "indeterminacy of affect," which draws the viewer in even as it withdraws.[14] Out of touch, lacking detailed information, and perhaps unwilling to engage in an assault on

---

[12] Alan Liu analyzes distance and detachment and their role in criticism in "Local Transcendence: Cultural Criticism, Postmodernism, and the Romanticism of Detail," *Representations* 32 (Autumn 1990): 97–99; his argument turns on the use by critics of local detail as a means or medium for approaching the "immanence" of culture. In the images I consider, distance is *not* mediated by detail; more often than not, detail is withheld.

[13] Beth Fowkes Tobin argues that Hodges's Indian landscapes erase the present facts of warfare, using a mode of picturesque which represses conflict to promote "only a serene and ancient [view of] India." *Colonizing Nature: The Tropics in British Arts and Letters, 1760–1820* (Philadelphia; U of Pennsylvania P, 2004), 136. In the Indian landscapes under discussion here, I emphasize rather what Kate Teltscher refers to as "a fundamental sense of insecurity which can rarely be allowed direct expression." *Indian Inscribed: European and British Writing on India, 1600–1800* (Delhi: Oxford UP, 1995), 151 (qtd. in Tobin, 133).

[14] W.J.T. Mitchell, ed., *Landscape and Power: Space, Place, and Landscape,* 2nd ed. (Chicago: U of Chicago P, 2002), viii, vii.

sensibility, these landscapes allow a prospect of and a feeling for distant war that has grown all but impossible in an age of instantaneous communication. In their very insistence upon distance and vacancy, they speak of desolation. In their suspension of linear time, they open up correspondence between realms otherwise divided by the temporal and spatial mapping of historicism. And they invite what Sontag seems to desire: a cosmopolitan response.

Worlding India

> Is India free? . . .
> Or do we grind her *still*?[15]

When the Indian landscape was first brought to the eyes of the British public in the 1780s and 1790s, it came as a landscape of war.[16] In this sense it was a landscape wounded, defaced, and overrun by a series of military campaigns between the armies of the British East India Company and those of the French, the Marathas, and, most recently, the rulers of Mysore, Haidar Ali (1761–1782) and his son, Tipu Sultan (1782–1799). "Between Agra and Delhi," William Daniell writes to his mother in 1790, "the country not long ago was uncommonly beautiful, but such destruction has been brought to it by war, scarcely a tree or blade of grass is to be seen."[17] Visual accounts of the Company's campaigns in India became available in the new genre of illustrated campaign book, popular into the Victorian period.[18] To a great degree, this desolation of the land was understood by the British public to be the grievous, in Cowper's words *grinding* effect of mercantile imperialism. Even those books sponsored by the Company seem unable or unwilling to shake this awareness of desolation; their registration of distance especially evokes and shapes desolation.[19] Before turning to the more accomplished and professional work of the Daniells, therefore, I consider two series of war images from India produced by military artists in the 1790s, Lieutenant Robert Colebrook and Richard Home,

[15] William Cowper, *The Task*, in *The Complete Poetical Works*, ed. H. S. Milford, 4th ed. (Oxford: Oxford UP, 1967), IV: 28–30; emphasis added.

[16] See Tobin, esp. 117–43; Mildred Archer et al., *India Observed* (London: Victoria and Albert Museum in association with Trefoil Books, 1982); and Jagmohan Mahajan et al., *Picturesque India* (New Delhi: Lustre Press under arrangement with Rupa & Co., 1983).

[17] "William Daniell's letter to his mother," transcribed by Joseph Farington, in Sir Evan Cottam, "The Daniells in India," *Bengal Past and Present* 25 (1923): 15.

[18] Archer, *India Observed* 82.

[19] These illustrated books by British army officers offered "some of the earliest views—though of a limited part—of south India by British artists" (Mahajan 95). In her reading of Hodges's paintings, commissioned in the 1780s mostly by Warren Hastings, East India Company representative and governor-general of Bengal, Tobin finds melancholy leading to a firming-up of imperial ambitions in India (117–43).

to show how their use of distance calls into question what has been won—and lost—in the desolation of fighting. Spatializing Cowper's interrogatory "still," their work shows how distance can manufacture views resistant to the narratives of history.

India was at this time, as Gayatri Spivak put it, a landscape newly "worlded" into British consciousness, a "supposedly uninscribed territory" being made into science and art, into "an object to be understood."[20] At the distance now of two hundred years, the general outlines of that inscription have grown familiar and legible. But the worlding of India was not a continuous, or as Spivak herself warns, homogeneous process. Nor was it always felt to be desirable or inevitable, as recent historians have pointed out.[21] The first landscapes by Britons attempting to depict Hindustan, many of them produced by military men, often approached the land through the violent operations and dislocations of regional and imperial wars, wars which kept the consolidation, the understood identity of the subcontinent, in doubt. Consider that, in the 1790s especially, the East India Company's campaigns were led by Lord Cornwallis, the man forced to surrender to George Washington at Yorktown a decade earlier. The dismal equation of America with India was common in England, invoked often in the 1780s to criticize imperial ambition.[22] Consider too that having checked him once at the beginning of the 1790s, Cornwallis was required to wage a second campaign in the south of India against Tipu Sultan, now ally of Napoleon, prompting the Fourth (and finally decisive) Mysore War in 1799. (To a certain degree, the threat of Napoleon's return after the Treaty of Amiens and again in the Hundred Days must have echoed for the British the indomitability of Tipu, the self-styled Tiger of Mysore.)[23] As with the multiple Anglo-Maratha wars fought in central Hindustan, the British in India seemed to be going over the same ground again and again, an experience that, as we will see, shadows their representation of the landscape. In this period before imperial settlement, there was no guarantee that Britain would maintain its Indian holdings or successfully realize their "worlding." What Suvir Kaul contends about the long poem in the eighteenth century could

[20] Gayatri Chakravorty Spivak and Sarah Harasym, *The Post-Colonial Critic: Interviews, Strategies, Dialogues* (New York: Routledge, 1990), 1. See also Teltscher, *India Inscribed.*

[21] C. A. Bayly, *Imperial Meridian: The British Empire and the World, 1780–1830* (London: Longman, 1989), 95–99; Kathleen Wilson, *The Island Race* (London: Routledge, 2003), 50–51; and Linda Colley, *Captives* (New York: Pantheon, 2002), 257–307.

[22] After the British defeat at Pollidur in 1780, Horace Walpole predicted, "India and America are alike escaping" (qtd. in Colley 270–71).

[23] Both Tipu and his father, Haidur Ali, were frequently referred to in British publications as "usurpers" and "tyrants." Once Tipu Sultan allied himself with Napoleon, the British were increasingly ready to view him as their Bonaparte in the East. As Colley puts it, "Tipu and Napoleon . . . became two sides of the same coin" (297).

apply as well to prospect painting. Both instruments of "worlding" aimed to enounce "a puissant (and plastic) vocabulary of nation, particularly one of Britain proving itself (in fits and starts, to be sure) great at home and abroad."[24] Yet those "fits and starts" step out of their parentheses and query any historical "to be sure" in the Indian landscapes of this period. The un-worlding effects of warfare kept ripping apart, like Penelope at her weaving, British attempts to make India into art.[25] Early representations of Indian landscape and of the wars conducted there thus allow an intermission—however tenuous—in what might now appear the rapid and inevitable movement of imperial conquest.

Robert H. Colebrook, "Lieutenant in the service of the Honourable East India Company, who attended the Army in the Capacity of Surveyor" published his *Twelve views of places in the kingdom of Mysore, the country of Tippoo Sultan, from drawings taken on the spot* in 1793, intending it primarily for an audience of military men, company men, and their close associates. Its publication date marked the successful conclusion of three years of intense fighting in the Third Mysore War, where Tipu Sultan Fath Ali Khan was forced to yield parts of the region and several forts, along with a large remuneration, to the East India Company. This victory in Mysore suggested a reversal of British military fortunes after the loss in America (1776–81) and after two previous humiliating outings in the south (First and Second Mysore wars, 1767–69 and 1780–84). Colebrook's *Twelve views* superimpose themselves upon those previous defeats without obliterating them. The large-format book (roughly twenty-four by thirty-six inches) features a series of landscape views of the southern kingdom; each of John William Edy's copperplate engravings of Colebrook's drawings is faced with the author's "concise descriptions of the places drawn, with a brief detail of part of the operations of the army under the Marquis of Cornwallis, during the late war, and a few other particulars."[26] Colebrook's attention to fortresses in this region, understandable given the course of the campaign, proved influential for later images of the subcontinent.[27] From the

[24] Suvir Kaul, *Poems of Nation, Anthems of Empire* (Charlottesville: U of Virginia P, 2000), 5.

[25] To get at the "semiosis of imperialism," Spivak coins the term "worlding," borrowing and extending Martin Heidegger's notion of the work of art as that which "emerges in the gap between earth and world." Though "gap" is a common translation for the German *Riss,* Spivak insists on a more literal reading: "*Riss* in Heidegger has the violent implication of a fracture—'fighting of the battle,' 'the intimacy of opponents'—rather than the relatively 'cool' connotations of a gap." Landscape painting of India emerged precisely in—and not fully *out of*—such a fracture. It may be no accident that the medium most common and effective for representing views of India in these years was engraving, itself, as William Blake insisted, born out of violent inscription. See Gayatri Chakravorty Spivak, "The Rani of Sirmur: An Essay in Reading the Archives," *History and Theory* 24 (1985): 253.

[26] Robert H. Colebrook, *Twelve views of places in the kingdom of Mysore* (London: [n.p.], 1793), title page.

[27] See Hermione DeAlmeida and George G. Gilpin, *Indian Renaissance: British Romantic Art and the Prospect of India* (Aldershot, UK: Ashgate, 2005), 176. Hodges's *Travels In India,* also

Figure 4   "East View of Bangalore" by Robert H. Colebrook. *Twelve views of places in the kingdom of Mysore* (London: [n.p.], 1793). Courtesy of Duke University Special Collections.

siege of Bangalore to Tipu's surrender at the fortress of Seringapatam, the order of engravings more or less follows the last stage of Cornwallis's campaign against the Sultan's armies. Colebrook's designation as military surveyor and the phrase "taken on the spot," moreover, advertise the professional knowledge of the artist as well as his proximity to events of the campaign. The written text of Colebrook's *Twelve views*, with its promise of a "brief detail" and "concise description," fulfills journalistic expectations that the trained observer on the scene will provide a fine-grained account informing the reader of significant events. The engravings, on the other hand, never come close.

Colebrook's initial plate, "East View of Bangalore," starkly represents the discrepancy between text and image (fig. 4). The prose "detail" attends first to the impressive fortress, describing the innovations and "modernizations" wrought by Tipu Sultan and Haidar Ali upon the walled city of Bangalore. Lest the technological update make the Mysorean rulers appear too enlightened, the description turns quickly to the ornamentation of the palace

---

published in 1793, places a similar emphasis on hill forts, but in the northern region around Benares, where Hastings had fought a decade earlier.

within: "it is painted in gilt, in a most gorgeous style. The contrast between this fabric [of palace and fort] and the surrounding huts conspicuously marks the distinction between the despot and his subjects." From formidable fort and gilt palace, the narrator zooms in on these small hovels, "in one of which," we are told, British officers were taken prisoner in the previous war (the Second Mysore War) and "treated with inhumanity, rigour, and insolence." Sudden proximity to the confined, mistreated bodies of British gentlemen in Mysore elicits readerly identification, compassion, horror, perhaps outrage. This quick point of contact, then, serves as justification for the subsequent description of Cornwallis's assault upon Tipu's fortress, and for the assault itself.[28] Here, the narrator's fascination with the British army's swift military movements aims to correct for the image of captive and humiliated officers. Swiftness also characterizes the narrative: the two weeks Cornwallis's troops "sit" before the walls of Bangalore are telescoped into a few crucial days of action and the final assault, where "the whole contest did not last more than an hour." When British soldiers stormed the fort, "a dreadful slaughter of the enemy ensued": roughly sixty British lives were lost against Mysore's five hundred. Numbers, however, soon give way to the face of the enemy as the concluding sentences swoop in for the emotional close-up. The loss of Bangalore was such a blow to Tipu Sultan, we read, "that he is said to have wept, and exhibited the most frantic symptoms of unavailing sorrow and despair." Yet if the rapid trajectory of the narrative works to replace the imprisoned officers with the emasculated Sultan, to substitute righteous for tyrannical warfare in "no more than an hour," it fails to move forward, or, rather, it circles back again. "He [Tipu] soon after wrecked [sic] his vengeance on some unfortunate British prisoners, . . . detained . . . since 1783, by ordering them to be put to death." This historical remainder, the prisoners left over from the previous conflict, will surface again in the prose text, forever complicating the narrative of the campaign. For now, though, their retaliatory execution at Bangalore propels and warrants the series of sieges to come, until Tipu himself is "reduced to his last stake" at Seringapatam.

In contrast to the propulsive movement of the narrative, with its dramatic swings from framing shot to detailed, emotionally charged close-up, Colebrook's "East View of Bangalore" is all stillness and distance. A placid sky stretches over the land, whose smooth horizon is punctuated only by a partly shadowed roadside shrine on the rising ground to the left; in the extreme distance, by the dim silhouette of mountains; and, to the right, by a vaguely discernible tower with its vaguely discernible (and unidentifiable) pennant. Even

---

[28] See Colley 269–307 for the way that stories of captive British officers in India were turned, after 1792, from embarrassments to effective propaganda for imperialism.

Figure 5   Detail of "East View of Bangalore" by Robert H. Colebrook. *Twelve views of places in the kingdom of Mysore* (London: [n.p.], 1793). Courtesy of Duke University Special Collections.

these breaks in the line move the eye horizontally, left to right. A small human figure squats by a horse, halted by the shrine. Other, very small figures of people work in the level field to the right; cattle graze. What holds the eye most is probably the long, dark line of cypress trees, which cuts the ground of the image, the front from the back. The very force and distinctness of that windbreak challenge the viewer to peer at the prohibited ground beyond (where yet another tree impedes the view). There, almost hugging the ground, and hard to differentiate from that ground (their empty spaces correspond to patches of dirt in the foreground), are the minuscule walls of the vast fortress of Bangalore, trailing off laterally into the distance, repeating but hollowly the barrier of cypress. With effort you can discern what occupies the center of the engraving: a number of tents and perhaps soldiers, scattered before the fortress walls (fig. 5). Yet to enlarge by focusing upon such details seems misguided, for the image itself pulls away from detailing, positioning specifics at such a distance as to remind the viewer of her inability to ascertain much at all—even in this large-format, expensively reproduced print.

At least three responses are ready at hand for such an image, over each of which I hesitate. Reading it in concert with the accompanying prose, for example, I cannot convincingly advance the argument that "East View of Bangalore" attempts to suppress or gloss over warfare, naturalizing its effects. Instead, in the image and thanks to the prose, the details of violence either go without saying or do not say enough, requiring the ample insufficiency of this visual supplement. I might then be tempted to read Colebrook's prospect of Bangalore as advertisement: look at this broad stretch of arable land which Britain now commands, thanks to the efforts of Lord Cornwallis. In this second interpretation, the remote image of the fort, with its military connotations, can now be diminished in favor of the closer promise of fertile cultivation and cultured contemplation. Part of the work of a surveyor, like Colebrook, would be to produce a vision of the conquered land now ready for exploitation. Yet a military surveyor also maps the lay of the land to be invaded, what military

engineers called "the Ground, with all its inequalities." [29] "East View of Bangalore" fulfills this role as well. There is at least as strong a pull to read the open
book from left to right, from the prose to the image, so that the massive movement of troops, artillery, horses, and elephants, not to mention the "dreadful
slaughter" described in the accompanying text, is poised to invade this otherwise serene landscape, destroying its agricultural prospects. Recall Daniell's
comment about the land around Agra: "such destruction has been brought to
it by war, scarcely a tree or blade of grass is to be seen." It is probably impossible to tell, in other words, whether the engraving depicts the landscape around
Bangalore before or after the military operations described. Is this a landscape
about to be ravaged or one that survives impassively the onslaught of Cornwallis's army? Whose tents are those (they could be traders', or travelers')? whose
pennant? and finally, whose fort, indeed whose landscape? With the distance it
inscribes, the engraving raises such questions without providing the specifics
necessary to answer them. If you want particulars, and with them proprietary
certainty, you must let in the violence of the written text.

The third response common to such an image addresses its temporality, the
curious stillness or suspension from history evoked here. In her work on nineteenth-century watercolors of Algeria by European women, Deborah Cherry
provides a succinct version of this response. The paintings she studies "portray
a land before and after colonisation, rather than a society caught up in and
traumatized by its chaotic intervention." [30] Orientalist painting in general, she
writes, "gives the impression of a population arrested in time and space. The
native figures are as immobile as the architecture they accompany. . . . [They]
convey the simplicity of a culture in which time passes imperceptibly" (90–91).
The temporality posed by these landscapes stands outside of the progressive,
even destructive movements of modernity and, indeed, historicism. Yet I
would alter Cherry's characterization, taken as it is from later colonial landscapes, and describe the "East View of Bangalore" not as comfortably "before
and after colonisation"—but uncomfortably *either* before *or* after, its sense of
temporality not simply "arrested" but hanging in doubt of the possibility of
colonization. The doubtful quality of time in the image accompanies the
written military history, broadening but also potentially undermining it.

---

[29] This phrase is taken from the description of curriculum overseen by the chief drawing master
at the Royal Military Academy. Royal Military Academy, Woolwich. *Rules and Orders for the Royal
Military Academy at Woolwich* (London: J. Bullock, 1776). *Eighteenth Century Collections Online*
(*ECCO*). Gale Group. http://galenet.galegroup.com/servlet/ECCO.

[30] Deborah Cherry, *Beyond the Frame: Feminism and Visual Culture in Britain, 1850–1900* (London: Routledge, 2000), 87. Tobin argues similarly about Orientalist versions of India (*Colonizing
Nature* 131). On many points, Cherry's and Tobin's analyses serve as a helpful counter to my own.
For general treatments of temporality and colonialism, see Dipesh Chakrabarty, *Provincializing Europe: Postcolonial Thought and Historical Difference* (Princeton: Princeton UP, 2000).

Figure 6   "East View of Seringapatam" by Robert H. Colebrook. *Twelve views of places in the kingdom of Mysore* (London: [n.p.], 1793). Courtesy of Duke University Special Collections.

Something slower, drawn-out, and inconclusive might be acknowledged here, even if it is only the much bigger picture of the halting process of colonization itself. A vast expanse of ground separates the viewer from Bangalore. The movement of eye to fortress is variously impeded. Slow consideration is required before the distant prospect can be related to the prose "detail" of Cornwallis's campaign.[31] In the final recognition of how little one can determine here, "East View of Bangalore" might restore to the understanding of war some recognition of the ground and *durée* we have seen Paul Virilio advocate so strenuously.

The temporal hesitation or intermission of this image, which is repeated in nearly all of the plates, leads less to a complacent vision of the premodern than to an anxiety over the reversals and indeterminacies of wartime history. Yes, the penultimate plate, "East View of Seringapatam" (fig. 6), finally represents the British and allied troops in full pageantry, fanning out in the plains with

[31] In Niklas Luhmann's analysis, the news has its "selectors" bent on providing distinctions, new newness, surprise, and a certain recursivity—and therefore identifiability—to people, places, things and events. *The Reality of the Mass Media* (Stanford: Stanford UP, 2000). All of these selectors are baffled here; surprise is especially baffled by the elegiac content of Colebrook's views.

no real impediment between them and Tipu's citadel; and the accompanying prose efficiently reports that here the assembled armies "sat down before" Seringapatam "and it was forced to yield" without a shot fired, Tipu forced to "accommodate" his pursuers. Yet the final plate unravels what might appear a successful coming to terms. The "West View of Seringapatam" shows another face altogether. It reverts to Colebrook's distanced, almost desolate treatment of landscape: the fortress recedes from view, all activity is erased. And the prose narrative, having settled matters with Tipu, turns back to resurrect his father, the "usurper" Haidar Ali (whose tomb was depicted in another plate) and recount his ruthless rise to power in the southern part of the subcontinent. The end of the Third Mysore War, in other words, leads back to the beginning of the First Mysore War, the usurper Haidar Ali resurfaces at the defeat of his son, the usurper Tipu Sultan. Why reopen this violent history at the end of the account, as if the twelfth prospect were in fact a retrospect, the next step a recurrence to the past? Indeed within five years of the appearance of Colebrook's work, there would be another Mysore war, another siege of Seringapatam, and beyond India, another usurper for the British to confront.

The disquiet and perplexity lurking in these distant prospects of war in India are only heightened by this suggestion of historical reversibility (east view or west?) and endless substitutions. Colebrook's refusal or failure to capture the landscape of Mysore, which, as his title tells, still remains "the kingdom of Tipoo Sultan," mimics a more general ambivalence in the military enterprise. The inability to capture calls attention to those moments in the prose narrative where, as at Bangalore, the British themselves fail to recapture what Tipu Sultan captured: those captive British officers from the previous wars. At Sewandroog and Outram-Durang, two other fortresses on the route to Seringapatam, the narrative tells us, Tipu Sultan successfully shuffles British captives from one prison to another; prisoners escape and are recaptured, in an endless reminder of the substitutions and remainders of war.[32] Linda Colley reports that over the course of the four Mysore wars, probably thousands of British captives, predominantly officers, were held for years in the prisons of Tipu and his father; four hundred of them remained in Mysore until the 1790s. Some of these were executed by the monarch in the course of the campaign in 1792; some were freed as part of the eventual treaty; others shocked their countrymen by converting, willingly or not, to Islam and joining the Mysore army—and these conversions were widely reported (Colley 275–307). In terms of ground, bodies, and even souls, then, the question of what in India belonged to Britain was subject to continual reversals.

[32] The game of substitutions can be baroque and brutal: to honor the death of his cousin, fallen at Sattimungalum in 1790, Tipu sacrificed four British officers before the tomb of his father (Colebrook pl. 10).

Figure 7   "East View of Seringapatam" by Robert Home (1794). *Select Views in Mysore* (London: Boyer [republished and printed by Butters], 1808). Courtesy of Duke University Special Collections.

Robert Home's *Select Views in Mysore, The Country of Tippoo Sultan; from Drawings Taken on the Spot* shares with Colebrook's series this awareness of substitutions, remainders, and reversals. First published in 1794, and reprinted in 1808, Home's *Select Views* continues Colebrook's meditation on distance and *durée* under the weight of elegy. Home repeats many of the same views, and reprints nearly verbatim Colebrook's account of the siege of Bangalore. Yet his engravings dedicated to fortresses offer even more attenuated prospects: Home's rendition of Seringapatam, for example, offers only a ghostly, hovering structure in the far distance.[33] Yet with Bangalore in particular, Home demonstrates a strong desire to overcome the barriers of distance with its haunting effects. The culminating suite of engravings in the volume provides a nearly step-by-step buildup to the capture of Bangalore and with it a new vantage on the landscape. A distant view "two days march from Bangalore" advances to a more accessible scene, "Inside the Pettah [lower fort] of Bangalore," which leads to the "Inside gateway where Capt. Moorhouse Fell," and from there to the interior "Inside Gate with Guard Room" and, finally, "Inside View of the Palace," establishing the viewer in the empty but beautiful hall, complete with a view out onto the landscape. Bangalore captured. But the capture soon turns inside out. The very last engraving, the

[33] Robert Home, *Select Views in Mysore, The Country of Tippoo Sultan; from Drawings Taken on the Spot* (London: Bowyer [republished and printed by R. Butters], 1808).

Figure 8   "Inside View of the Palace at Bangalore" by Robert Home (1794). *Select Views in Mysore* (London: Boyer [republished and printed by Butters], 1808). Courtesy of Duke University Special Collections.

end of the suite, depicts a gloomy view of memorials ornamented with funeral urns, erected to the "Memory of those Officers who fell at the Taking of Bangalore." This is the final proximity; the British are irrevocably "inside" the landscape.

Unlike Colebrook's account, which anchors itself, albeit nominally, in the capture of fortresses, Home's series of plates begins and ends with tombs and memorials, visible signs on the terrain of the bodies buried within. *Select Views* opens with a frontispiece showing the mausoleum of Haidar Ali and closes with the British memorials. In this way, the land that had held Haidar is now shown to hold these British heroes; but it remains unclear how reassuring such a substitution is meant to be. Anthropologists have argued that "the surest way to take possession of a place and secure it as one's own is to bury one's dead in it." At the same time, however, the place marked by the grave or tombstone speaks of human limitation, especially in time. Temporality pools around such markers, stilling the onward movement of history: the grave remains "a place where time reflects back on itself[.] The grave marks a site in the landscape where time cannot merely pass through or pass over."[34] Fittingly, even the order of this substitution is insecure, for the series of Home's engravings actu-

[34] Robert Pogue Harrison, "Hic Jacet," in *Landscape and Power: Space, Place, and Landscape*, ed. W.J.T. Mitchell, 2nd ed. (Chicago: U of Chicago P, 2002), 354, 353.

Figure 9   "View of the Burial Ground at Bangalore" by Robert Home (1794). *Select Views in Mysore* (London: Boyer [republished and printed by Butters], 1808). Courtesy of Duke University Special Collections.

ally runs counter to chronology. Though the suite of views of Bangalore is chronologically (and geographically) sequential in itself, it forms the end of the series, whereas views of Seringapatam, the endpoint of the campaign, initiate the series. Home depicts the story of the campaign in reverse, concluding not with the triumph at Seringapatam but with the British buried in this alien land. That reversal is only exacerbated in the 1808 version, where the list of illustrations switches the order of all the plates: the list tells us that the burial ground at Bangalore should open the volume; that the Mausoleum of Haidar Ali should end the set. Temporal and spatial dilemmas structure Home's *Select Views*: war at a distance offers haunting prospects but proximity offers death; and, whichever way you spin the chronology of the campaign, you begin and end with the bodies fallen into this landscape.

These illustrated books of war, meant as guides for the British public to distant fighting on the subcontinent, evoke both narrative and affective ambivalence through the distance of their views. Resisting the desire for a capturing "shot" or, relatedly, for detailed information (and with it proprietary certainty), they signal the complicity of those urges with violence and death. As an effect of the inescapable distance to which they bear witness, these images fall short of locating southern India, of "worlding" it in either a secure location or a definite historical episode. The vacancy and stillness they exhibit—not unlike the vacancy and stillness found in Cowper's poetry and its imitators—together with what seems the concerted insufficiency of their visual reporting suggest a halt in the history of British imperialism, an opening for questions that may now seem foreclosed. They resurrect the prospect of a picture of war that dismantles speed and mobility, grounding itself not on the collapse of space and time but on the fragile, maybe mortal, acknowledgment of physical and epistemological distance.

As we saw with the poems of chapter 2, these prospects propose another deconstruction of modern journalism. Within the system of the news, to recall Luhmann's critique, "a *form* develops whose inside is characterized by reusability and outside disappears from view" (37). Home and Colebrook do both report in prose on the wars in Mysore, but in the supplemental images, it's as if the *inside,* the information, the familiar form itself of news, threatens to disappear from view, disclosing instead that outside which the news cannot capture, the "'unmarked space' of the rest of the world."[35] In their brooding ambivalence the images of Mysore provide an early and prescient answer to the question raised by Luhmann: "what kind of reaction [is] there. . . in the system of the mass media itself to the aporia continually reproduced by being helplessly and despairingly informed?" (40).[36]

Even within the emergence of war photography, the legacy of this answer or prospect can be glimpsed. Here is Roger Fenton's shot of the "Tombs of the Generals" in Crimea, the effect of which chimes closely with Home's Bangalore memorials (fig. 10). The desolation of distance, the unraveling of a world to-be-built on the science of detailed knowledge, and the nearly unbearable stillness recorded by the military artists in India, return even more powerfully in Fenton's most famous image from the Crimea, "Valley of the Shadow of Death" (1855) (fig. 11). Fenton understood his role as observer in marking the distance between himself and the army, and between his viewers and the carnage he was asked to witness. He chided the graphic illustrations in the contemporary press for their "bits of artistic effect," noting that they avoided what his photographs understood: "All the sketches at home seem to err in making it [the contested fort of Sebastopol] much too *near* and in making the details too large in order to obtain *distinctness*" (emphasis added). For Fenton, nearness and distinctness demonstrate what he called a "total want of likeness to

[35] The campaign images differ distinctly from, and provide a countering supplement to the several pamphlet accounts that appeared soon after the end of the campaign. Daniel O'Quinn gives a thorough reading of these other accounts and the ideological work they perform in *Staging Governance: Theatrical Imperialism in London, 1770–1800* (Baltimore: Johns Hopkins UP, 2005), 315–32.

[36] In citing Luhmann, I mean to suggest not that these images stand outside the system of news or mass media, but that they participate in ways that make visible the aporia inherent in that system. "The mass media," Luhmann writes, "'deconstruct' themselves since they reproduce the constant contradiction of their constative and their performative textual components within their operations" (*Reality* 39).

Figure 10   "Tombs of the Generals on Cathcart Hill" by Roger Fenton (1855).
Courtesy of the United States Library of Congress.

Figure 11   "Valley of the Shadow of Death" by Roger Fenton (1855).
Courtesy of the J. Paul Getty Museum.

reality" in the Crimea.[37] Fenton finds in war a reality built of distance and the inability to distinguish: are those rocks or cannonballs or skulls? Even the title, "Valley of the Shadow of Death," raises a question: where on earth is the viewer to locate such a landscape? As one critic notes in his recent review of Fenton's work, the photographer's stance was not determined by supposed midcentury squeamishness about viewing blood and guts; even in high art it had become "standard practice to depict actual battles, ferocious encounters, in gory detail"; his was rather an ethical as well as an aesthetic stance (Fenton 40).

As Fenton's comments and work make clear, the profound belatedness and unfamiliarity of the images of war I've been discussing took their place within a culture already anticipating photography and film, and anticipating with them the "quintessential modern experience" of war that absorbs current thinkers like Sontag and Virilio.[38] My analysis of these images, I hope, suggests that their sense of temporality and distance should be regarded not as anterior to modernity, but as possibilities within the modern visual experience of distant war.

The Historical Sublime

Over any discussion of the visual culture of this period, and especially in its representation of distant scenes of battle, the sublime hangs as heavily as gunsmoke. Aspects of the sublime are obviously at work in all these images, but it is the historical sublime, in its linking of the aesthetic with the historical, that is most pertinent. And it is pertinent not because the images in which I am most interested engage it fully. Indeed, I argue that those images, unlike more familiar contemporary representations of war like the panorama, in fact forestall rather than further the sublime. The historical sublime is pertinent instead because attention to it will highlight the dilemmas attendant upon efforts to make history of the present or recent past. How is sublimity accomplished if an event stands close in time but appears to be happening elsewhere, at a remove? Does the sublimity so frequently associated with distance operate differently when temporal and geographical distances do not match up; or, as in the instance of the panorama, when they collapse too violently? These dilemmas in turn open onto the formal and affective differences at the heart of competing views of distant war available in the Romantic period.

---

[37] Qtd. in James Fenton, "The Photograph Man," review of *All the Mighty World: The Photographs of Roger Fenton, 1852–1860*, by Gordon Baldwin, Malcolm Daniel, and Sarah Greenough, *New York Review of Books*, January 13, 2005, 34.

[38] In addition to Sontag and Virilio, see Thomas Keenan, "Publicity and Indifference (Sarajevo on Television)," *PMLA* 117.1 (2002): 104–16.

At the end of the eighteenth century, writings about the past began to offer a newly sublime rendering of history. History writing, notes Mark Salber Phillips, evoked a "new emotion": the experienced remoteness of the past produced in the reader (or viewer) the freedom "to pursue his or her own inward vision of history," where "the associations of time and place [could] run together."[39] Precisely the temporal distance of a historical event, its obscurity to contemporary minds, initiates a psychological appropriation—both an owning and a coming closer. That coming closer was figured as physical but understood as psychological proximity. Thus William Godwin writes in his *Essay on Sepulchres* (1809), "They [the figures of the past] are not dead; . . . they still have their place, where we may visit them, and where, if we dwell in a composed and quiet spirit, we shall not fail to be conscious of their spirit."[40] Landscape—and not just the landscape of sepulchers—plays a crucial role here. Landscapes of historical significance came to offer greater play to imaginative remembrance than did the moral exemplars of classical history-writing; these sites or areas of ground anchored an intense engagement with temporally distant experience, an engagement "essentially spectatorial and inward" (Phillips, *Society* 324). The physical proximity of a site, in concert with the temporal distance of an event, promoted a sublime historical consciousness.

For Godwin and the Rev. Archibald Alison, another witness to the sublimity of history, contemplation of a historically drenched site initially produces a state of suspended animation, a "solemn reverie" (Godwin) or "a powerless state of reverie" (Alison) that nonetheless leads to a unifying experience.[41] In a softened echo of the process of the Kantian sublime, that initial, dreamy suspension succeeds in precipitating Godwin's consciousness of a powerful historical "spirit."[42] A marvelous dance of hazy apprehension and clear consciousness, of powerlessness and creation, generates this condensed experience of history. The archetypical setting for such a sublime encounter with history is the site of past battle. Stripped of arresting props, depopulated of actors, the now vacant battlefield lends itself all the more to promoting a viewer's historical imagination. In Alison's *Essay on the Nature and Principles*

---

[39] Mark Salber Phillips, *Society and Sentiment: Genres of Historical Writing in Britain, 1740–1820* (Princeton: Princeton UP, 2000), 330. Phillips extends his thoughts on distance in historiography in "Relocating Inwardness: Historical Distance and the Transition from Enlightenment to Romantic Historiography," *PMLA* 118.3 (2003): 436–49.

[40] William Godwin, *Essay on Sepulchres, The Political and Philosophical Writings of William Godwin*, ed. Mark Philp, vol. 6 (London: Pickering, 1993), 22–23; qtd. in Phillips 326.

[41] Godwin qtd. in Phillips, *Society* 323. Archibald Alison, *Essays on the nature and principles of taste. By the Revd. Archibald Alison* (Dublin, 1790), 14. ECCO. Gale Group. http://galenet.galegroup.com/servlet/ECCO.

[42] "Suspended animation" is Phillips's term (*Society* 329). See also Neil Hertz, *The End of the Line: Essays on Psychoanalysis and the Sublime* (New York: Columbia UP, 1985).

of Taste, for instance, ancient battlefields supply his central example of history's sublime effect:

> No man, acquainted with English history, can behold the field of Agincourt without some emotion of this kind. The additional conceptions which this association produces, and which fill the mind of the spectator on the prospect of that memorable field, diffuse themselves in some measure over the scene, and give it a sublimity which does not normally belong to it. The majesty of the Alps is increased by the remembrance of Hannibal's march over them; and who is he who could stand on the banks of the Rubicon, without feeling his imagination kindle and his heart beat high![43]

Here the diffusive yet oddly kindling effect of the battlefield prospect is fully mediated by historical knowledge: the viewer must be "acquainted with English history" to experience the site's sublimity. Without historical knowledge, by contrast, the field remains for the viewer unfilled and therefore difficult to appropriate. "Take from a man these associations [gained from historical knowledge]," writes Alison, "and how different would be his emotion!" (28). With the benefit of historical knowledge—the effect of Spivak's *worlding*—the imagination can respond to the dimness and remoteness of history so as to give it vivid detail and bring it emotionally, psychically close; even, as Phillips suggest, to bring it inward. As Alison explains, the obscurity which shrouds prospects of the distant past "stimulate[s] his fancy to fill up by its own creation those long intervals of time of which history has preserved no record"; his contemplations "seem to approach him still nearer to the ages of his regard" and the feeling is exhilarating (27–28). The scaffolding upon which his fancy operates, however, continues to be the historical record. The practice of history in the nineteenth century would appear to have absorbed this dynamic as dogma, so that Thomas Babington Macauley, writing in 1828, would begin his definition of the duty of a historian thus: it is "[t]o make the past present, to bring the distant near, to place us in the society of a great man on an eminence who overlooks the field of a mighty battle."[44] (Note, however, that even this image of proximity keeps its distance from the ugliness of battle itself, securing more elevated and unifying impressions.)

---

[43] On the relationship between nation and sublime feelings, see Alison 20 (qtd. in Phillips, *Society* 329).

[44] Thomas Babington Macauley, *Historical and Miscellaneous Essays*, 3 vols. (New York: Albert Cogswell, 1859), 1: 310; qtd. in Phillips, *Society* 347. Macauley's other examples climb down from this height, until we are "seated at the table" with "our ancestors" (1: 308). Warfare thus posed as an obstacle to the practice of sympathetic insight (*Verstehen*) which, as Phillips argues, "came to be understood as the central feature of historical understanding" (347).

In these operations of the historical sublime, then, knowledge appears the correlative of temporal distance: distance opens the space to be filled in by (1) historical information, (2) the imaginative associations such information provokes, and (3) identifiably sublime emotion. Without that distance, the imagination has little room to maneuver; without the enabling knowledge of outcomes and effects, those "long intervals of time" cannot be imaginatively bridged, and the emotion imparted remains unidentified, if not unidentifiable: "Take from a man these associations [gained from historical knowledge]," writes Alison, "and how different would be his emotion" (28). The reassuring operations of the historical sublime will in this case be blocked; you will not be free to cultivate your "own inward vision of history," but will rather confront an epistemologically and aesthetically inadequate field; not knowing enough, you will not know how to feel. In such a situation, there can be no sense of suspended animation tending toward the private production of a site's historical spirit. The suspension endures perhaps, but without achieving the commemorative and exhilarating effects of the historical sublime. This is the situation of the engravings from Mysore in the 1790s, where in fact the viewer has not had enough temporal distance to know the clear outcomes and effects of the military campaign. Here the imagination must work with uncertainty rather than certainty, and emotion remains unanchored, "different" from expectation. To make my earlier point in a different way: the insistence with which these images underscore spatial distance and its obscurities cannot be overcome by unifying efforts of historical sublimity, dependent as it is on the liberating vantage of temporal distance and historical knowledge. In this situation, distance in time does not trump distance in space. Solemn reverie, though palpable in these depictions of the southern Indian landscape of battle, does not result in a transcendent "spirit": it continues to brood, laden with unidentifiable affect.

If brooding over distance from war offered one alternative in the visual culture of the 1790s and after, another alternative pressed past brooding, past romantic reverie into full-blown awe: the phenomenally popular panorama. In their rendering of distant war, the precinematic technologies of the panorama—along with stage spectacles of the day—achieved an historical sublime where the distances of time and space were overcome simultaneously in an experience overwhelming to contemporary audiences. Instead of cultivating that reverie productive of "an essentially spectatorial and inward," private historical consciousness, the panorama provoked a sensationally distracting response, productive instead of collective national identity. My account will be brief, in part because extensive critical work has already been done on these technologies and their effects; in part because the contrasting view of war they offer is both sharp and familiar.

Panoramas burst onto the visual scene in the 1790s, beginning with Barker's "Panorama of London" (1792–93), and were wildly popular for the following three decades. Self-consciously modern inventions, these wartime entertainments provided an alternative version of pictorial journalism in the romantic era. Enormous buildings, several stories high, were constructed in the capitals of Europe, and later North America; the core of the structure was a single, vast, circular room, on whose walls hung one, sometimes two (on different levels), continuous paintings, the larger perhaps thirty feet high. A system of stairways and catwalks led viewers through a tour of the panorama, placing them in close proximity to each information-laden section.

Here, according to Richard Altick, "the literate public repaired to visualize what it read about in the newspapers, with the same expectations with which, in the twentieth century, it would watch first newsreels, and then newsreels' successors, television news programs."[45] The wonder of the panorama was its sweeping, 360-degree vantage of a scene (itself a virtuoso manipulation of the laws of perspective) as well as a registration of detail that seemed beyond the limits of mere human perception. It seemed as if the viewer were given a bird's-eye view but with that view magnified to life size. An early panorama of the cityscape of London, drawn from the top of St. Paul's cathedral, could show a small lane, a shop sign, a person hanging out a window, each rendered with stunning exactness. The panorama thus provided, Altick says curtly, a "superior illusion" (137). It presented an apparently impossible view: actions which took place over a series of minutes or hours, for instance, could be assembled together on the canvas as if they happened simultaneously. Though such simultaneity was available in the practice of history painting, here it presented itself with the awareness that no individual viewer could keep up, could view the diversity all at once. For unlike the experience of a conventional painting, here one could not contemplate the panorama as a whole, even as the panorama inserted each viewer within its totality. In this form of news-entertainment, distance of various sorts was dizzyingly, dazzlingly overcome not by the viewer's imagination but by the technology itself.

A wealth of recent critical studies has shown how the panorama especially taught the public to "see" and to see as a nation; its enormous, encircling canvases dismantling the priority of the individual viewer and assembling instead a mobilized and nationalized public.[46] The panorama's scale, together with its effect of simultaneous and instantaneous activity, overwhelmed—Sontag might

---

[45] Richard Altick, *The Shows of London* (Cambridge: Belknap, 1978), 176.

[46] See William Galperin, *The Return of the Visible in British Romanticism* (Baltimore: Johns Hopkins UP, 1993), 34, 39; Jonathan Crary, *Techniques of the Observer: On Vision and Modernity in the Nineteenth Century* (Cambridge: MIT P, 1990), 113–14; Gillian Russell, *The Theatres of War: Performance, Politics, and Society 1993–1815*, (Oxford: Clarendon 1995), 75–78.

say "assaulted"—its viewers. Without the mediating effect of frame or prosce-
nium, viewers were thrown into the life-sized scene itself, given "the impression that 'this' was what it was really like" (Russell 77). Thus a contemporary
viewer applauds William Daniell's 1829 panorama of Madras for the

> fidelity with which all that is characteristic of Indian climate and scenery
> in general and of the Madras variety of it in particular . . . has been pre-
> served. . . . [T]he figures are drawn with such perfect truth that we can
> almost see the natives moving about, we fancy we can catch the sound
> of the palankeen bearers' voices as they bustle along. . . . Every square
> inch is redolent of hot climates crowded with Asiatic images and fertile
> in what may be called historical and political associations peculiar to our
> Indian administration.[47]

Both the date of the panorama and the bent of this response indicate a more
settled picture of India (postsettlement) than those of the campaign books.
The superior illusion of the panorama resolves itself into the fertile cultivation
of "associations" related to the knowledge of "our Indian Administration." The
invention or "gift" of the panorama was to make this loss of detachment "en-
ticing," a "desideratum" of modern life, a desirable way to "view differently."[48]
Velocity and movement were associated with these spectacles at every level:
not only did palankeen bearers bustle on the canvas, but the artists themselves
rushed to transfer newspaper reports onto the enormous canvas screens. Viewers raced to see them (contemporary accounts say Joshua Reynolds came out
in his dressing gown and slippers to view the first panorama [Altick 172]), and
customers were shuttled through tunnels and stairways as part of a carefully
mechanized (even patented) viewing experience. The inherent motion, speed,
and currency of the panorama thus pushed away the privatized, reflective, and
"meditative disposition" of other contemporary versions of landscape painting
(Galperin 39). There was not time or space to think alongside such "visceral
wonder" and "distraction": Queen Charlotte felt seasick; young women fainted.
One looked "with a shuddering awe," a viewer reported, "and retreat[ed]
shuddering."[49]

The language of retreat is not incidental: the major subject for panoramas,
besides cityscapes, was the military siege. Events from the Napoleonic wars account for half of all panoramas shown up until the 1820s. Discernible in the

---

[47] Qtd. in Maurice Shellim, *The Daniells in India and the Waterfall at Papanasam* (Calcutta:
Statesman, 1970), 81.

[48] "Its success," according to Galperin, "owed to a confusion in which the act of viewing was less
a matter of being wrenched and startled than of being enticed *into being startled* from a stable and
commanding vantage" (41–42; emphasis original).

[49] Qtd. in Altick 135.

panorama is a technology of citizenship which seeks to "view differently" one's relationship to the city as *polis*, and alongside that to "view differently" one's relationship to war, especially war as the besiegement of cities. Even before the detention camps Sebald finds in *Austerlitz*, the panorama is where the science of siege craft relocated and updated itself. More often than not, in submitting to the machinery of the panorama, one submitted to a specific, passive position within the modern view of war. Taking advantage of its effect of visual assault, contemporary stage productions borrowed from the panorama for their depiction of battle scenery, adding the special effects of mechanized animals and live explosives, flames from artillery that erupted close, but not too close, to the audience. As Gillian Russell and Daniel O'Quinn have argued, both panoramic and theatrical representations of battles in this period introduced the public to an experience of mechanized war, war performed, as Russell concludes, "without the mediation of actors" (78).[50] Similarly, in *The Rhetoric of English India*, Sara Suleri understands the British theater's spectacular mechanization of destruction in terms of the audience's "surrender" to the "brute force of side effects," the very "mechanization of power." "From [Richard Sheridan's 1799] *Pizarro* on, theatergoers would watch contemporary drama . . . for its cumbersome enactment of illusion: for bridges to break down, for castles to collapse."[51] Combining panoramic scenery and stage machinery, stage spectacles provided a potent modern prospect of war, where destruction was as much expectation as illusion. War happened, it happened all around you and your fellow citizens, you were up close to it but had no role other than spectator. It was all captured for you in this overwhelming instance—and then you retreated, shuddering.

In the spring of 1800, at no great distance from the Royal Academy, where the Daniells' *Rope Bridge* was hanging on display, Robert Ker Porter's 2500-square-foot *Siege of Seringapatam*, itself a marvel of speed and engineering, was exhibited at Barkley's Panorama (Porter is said to have spent six weeks—excepting Sundays—working round the clock on the project).[52] I will keep *The Rope Bridge* hanging just a bit longer. But even without it as a reference point, one can easily discern the conceptual and emotional distance between Porter's panoramic view of the citadel, adapted from published reports of the British victory, and the versions by Colebrook and Home, taken so remotely "on the spot" in the prior war. The sublime effect of Porter's depiction of the

[50] O'Quinn elaborates on this thought to consider "mechanized war" more generally, 340–48.

[51] Sara Suleri, *The Rhetoric of English India* (Chicago: U of Chicago P, 1992), 69.

[52] See the account of his sister, the novelist Jane Porter, cited in Altick 135. "Wonder" and "marvel" are the words continuously associated with Porter's "Seringapatam," painted when he was nineteen and a student at the Royal Academy.

siege depended both on the simultaneity of the military action and its im-
mense detail (a whole day's worth of fighting represented as if happening at
once), but also on its historicity: everyone knew the siege was in the past, that
Tipu Sultan had been killed and the British had achieved, as reviews of the
panorama put it, a "decisive victory." In London, in Barkley's Panorama build-
ing, Seringapatam was irrevocably taken—to "shuddering" effect—every day
the doors were open.

Perhaps too the constant rehearsal of victory—in which all viewers could
participate—helped erase the repeated military reversals of the previous two
decades. Just as there was no space left to be filled in the panorama, so there
was nothing left to be done in Mysore. Coming in the midst of the war with
France, just as Napoleon's army was crossing the Alps into Italy, the closure of
the south Indian front no doubt produced a particularly spectacular effect.
The panoramic siege thus insisted on close and elaborated information: a
booklet sold at the entrance identified more than two hundred (primarily
British) life-size figures by name and rank, inviting viewers to get up-close and
personal with their national heroes while offering the "superior illusion" that
all bodies sacrificed in war were meaningful—or rather that all meaningful
bodies were accounted for (by some counts there were more than seven hundred human figures in Porter's *Siege*). The booklet organized the chaos of warfare in tidy narratives and lists, even as Porter's *Siege* organized its viewers in a
procession of unidirectional movement, through a landscape of war captured,
like the enemy fort itself, on the enormous canvas. Finally, as I mentioned earlier, Porter's panorama depended upon even as it produced a powerful sense of
collective identity, a national "we" who could afford to pay a few shillings to
be moved by the visceral wonder and distraction of a war now completed in
India.

The panorama, in other words, offered a surfeit of the historical sublime,
removing it from the inward motions of the individual imagination and projecting it outward as moving, technological marvel. In doing so, it anticipates
the assaulting logic that Sontag delineates in contemporary photojournalism.
Through the elimination of distance and the offer of unbearable detail, it surpasses the unifying spirit of the historical sublime. It nationalizes history and
its audience, and in doing so harnesses the event to an overwhelming, incon-
trovertible force. The desolate landscapes of Colebrook and Home are unsettling in part because so much is left ambiguous or unsettled; the panorama, by
contrast, filled to the breaking point with detail ("every square inch . . .
crowded with Asiatic images"), aims at settlement here and now. As if there
were nothing left unresolved, nothing left to know, no need to go over that
ground again.

Figure 12   "The Bridge of Serinagur [Srinagar]" by William and Thomas Daniell. From *Oriental scenery. One hundred and fifty views of the architecture, antiquities, and landscape scenery of Hindoo-stan.* (London: The authors, 1812–16). Courtesy of the University of Chicago Special Collections.

The Rope-Bridge

> And the cries of India are given to seas and winds, to be blown about . . .
> over a remote and unhearing ocean.[53]

The painting that compels my attention now is usually known as *The Rope Bridge of Serinagur* [Srinagar], though it is occasionally titled "*The Siege of Srinagar*" (fig. 12). It was first exhibited at the Royal Academy in 1800 and later included as an aquatint engraving in the fourth volume of William and Thomas Daniells' *Oriental Scenery* (1805). Following the analysis of military landscapes of southern India and panoramic treatment of such landscapes, this painting turns us to a third treatment of distance in the representation of war. The Daniells' image of war in India avails itself, like the engravings by Colebrook and Home, of a distance and obscurity or lack of information that forestalls sublimity. Relying upon suspense or the "sense of intermission" I invoked earlier, and removing itself from the settled ground of the panorama, this image proposes in place of a collective sublime a picturesque landscape, from which emerges the possibility of a cosmopolitan view. It aligns the Daniells' *Rope Bridge* with the "romantic, interested, melancholy and cosmo-

[53] Edmund Burke, Speech in Commons, 1783.

politan" view that Ian Baucom, following Jacques Derrida, assigns to the historical witness.[54]

At first glance there seems little reason to see the Daniells as source for a particularly cosmopolitan view. Upon returning from their travels in Asia, for instance, William took the skills honed in India and used them to produce a series of engravings of the coastline and ports of Great Britain, an ostensibly nationalist project often cited as the finest book of engravings produced in the period.[55] Yet the first volume of this *Voyage Round Great Britain* (1814) concludes with the image of another rope bridge, this one suspended in agitation above the port of Holyhead, on the Welsh island of Anglesey, the major ferry station for travel to Ireland. Acknowledging its kinship to *The Rope Bridge of Serinagur* suggests that William Daniell's limning of Britain's borders—its entry and exit points—might offer a rather complicated meditation on the island empire's place in the world in 1813–14.[56] One might say this second rope bridge provides flimsy—and obscure—support for the work of cosmopolitanism. Indeed. So it is with tricky engineering and some tentativeness, like the rope bridge itself, that I employ the Srinagar painting to evoke a third type of emotional landscape for the British home front in wartime. How might it feel to be cognizant of, yet removed from, the ravages of war? How might one view war from a distance and acknowledge, let alone bridge, that distance?

My preoccupation with this scene mimics the artists' own: the Anglesey image aside, the Daniells reworked it at least nine different times, with often telling changes. The image, in other words, was not fixed or final for them, as if even years later the suspense it involved was never settled.[57] All versions of *The Rope Bridge of Serinagur* place the bridge in the middle distance, where it offers the most slender communication between a small walled fort and the opposite shore of a broad river, the Alaknanda.[58] The river itself is divided into

[54] Ian Baucom, *Specters of the Atlantic: Finance Capital, Slavery, and the Philosophy of History* (Durham: Duke UP, 2005), 173–78.

[55] See Shellim 112–36 for a good account of William's later career. Having been made a member of the Royal Academy and before turning to panoramas, William Daniell exhibited a series of naval battle pieces (*The English Fleet at Trafalgar, Battle of Trafalgar, The Battle of the Nile,* etc.) (118).

[56] Shellim also links the rope bridge at Anglesey with that of Srinagar, but emphasizes the artist's consistent condescending view of the locals, "still little advanced from a state of savagery" (124).

[57] They rework this episode in their writing as well. It first appears in William's journal of 1789: having been welcomed with great hospitality by the Raja of Srinagar, the Englishmen were asked the next day to depart; the Raja's troops had been defeated elsewhere and the conquering army was on its way to capture the city. The Bridge of Ropes by which they all fled was so crowded, according to William, "we thought at times it would have broke, taking their Chesebust [belongings] with them" (qtd. in Mahajan et al. 28). The detachment evident in that gap between the "we" and "they" on the bridge grows in a still later account, published in the Notes to *Views of Hindoostan*. There the artists are off the bridge altogether.

[58] The Daniells referred to this river as the Ganges, though technically the Ganges is formed south of Srinagar, where the Alaknanda joins the Bhagirathi River.

two areas, turbulent below and calm above the line of the bridge, as if register-
ing a temporal and psychological halt along that axis. Barely discernible on the
bridge, hardly more than dark marks, isolated individuals, some hauling baggage on their backs, flee the city in anticipation of a siege. Reports of the 1800
Royal Academy oil painting of this scene indicate that crowds jammed the
bridge, echoing William Daniell's note in his journal that "we feared at times
it would have broke, taking their . . . [belongings], cots, etc. with them."[59] (It
echoes as well Suleri's comment about romantic stage spectacles, where audiences waited for "bridges to break down, castles to collapse" [69]). In subsequent engravings, however, the image becomes considerably depopulated as
bodies are scattered at a distance from one another across the rope bridge.[60] In
the background stands an impervious range of mountains; the foreground is
half rushing water, half rocky river bank. In many ways, the painting seems to
operate within a familiar picturesque aesthetic[61]—except for the small detail
of civic and presumably domestic devastation, visible yet out of reach in the
middle distance; and except for that element of suspense provided by the rope
bridge: will it hold, and for how long? In some versions the landing of the
bridge, its leftmost extreme, nearly fades from view. That is, the Daniells provide no end point for the flight of the people of Srinagar. The scene includes
nearby villages, serving almost as visual stepping-stones for a flight to the distant hills, but these dwellings might also be vulnerable to the approaching
army. No obvious haven awaits the refugees at the end of the bridge: they head
into shadow.

"A world of possibility shadows the probable and representable world" of
the picturesque, writes William Galperin, referring to Jane Austen's novels
(67). I would like to claim a more shadowy shadow, with less utopian possibilities, for the Daniells' art. The effects of war—the siege itself, the fate of these
refugees, the escalation of violence—are possible if not quite representable in
this image which seems thereby to incline the picturesque toward dreadful
suspense. The Daniells are usually categorized as picturesque painters (one
standard book on their work is titled *Picturesque India*; and contemporaries
hailed their "exquisite specimens of the picturesque scenery of India").[62] Yet to
view this painting through the standard protocols of the picturesque, it seems

[59] Qtd. in Mahajan et al. 28.

[60] N. R. Ray, *A Descriptive Catalogue of the Daniells['] Work in the Victorian Memorial* (Calcutta:
N. R. Ray on behalf of the Trustees of the Victoria Memorial, 1976), 3. Ray says that the crowds of
people in the 1800 oil painting exhibited at the Royal Academy do not appear in the engravings, by
which he must mean that they dwindle considerably.

[61] The rocky promontory on the right recalls Welsh and Scottish ruins painted by Paul Sandby,
member of the Royal Academy, inventor of aquatint engraving (the method used by the Daniells),
and the drawing master at Woolwich. Sandby probably taught Colebrook and Home.

[62] *The Morning Chronicle*, 13 November 1798.

to me, leads to frustration and helplessness, in contradistinction to the exhilaration or nationalized awe provided by the sublime panoramas.

The artists do not bring the human figures close to our view—or to our hearts, quite; this is no sentimental tableau inviting identification. And yet, suspended on that man-made bridge, the figures do not quite recede into nature either. What to do with them? The position of these human figures and the problem of identification that they pose, neither close enough to attach themselves nor far enough to be dismissed, organize the painting. Which is to say that the technology of the suspended bridge organizes the painting. This point is supported both by the Daniells' extensive notes in *Oriental Scenery* (half of which they devote to the rigging up of the rope bridge, with an emphasis on its temporary, provisional nature) and by the alliance between this feat of engineering and their art (with its own provisional drafts and sketches as well as its science of line and distance, and, in the case of aquatint engraving, the intervention of water). In making these claims I assume that, through the bridge of the middle distance, a viewer is nevertheless challenged to recognize the hard-to-identify strangers, those merest hints of human form on a bridge, moving somewhere halfway across the globe.[63]

In a prescient essay titled "Distance," Raymond Williams would appear to argue with my assumptions. Responding to television coverage of Britain's war in the Falklands in 1982, he decries the "culture of distance" which spins the geographical distance of the violence into something like the picturesque, "within which men and women are reduced to models, figures and the quick cry in the throat." "The sovereign power to order war," he writes, "operates within the cultural power to distance," especially to distance the mortal reality of human bodies.[64] Yet Williams complicates his condemnation of distance in at least two ways. Distance, it turns out, is foremost a manipulation of tempo (like his own "quick cry in the throat"). Williams astutely describes the "long slow rhythm," "the dragging but limited time" of television broadcasting leading up to the war, with its effect of pushing viewers to such impatience that

[63] John Barrell makes a strong counterclaim, in *The Dark Side of the Landscape: The Rural Poor in English Painting, 1730–1840* (Cambridge: Cambridge UP, 1980), especially in reference to Constable's landscapes. The figures of laborers work, in Constable, "in the distance, for the resentments of the poor are now [1790s] known to us all, and those resentments could not be concealed in any credible image of the poor except *by hiding them in the middle ground*, where we can see their labours but not their expressions" (21; emphasis added). Constable places his figures insistently "in the middle ground, until they become almost invisible in the landscapes they have made" (32). Without discounting the importance of Barrell's argument, I argue that in *The Rope Bridge*, the bridge itself reminds the viewer that this is neither a "natural" nor an agricultural scene; and flight from a siege alters what the threat of invisibility might signal to the viewer.

[64] Raymond Williams, "Distance," in *What I Came to Say* (London: Century Hutchinson, 1989), 43. For a helpful analysis of Williams's response to distance, see Bruce Robbins, *Secular Vocations: Intellectuals, Professionalism, Culture* (London: Verso, 1993), 57–72.

they can only respond, "'Let's get it over with'" (37, 40).[65] In this "induced urgency," chiastically related to the distancing effects of modern media, Williams
finds a serious threat to democracy and peace:

> The sovereign power to order war operates with the cultural power to
> distance. . . . The modes interact, for the war is fast and is made to ap-
> pear fast. And there can be no hanging about when the threat is urgent
> and the blood is roused. (42)

No hanging about, no toleration of suspense, only a rousing rush to settle
matters. Rushing aims to obliterate distance, the temporal breadth between
now and a future then. Send troops far away to secure the outcome *now*. For,
as Hannah Arendt observes simply, justification for the violence of war "loses
its plausibility the farther its intended end recedes into the future."[66] It justi-
fies itself through urgency and immediacy. At the same time, however, such
rushing works to restore distance: a quick settlement often means we can keep
that bit of the world at a distance.

When Williams meshes distance with tempo, he sends us back with questions to the hanging rope bridge, where distant figures of men and women appear to flee with so little urgency. In spite of what William Daniell records in
his diary, or perhaps on second or third thought, the artists do not give us
people who are hurrying. The span of their flight from then to now hangs
about, defying the rush to collapse time and space. Precisely by resisting the
rush, though, the image opens up to suspense and its range of possibilities:
Will they cross in time? Will the bridge hold? Will they find safety? What will
become of them? The picturesque, Jill Heydt-Stevenson and Gary Harrison
suggest, operates by "putting people in motion," but at what speed and for
how long?[67] "Putting people in motion" for these critics harkens to the mobilization of bodies in practices of picturesque tourism, but in wartime the
phrase shadows forth altered meanings.

The second complication in Williams's plaint against distance is his admis-
sion that distance *enables* his own critique of the war—not just geographic distance, but also distance born of displacement from the nation. Getting his first
news of the Falklands war from Ireland, in the Irish newspapers, Williams discovers that "Distance in that form had particular [and valuable] effects. Every
contradiction seemed heightened." What he calls the "cool and informative"

---

[65] Williams likes the play of "telos" with the word "television"; see 36. Niklas Luhmann makes a
similar point about the rhythm of the news: "Events have to be dramatized as events—and have to
be suspended in time, a time which thus begins to flow more quickly" (*Reality* 26).

[66] Hannah Adrendt, *On Violence* (New York: Harcourt Brace & Co., 1970), 52.

[67] Gary Harrison and Jill Heydt-Stevenson, "Variations on the Picturesque: Authority, Play and
Practice," *European Romantic Review* 13 (2002): 3–10.

Irish press granted him a "supporting sense of the real complexity of events . . . making any simple opinion or position impossible" (39). Neither the managed distance of television, nor the violent rush to certainties, this other mode of distance (with a little Irish on it) makes simple positioning—political or geographical—"impossible," spinning distance itself into something quite variable and provisional. In this mode, can we really determine how far we are from war? Williams pursues the question when, back in England, he sees a bonfire of oil and rags, the sight unleashing a memory that puts him in deadly proximity to disaster: "in an overwhelming moment, I was in a field in Normandy, and the next tank, with my friends in it, was burning and about to explode" (40). If, under pressure from a war off the coast of Argentina, an English village reveals itself as a field in Normandy, what sights might a hill town and its refugees in northern India reveal under pressure of global war? More pointedly, Williams reminds us how the human figures in the middle distance of *The Rope Bridge at Serinagur* knock our sense of location off-balance even as they problematize any identification with them: as refugees, they display the loss of place, the dislocation from home or city or state that turns distance and the positions that underwrite it into questions rather than facts.

I've been suggesting three points about *The Rope Bridge of Serinagur* and the unsettling effects of its use of distance. First, that the position of the human figures in the painting, neither close enough to identify as individuals nor far enough away to naturalize or dismiss, raises the question of the viewer's moral response to the painting. How does one respond to these distant, mere mentions of suffering humanity? Second, the curious suspension of time in the painting—drawn out in the lines of the rope bridge and the disposition of the figures, perhaps even the strange bifurcation of the river's movement—resists the rush to foreclosure that Williams otherwise identifies with a "culture of distance" promoting war. The painting's distance holds in suspense the effects of war, its outcomes; it grants no settlement. Third, there is a mode of distance which in fact rearranges the ground beneath our feet, the position in the world we had simply assumed. Look again at *The Rope Bridge of Serinagur*: not only is the figural ground primarily liquid in this image—a river—but the perspective of the painters—and the viewer—is itself eerily suspended. Rather than a perspective of divine impassivity, though, the image hints that the viewer occupies a distant position no more stable than that of the fleeing refugees. (Indeed, the Daniells themselves were forced to flee Srinigar under the threat of siege.)

Wartime is particularly likely to effect such situational mutability, as when a local feud in India (such as this one) might indeed inflect the strategic plans of Napoleon, the Russian czar, the Shah of Persia, and William Pitt; or where France's invasion of Egypt propels the British to secure the Cape of Good

Hope in southern Africa and crush the ambitions of Tipu Sultan in Mysore. Perhaps now is the moment to evoke the gravity of India in the plans of both Napoleon and the Russian emperor, not to mention its importance to Great Britain; to recognize the alliance between Napoleon and Tipu Sultan to halt British imperialism on the subcontinent (the sultan had earlier joined the Jacobin club and renamed himself Citizen Tipu); and to recall the strategic value of the Garwhal mountain of India, depicted here, as possible passageway for troops from Afghanistan into the subcontinent (the impetus for the early topographical military missions described in Peter Hopkirk's *The Great Game*). The cities and hill towns of India are intimately connected to Paris and St. Petersburg, Capetown and Alexandria, as well as to London. I try to imagine those in England who viewed the Daniells' images of India between, say, 1800 and 1805 and ask at what remove they beheld them: was this 1789 siege of Srinagar much more distant than the 1799 siege of Seringapatam? Or of Malta? Or the 1802 siege of Copenhagen? Or, indeed, the 1803 invasion threatened from across the channel, which might turn them all into refugees? Distance, along with location, becomes a provisional matter, achieved only to be forfeited in Williams's "overwhelming moment," in the anticipation or memory of military attack.

The effects of distance in *The Rope Bridge of Serinagur* come close to a cosmopolitan view, but if so, this view sees itself not providing hospitality or refuge to others, but rather acknowledging a world of potential upheavals and dispossessions. Such a view requires a complex response to images—even picturesque images—of distant war. The rearrangement of location by techniques of distancing seems one point of communication between the cosmopolitan view and the picturesque landscape. A recent argument by David Marshall identifies the picturesque mode as in fact a "problem of distance," and though he takes that distance aesthetically and metaphysically, we might bend it back toward space and time. Because of its familiar framing ordinances, "The beholder of the picturesque," writes Marshall, "identifies with another beholder, experiences someone else's point of view . . . through a double perspective that is divided between a sight and someone else's view of it."[68] The mediating identification is never total or stable: hence the "discomfort," the "anxiety," and—to underline the problematic of ground—the "vertiginous space" Marshall finds in the picturesque. This is the off-balancing mode of distance described by Williams and operative in the Daniells' *Rope Bridge*. How much more would this vertiginous space be activated if the very ground to be viewed, from however many points of view, were the contested ground of warfare?

[68] David Marshall, "The Picturesque," in *The Cambridge History of Literary Criticism, Vol. IV: The Eighteenth Century*, ed. H. B. Nisbet and Claude Rawson (Cambridge: Cambridge UP, 1989), 430.

The two-step between identification and separation that shapes the middle distance in this case resembles what Amanda Anderson, in *The Powers of Distance: Cosmopolitanism and the Cultivation of Detachment*, calls "reflective distance," a dialogue between one's own cultural position and that of others, suspending oneself between one's given worldview and someone else's view of it.

> Such achieved distance, should in turn promote not a sustained or absolute disengagement . . . but rather cultivated partiality, a reflective return to [one's] cultural origins that one can no longer inhabit in any unthinking way.[69]

This achieved or dialogic distance recalls Williams's privileged mode of distance, where simple (and, for him, national) positions become impossible and "the real complexity of events" becomes visible. Sometimes, Anderson tells us, such detachment risks "lapsing into [a] cosmopolitan indifference equivalent to cynicism."[70] That indifference might derive from a distance that is too strong, perhaps too solipsistic, so that the detached observer beholds all others without distinction, casting them, you might say, into shadow or background or—to invoke an example from earlier in this book—into snow.[71] Or detachment could be the by-product of too much attachment or sympathy leading, in the mode of liberal guilt, to a foregrounded sense of impotence and resignation, of being, to quote Luhmann again, "helplessly and despairingly informed"—as if all this were too much, too impossible for me.[72] In the first case, you have a hardened or willful distance; in the other, a resigned or passive distance. Between them stretches the bridge of the middle distance—the tentative and constantly reconstructed distance that hangs in suspense. Anderson gestures to something like this when she describes cultivated or achieved distance "in its most promising form . . . as an aspiration rather than a certainty," a "temporary achievement." She dedicates her book to those practitioners of distance "who are ambivalent, hesitant, uneasy, and sometimes quite thoughtfully engaged in a complex process of self-interrogation and social critique" (32–33)—practitioners not unlike Susan Sontag in *On Regarding the Pain of Others* or Raymond Williams in "Distance." In this Anderson chimes with Dominick LaCapra, who supports a sort of response he calls "empathic unsettlement" which "involves a kind of virtual experience through which one puts oneself in the other's

[69] Amanda Anderson, *The Powers of Distance: Cosmopolitanism and the Cultivation of Detachment* (Princeton: Princeton UP, 2001), 121.
[70] George Eliot qtd. in Anderson 131.
[71] See Interlude 1: Still Winter Falls.
[72] On liberal guilt, see Julie Ellison, *Cato's Tears, and the Making of Anglo-American Emotion* (Chicago: U of Chicago P, 1999). Dominick LaCapra critiques these two extremes, which he describes as fantasies of mastery and fantasies of victimization or self-victimization. "Trauma, Absence, Loss," *Critical Inquiry* 25.4 (1999), esp. 717–20.

position while recognizing the difference of that position and hence not taking the other's place" (722).[73] Anderson and LaCapra both acknowledge the careful if provisional engineering involved in this mode of distance, so similar to Marshall's picturesque, and they grant that work its value as well as its characteristic affect (ambivalence, hesitancy, unease), so that it is no longer mistaken for the distance of pure abstraction or rationalization.

Could the Daniells' painting prompt a similar argument about the value and felt experience of distance in a time of global war? Despite its seeming belatedness compared to our contemporary media, its vision of war derives from an age already anticipating photography and film, as seen with the contemporaneous phenomenon of the panorama. Despite its place in a technology and a sense of temporality that appear anterior to modernity, the questions posed by this painting, I believe, have only intensified over the past two centuries. Against the sensations of shock and awe offered by some media, the questions of the rope bridge open up again the problem of feeling and unfeeling in wartime, a problem which has persisted throughout this book. They ask us to reconsider the charge of indifference, often laid at the feet of the cynical cosmopolitan, and leveled by many critics against the complacent practices of the picturesque, especially in its presentation of the human form. An inability to identify (or identify with) figures at a distance may promote indifference, but it may also demand a specific awareness of the forces that obscure features of the human—as in the Daniells' painting, as in Thomson's figure of the man "bleached" by the snows, as in warfare. (Consider the anonymity of modern warfare: the unmarked graves; the unknown soldiers; the faceless statistics given to mass armies ushered in by the Napoleonic wars; and Byron's remark that soldiers—and who knows how many noncombatants—lie "buried in the heap of such transactions / Their names . . . rarely found, nor often sought.")[74] If the Daniells' painting prompts indifference, it is a disturbed, anxious, uneasy indifference.

In his lecture "On Cosmopolitanism," the late Jacques Derrida resists the inclination to individuate and differentiate, suggesting another response to those dispossessed by violence. He advocates "a new cosmopolitics" responsive to "the foreigner in general, the immigrant, the exiled, the deported, the state-

---

[73] The terms of LaCapra's analysis bear closely on my own:

> Without discounting all forms of critical distance (even numbing "objectivity") that may be necessary . . . one may also appeal to the role of empathy in raising doubts about positivistic or formalistic accounts that both deny one's transferential implication in the problems one treats and attempt to create maximal distance from them—and those involved in them—through extreme objectification. (723)

[74] Byron, *Don Juan*, VII: 267–68. Canto VII continues the poet's cry against the dehumanizing anonymity of the war, exacerbated by the fickleness of print media.

less or the displaced person."[75] This responsiveness is, in its way, indifferent:
the unconditional law of hospitality that Derrida recommends welcomes "all
who might come, without question or without even having to identify who
they were or whence they came" (18). He recalls here Kant's essay on "Perpetual Peace" where, as we have seen, every person holds "a *Right of Resort* or of
visitation" ("Perpetual Peace," 105). Yet Derrida returns again and again in this
essay to the anonymity of the dispossessed, treating it with caution, as a way
of honoring their unique status.[76] Thus, when he lists those in the world who
compel the hospitality of the cosmopolitan, he hesitates:

> Let us not proffer an example, for there are too many, and to cite the
> best known would risk sending the anonymous others back into the
> darkness (*mal*) from which they find it hard to escape, a darkness which
> is truly the worst and the condition of all others. (6)

It is hard not to recollect with these words the anonymous strangers on a winter's evening, flickering into view and then back into darkness in the various
poems considered in this book's opening prelude. To differentiate here would
be to offer special treatment, to highlight some at the risk of sending others
into the shadows. Anonymity, then, or a lack of identification, might in this
instance demand an in-difference, a refraining from differentiation that is
nonetheless deeply aware of the difficulty and dangers of these unidentified
strangers.

Just as there are reasons to hesitate before a collective "we" (or "them"),
there are reasons not to differentiate too urgently, but rather to suspend identi-
ties and positions in the middle distance. Here at the end, let us take seriously
Derrida's question, at the beginning of "On Cosmopolitanism": "Is it not the
case that cosmopolitanism has something to do either with all the cities or
with all the states of the world?" (3). How distant is this scene of the *Rope
Bridge*? If it is a generic picturesque, can it be cordoned off by its viewers as
only one, far-removed corner of the world? Or could this scene, in part because of its framed, generic quality, be played out throughout the world, not
in one mountainous terrain but in any mountainous terrain? Not in one city
but in any city? What is to keep this in-different scene from recurring all the
time and at no great distance, if not its potential to make someone question
her position in the world? Here, I believe, lies the endless suspense of the picturesque siege.

---

[75] Jacques Derrida, *On Cosmopolitanism and Forgiveness* (London: Routledge, 2001), 4.
[76] See also his citation of Hannah Arendt on "fame and anonymity," 15.

CODA

Undone

I tell a story about the relations I choose, only to expose, somewhere
along the way, the way I am gripped and undone by those very
relations. My narrative falters, as it must.

Let's face it. We're undone by each other. And if we're not, we're
missing something.

—Judith Butler[1]

This book began with the problem of modern wartime, that is, the problem of
coordinating an awareness of violence elsewhere with everyday movements
here, at a distance from the fighting. The book ends with the problem of cosmopolitanism. Another way of characterizing this trajectory would be to say it
looks from the familiar scene at hearth and home to the more foreign scene of
a suspension bridge set in a distant land—then looks back again. Holding together these two scenes is difficult: in one you might sit as a violent world
comes to you; in the other you might be forced out of home and into an un-
welcoming world. The former scene holds the danger that these threats will be
domesticated and made familiar as "news" and an alienated response to news.
The latter holds the threat of violence, homelessness, and falling. These are my
bookends, then, and a broad shelf spans the distance between them, a shelf
which, as I survey it now, tilts uneasily one way and then the other.

Looking back to the poems in my opening pages reveals an inclination
away from the precarious and toward domestication, especially in the treatment of the stranger in wartime. Welcoming that strange figure at the hearth,
granting it, as Samuel Taylor Coleridge does briefly, "dim sympathies" with
himself, seems to require that he assimilate its strangeness. In his midnight
meditation Coleridge recollects Cowper's fireside stranger only to relocate the
"unquiet thing" in personal memory (line 16). Once inserted into the poet's
own past, the stranger is greeted—but transformed: "For still I hoped to see

---

[1] Judith Butler, *Precarious Life: The Powers of Mourning and Violence* (London: Verso, 2004), 23.

the *stranger's* face, / Townsman, or aunt, or sister more beloved . . . (41–42). The face Coleridge longs to see travels a path of increasing identification, moving ever closer to himself until, after his beloved sister, the poet faces his infant son "cradled by my side" (44). C. K. Williams, writing in 2003, follows Coleridge's lead. His poem "The Hearth" watches a strange "creaturely thing" melting in the fire, which then prompts a memory of an old friend. By the end of his poem, facing the prospect of unending war, even friend cedes to family:

I was thinking,
as I often do these days, of war;
I was thinking of my children, and their children,
of the more than fear I feel for them. . . .[2]

That shifting, from unidentifiable thing to remembered friend to "my children," seems a deliberate attempt to leave behind the unease aroused by unquiet things intruding upon a quiet evening. The *unheimlich*, the uncanny thing that does not belong in the home, turns *heimlich*, homely and familiar. By giving the stranger a face and relation, Coleridge and Williams recall identifiable feeling (hope or fear) to the scene.

But what if, in the time of modern war, you face a world where as William Cowper suggests on that winter evening, "the face of Things" or "earth's universal face" can no longer be delineated? What if the strangers appearing in your home, like the strangers on the bridge, remain unidentified, your relations to them unknown and the feelings they evoke—strange? And how do you respond if no tangible body stands on your doorstep but instead a flickering image, a mediated apparition?

The gesture of hospitality, of bringing the stranger into the home, underwrites a conventional understanding of cosmopolitanism we have seen enunciated by Kant. Kant grants the stranger "a *Right of Resort* or of visitation," and unconditional hospitality.[3] Yet does this gesture require that in welcoming the stranger we ourselves feel comfortable and at home? David Simpson claims as much, writing that such cosmopolitan hospitality "presupposes the foundational security of hearth and home, whose assumed fixity is what allows us to think of strangers as strangers" and to know ourselves as secure.[4] It also presupposes—or at least anticipates—the unmediated presence of actual persons,

[2] Thanks to Julie Carlson for pointing out the familial bias of these two poems. See her *England's First Family of Writers: Mary Wollstonecraft, William Godwin, Mary Shelley* (Baltimore: Johns Hopkins UP, 2007).

[3] Immanuel Kant, "Perpetual Peace: A Philosophical Essay," in *Kant: Political Writings*, ed. Hans Reiss (Cambridge: Cambridge UP, 1991), 105.

[4] David Simpson, "Wandering Spooks," *London Review of Books* 30.16 (14 August 2008): 12.

bodies to be welcomed and tended to. By contrast, the cosmopolitanism prompted by the scene of the rope bridge has to forgo such fixity, identification, and tangibility. As I have tried to show in reading the Daniells' painting, this other possibility emerges: a cosmopolitanism that ventures into unknown territory to risk failure and falling; one that declines, or finds impossible, the emotional consolation of a present body or a familiar face. It may not be able to embrace the strange but it does let the strange, however unknowable and unsettling, abide.

This sense of a radical un-housing extends from the early nineteenth century to the present time of war. It lies, for instance, at the heart of Judith Butler's meditations in *Precarious Life*, written in the aftermath of the attacks of September 11, 2001. Striving to find an adequate response to that violence and the wars it sponsored, Butler arrives at the thought that her response must initiate "a re-imagining of the possibility of community" not on the basis of security and home, but "on the basis of vulnerability and loss" (20). Butler sidesteps the term cosmopolitanism, and replaces its capacity for hospitality with "a capacity to mourn in global dimensions" (12). Her emphasis on the dispossession of identity, its necessary instability and implication in a violent world, gives her wartime reflections a kinship with Derrida's remarks on cosmopolitanism. They recall as well Cowper, who briefly trades his fireside complacency for an imagination claimed by the "strange visages express'd" in his fireplace.

In fact Butler's embrace of precarious life moves in a direction exactly counter to that traced by Coleridge and Williams. She begins with the loved one, friend and familiar, who has been taken away, who is no longer here. She then writes movingly about how that experience of loss can lead you away from yourself, to confess you are "undone," "no longer master" of yourself, and "faced with something enigmatic," unaccountable and strange (21). If the personal experience of loss and grief exposes the ways in which you are "undone" by your relations, it also moves you beyond the autonomy—the fixity and security—of the private. It moves you toward (at least this is the possibility Butler imagines) mindfulness of a more general vulnerability and thereby toward a larger and more complex "sense of political community" (22). A pulling away from the hearth to that suspended bridge.

Butler's ethics of mourning dispenses with the problem of the insubstantiality of the stranger at the hearth in ways that ask me to review that stranger's precursors. Butler repositions the ontological question as temporal and historical: you respond to such an apparition not because it can touch you, but because at some prior moment you have been touched. Reading romantic texts has revealed how that figure's flickering, apparitional quality looks forward to technologies of modern media. It signals the after-effects of reading a newspaper or book, listening to the radio, or watching television. Precisely in its precarious being as "unquiet thing," it raises the question of its own humanity and reality: can you be touched by such beings? If not, if you remain unmoved, the consequences could be dire. For in a world where the injurious effects of war are distributed differentially, from one place or scene to another,

> violence is done against those who [appear] unreal. . .[.] From the perspective of violence, it [violence] fails to injure or negate those lives since they are already negated. But they have a strange way of remaining animated and so must be negated again (and again). (33)

Reading romantic literature, I have tried to recover a history of writers and readers who had been touched and moved by the unaccountable violence of war. The effort was, in part, to recognize what many of them seemed able to diagnose: the obstacles to such responsiveness, the negating effects of modern war and modern mediation of war. Equally strong was the desire to call up past feelings for the present, on behalf of the present. I found that like other negated things, feelings from the past too have a strange way of reanimating themselves. The words of romantic writers have brought me to the experience of wartime and left me at a loss. If these words have any life, then this project must be left undone.

ACKNOWLEDGMENTS

At the end of this project two kinds of acknowledgment call out, and before those of gratitude I turn to those of—for lack of a better word—history.

I once thought this project arose from a specific time of war, the first Gulf War, which forced me to think about a civilian's long-distance and mediated experience of state-sponsored violence. Yet my dating proved faulty; subsequent and previous wars have contributed no less. How much shaping force had the Vietnam War, which shrouded my childhood both certainly and indistinctly? (Years later I understood why, in that wartime, my sixth-grade teacher made us memorize Tennyson's "The Charge of the Light Brigade.") What impressions did the Second World War leave, a war my father just missed while in training at West Point, from which he graduated in June 1945? Shortly after my birth, during the Cuban Missile Crisis, he had a civilian job at the Pentagon; the office where he once worked was later destroyed by a hijacked plane on September 11, 2001. And so on, each war cascading into other wars, with their elusive causes and incalculable consequences.

In many ways this project has also been an attempt to figure out how a set of personal losses led me to contemplate distant histories of war—and that attempt remains unresolved. In the second- and third-hand manner that seems to characterize this book, these experiences have nevertheless left their imprint on the writing. If I have been able to attune my words to the experience of fallen lives, these losses are probably responsible.

Much more gratefully, I acknowledge the friends and colleagues who have given me abundant gifts. Through times when I did not believe this book would be written, there were those who did believe and prodded me in ways subtle and generous. No words are fine enough to thank Andrew Miller for his patience, wisdom, and love. Susan Gubar and Don Gray each befriend me almost daily, but never more than by reminding me that grace, humor, and humanity can be united in the person of a literary critic. Sonia Hofkosh, friend wise and true, reminds me what really matters. Ken Johnston makes the crossroads of scholarship, Romanticism, and Bloomington—and London!—seem a happy place to spend one's time. Many others have had reason to thank Jim Chandler in their acknowledgments, but he has also helped me uniquely; the profession is a better, more stimulating and human place because it includes him. Marshall Brown, Claudia Johnson, Frances Ferguson, and Billy Galperin have all called me to aspire to their high standards of critical writing. I cannot reckon the full value of their various encouragements. David Clark, Celeste Langan, and Kevis Goodman each brought a highly charged intelligence to this project, reading it with generosity and sending it back to me redeemed— or nearly.

Friends and colleagues at Indiana University have brought me riches: their knowledge and ideas, their various styles and jokes, but also their sympathy and special liveliness. I owe a special debt to two of them, whose advice made it possible for me to conceive this book. Jonathan Elmer has been a brother to me over the years, and a constant reminder of the pleasures of thinking. Deidre Lynch's magnanimity and too-brief presence in Bloomington benefit many sections of this book. She pointed me to Cowper's *The Task*, after which everything made sense. Others at Indiana have read versions of this material or offered suggestions that spurred the writing and I am happy to thank them here: Tim Campbell, Linda Charnes, Ed Comentale, Jen Fleissner, Paul Gutjahr, Patty Ingham, Josh Kates, Richard Nash, Eric Sonstroem, Janet Sorensen, Lee Sterrenburg, Paul Westover, and Nick Williams. As department chairs, Christine Farris, George Hutchinson, Ken Johnston, and Steve Watt have made the English department a generative and supportive place.

The Center for Eighteenth-Century Studies at Indiana University has provided that rare thing: an encouraging and stupendously smart group of colleagues from various disciplines. Dror Wahrman, the center's director, has been an inspiration and a warm friend. Fritz Breithaupt, Michel Chaouli, Konstantin Dierks, Constance Furey, Sarah Knott, Richard Nash, Rebecca Spang, Jonathan Sheehan, Janet Sorenson, Johannes Turk, and, again, Deidre Lynch and Jonathan Elmer, have together and individually made this a better project while offering their good company. Sections of the book were presented in early form at the center's annual workshop, and visiting participants there provided sharp and productive feedback.

Two recent books, Kevis Goodman's *Romanticism and Georgic Modernity* and William Galperin's *The Historical Jane Austen*, prompted such a powerful sense of gratitude and affinity that I wrote their authors, who promptly wrote back, initiating a real and productive intellectual exchange. Their support and intelligence as readers, as much as their own writing, gave this project new possibilities. Thanks as well to a selfless community of scholars in romantic studies. Sam Baker, John Barrell, Marilyn Butler, Luisa Cale, Julie Carlson, Jeff Cox, Anne-Lise François, Tim Fulford, Michael Gamer, Kevin Gilmartin, Joshua Gonsalves, Harriet Guest, Lily Gurton-Wachter, Jill Heydt-Stevenson, William Keach, Theresa Kelley, Jacques Khalip, Marjorie Levinson, Richard Maxwell, Rob Mitchell, Jeanne Moskul, Danny O'Quinn, Adela Pinch, Ann

Rowland, Esther Schor, Philip Shaw, Katie Trumpener, and Susan Wolfson each left a mark on this book. Audiences from York to Houston, Boston to Boulder tried to alert me to what did and did not work in these pages. Thanks especially to Mark Salber Phillips, David Bell, Jonathan Freedman, Ranjana Kanna, and Betty Joseph.

A fellowship at the Bunting Institute at Radcliffe (now the Radcliffe Institute) gave me the first inkling of this project. Later a Delta Delta Delta fellowship at the National Humanities Center gave the writing room and time to breathe. It also brought me close to the radiance of Laurie Langbauer and Terry Holt. Thanks to all my lunch mates, and especially Cara Robertson and Roger Chickering, Georgia Warnke and Wendy Allenbrook, Geoff Harpham and Kent Mullikin. Special thanks to the center's magnificent librarians, as well as the special collections librarians at Duke University.

Sections of this book were previously published and improved by editors and readers at various journals. A shorter version of "War in the Air" was published in *MLQ: Modern Language Quarterly*; an early version of "Everyday War" appeared in *ELH: English Literary History*; "Still Winter Falls" appeared in *PMLA*'s special issue on war, ed. Srinivas Aruvamudan and Diana Taylor. Richard Higgins performed heroically in preparing this manuscript; Jamie Horrocks also read it with care. I feel a large debt to them, and to Hanne Winarsky, Beth Clevenger, and Carole Schwager at Princeton University Press, who brought to the text their thoughtful and sensitive editing. Deep thanks to Charles K. Williams for his generosity. Permission to reprint Mr. Williams's poems has been granted by Farrar, Straus and Giroux, publishers of *The Singing* (New York, 2004) and in the United Kingdom and British Commonwealth by Bloodaxe Books, publishers of C. K. Williams, *Collected Poems* (Tarset, UK, 2006).

A heartfelt thanks to those who gave me other things to think about, especially my dear friends Alexandra Morphet, Dawn Johnsen, and John Hamilton; my swim team, Mary Clare Bauman and Cathy Gutjahr; my parents, Andy and Loretta, my sisters, La and Babe; and other far-flung family members. Before and after and throughout the writing, Benedict, Cassandra, and Andrew fill my life. They are my joy.

BIBLIOGRAPHY

N.B. All citations marked with *ECCO* refer to the *Eighteenth Century Collections On-line*. Gale Group.

Abrams, M. H. *Natural Supernaturalism*. New York: Norton, 1973.

Aikin, John. *General biography; or lives, critical and historical, of the most eminent persons of all ages. . . .* London: G.G. and J. Robinson, 1799–1815. *ECCO*

Alison, Archibald. *Essays on the nature and principles of taste. By the Revd. Archibald Alison*. Dublin, 1790. *ECCO.*

Althusser, Louis, and Étienne Balibar. *Reading "Capital."* Trans. Ben Brewster. London: Verso, 1970.

Altick, Richard. *The Shows of London*. Cambridge: Belknap, 1978.

Anderson, Amanda. *The Powers of Distance: Cosmopolitanism and the Cultivation of Detachment*. Princeton: Princeton UP, 2001.

Anderson, Benedict. *Imagined Communities: Reflections on the Origins and Spread of Nationalism*. 2nd ed. London: Verso, 1991.

Andrews, John. *History of the War with America, France, Spain, and Holland*. Vol. 2. London: John Fielding, 1785–86. *ECCO*

The Annual Register. London: Dodsley, 1758–1790.

Anon. *The Alarmist, No. 1*. London: J. Owen, 1796.

Anon. *An appeal to the head and heart of every man and woman in Great Britain, respecting the threatened French invasion, and the importance of immediately coming forward with voluntary contributions*. London: J. Wright, 1798. *ECCO.*

Anon. *The Meteors*. London: A. and J. Black, and H. D. Symonds, 1799.

Anon. *Observations on the Art and Trade of Clock and Watchmaking*. London: J. Richardson, 1812.

Anon. Rev. of *Jane Fairfax*, by Naomi Royde Smith. *Times Literary Supplement*, 28 September 1940.

Anstey, Christopher. *The Poetical Works*. London: T. Cadell, 1808. English Poetry Database. http://gateway.proquest.com.

Aravamudan, Srinivas. "The Return of Anachronism." *MLQ: Modern Language Quarterly* 62.4 (2001): 331–53

Archer, Mildred, et al. *India Observed*. London: Victoria and Albert Museum in association with Trefoil Books, 1982.

Archibald, Sasha, and Daniel Rosenberg. "A Timeline of Timelines." *Cabinet Magazine* 13 (Spring 2004). http://www.cabinetmagazine.org/issues/13/timelines.php.

Arendt, Hannah. *On Revolution*. Westport, CT: Greenwood, 1982.

———. *On Violence*. New York: Harcourt, Brace & World, 1970.

Arnold, Matthew. *Essays in Criticism, Second Series*. Ed. S. R. Littlewood. London: Macmillan, 1958.

Ash, John, ed. *The New and Complete Dictionary of the English Language*. Vol. 2. London: E. and C. Dilly, 1775. *ECCO*.

Auerbach, Nina. *Communities of Women: An Idea in Fiction*. Cambridge: Harvard UP, 1978.

Austen, Jane. *Northanger Abbey*. Eds. Barbara M. Benedict and Deirdre Le Faye. Cambridge: Cambridge UP, 2006.

———. *Persuasion. The Novels of Jane Austen*. Vol. 5. 3rd ed. Oxford: Oxford UP, 1933, 1988.

———. *Persuasion*. Ed. Linda Bree. Peterborough, Ont.: Broadview, 1998.

Bailey, Nathan. *The New Universal Etymological English Dictionary*. 5th ed. London: Cavell, 1775. *ECCO*.

Baillie, Joanna. *Poetical and Dramatic Works*. London: Longman, Brown, Green and Longmans, 1851.

Bainbridge, Simon. *British Poetry and the Revolutionary and Napoleonic Wars: Visions of Conflict*. Oxford: Oxford UP, 2003.

Balfour, Ian. *The Rhetoric of Romantic Prophecy*. Stanford: Stanford UP, 2002.

Barbauld, Anna Letitia. "On the Uses of History." *A Legacy for Young Ladies*. Ed. Lucy Aikin. 2nd ed. London: Longman, Rees, Orme, Brown, and Green, 1826.

———. *Selected Poetry and Prose*. Ed. William McCarthy and Elizabeth Kraft. Toronto: Broadview P, 2002.

Barlow, Joel. *The History of England, from the Year 1765, to the Year 1795*. Vol. 2. London: J. Parsons, 1795. *ECCO*.

Barrell, John. *The Dark Side of the Landscape: The Rural Poor in English Painting, 1730–1840*. Cambridge: Cambridge UP, 1980.

———. *English Literature in History, 1730–1780*. London: Hutchinson, 1983.

———. *Imagining the King's Death: Figurative Treason, Fantasies of Regicide, 1793–1796*. Oxford: Oxford UP, 2000.

Baucom, Ian. *Specters of the Atlantic: Finance Capital, Slavery, and the Philosophy of History*. Durham: Duke UP, 2005.

Bayly, C. A. *The Birth of the Modern World, 1780–1914: Global Connections and Comparisons*. Malden, MA: Blackwell, 2004.

———. *Imperial Meridian: The British Empire and the World, 1780–1830*. London: Longman, 1989.

Bell, Alexander, and Colin MacFarquhar. *Encyclopedia Britannica*. 3 vols. Edinburgh: A. Bell and C. MacFarquhar, 1771. *ECCO*.

Bell, David A. *The First Total War: Napoleon's Europe and the Birth of Warfare as We Know It*. Boston: Houghton Mifflin, 2007.

Benjamin, Walter. *Illuminations: Essays and Reflections*. Ed. and intro. Hannah Arendt. Trans. Harry Zohn. New York: Schocken, 1968.

Bennett, Betty T., ed. *British War Poetry in the Age of Romanticism, 1793–1815*. New York: Garland, 1976.

Benveniste, Emile. "'Hiver' et 'Neige' en Indo-Européen." *Mnemes Xaron; Gedenkschrift Paul Kretschmer*. Ed. Heinz Kronasser. Gottingen: Hubert & Co. 1956.

Bergson, Henri. *Matter and Memory*. New York: Zone Books, 1988.

Berman, Russell. "Politics: Divide and Rule." *MLQ: Modern Language Quarterly* 62.4 (2001): 317–30.

Bhabha, Homi K. *The Location of Culture*. London: Routledge, 2004.

Blake, William. *Blake: Complete Writings*. Ed. Geoffrey Keynes. London: Oxford UP, 1971.

Blanchot, Maurice. "Prophetic Speech." *The Book to Come*. Trans. Charlotte Mandell. Stanford: Stanford UP, 2003. 79–85.

Blanqui, Jerome-Adolphe. *A History of Political Economy in Europe*. Trans. Emily Josephine Leonard. New York: G. P. Putman's Sons, 1885.

Bodle, Wayne K. *The Valley Forge Winter*. University Park: Pennsylvania State UP, 2002.

Bolter, Jay David, and Richard Grusin. *Remediation: Understanding New Media*. Cambridge: MIT P, 1999.

Brewer, John. *The Sinews of Power: War, Money and the English State, 1688–1783*. Cambridge: Havvard UP, 1990.

Bromwich, David. "Euphemism and American Violence." *New York Review of Books* 55.5 (April 3, 2008).

Brooks, Cleanth. "Wordsworth and Human Suffering: Notes on Two Early Poems." *From Sensibility to Romanticism*. London: Oxford UP, 1965. 373–88.

Brothers, Richard. *Brothers's prophecy of all the remarkable and wonderful events which will come to pass in the present year: foretelling, . . . the downfall of the Pope; a revolution in Spain, Portugal, and Germany; . . . Also, a dreadful famine, pestilence, and earthquake*. London: 1795? ECCO.

———. *A corroborating proof from the holy scriptures, of the truth of the chronology of the world, as given by revelation to Richard Brothers*. London, 1795. ECCO.

———. *An exposition of the Trinity: with a further elucidation of the twelfth chapter of Daniel; one letter to the King, and two to Mr. Pitt, &c. by Richard Brothers. The descendant of David, King of Israel, &c*. London, 1795. ECCO.

———. *A letter from Mr. Brothers to Miss Cott, the recorded daughter of David, and future Queen of the Hebrews. With an address to the members of His Britannic Majesty's Council*. Edinburgh, 1798. ECCO.

———. *A revealed knowledge of the prophecies & times. Book the first. Wrote under the direction of the Lord God, . . . it being the first sign of warning for the benefit of all nations; containing, with other great and remarkable things, not revealed to any other person on earth, the restoration of the Hebrews to Jerusalem, by the year 1798*. London, 1794. ECCO.

———. *A revealed knowledge of the prophecies and times. Particularly of the present time, the present war, and the prophecy now fulfilling. . . . Book the second. Containing, with other great and remarkable things, not revealed to any other person on earth, the sudden and perpetual fall of the Turkish, German, and Russian empires.* London, 1794. *ECCO.*

Brothers, Richard. *Wonderful prophecies. Being a dissertation on the existence, nature, and extent of the prophetic powers in the human mind . . . .* 3rd ed. London: B. Crosby, 1795.

Brown, Ivor. Review of "Emma" [stage production]. "Theatre and Life." *The London Observer*, 11 February 1945: 2.

Buonaparte, Napoléon, *An Account of the French Expedition in Egypt.* 2nd ed. Leeds: Edward Baines, 1800.

Burke, Augusta. Notebooks of Augusta Burke. Burke Collection. Goucher College Library.

Burke, Edmund. *Reflections on the Revolution in France.* New York: J. Dodsley, 1790.

Busch, Noel Fairchild. *Winter Quarters.* New York: Liveright, 1974.

Butler, Judith. *Precarious Life: The Powers of Mourning and Violence.* London: Verso, 2004.

Byron, George Gordon. *Don Juan.* Ed. T. G. Steffan, E. Steffan, and W. W. Pratt. New Haven: Yale UP, 1982.

Cadava, Eduard. *Emerson and the Climates of History.* Stanford: Stanford UP, 1997.

Carlson, Julie. *England's First Family of Writers: Mary Wollstonecraft, William Godwin, Mary Shelley.* Baltimore: Johns Hopkins UP, 2007.

Caruth, Cathy. *Trauma: Explorations in Memory.* Baltimore: Johns Hopkins UP, 1995.

———. *Unclaimed Experience: Trauma, Narrative, and History.* Baltimore: Johns Hopkins UP, 1996.

Cavell, Stanley. *Disowning Knowledge: In Six Plays of Shakespeare.* Cambridge: Cambridge UP, 1987.

———. *In Quest of the Ordinary: Lines of Skepticism and Romanticism.* Chicago: U of Chicago P, 1988.

Certeau, Michel de. *The Practice of Everyday Life.* Trans. Steven Rendall. Berkeley: U of California P, 1984.

Chakrabarty, Dipesh. *Provincializing Europe: Postcolonial Thought and Historical Difference.* Princeton: Princeton UP, 2000.

Chandler, James. "About Loss: W. G. Sebald's Romantic Art of Memory." *South Atlantic Quarterly* 102.1 (Winter 2003): 235–62.

———. *England in 1819: The Politics of Literary Culture and the Case of Romantic Historicism.* Chicago: U of Chicago P, 1998.

Chartier, Roger. "Do Books Make Revolutions?" *The Cultural Origins of the French Revolution.* Durham: Duke UP, 1991. 67–91.

Cherry, Deborah. *Beyond the Frame: Feminism and Visual Culture in Britain, 1850–1900.* London: Routledge, 2000.

Chickering Roger. "Total War: The Use and Abuse of a Concept." *Anticipating Total War: The German and American Experiences, 1871–1914.* Ed. Roger Chickering and Stig Forster. Cambridge: Cambridge UP and Washington, DC: The German Historical Institute, 1999.

————, and Stig Forster, eds. *War in the Age of Revolution*. Cambridge: Cambridge UP, 2009.

Christensen, Jerome. *Romanticism at the End of History*. Baltimore: Johns Hopkins UP, 2000.

Clausewitz, Carl von. *On War*. Eds. and trans. Michael Howard and Peter Paret. New York: Oxford UP, 2007.

Cobbett, William. *Paper against Gold: The History and Mystery of the Bank of England*. New York: John Doyle, 1834.

Cocker, Edward. *Cocker's English Dictionary*. London: Back and Bettesworth, 1704. *Eighteenth Century Collections Online ECCO*.

Cohen, Monica. "Persuading the Navy Home: Austen and Married Women's Professional Property." *Novel* 29.3 (Spring 1996): 346–66.

Colebrook, Robert H. *Twelve views of places in the kingdom of Mysore*. London: [n.d.], 1793).

Coleridge, Samuel Taylor. *The Complete Poems*. Ed. William Keach. New York: Penguin, 1997.

————. "The War and International Law." *The Friend*. 1803. *Collected Works*. Ed. Barbara Rooke. Vol. 4. London: Routledge and Kegan Paul, 1969. 265–67.

Colley, Linda. *Britons: Forging the Nation, 1707–1837*. New Haven: Yale UP, 1992.

————. *Captives*. New York: Pantheon, 2002.

Connor, Steven. "Michel Serres's Milieux." Paper presented at ABRALIC (Brazilian Association for Comparative Literature), "Mediations," Belo Horizonte, July 23–26, 2002. http://www.bbk.ac.uk/english/skc/milieux/.

Cottam, Sir Evan. "The Daniells in India." *Bengal Past and Present* 25 (1923).

Cowper, William. *The Iliad and Odyssey of Homer, translated into English Blank Verse*. London: J. Johnson, 1791. *ECCO*.

————. *The Letters and Prose Writings of William Cowper*. Ed. James King and Charles Ryskamp. 3 vols. Oxford: Clarendon, 1979–86. I: 247.

————. *The Task*. *Poetical Works*, Ed. H. S. Milford. 4th ed. Oxford: Oxford UP, 1967. 129–241.

————. *The Task and Selected Other Poems*. Ed. James Sambrook. London: Longman, 1994.

Crabbe, George. "The Newspaper." *Poems*. London: J. Hatchard, 1807. 165–87.

Crary, Jonathan. *Techniques of the Observer: On Vision and Modernity in the Nineteenth Century*. Cambridge: MIT P, 1990.

Crawford, Rachel. "English Georgic and British Nationhood." *ELH: English Literary History* 65.1 (1998): 123–58.

Cunningham, George Godfrey, ed. *Lives of Eminent and Illustrious Englishmen*. 8 vols. Glasgow: A. Fullarton, 1838.

Cuomo, Chris J. "War Is Not Just an Event: Reflections on the Significance of Everyday Violence." *Hypatia* 11.4 (Autumn 1996): 30–45.

Curran, Stuart. "The 'I' Altered." *Romanticism and Feminism*. Ed. Anne Mellor. Bloomington: Indiana UP, 1988. 185–207.

Dalton, John. *Meteorological Observations and Essays*. London: W. Richardson, 1793.

Darnton, Robert. *Literary Underground of the Old Regime*. Cambridge: Harvard UP, 1982.

Davidoff, Leonore, and Catherine Hall. *Family Fortunes: Men and Women of the English Middle Class, 1780–1850*. Chicago: U of Chicago P, 1987.

de Man, Paul. *Blindness and Insight*. Intro. Wlad Godzich. 2nd ed. Minneapolis: U of Minnesota P, 1983.

DeAlmeido, Hermione, and George G. Gilpin. *Indian Renaissance: British Romantic Art and the Prospect of India*. Aldershot, UK: Ashgate, 2005.

DeQuincey, Thomas. "The English Mail Coach." *Confessions of an English Opium-Eater and Other Writings*. Ed. Grevel Lindop. Oxford: Oxford UP, 1996. 183–233.

Derrida, Jacques. *Apprendre à vivre enfin: Entretien avec Jean Birnbaum*. Paris: Galilee, 2005.

———. *The Ear of the Other: Otobiography, Transference, Translation*. Ed. Christie V. McDonald. Trans. Peggy Kamuf. Lincoln: U of Nebraska P, 1988.

———. *On Cosmopolitanism and Forgiveness*. London: Routledge, 2001.

Dolan, John. "'Today the Mind Is Not Part of the Weather': Cognitive and Rhetorical Perspectives on the Construction of Poetic Metaphor." *Qui Parle* 7.2 (Spring/Summer 1994): 57–77.

Elfenbein, Andrew. "'Stricken Deer': Secrecy, Homophobia, and the Rise of Suburban Man." *Genders* 27 (1998).

Eliot, T. S. *The Waste Land*. Ed. Frank Kermode. Harmondsworth, UK: Penguin, 2003.

Ellison, Julie. *Cato's Tears and the Making of Anglo-American Emotion*. Chicago: U of Chicago P, 1999.

———. "News, Blues, and Cowper's Busy World." *MLQ: Modern Language Quarterly* 62.3 (2001): 219–37.

Encyclopedia; or, A dictionary of arts, sciences, and miscellaneous literature . . . Compiled from the writings of the best authors, in several languages. . . . 1st American ed. Philadelphia, 1798. *ECCO*.

Erdman, David. *William Blake: Prophet against Empire*. Princeton: Princeton UP, 1977.

Faust, Drew Gilpin. *This Republic of Suffering: Death and the American Civil War*. New York: Alfred A. Knopf, 2008.

Fawcett, Joseph. *The Art of War*. London: J. Johnson, 1795.

———. *War Elegies*. London: J. Johnson, 1801.

Fenton, James. "The Photograph Man." Review of *All the Mighty World: The Photographs of Roger Fenton, 1852–1860*, by Gordon Baldwin, Malcolm Daniel, and Sarah Greenough. *New York Review of Books*. 13 January 2005.

Ferguson, Frances. "Malthus, Godwin, Wordsworth, and the Spirit of Solitude." *Literature and the Body: Essays on Populations and Persons*. Ed. Elaine Scarry. Baltimore: Johns Hopkins UP, 1988. 106–24.

Ferguson, Niall. *Empire: The Rise and Demise of the British World Order and the Lessons for Global Power*. New York: Basic Books, 2004.

Fisher, Philip. *The Vehement Passions*. Princeton: Princeton UP, 2002.

Fitzpatrick, John C., ed. *The Writings of George Washington from the Original Manuscript Sources*. Washington, DC: U.S. Government Printing Office, 1933.

Foucault, Michel. *Discipline and Punish: The Birth of the Prison*. Trans. Alan Sheridan. 2nd ed. New York: Vintage, 1995.

———. *The Order of Things: An Archaeology of the Human Sciences*. New York: Vintage, 1973.

———. *"Society Must Be Defended": Lectures at the College de France, 1975–76*. Ed. Mauro Bertani and Alessandro Fontana. Trans. David Macey. New York: Picador, 2003.

François, Anne-Lise. *Open Secrets: The Literature of Uncounted Experience*. Stanford: Stanford UP, 2007.

———. "Unspeakable Weather, or the Rain Romantic Constatives Know." *Phantom Sentences: Essays in Linguistics and Literature Presented to Ann Banfield*. Ed. Robert S. Kawashima et al. Bern: Peter Lang, 2008. 147–61.

Freud, Sigmund. *Beyond the Pleasure Principle*. Ed. and trans. Lytton Strachey. Intro. Gregory Zilboorg. New York: Norton, 1961.

———. "Mourning and Melancholia." *On Metapsychology: The Theory of Psychoanalysis*. Ed. Angela Richards. Harmondsworth, UK: Penguin, 1984.

Frost, Robert. *Mountain Interval*. New York: H. Holt and Company, 1916.

Frye, Northrop. *Anatomy of Criticism*. Princeton: Princeton UP, 1971.

———. *Fearful Symmetry*. Princeton: Princeton UP, 1947.

Fulford, Tim, ed. *Romanticism and Millenarianism*. New York: Palgrave, 2002.

———. "Romanticizing the Empire: The Naval Heroes of Southey, Coleridge, Austen, and Marryat." *MLQ: Modern Language Quarterly* 60.2 (June 1999): 161–96.

———. "Sighing for a Soldier: Jane Austen and Military Pride and Prejudice." *Nineteenth-Century Literature* 57.2 (September 2002): 153–78.

———. Debbie Lee, and Peter J. Kitson. *Literature, Science and Exploration in the Romantic Era: Bodies of Knowledge*. Cambridge: Cambridge UP, 2004.

Fussell, Paul. *The Great War and Modern Memory*. New York: Oxford UP, 1975.

———. *Wartime: Understanding and Behavior in the Second World War*. New York: Oxford UP, 1989.

Galperin, William. *The Historical Jane Austen*. Philadelphia: U of Pennsylvania P, 2003.

———. *The Return of the Visible in British Romanticism*. Baltimore: Johns Hopkins UP, 1993.

Galt, John. *Annals of the Parish*. London: Henry Frowde, 1908.

Godwin, William. *An Enquiry Concerning Political Justice*. 2 vols. London: G. G. and J. Robinson, 1796. *ECCO*

———. *Essay on Sepulchres. The Political and Philosophical Writings of William Godwin*. Ed. Mark Philp. Vol. 6. London: Pickering, 1993.

Goodman, Kevis. *Georgic Modernity and British Romanticism: Poetry and the Mediation of History*. Cambridge: Cambridge UP, 2004.

————. "The Loophole in the Retreat: The Culture of News and the Early Life of Romantic Self-Consciousness." *South Atlantic Quarterly* 102.1 (Winter 2003): 25–52.

Gould, Eliga. "Zones of Law, Zones of Violence: The Legal Geography of the British Atlantic, circa 1772." *William and Mary Quarterly* 60.3 (July 2003): 471–510.

Grafton, Anthony. *Joseph Scaliger: A Study in the History of Classical Scholarship, Vol. 2: Historical Chronology.* Oxford: Clarendon, 1993.

Guiomar, Jean-Yves. *L'invention de la guerre totale, XVIIIe–XXe siècle.* Paris: Le Félin Kiron, 2004.

Guyer, Sara. "The Rhetoric of Survival and the Possibility of Romanticism." *Studies in Romanticism* 46. 2 (2007): 247–64.

Hamblyn, Richard. *The Invention of Clouds: How an Amateur Meteorologist Forged the Language of the Skies.* New York: Farrar, Straus and Giroux, 2001.

Hardt, Michael, and Antonio Negri. *Empire.* Cambridge: Harvard UP, 2000.

Harrison, Gary, and Jill Heydt-Stevenson. "Variations on the Picturesque: Authority, Play and Practice." *European Romantic Review* 13 (2002): 3–10.

Harrison, J.F.C. *The Second Coming: Popular Millenarianism, 1780–1850.* New Brunswick, NJ: Rutgers UP, 1979.

Hartman, Geoffrey H. *Beyond Formalism: Literary Essays 1958–1970.* New Haven: Yale UP, 1970.

————. "Poetics of Prophecy." *High Romantic Argument: Essays for M. H. Abrams.* Ed. Lawrence Lipking. Ithaca: Cornell UP, 1981. 15–40.

————. *Saving the Text: Literature, Derrida, Philosophy.* Baltimore: Johns Hopkins UP, 1981.

Hazlitt, William. *The Selected Writings of William Hazlitt.* Ed. Duncan Wu. Vol. 9. London: Pickering & Chatto, 1998.

Hegel, G.W.F. *The Philosophy of History.* New York: Dover, 1956.

Heidler, David Stephen. *Daily Lives of Civilians in Wartime Early America: From the Colonial Era to the Civil War.* Westport, CT: Greenwood Press, 2007.

Heinzelman, Kurt. "Roman Georgic in the Georgian Age: A Theory of Romantic Genre." *Texas Studies in Literature and Language* 33 (1991): 182–214.

Herbert, Christopher. *Culture and Anomie: Ethnographic Imagination in the Nineteenth Century.* Chicago: U of Chicago P, 1991.

Hertz, Neil. *The End of the Line: Essays on Psychoanalysis and the Sublime.* New York: Columbia UP, 1985.

Heydt-Stevenson, Jill. "'Unbecoming Conjunctions': Mourning the Loss of Landscape and Love in *Persuasion*." *Eighteenth-Century Fiction* 8.1 (October 1995): 51–71.

Higgins, David Minden. *Romantic Genius and the Literary Magazine.* London: Routledge, 2005.

Hodges, William. *Travels In India, during the years 1780, 1781, 1782, & 1783.* London: J. Edwards, 1793.

Holmes, Richard. *Coleridge: Early Visions, 1772–1804.* New York: Viking, 1989.

Home, Henry (Lord Kames). *Sketches of the History of Man.* Edinburgh, 1788. ECCO.

Home, Robert. *Select Views in Mysore, The Country of Tippoo Sultan; from Drawings Taken on the Spot.* London: Bowyer (republished and printed by R. Butters), 1808.

Hope-Jones, Arthur. *Income Tax in the Napoleonic Wars.* Cambridge: Cambridge UP, 1939.

Howard, Luke. *The Climate of London.* 2 vols. London: W. Phillips, 1818–1820.

———. *On the Modifications of Clouds, and on the Principles of their Production, Suspension and Destruction, etc.* London: J. Taylor, 1803.

Hugo, Victor. *Les Misérables.* Trans. Charles E. Wilbour. New York: Modern Library, 1992.

Hume, David. *An Enquiry Concerning the Principles of Morals.* London: A. Millar, 1751.

———. *Essays and Treatises on Several Subjects.* 2 vols. Edinburgh and London: George Caw, Cadell and Davies, 1800.

———. *A Treatise of Human Nature.* London: John Noon, 1739–40. ECCO.

Jameson, Fredric. "The End of Temporality." *Critical Inquiry* 29 (Summer 2003): 695–718.

Janković, Vladimir. *Reading the Skies: A Cultural History of English Weather, 1650–1820.* Chicago: U of Chicago P, 2001.

Jeffrey, Francis. Review of "Hayley's Life of Cowper." *Edinburgh Review* 2 (1803): 64–86.

Johnson, J. W. "On Differing Ages and Climes." *Journal of the History of Ideas* 21 (October–December 1960): 465–80.

Johnson, Samuel. *Dictionary of the English Language.* Vol. 2. London, 1756. ECCO.

———. *The Idler, No. 11. The Yale Edition of the Works of Samuel Johnson.* Ed. Walter J. Bate, J. M. Bullitt, and L. F. Powell. New Haven: Yale UP, 1963.

———. *The Plan for a Dictionary of the English Language.* London: J. and P. Knapton, T. Longman and T. Shewell, C. Hitch, A. Millar, and R. Dodsley, 1747. ECCO.

Jones, William. "On the Appearances, Causes, and Prognostic Signs of the Weather." *The Theological, Philosophical and Miscellaneous Works of the Rev. William Jones.* London: F. and C. Rivington, 1801.

Kant, Immanuel. "Perpetual Peace: A Philosophical Sketch." *Kant: Political Writings.* Ed. Hans Reiss. Cambridge: Cambridge UP, 1991.

Kaplan, Alice, and Kristin Ross."Introduction." *Yale French Studies: Special Issue on Everyday Life* 73:9 (1987): 1–4.

Kaul, Suvir. *Poems of Nation, Anthems of Empire.* Charlottesville: U of Virginia P, 2000.

Keegan, John. *The Face of Battle.* Harmondsworth, UK: Penguin, 1976.

———, ed. *The Book of War.* New York: Viking, 1999.

Keenan, Thomas. "Publicity and Indifference (Sarajevo on Television)." *PMLA* 117.1 (2002): 104–16.

Kersey, John. *A New English Dictionary.* London: Robert Knaplock, 1713. ECCO.

Kinser, Samuel. "Everyday Ordinary." *diacritics* 22.2 (Summer 1992): 79.

Knapp, Stephen. *Personification and the Sublime: Milton to Coleridge.* Cambridge: Harvard UP, 1985.

Koselleck, Reinhart. *Futures Past: On the Semantics of Historical Time*. Trans. Keith Tribe. New York: Columbia UP, 2004.

———. "Time and History." *The Practice of Conceptual History: Timing History, Spacing Concepts*. Trans. Todd Samuel Presner et al. Stanford: Stanford UP, 2002. 100–14.

Krugman, Paul. *The Great Unraveling: Losing Our Way in the New Century*. New York: Norton, 2004.

LaCapra, Dominick. "Trauma, Absence, Loss." *Critical Inquiry* 25.4 (1999): 696–727.

Lamb, Charles. *The Life and Works of Charles Lamb*. Ed. Alfred Ainger. 2 vols. London: Macmillan, 1899.

Landa, Manuel de. *War in the Age of Intelligent Machines*. New York: Zone Books, 1991.

Langan, Celeste, and Maureen McLane. "The Medium of Romantic Poetry." *Cambridge Companion to British Romantic Poetry*. Ed. James K. Chandler and Maureen McLane. Cambridge: Cambridge UP, 2009.

Langbauer, Laurie. "Cultural Studies and the Politics of the Everyday." *diacritics* 22.1 (Spring 1992): 47–65.

Lefebvre, Georges. *Napoleon*. New York: Columbia, 1990.

Lefebvre, Henri. *Critique of Everyday Life*. Trans. John Moore. Pref. Michel Trebitsch. London: Verso, 1991.

———. *Everyday Life in the Modern World*. Trans. Sacha Rabinovitch. Piscataway, NJ: Transaction, 1984.

Liu, Alan. "Local Transcendence: Cultural Criticism, Postmodernism, and the Romanticism of Detail." *Representations* 32 (Autumn 1990): 75–113.

———. "Remembering the Spruce Goose: Historicism, Postmodernism, Romanticism." *South Atlantic Quarterly* 102.1 (Winter 2003): 263–75.

———. *Wordsworth: The Sense of History*. Stanford: Stanford UP, 1989.

Locke, John. *An Essay on Human Understanding*. Ed. Alexander Campbell Fraser. Oxford: Clarendon, 1894.

Low, Anthony. *The Georgic Revolution*. Princeton: Princeton UP, 1985.

Lowe, Donald. *History of Bourgeois Perception*. Chicago: U of Chicago Press, 1982.

Luhmann, Niklas. *The Reality of the Mass Media*. Trans. Kathleen Cross. Stanford: Stanford UP, 2000.

Lukács, Georg. *The Historical Novel*. Lincoln: U of Nebraska P, 1983.

Lynch, Deidre. "Homes and Haunts: Austen's and Mitford's English Idylls." *PMLA* 115.5 (October 2000): 1103–8.

Macauley, Thomas Babington. *Historical and Miscellaneous Essays*. 3 vols. New York: Albert Cogswell, 1859.

Mahajan, Jagmohan, et al. *Picturesque India*. New Delhi: Lustre Press under arrangement with Rupa & Co., 1983.

Mahoney, Charles. "Periodical Indigestion: Hazlitt's Unpalatable Politics." *Romanticism and Conspiracy, Romantic Circles Praxis Series*. Ed. and intro. Orrin N. C. Wang. College Park: U of Maryland P, 1997. http://www.rc.umd.edu/praxis/conspiracy/mahoney.

Marshall, David. "The Picturesque." *The Cambridge History of Literary Criticism, Vol 4: The Eighteenth Century*. Ed. H. B. Nisbet and Claude Rawson. Cambridge: Cambridge UP, 1989.

Massumi, Brian. *Parables for the Virtual: Movement, Affect, Sensation*. Durham: Duke UP, 2002.

Mattingly, Garrett. "No Peace beyond What Line?" *Transactions of the Royal Historical Society, 5th Ser.* 13 (1963): 145–62.

McCalman, Iain, ed. *An Oxford Companion to the Romantic Age*. Oxford: Oxford UP, 1999.

McHugh, Heather. "Presence and Passage: A Poet's Wordsworth." *MLQ: Modern Language Quarterly* 63.2 (June 2002): 167–96

McLane, Maureen N. *Romanticism and the Human Sciences: Poetry, Population, and the Discourse of the Species*. Cambridge: Cambridge UP, 2000.

McNeil, David. "*Tristram Shandy*: The Grotesque View of War and the Military Character." *Studies in the Age of Voltaire and the Eighteenth Century* 266 (1989): 411–32.

Mee, Jon. *Dangerous Enthusiasm: William Blake and the Culture of Radicalism in the 1790s*. Oxford: Clarendon Press, 1992.

———. *Romanticism, Enthusiasm, and Regulation: Poetics and the Policing of Culture in the Romantic Period*. Oxford: Oxford UP, 2005.

Mellor, Anne. *Mothers of the Nation*. Bloomington: Indiana UP, 2000.

Miller, D. A. "Austen's Attitude." *Yale Journal of Criticism* 8.1 (Spring 1995): 1–5.

Milton, John. *Paradise Lost*. Intro. Philip Pullman. Oxford: Oxford UP, 2005.

Mitchell, W.J.T., ed. *Landscape and Power: Space, Place, and Landscape*. 2nd ed. Chicago: U of Chicago P, 2002.

The Monthly Magazine. London: R. Phillips, 1796–1800.

Moody, Jane. *Illegitimate Theatre in London, 1770–1840*. Cambridge: Cambridge UP, 2000.

Morris, Edward. *Constable's Clouds: Paintings and Cloud Studies by John Constable*. Edinburgh: National Galleries of Scotland, 2000.

Muir, Rory. *Tactics and the Experience of Battle in the Age of Napoleon*. New Haven: Yale UP, 1998.

Muller, John. *A Treatise Containing the Elementary Part of Fortification, Regular and Irregular*. London: J. Nourse, 1746. *ECCO*.

Nora, Pierre. *Les Lieux de Mémoire*. 7 vols. Paris: Gallimard, 1984–92.

Officers. *A Military and Sea Dictionary, Explaining All Difficult Terms in the Martial Discipline*. 4th ed. London: J. Morphew, 1711. *ECCO*.

Oken, Lorenz. *Elements of Physiophilosophy*. Trans. Alfred Tulk. London: Ray Society, 1847.

O'Quinn, Daniel. *Staging Governance: Theatrical Imperialism in London, 1770–1800*. Baltimore: Johns Hopkins UP, 2005.

Paley, Morton D. *The Traveller in the Evening: The Last Works of William Blake*. Oxford: Oxford UP, 2003.

Paley, Morton D. "William Blake, the Prince of the Hebrews, and the Woman Clothed with the Sun." *William Blake: Essays in Honour of Sir Geoffrey Keynes*. Ed. Morton D. Paley and Michael Phillips. Oxford: Oxford UP, 1973. 260–93.

Pasley, Charles William. *Essay on the Military Policy and Institutions of the British Empire*. 2nd ed. London: A. J. Valpy, 1811.

———. "Letter to The Times." *Times of London*, 5 March 1795.

———. *The Military Policy and Institutions of the British Empire*. Ed. and intro. B. R. Ward. 5th ed. London: W. Clowes and Sons, 1914.

Peach, Lucinda. "An Alternative to Pacifism? Feminism and Just-War Theory." *Hypatia* 9.1 (1994): 152–72.

Phillips, Adam. *On Kissing, Tickling and Being Bored: Psychoanalytic Essays on the Unexamined Life*. Cambridge, MA: Harvard UP, 1993.

Phillips, Edward. *The New World of Words, or, Universal English Dictionary*. London: J. Phillips, 1706. ECCO.

Phillips, Mark Salber. "Relocating Inwardness: Historical Distance and the Transition from Enlightenment to Romantic Historiography." *PMLA* 118.3 (2003): 436–49.

———. *Society and Sentiment: Genres of Historical Writing in Britain, 1740–1820*. Princeton: Princeton UP, 2000.

Pinch, Adela. *Strange Fits of Passion: Epistemologies of Emotion, Hume to Austen*. Stanford: Stanford UP, 1996.

Pocock, J.G.A. "Political Thought in the English-Speaking Atlantic, 1760–1790." *The Varieties of British Political Thought, 1500–1800*. Cambridge: Cambridge UP, 1993.

Poovey, Mary. *A History of the Modern Fact*. Chicago: U of Chicago P, 1998.

Pope, Alexander. *The Iliad of Homer: Translated by Mr. Pope*. London: Bernard Lintot, 1715–20. ECCO.

Priestley, Joseph. *History of the Present State of Electricity, with Original Experiments*. 2 vols. London: C. Bathurst and T. Lowndes, 1775.

Rawlinson, Mark. "Invasion! Coleridge, The Defence of Britain and the Cultivation of the Public's Fear." *Romantic Wars: Studies in Culture and Conflict, 1793–1822*. Ed. Philip Shaw. Aldershot, UK: Ashgate, 2000.

Ray, N. R. *A Descriptive Catalogue of the Daniells['] Work in the Victorian Memorial*. Calcutta: N. R. Ray on behalf of the Trustees of the Victoria Memorial, 1976.

Reed, Arden. *Romantic Weather: The Climates of Coleridge and Baudelaire*. Hanover: UP of New England, 1983.

Ricardo, David. *The High Price of Bullion a Proof of the Depreciation of Bank-notes*. London: John Murray, 1810.

Riley, Denise. *Impersonal Passion: Language as Affect*. Durham: Duke UP, 2005.

Robbins, Bruce. *Secular Vocations: Intellectuals, Professionalism, Culture*. London: Verso, 1993.

Robinson, Mary. *The Poetical Works . . . In Three Volumes*. London: Richard Phillips, 1806.

Rosenberg, Daniel. "Joseph Priestley and the Graphic Invention of Modern Time," *Studies in Eighteenth-Century Culture* 36.1 (2007): 55–103.

———. "The Trouble with Timelines." *Cabinet Magazine* 13 (Spring 2004).

Rosenmeyer, Thomas G. "On Snow and Stones." *California Studies in Classical Antiquity* 11 (1979): 209–25.

Ross, Andrew. "The Work of Nature in the Age of Electronic Emission." *Social Text* 18 (Winter 1987/88): 116–28.

Rounce, Adam. "Cowper's Ends." *Romanticism and Millenarianism*. Ed. Tim Fulford. New York: Palgrave, 2002. 23–36.

Royal Military Academy, Woolwich. *Rules and Orders for the Royal Military Academy at Woolwich*. London: J. Bullock, 1776. ECCO.

Russell, Gillian. *The Theatres of War: Performance, Politics, and Society, 1793–1815*. Oxford: Clarendon, 1995.

Scarry, Elaine. *The Body in Pain: The Making and Unmaking of the World*. New York: Oxford UP, 1985.

Schmitt, Carl. *The* Nomos *of the Earth*. New York: Telos, 2003.

Schott, Robin May. "Gender and 'Postmodern War.'" *Hypatia* 11.4 (1996): 19–29.

Scott, Walter. *The Antiquary*. New York: Columbia UP, 1995.

———. *The Lay of the Last Minstrel*. Oxford: Woodstock Books, 1992.

———. *The Poetical Works of Sir Walter Scott*. The Oxford Complete Edition. Ed. J. Logie Robertson. London: Henry Frowde, 1908.

———. *Redgauntlet*. Ed. Kathryn Sutherland. Oxford: Oxford UP, 1985.

[———.] "Unsigned Review of *Emma*." *Quarterly Review*. 14 March 1816. Rpt. in *Jane Austen: Critical Assessments*. Ed. Ian Littlewood. Vol. 1. Mountfield, UK: Helm Information, 1998.

Sebald W. G. *Austerlitz*. Trans. Anthea Bell. New York: Random House, 2001.

Sedgwick, Eve Kosofsky. *Touching Feeling: Affect, Pedagogy, Performativity*. Durham: Duke UP, 2003.

Serres, Michel. *The Parasite*. Trans. Lawrence R. Schehr. Baltimore: Johns Hopkins UP, 1982.

Shakespeare, William. *The Winter's Tale*. Ed. Susan Snyder and Deborah T. Curren-Aquino. Cambridge: Cambridge UP, 2007.

Shaw, Philip. *Waterloo and the Romantic Imagination*. Basingstoke, UK: Palgrave Macmillan, 2002.

———, ed. *Romantic Wars: Studies in Culture and Conflict, 1793–1822*. Burlington, VT: Ashgate, 2000.

Shellim, Maurice. *The Daniells in India and the Waterfall at Papanasam*. Calcutta: Statesman, 1970.

Sherman, Stuart. *Telling Time: Clocks, Diaries and English Diurnal Form, 1660–1785*. Chicago: U of Chicago P, 1996.

Simic, Charles. "Archives of Horror." Rev. of *Regarding the Pain of Others*, by Susan Sontag. *New York Review of Books*, 1 May 2003.

Simpson, David. *9/11: The Culture of Commemoration*. Chicago: U of Chicago P, 2006.

———. "Derrida's Ghosts: The State of Our Debt." *Studies in Romanticism* 46.2 (Summer–Fall 2007): 183–202.

———. "Wandering Spooks." *London Review of Books* 30.16 (14 August 2008): 12.

Simpson, David. "Raymond Williams: Feeling for Structures, Voicing 'History.'" *Social Text* 30 (1992): 9–26.

Siskin, Clifford. *The Work of Writing: Literature and Social Change in Britain, 1700–1830.* Baltimore: Johns Hopkins UP, 1998.

Smith, Adam. *The Theory of Moral Sentiments.* Amherst, NY: Prometheus, 2000.

Smith, Charlotte. *The Poems of Charlotte Smith.* Ed. Stuart Curran. New York: Oxford UP, 1993.

Sobel, Dava. *Longitude: The True Story of a Lone Genius Who Solved the Greatest Scientific Problem of His Time.* New York: Walker, 1995.

Sontag, Susan. *Regarding the Pain of Others.* New York: Farrar, Straus and Giroux, 2003.

Sorenson, Janet. *The Grammar of Empire in Eighteenth-Century British Writing.* Cambridge: Cambridge UP, 2000.

Southey, Robert. "History of the Peninsular Wars." *Select Prose of Robert Southey.* Ed. with intro. Jacob Zeitlin. New York: Macmillan, 1916.

———. "Review of Pasley's *Essay on Military Policy and Institutions of the British Empire.*" *Quarterly Review* 5 (May 1811): 432–33.

Spitzer, Leo. "Milieu and Ambiance." *Essays in Historical Semantics.* New York: S. F. Vanni, 1948.

Spivak, Gayatri Chakravorty. "The Rani of Sirmur: An Essay in Reading the Archives." *History and Theory* 24 (1985): 247–72.

———, and Sarah Harasym. *The Post-Colonial Critic: Interviews, Strategies, Dialogues.* New York: Routledge, 1990.

Stafford, Barbara Maria. *Visual Analogy: Consciousness as the Art of Connection.* Cambridge: MIT P, 1999.

St. Clair, William. *The Reading Nation in the Romantic Period.* Cambridge: Cambridge UP, 2004.

Stephen, Leslie. "Forgotten Benefactors." *Social Rights and Duties.* London: Swan Sonnenschein, 1896.

Stevens, Wallace. *The Collected Poems of Wallace Stevens.* New York: Vintage, 1982.

———. *Opus Posthumous.* Ed. Milton J. Bates. Rev. ed. New York: Alfred A. Knopf, 1989.

Stevick, Peter. "Miniaturization in Eighteenth-Century Literature." *University of Toronto Quarterly* 38 (1969).

Stewart, Susan. *On Longing: Narratives of the Miniature, the Gigantic, the Souvenir, the Collection.* Durham: Duke UP, 1992.

———. *Poetry and the Fate of the Senses.* Chicago: U of Chicago P, 2002.

Stromberg, Joseph R. "Strategies of Annihilation: Total War in U.S. History." *LewRockwell.com.* http://www.lewrockwell.com/stromberg/stromberg22.html.

Suleri, Sara. *The Rhetoric of English India.* Chicago: U of Chicago P, 1992.

Sutton, Thomas. *The Daniells: Artists and Travellers.* London: Bodley Head, 1954.

Taylor, Irene. *The War Diaries: An Anthology of Daily Wartime Diary Entries Throughout History.* Edinburgh: Canongate, 2004.

Teltscher, Kate. *India Inscribed: European and British Writing on India, 1600–1800.* Delhi: Oxford UP, 1995.

Tempelhoffe, George Friedrich von. *Extracts from Colonel Tempelhoffe's History of the Seven Years War*. Trans. Colin Lindsay. Vol. 2. London: T. Cadell, 1793.

Terada, Rei. *Feeling in Theory: Emotion after the "Death of the Subject."* Cambridge: Harvard UP, 2001.

———. "Phenomenality and Dissatisfaction in Coleridge's Notebooks." *Studies in Romanticism* 43.2 (Summer 2004): 257–75.

Thompson, E. P. "Time, Work-Discipline, and Industrial Capitalism." *Past and Present* 38 (December 1967): 56–97.

Thomson, James. "Winter." *The Seasons*. New York: A. S. Barnes, 1860.

Thornes, John E. *John Constable's Skies: A Fusion of Art and Science*. Birmingham: U of Birmingham P, 1999.

The Times. London. 1788–.

Tobin, Beth Fowkes. *Colonizing Nature: The Tropics in British Arts and Letters, 1760–1820*. Philadelphia: U of Pennsylvania P, 2004.

Trumpener, Katie. *Bardic Nationalism: The Romantic Novel and the British Empire*. Princeton: Princeton UP, 1997.

Trussell, John B. B. Jr. *Birthplace of an Army: A Study of the Valley Forge Encampment*. Harrisburg: Commonwealth of Pennsylvania, Pennsylvania Historical and Museum Commission, 1976.

Tuck, Richard. *The Rights of War and Peace: Political Thought and the International Order from Grotius to Kant*. Oxford: Oxford UP, 1999.

Unsworth, Barry. *Losing Nelson*. London: Hamish Hamilton, 1999.

Vetch, R. H. "Pasley, Sir Charles William (1780–1861)." Rev. John Sweetman. *Oxford Dictionary of National Biography*. Ed. H.C.G. Matthew and Brian Harrison. Oxford: Oxford UP, 2004. http://www.oxforddnb.com/view/article/21500.

Virgil, *The Georgics*. Trans. L. P. Wilkinson. Harmondsworth, UK: Penguin, 1982.

Virilio, Paul. *Desert Screen: War at the Speed of Light*. London: Continuum, 2002.

———. *Pure War*. New York: Semiotexte, 1997.

Wahrman, Dror. *The Making of the Modern Self: Identity and Culture in Eighteenth-Century England*. New Haven: Yale UP, 2004.

Ward, B. R. Preface to Fifth Edition. *The Military Policy and Institutions of the British Empire*. Ed. and intro. B. R. Ward. 5th ed. London: W. Clowes and Sons, 1914.

Watson, J. R. *Romanticism and War: A Study of British Romantic Period Writers and the Napoleonic Wars*. Basingstoke, UK: Palgrave Macmillan, 2003.

Wetherell, John. *The Adventures of John Wetherell*. Ed. C. S. Forester. London: Michael Joseph, 1994.

White, Matthew, ed. "Statistics of Wars, Oppressions and Atrocities of the Nineteenth Century." *Historical Atlas of the Twentieth Century*. http://users.erols.com/mwhite28/wars19c.htm.

Whitman, Walt. *Prose Works 1892, Vol. 1: Specimen Days*. Ed. Floyd Stovall. New York: New York UP, 2007.

Williams, C. K. *The Singing*. New York: Farrar, Straus and Giroux, 2003.

———. "Doves." Speech for the National Book Award in Poetry (2003). http://www.nationalbook.org/nbaacceptspeech_ckwilliams.html.

Williams, Raymond. *Marxism and Literature*. New York: Oxford UP, 1977.

———. *Politics and Letters*. London: New Left Books, 1979.

———. *What I Came to Say*. London: Century Hutchinson, 1989.

Wilson, C. R. "General Sir Charles William Pasley." *Royal Engineers Museum*. http://www.remuseum.org.uk/biography/rem_bio_pasley.htm.

Wilson, Kathleen. *The Island Race*. London: Routledge, 2003.

———. *The Sense of the People: Politics, Culture, and Imperialism in England, 1715–1785*. New York: Cambridge UP, 1995.

Wiltshire, John. *Jane Austen and the Body: "The Picture of Health."* Cambridge: Cambridge UP, 1992.

Woodward, John. *An Essay toward a Natural History of the Earth: And Terrestrial Bodies, Especially Minerals: As also of the Sea, Rivers, and Springs. With an Account of the Universal Deluge: And of the Effects that it had upon the Earth*. London: R. Wilkin, 1695.

Woolf, Virginia. "The Leaning Tower." *The Moment and Other Essays*. New York: Harcourt Brace, 1948. 130–31.

Wordsworth, William. *The Excursion. Wordsworth: Poetical Works*. Ed. Thomas Hutchinson, rev. Ernest de Selincourt. Oxford: Oxford UP, 1904; 1981.

———. *The Poems*. Ed. John O. Hayden. 2 vols. Harmondsworth, UK: Penguin, 1977.

———. "Preface." In *Lyrical Ballads with other poems, in two volumes*. 2nd ed. Bristol, UK: T.N. Longman and O. Rees, 1802.

———. *The Prelude, 1799, 1805, 1850*. Ed. Jonathan Wordsworth, M. H. Abrams, and Stephen Gill. New York: Norton, 1979.

———. "Reconciling Addendum to 'The Ruined Cottage.'" *The Poetical Works of William Wordsworth*. 5 vols. Ed. Ernest de Selincourt and Helen Darbishire. Oxford: Clarendon, 1949.

INDEX